THE NOVELS OF *William Faulkner*

N.L. Terteling Library

Swisher Memorial Collection

THE NOVELS

A CRITICA

Louisiana

State

University

Press

Baton Rouge
and
London

William

OF Faulkner

INTERPRETATION BY OLGA W. VICKERY

TO F. J. HOFFMAN

Library of Congress Catalog Number 64-23150
Copyright © 1959, 1964 by Louisiana State University Press
All rights reserved
Manufactured in the United States of America
Designed by Theo Jung
Revised edition published 1964

The paper in this book meets the guidelines for permanence and
durability of the Committee on Production Guidelines for Book
Longevity of the Council on Library Resources. ∞

ISBN 0-8071-2006-5 (paper)

Louisiana Paperback Edition, 1995
04 03 02 01 00 99 98 97 96 95   5 4 3 2 1

PREFACE

This study offers a critical interpretation of the novels of William Faulkner. More particularly, its primary concern is to illuminate Faulkner's themes and characters by attending to his use of point of view and structure in individual novels. Throughout, a radically inductive method is followed. Each novel is analyzed, so far as possible, as a unique work none of whose parts or aspects can be slighted. The aim of this inductive approach has been to avoid preconceptions and to minimize the likelihood of confusing partial insights with complete interpretations.

Accordingly, Part One is devoted solely to a consideration of the individual novels. Each chapter constitutes a self-contained unit, though interrelations are, of course, indicated when pertinent to the topic under discussion. *Go Down, Moses* and *The Hamlet* have both received detailed treatment since they are clearly in the mainstream of Faulkner's fiction and also because they are more nearly experimental novels than collections of short stories.

Part Two discusses those patterns or major themes which recur throughout the novels and suggests the relations which exist between them.

In arriving at my interpretation, I have been aided, needless to say, by the works of other critics of Faulkner. Their arguments have served both to buttress my own interpretations and to spur me to a clearer formulation of my own views on particular issues. Of a more personal order is my indebtedness to three persons. Professor F. J. Hoffman urged me to undertake this study, gave me the benefit of his knowledge and acumen, and provided me with a model of critical responsibility. The dedication of this book to him is an inadequate but sincere avowal of my gratitude. My debt to my husband is also great. His familiarity with philosophical problems and his insistence that I face critical issues helped me to eliminate many inconsistencies and to clarify many difficult points. His encouragement and aid, often at the expense of his own work, was unfailing. Another person to whom I am heavily indebted is Professor Helen Griffith (Emeritus) of Mount Holyoke College. Her enthusiasm for Faulkner and her abiding interest in the progress of this study were as heart-warming as they were helpful.

Certain parts of this book have previously appeared elsewhere. I should like to acknowledge the kindness of the editors of the following periodicals for permitting me to republish these articles: the first section of chapter 1, titled "Faulkner's First Novel" in *The Western Humanities Review*, Vol. XI, No. 3 (Summer, 1957), 251–56; the second section of chapter 1, titled "Faulkner's *Mosquitoes*" in *The University of Kansas City Review*, Vol. XXIV, No. 3 (Spring, 1958); chapter 2, titled "The Making of a Myth: *Sartoris*" in *The Western Review* (Spring, 1958); a longer version of chapter 3, titled "*The Sound and the Fury*: A Study in Perspective" in *PMLA* (December, 1954), 1017–37; a much altered form of chapter 4 in *Perspective* (Autumn, 1950), 179–91; chapter 14, titled "Faulkner and the Contours of Time" in *The Georgia Review*, Vol. XII, No. 2 (Summer, 1958), 192-201; chapter 18, titled "William Faulkner and the Figure in the Carpet" in *The South Atlantic Quarterly*, Vol. LXIII, No. 3 (Summer, 1964), by permission of the copyright holder, Duke University Press.

Of a similar order is the generosity of Lake Forest College whose grant from the Given Fund helped defray the costs in preparing the typescript for the publisher and of Purdue University whose XL Grants provided me with uninterrupted time to make revisions and additions for the present edition.

Finally, I wish to acknowledge the publishers of Faulkner's works quoted in this study. All quotations are either from the novel being analyzed (Part I) or are identified in the body of the text (Part II). The works quoted are:

Absalom, Absalom! New York, Modern Library, 1951.

A Fable. New York, Random House, 1954.

As I Lay Dying. New York, Modern Library, 1946.

Go Down, Moses. New York, Random House, 1942.
The Hamlet. New York, Random House, 1940.
Intruder in the Dust. New York, Random House, 1948.
Knight's Gambit. New York, Random House, 1949.
Light in August. New York, Modern Library, 1950.
The Mansion. New York, Random House, 1959.
Mosquitoes. New York, Liveright, 1927.
Pylon. New York, H. Smith & R. Haas, 1935.
The Reivers. New York, Random House, 1962.
Requiem for a Nun. New York, Random House, 1951.
Sanctuary. New York, Modern Library, 1932.
Sartoris. New York, Harcourt, Brace, 1929.
Soldiers' Pay. New York, Liveright, 1926.
The Sound and the Fury. New York, Modern Library, 1946.
The Town. New York, Random House, 1957.
The Unvanquished. New York, Random House, 1938.
The Wild Palms. New York, Random House, 1939.

Olga W. Vickery

TABLE OF CONTENTS

PART TWO

THE GRAND PATTERN

THE NOVELS OF *William Faulkner*

1 : THE APPRENTICESHIP

Soldiers' Pay
and *Mosquitoes*

William Faulkner's first two novels, *Soldiers' Pay* and *Mosquitoes*, constitute his literary apprenticeship. In them he tends to employ traditional narrative forms and techniques, yet at the same time one can detect unmistakable signs of those qualities of mind and art that are to stamp the later mature novels with their author's particular originality. Despite the uncertainty and even crudeness with which themes and techniques are handled, these novels provide an invaluable, if limited, insight into Faulkner's habit of mind since they contain, though in unassimilated fashion, most of those preoccupations which we associate with his mature work. The difference between his major novels and these early studies lies largely in a deepening of his essential view of man and the world and in an increased perception of the complex implications of that view. His continual innovations in form and technique are both the cause and a reflection of this mental development.

In *Soldiers' Pay* and *Mosquitoes* Faulkner presents the themes of post-war disillusionment and pseudo-intellectual Bohemia. Beneath these, however, can be discerned interests more germane to his later work, such as his fascination with the multiplicity of responses which mankind makes to a common experience, with time, with language and action, and with man's endeavor to define himself. These concerns inevitably clash with his attempted imitations of the early T. S. Eliot and Aldous Huxley; his passionate engagement is continually at odds with his ironic detachment. In these two novels his own preoccupations become gigantic irrelevancies disturbing the tone and texture which he was ostensibly imitating. Techniques later employed to advantage in *The Sound and the Fury*, *As I Lay Dying*, and *Light in August* are here incompletely realized and hence too cumbersome and inflexible for the themes he has elected. In short, Faulkner is using a steam shovel to lift a grain of sand; and yet, for this very reason, *Soldiers' Pay* and *Mosquitoes* merit more careful consideration than they have received to date.

In *Soldiers' Pay* Faulkner appears to be one of those bitter young men who brooded over their pain and frustration in print, thereby contributing to the ever-increasing mass of undistinguished post-war fiction. His characters are seldom more than types—the sensitive veteran, the unfaithful sweetheart, the bereaved mother, the envious youngsters, and the callous civilians—all of whom move woodenly through stock situations. Nevertheless, out of the collision of two groups, one immersed in the violence of war, the other scarcely touched by it, Faulkner has created a story whose multiple ironies pencil in that basic distinction between superficial and profound reactions to violence which is to become increasingly important in his works. It is the pervasive irony, broadening at times into farce, that prevents the novel from being merely another recital of the post-war slump or an introverted probing of familiar wounds. Admittedly, the irony is glib and superficial and on occasion gives way to sentimentality and bathos, but these two extremes correspond to the two unrelated levels of action. The first, dominated by Januarius Jones, describes post-war society in terms of bitter comedy; the second, independent of time and place, is tragic or, more accurately, pathetic in its implications. The former most clearly reveals Faulkner's borrowings, while the latter marks the first tentative manifestations of his concern with time and the individual consciousness.

Jones's intrusion into the rector's garden and his amorous pursuit of Cecily and Emmy form a plot sequence that is quite independent of Donald Mahon's reappearance in Charlestown. Donald, of course, is oblivious to the very existence of Jones, who, in turn, deliberately ignores Donald's presence except for an occasional misuse of his name. The two neither meet nor establish any direct awareness of each other. If the novel was meant to be built around the dramatic tension between these two figures, then it fails, for Donald's complete passivity is an insufficient foil for Jones's rampaging vitality. Similarly, if either of them is meant to be the dramatic center of the book, then the treatment accorded the other is disproportionate.

There is, however, at least a partial explanation for the equal attention given these two characters. They mirror in their own persons the separation of past and present and the alienation of individuals which is the underlying theme of the novel. Jones, who is a caricature of the civilian group, is wholly indifferent to the past, while Mahon in a semi-coma is unconscious of any present. Communication between them is clearly impossible because of that dislocation in time and consciousness which Mahon's coma symbolizes. The other characters simply act or react between these two poles. Because of this dislocation, Charlestown is split into two groups each of which is a stranger to the other. Even verbal communication ceases, for while death has become an integral part of the veterans' experience, it is, if not meaningless, then only a symbol of romance, of "something true and grand and sad" (52) for the non-combatants.

In Chapter 5, the approximate middle of the book, Faulkner completely ignores the central story in order to dramatize the isolation of each of the characters and the part played by time in the creation of this predicament. The conventional comments made in the rector's drawing room are accompanied by recurrent motifs: Margaret's "Dick, Dick, How young, how terribly young"; the rector's "Yes, that was Donald. He is dead"; Mrs. Burney's "Dewey, Dewey. So young he was, so big and brave." The thoughts of each travel separate ways into the past which bereaved them. Madden also has his memory of the past, a recurring image of a soldier suffering a horrible death. The violence and death which each has had to confront, if only imaginatively, excludes them from the ephemeral movements of the dance.

In the extreme case time can even alienate man from himself. The scar on Donald's forehead marks the difference between the youth with "the serenity of a wild thing, the passionate serene alertness of a faun" (82–83) and the man who sleeps "in all the travesty of his wings and leather and brass." (31) These two pictures are static and self-contained; there can be no modulation from one to the other since " 'the man that was wounded is dead and this is another person.' " (118) The extent of this divergence is underscored by the fact that young

Donald, the Donald who is dead, resembles Jones in his egoism and indifference to others. Similarly, both Emmy and the chemise acquired in France indicate Donald's prowess in a field that Jones makes his own. The faun and the satyr are both followers of the great god Pan who flouted tradition and social respectability. Donald, however, had disclaimed the social order to live in close and harmonious contact with nature, while Jones seeks merely to fulfill his own stultifying desires.

The sharp contrast between the living Donald of the past and the dying Donald of the present is forcefully impressed on all the characters. Their motives and actions stem from their awareness of and reactions to it. On the other hand, Donald himself is only dimly aware of the disturbances created by his return. His fumbling, half-articulate " 'Carry on Joe' " expresses his total indifference to the world about him; he is no longer even trying to link his past to the present but only to remember the point at which his life had terminated. The elusive past is finally recaptured as he remembers the encounter with the enemy plane, and the two Donalds, one dying, the other dead, are reunited at the point where they had diverged three months earlier.

The lack of relation between the Donald of the past and the apathetic man who returns to Charlestown is crucial not so much for him as for his friends. For each of them he represents a lacuna in time that flaunts the discontinuity of human experience. Thus, Emmy centers her emotional life wholly in the memory of her lover who, for a brief moment, had lifted her from a monotonous life into a romantic world of passionate enchantment. Despite the objective proof of the scar, the withered hand, and the blindness, Emmy at first sees only her lover in the dying man. Eventually, however, she learns to separate lover and invalid, and with this her passion becomes a part of the past and her care of the dying man efficient but impersonal. The completeness of this separation is indicated by her immediate rejection of Margaret's suggestion that she marry Donald and her refusal to attend his funeral. Instead she sits alone, "remembering that night long, long ago, the last time she had seen Donald, her Donald—not that one! and he had said, 'Come here, Emmy,' and she had gone to him. Her Donald was dead long, long ago." (297) At the same time Jones's touch reasserts present reality and her dream of Donald loses substance. Thus, her surrender to Jones is an acceptance of her own continuing involvement in experience. And with this acceptance she makes peace with her past. She still remembers Donald, but for the first time she herself becomes a dream figure associated with a dream lover. The swift, naked figure of the girl she sees swimming with Donald in the pool has no connection with the Emmy who "rose slowly, feeling her damp clothes, thinking of the long walk home." (301)

While Emmy finds the whole meaning of her life compressed into one past experience, Cecily exists only in and for the present moment. She had become engaged to Donald because he possessed the flier's aura of romance, danger, and fame. Hence, even before his return, she is already emphasizing the chasm between then and now, and the impossibility, at least for her, of bridging it. When she does see him, the scar serves as an incessant reminder of the ineluctable difference between past and present. Others, however, expect her not only to remember the past but to act in accordance with it. Although she shrinks from marrying the horribly disfigured Donald, she is not strong enough to reject him. Instead, she is continually swayed both by her own fleeting impulses and by the convictions of others. She shares her mother's calculated repudiation of the engagement, but at the same time she is disturbed by her father's uneasy sense of duty and responsibility to this promise from the past. Her subsequent marriage to George, prompted by her desire to escape the past and its obligations, inevitably fails, for Cecily is essentially fickle, capable only of the most transitory attachments. Unlike Emmy she does not resolve her problem by acquiescence but seeks to evade it by flight.

While Cecily and Emmy have a direct connection with Donald, Margaret creates one. Knowing nothing about the wounded man on the train, she, nevertheless, decides to assume the task of caring for and about him. Her decision stems from the sight of his disfigured face which to her mind identifies him with her dead husband. Her marriage to Dick Powers, the hero departing for the war, was an impulsive gesture since she, like Dick, believed that " 'what you did to-day would not matter to-morrow, that there really wasn't a to-morrow at all.' " (162–163) But as his last letter had indicated, Dick had come to see their marriage a permanence capable of withstanding whatever change they themselves might suffer. As a result Margaret reproaches herself with her failure of imaginative sympathy. Guiltily she recalls her feeling that it was as if Dick Powers, her husband and an officer, were two distinct and unrelated persons. At this juncture she sees an opportunity of making amends; the faith she had broken with Dick can be transferred to Donald whose scarred face is a visible symbol of the violence that Dick too endured. Hence, she embarks on a series of desperate efforts to make things approximate the condition in which Donald had left them. Her aim is to provide him with the reassuring sense of permanence she had denied Dick. Thus, she endeavors to force Cecily back into her engagement, and then to persuade Emmy to marry him. Finally, when both these attempts fail, she marries him herself. Like Emmy and Cecily, Margaret endeavors to cope with the human problem embodied in the wounded Donald. But whereas Emmy performs an act of memory and Cecily one of withdrawal, Margaret engages in an act of expiation. And in so doing, they each provide a revelation of character and a distinct perspective on the central theme.

Throughout the series of emotional crises occasioned by Donald's return, the rector preserves a balance and sanity lacking in the other characters. The source of his calmness is his acceptance of the inevitability of all experience and the necessity of change. Human life is a matter of both love and death, sorrow and happiness; they do not cease to exist simply because men repudiate them, nor can they be made immune to change or destruction. Whatever form it takes, experience can neither be restricted nor controlled. Like the Compson children, Cecily, Emmy, and Margaret each attempt to deny some aspect of their experience. Inevitably, the partial redemption of the latter two depends upon their learning to accept and endure whatever time brings.

Whereas all these characters focus their attention on the past, Januarius Jones lives wholly in the present where he pursues sensuous and sensual experiences for the delight afforded by their novelty and immediacy. Significantly, the satyr and the goat, both emblems of lust, are constantly associated with him. The satyr, in addition, is a symbol of social disorder and disregard for established traditions, while the goat suggests the scavenger. And Jones appropriately shows an unfailing ability to disrupt social occasions, either by his deliberate efforts to shock, as at the rector's, or by his disregard for convention, as

6

at the dance. The scavenger quality is emphasized by the fact that he is unable to initiate any ultimately successful move, though time and again he takes advantage of a situation already in existence and turns it to his own profit. This pattern emerges most clearly in the advances he makes to the three women. His ultimate conquest of Emmy succeeds only after he forfeits his identity and takes advantage of her dream-filled mind intent on its own sorrow. Both Cecily and Margaret elude his advances and defeat his elaborately complacent attempts to dominate them. In each case he is made to appear ludicrous and exposes himself to the jibes of the other characters.

These forays and pursuits by Jones provide the novel with the bulk of its comedy. Jones, of course, has an essentially serious and sober view of himself, but set over against this is the comic view of his personality and behavior which Faulkner and the reader share. Unfortunately, this treatment largely fails as humor. Faulkner's comic potential is simply not plumbed by the shallow cleverness of the drawing room which relies principally on isolated witty remarks at the expense of such individuals as Jones. At its best, Faulkner's humor is cumulative and derives from the presentation of a rationally absurd situation in which persons believe they are, and in a sense are, acting in the only intelligent way possible in that situation. Unlike *The Hamlet*, which is a brilliantly uproarious study in incongruities, *Soldiers' Pay* lacks both the right locale and the involved yet ironically detached focal character through whom the scenes gain their perspective. The irony here is at once too diffused yet too committed and angry on the subject of war and its aftermath to accept the humor of despair, as do such characters as Jason Compson in *The Sound and the Fury*, or to see the farce implicit in catastrophe, such as is revealed in *As I Lay Dying*.

This together with other structural and stylistic flaws discloses the apprentice at work. At the same time, however, they hint at the direction to be taken in his subsequent development. To recognize that Faulkner is already concerned with time as the source of motives and with situations which are revealed rather than developed is to avoid the danger of seeing him as shifting suddenly from pure imitativeness in *Soldiers' Pay* and *Mosquitoes* to pure originality in *The Sound and the Fury* and *As I Lay Dying*. Seeing in *Soldiers' Pay* merely an

7

example of post-war fiction obscures the devotion and integrity with which Faulkner has attended the gradual crystallization of his own highly individual style and vision.

*

Mosquitoes is generally considered to be Faulkner's weakest novel, probably because both the intention and the content seem superficial. Most frequently it has been dismissed as a bad imitation of Aldous Huxley. Although it is impossible, in all honesty, to quarrel with this judgment, nevertheless one may wonder whether it properly assesses the role played by *Mosquitoes* in Faulkner's development. With the work of nearly thirty years before us, the novel's imitative surface fades into insignificance, while Faulkner's enduring interests and preoccupations stand out in bold, though sketchy, relief.

One of the basic attitudes running throughout all his work is the view that language and logic act to obscure truth rather than to reveal it. Accordingly, a primary concern is to demonstrate the barrenness that attends all discussion. Here, as in the later novels, truth is dependent not on words but on a moment of comprehension which usually occurs when the individual is least concerned with intellectual activity. As a result of this linguistic scepticism, the element of farce in the novel is not confined to the actions of the characters, such as the ill-fated attempt to free the stranded *Nausikaa*. It is an integral part of the conversations not only when Al Jackson's exploits are involved, but also when the "serious" subject of art is being debated. Each conversation is marked by the presence of at least one character, usually Julius or Eva Wiseman, who reveals the absurdity of the discussion, or else through exaggeration turns it into something as fantastic as Fairchild's tales about Al Jackson.

Although art, and literature in particular, is the dominant topic of conversation in *Mosquitoes*, religion, education, social clubs, sex, the war and its aftermath are all touched upon. In no case does the discussion reach a profound level, even though some one of the characters, usually Fairchild, is in dead earnest. The endless discussion is succinctly characterized as "Talk, talk, talk: the utter and heartbreaking stupidity of words. It seemed endless, as though it might go on forever. Ideas, thoughts, became mere sounds to be bandied about until they were dead." (186) This distinction between words and ideas also holds, according to Fairchild, between words and actions: " 'Well, it is a kind of sterility—Words,' Fairchild admitted. 'You begin to substitute words for things and deeds, like the withered cuckold husband that took the Decameron to bed with him every night, and pretty soon the thing or the deed becomes just a kind of shadow of a certain sound you make by shaping your mouth a certain way.' " (210) Thus, Gordon, who is the only genuine artist in the group, has the least to do with talk. Talliaferro, on the other hand, verbalizes all possible approaches to action, and for that very reason is incapable of performing any act.

The separation of words and deeds is occasioned or at least paralleled by a distinction between living and consciousness of living. This is most clearly articulated in Fairchild's assertion:

"When youth goes out of you, you get out of it. Out of life, I mean. Up to that time you just live; after that, you are aware of living and living becomes a conscious process. Like thinking does in time, you know. You become conscious of thinking, and then you start right off to think in words. And first thing you know, you don't have thoughts in your mind at all: you just have words in it. But when you are young, you just be. Then you reach a stage where you do. Then a stage where you think, and last of all, where you remember. Or try to." (231)

The state of "just being" and of instinctively knowing, which precedes self-consciousness and verbalization, is one of the constant sources of value and strength in Faulkner's novels. It is clearly bound up with the land, as we see at the conclusion of *Soldiers' Pay* where the profound feelings of Joe Gilligan and the rector become part of the Negro singing and of the land. Similarly, Fairchild has his moment of knowledge when he listens to the "dark and measured beating of the heart of things." (339) He learns that genius is the Passion Week of the heart when all the elements of life " 'brought together by chance in perfect proportions, take on a kind of splendid and timeless beauty.' " (339) Yet this identification with the rhythm of life is always in danger of being destroyed by words, precepts, or empty rituals. Once again it is Fairchild who suggests that some people vivify rituals and conventions by making them an integral part of life, while others destroy life by reducing it to a hollow and stultifying ritual. Acts, like words, may be either magical or trivial; mankind may order his life in accordance with significant or empty ritual.

The contrasts, discussed by Fairchild, between youth and age, ideas and words, existence and action determine the grouping of the characters in *Mosquitoes*. Thus, the book sketches the relations existing between creative artists and nonartists or laymen. Mrs. Maurier supports Art, Talliaferro appreciates it, and the others are uninterested, though Pat desires one particular specimen of it. Another division, that of age, links Talliaferro and Mrs. Maurier with the artists in contrast to Pat and her group whose youth is a barrier to the others. Finally, characters are grouped according to their attitudes toward "talk." Here, the younger set is relatively less voluble, while David, the steward, is almost completely inarticulate. But it is Gordon who emerges in splendid isolation as the character who talks the least yet comprehends the most.

None of the young people take any interest in the incessant discussions of art and life, primarily because they feel that such debates have no relevance to their lives. For the young, life itself is the dominant interest; consequently, they do not try to evoke emotions by words or to capture life by set forms of behavior. Jenny gently ignores the interminable shipboard conversations, while Pat cuts through their verbiage with a blunt directness that is at times palpably rude. The utter unimportance of words to Pat is indicated by her habit of calling her brother Ted, Jack, or Gus, as if the name itself made no difference. Furthermore, she is fascinated by a phrase known to Jenny not because of its possible usefulness but because " 'it sure sounds good.' " (147) Ted and Pete are even more indifferent to words than the two girls. Pete is wholly absorbed in guarding his hat and waiting for Jenny. And compared to the overwhelming importance of getting the parts of his pipe to fit, what people want of or say to Ted is of no significance to him. Neither Major Ayers' business propositions nor Fairchild's reminiscences can stir his interest.

In addition to their indifference to words, the young people all share, though to different degrees, in the secret richness of "just being." In Jenny this takes the form of a purely passive and unconscious self-centeredness. She is the soft, magnetic center which attracts without itself being moved. Like Eula Varner in *The Hamlet* or Lena Grove, she exists on the minimal level of consciousness, her mind comfortably immune to the uncertainties and anguish which even a limited ability to abstract and generalize can engender. The result is an inviolable serenity involving neither joy nor sorrow but only passive contentment.

In contrast to Jenny's passivity, Pat's self-centeredness manifests itself in an active pursuit of the varieties of sensation that life has to offer. Eagerly she touches the cool marble of Gordon's statue, strokes Jenny's flank, or plunges nude into the water. That she is completely absorbed in this world of sensations is suggested by her impatience with David's emotion-charged behavior. Her disappearance with him is not an attempt to escape the futility of the cruise. It represents rather her desire to translate a dream of adventure into a full-bodied experience capable of being savored in all its sensuous immediacy. The trip to Mandeville is to serve as a prelude to the grand European excursion which has stimulated her imagination. In effect, then, there are two trips—the imaginative idyll existing only in Pat's mind and the sorry journey through the swamp—and what they ultimately signify is the incalculable distance between dream and reality. The mosquitoes cannot be ignored; and though David can bathe her shoulders, give her his shirt, and even carry her part of the way, he cannot restore her dream. In undergoing the suffering that attends this escapade, Pat has been confronted, for the first time in her life, with sensations that are neither desirable, enjoyable, nor beautiful. She retreats, for the time being at least, to the security of the *Nausikaa* where conversation and social maneuvering replace the hard, intractable reality of experience.

Except for Gordon, the older people collect words in order to disguise some emptiness or inadequacy in themselves. Thus, Mark Frost's cerebral manipulation of words takes the place of any genuine creativity or imagination. His humorless belief that he is the best poet in New Orleans prevents his ever becoming aware of the ridiculous and futile cul-de-sac in which he lives. It is Fairchild, however, who is most sensitive to the problem inherent in words. As a novelist, he is aware of and bewildered by the perplexities and difficulties that confront man when he is attempting to relate words to the reality of experience. His earnest endeavors to articulate and thereby to solve the difficulty end in contradiction: he points out the impotence of words at one moment, and then endows them with a superior reality the next. Ironically enough, when he disregards the "problem" of art, he then becomes capable, almost unconsciously, of a high degree of creativity, as in his accounts of his childhood and in the farcical tales of Al Jackson.

The position in the novel of Julius, Mrs. Wiseman's brother, is an important one, especially in relation to Fairchild. He belongs, by choice, with the artistic group, but he is not merely a portrait of the "informed" critic designed as a contrast to the inanities of Mrs. Maurier and Talliaferro. The constant references to him as the Semitic man, even after his identity has been established, emphasize his isolation from all the people on the *Nausikaa*, artists and non-artists alike. This position outside the group enables him to understand, if not help, the other passengers. His awareness of the futility of all discussions allows him to assume toward ideas an attitude of irreverence which Fairchild never quite comprehends. Thus, over and over again he leads Fairchild into exaggerations or contradictions that reduce his ideas to absurdity. In this way Julius tries to free Fairchild from his habit of analyzing himself and his art, for he realizes that it is impeding Fairchild's development both as a man and as a novelist.

In contrast to the others, Gordon is the living embodiment of creative productivity; he exists naturally and easily in a state where disguises and fetiches are both impossible and unnecessary. Significantly, he is the most silent of the characters, ignoring both the social chatter of Mrs. Maurier and the artistic ramblings of Fairchild. He is as impervious to idle words as he is immune to mosquitoes. But by ignoring Mrs. Maurier's external characteristics and habits, he is able to apprehend the truth about her. What is important for him is the quality rather than the details of her past experience. This passionate concern with the quiddity of things and persons is disturbed, however, by Mrs. Maurier's niece, Pat. For a brief interval, she tempts him to express his feeling through words and actions. But he regains his independence and inviolability, for he knows intuitively that his language is sculpture and that the statue says everything he is capable of saying to her. His attitude is rendered explicitly in a final, terse comment that foreshadows major developments in the later novels: " 'Only an idiot has no grief; only a fool would forget it. What else is there in this world sharp enough to stick to your guts?' " (329)

The final appearance of Gordon, Fairchild, and Julius is marked by a flamboyant drinking spree reminiscent of the

Walpurgisnacht section of *Ulysses*. In the midst of chaotic and hallucinatory impressions of priests, rats, and women clad in animal skins, there is a moment in which things coalesce into a recognizable and familiar form: *"Then voices and sounds, shadows and echoes change form swirling, becoming the headless, armless, legless torso of a girl, motionless and virginal and passionately eternal before the shadows and echoes whirl away."* (339) With this vision Fairchild sees that genius, the ability to create, is in reality an " 'instant of timeless beatitude. . . . [a] passive state of the heart with which the mind, the brain, has nothing to do at all.' " (339) The truth which was withheld during all the discussions about art is suddenly and intuitively grasped in a single moment of rapt identification with the core of life itself.

In contrast to Fairchild's ultimate self-fulfillment, Talliaferro, Mrs. Maurier, and Dorothy Jameson are bedeviled by an awareness of some essential incompleteness in their lives. Each believes himself to have been cheated of love. Hence, each pursues that elusive emotion by indulging in flirtations, hoping that the ritual of pursuit will itself force the desired end into being. They try to overcome the fragmentary nature of their lives by artificially reconstructing what they have missed. At the root of Dorothy's discontent is her inability to forget either herself or the fact that men and sex are a "problem." Through her concentration on empty ritual and intellectualized verbal maneuverings, she consistently alienates the men with whom she comes in contact. Dorothy, however, is at least still conscious of some connection between the gestures she makes and her desires. Mrs. Maurier, on the other hand, has even forgotten the source of her behavior. As Fairchild remarks, " 'all she has left is a habit, the ghost of a need to rectify something the lack of which her body has long since forgotten about.' " (326) In Mrs. Maurier the gestures, the expression of infantile, trusting astonishment, the saccharine modulation of the voice, the glances of decayed coquetry, all have taken on an independent existence which has submerged, if not destroyed, the reality of life in and for her. It is Talliaferro, however, who affords the clearest illustration of the chasm between words and deeds and of the futility of words. From his childhood his impulses and actions were never allowed to coincide. Each move he makes is marked by a reliance on words, or, rather, by a search for "the" word which will produce miraculous results. The change of his name from Tarver to Talliaferro is a striking instance of this childlike belief in the magical efficacy of the word. The most appalling of his absurdities, however, is his failure ever to learn from experience. Even after Jenny deserts him at the dance, he rises phoenixlike from the ashes of his despondency for yet one more attempt: "He stopped utterly still in the flash of his inspiration. At last he had it, had the trick, the magic Word. It was so simple that he stood in amaze at the fact that it had not occurred to him before." (305)

Illuminating as the stoical integrity of Gordon, the earnest gropings of Fairchild, and the follies of Talliaferro may be, they do not make the novel an integrated work of art. Nevertheless, we may reasonably insist that *Mosquitoes* is more than merely an imitation of the ironic and intellectual comedy of Huxley. Faulkner was exploring a problem that was genuinely his own if its recurrence in the later novels be any proof. But, as in *Soldiers' Pay*, he is not yet capable of exercising full control over his material. A convenient index to his development is found in *The Sound and the Fury* and *As I Lay Dying* where the episodic method and the shifting points of view operate with a severely functional economy. By contrast, in *Mosquitoes* these same techniques diffuse the interest and distract from rather than emphasize the theme. Faulkner's concern with the separation of words and actions and with the dialectic of significant and empty ritual is obscured by, instead of integrated into, the "comedy of futility." The latter, involving such things as the clowning and madcap antics of Fairchild, the petulant self-esteem of Frost, and the interminable banalities of the card-playing, dancing, and drinking, constitutes a structural counterpoise to the words-action pattern. Unfortunately, however, the proper balance is never struck and the result is a scenic mélange, uneven in quality and varying widely in merit. In this respect, the Walpurgisnacht section mirrors accurately the achievement and the defects of the novel as a whole. The style suffers a similar failure of realization so that in the end a mixture of Faulknerian rhetoric, Joycean passages, echoes of Huxley, and possibly even something of Ronald Firbank's whimsicality waits for some unifying power to make them an essential part of the content. But at this stage of his career, Faulkner lacks the artistic maturity to effect such a fusion. He attempted a *tour de force* in which the sheer accumulation of words would show their very futility, but he fell short of it.

2 : THE MAKING OF A MYTH

Sartoris

In *Soldiers' Pay* Faulkner made a tentative and only partially successful effort to examine time as an integral part of experience rather than simply a medium for it. And in *Mosquitoes* he attempted to clarify the relationship of mind and of language to man's emotional and instinctual behavior. He concluded that language, particularly in its abstract and conceptual aspect, tends to destroy the total human response to experience and to substitute for it empty rituals and meaningless gestures. Man's excessive reliance on words may eventually confine him within a verbal universe where words do, in fact, replace things and thoughts replace actions. It is in *Sartoris*, however, that Faulkner, for the first time, is able to give dramatic embodiment to his concern with time and language and to put them to a predominantly functional use.

To grasp this fact is to realize that Faulkner is not a romantic seeing his characters and locale through a haze of glamor and melodrama. On the contrary, he handles quite realistically a theme—the making of a myth—which engenders romantic attitudes on the part of the characters. Time and again, the caustic remarks of Miss Jenny throw the romantic actions of young Bayard into perspective. Similarly, the frequent scenes of comedy provided by Simon's indiscretions, Caspey's homecoming, or old Bayard's wen militate against the brooding melancholy and despair which young Bayard shares with the traditional romantic hero. Despite his own grim earnestness, unrelieved by any trace of humor, the latter is not permitted to conduct his search for death on a tragic or even a serious level. After one escapade he is locked in jail for the night on Miss Jenny's order, like a recalcitrant schoolboy. After another he is rescued from the creek by two Negroes in a scene whose farcical elements threaten to deprive Bayard not only of his chance to achieve tragic grandeur but also of his dignity.

An analysis of the structure of *Sartoris* shows even more clearly that Faulkner is unimplicated in the romanticism of young Bayard. The actual events take place in approximately a year. In that time Bayard returns from France, makes a few determined efforts to kill himself, marries Narcissa and fathers her child, contributes to the death of his grandfather, and finally finds the death he has been seeking so persistently. This sequence of events, chronologically arranged, is sufficient to establish post-war disillusionment, *Weltschmerz*, and the death-wish as the theme of the novel, if that were Faulkner's intention. But the relative unimportance of this chronological progression is demonstrated by the fact that we only realize what is happening after it is already concluded. The ultimate significance of an event depends on the large temporal and causal pattern into which it fits. This can only be seen and comprehended in retrospect.

Accordingly, the thematic action of *Sartoris* takes place not over a period of months but in a time span covering four generations, flanked by the Civil and First World Wars and by the two John Sartorises. The position that Colonel John Sartoris holds with respect to this larger time pattern is duplicated by his great grandson's within the shorter period. The influence exerted by the former over his heirs is repeated in young John's more personal and immediate control over his brother's life. Consequently, young Bayard has to come to terms with both pasts, particularly since they reinforce and repeat one another.

A closer examination of the two temporal poles for the action, namely, the two wars, yields a clearer comprehension of the significance of Sartoris, both the novel and the name. In none of Faulkner's works is there much direct description of the actual fighting in either war. Many of his characters, however, reminisce about the wars and references to them are found in practically every novel. The emphasis on reminiscence suggests that any war is incomprehensible for the individual while he is caught up in the rush of its events. Some measure of perspective is necessary in order to realize, not what is happening, but what has happened. Thus, in *Sartoris* the characters' perspective on the war is conveyed by the obviously romantic descriptions of the Civil War which glorify the courage and gallantry of the Confederate soldiers.

What Faulkner stresses, however, is not values expressed in and through the Civil War, but precisely the fact that it has been over for a long time, long enough to become not only history but legend. In contrast, there has not been time enough for a "public" attitude embodied in legend to develop and perpetuate itself in connection with the World War. As Buddy MacCallum suggests, it conveys only "an impression of people, creatures without initiative or background or future, caught timelessly in a maze of solitary conflicting preoccupations, like bumping tops, against an imminent but incomprehensible nightmare." (320) Hence we get antithetical pictures of the recent struggle: there is little similarity between Cadet Lowe's envious glorification of battle and Sergeant Madden's painful memories in *Soldiers' Pay*, or between Chick Mallison's youthful vision of the glorious field of combat and his uncle's experiences of blood, dirt, and isolation in *Knight's Gambit*. Bayard himself has two different accounts: one of "young men like fallen angels, and of a meteoric violence like that of fallen angels, beyond heaven or hell and partaking of both," (126) the other of screaming nerves and unbearable fear. Even Caspey has a personal version of the fighting, comic in its exaggeration but completely valid for himself and his listeners.

The passing of time not only removes the confusion which accompanied the experience but permits and even encourages poetic license until, at last, the experience is formalized and expressed by a series of significant gestures or words. The "truth" of these legends is not in question since cold, unadorned facts, measurements and statistics are no substitute for the vision of the enthralled imagination and the passionate heart making out of the brutality and confusion an enduring spectacle of human courage and faith and self-sacrifice. Each post-war generation must rediscover disillusionment which must, in turn, be replaced by a renewed faith in the legend. In other words, the legend which has its source in history finally replaces history. Thus, it is time and the retelling that have made the Civil War glamorous and imaginatively compelling, filling it with gallantry and the splendor and gloom of old battles. The clash of the legend and the actual experience of war is responsible, in part at least, for Bayard's frustration.

That Faulkner is concerned to stress the myth-making of his characters and that he is aware of the gradual separation of such myths from the truth of the historical experience is clearly revealed in his description of Miss Jenny's storytelling:

It was she who told them of the manner of Bayard Sartoris' death prior to the second battle of Manassas. She had told the story many times since (at eighty she still told it, on occasions usually inopportune) and as she grew older the tale itself grew richer and richer, taking on a mellow splendor like wine; until what had been a harebrained prank of two heedless and reckless boys wild with their own youth had become a gallant and finely tragical focal point to which the history of the race had been raised from out the old miasmic swamps of spiritual sloth by two angels valiantly fallen and strayed, altering the course of human events and purging the souls of men. (9)

Just as the Civil War becomes a legend finer and more glamorous than the reality so the history of the family becomes a myth. The word "Sartoris" becomes pregnant with accumulated meanings and emotions. Gradually Colonel John Sartoris ceases to be remembered as an individual with certain specific physical and mental characteristics and with human weaknesses and inconsistencies. The concrete details of his appearance found in *The Unvanquished* are absent from *Sartoris* even though he is an integral part of the thematic action. What we have is a pageant in which the central figure is not a man but rather a symbol, namely, "Sartoris." As in Miss Jenny's account of her brother, old Will Falls refines Colonel John Sartoris into "a gallant and finely tragical focal point" for humanity. Yet when Bayard asks Will what all the fighting was about, he can only answer " 'be damned ef I ever did know.' " (227) His reply is understandable. History concerns itself with a rational account of causes and effects; legend is content to glorify those actions which stir human emotions and the imagination.

The legend of John Sartoris is much more potent and effective than the man could ever be. As long as he is alive, his role as hero is continually modified by his physical presence. Only death can free the creative imagination to make of him a patriarchal and cultural symbol, to "stiffen and shape that

which sprang from him into the fatal semblance of his dream."
(23) His son can still defy the precept, "the virus, the inspiration and example of that one which dominated them all,"
(375) and refuse to kill Redmond. But his great grandson is helpless before the cumulative force of the legend which demands his conformity in spite of circumstance and his own nature. Only in the few interludes when he is hunting or working the land can young Bayard escape the pressure of the past as revealed in the interlocking legends of the Civil War and Colonel John Sartoris. Imperceptibly, the legend has been transformed into a precept which both regulates and evaluates behavior.

The core of the Sartoris legend, however, has to be more than a personal example. Drusilla Hawk suggests that what John Sartoris represented was an unforgettable and highly influential dream. What Sartoris' dream is we can only gather by implication, for this man who provides a basis for the actions of all his descendants is never presented directly. His deeds are described and reactions to them outlined, but never are we allowed to see what he himself is thinking or feeling. In its effect, however, the dream becomes progressively more destructive as it takes on all the force of a categorical imperative for Colonel John Sartoris' descendants. Spontaneous reactions to experience are replaced by imitative rituals in which form becomes more important than meaning. The final result is apt to be either an outbreak of violence or complete paralysis. At its most extreme, devotion to the dead and their design can mean a complete denial of one's own life.

The repetition of the names John and Bayard through four generations of Sartorises, while confusing to the reader, is actually a way of stressing the power of the Sartoris dream and legend. The names not only repeat the past verbally but create an obligation for their bearers to do so in action. Colonel John Sartoris knowingly walks to his death; his son repeats the gesture, against his own inclination, because he is a Sartoris and it is expected of him. Young John goes up in his plane expecting death; two years later his brother finally succeeds in destroying himself in the same manner. Thus, the relation of a Bayard to a John Sartoris is re-enacted. Significantly, the actions of the two Bayards are conscious imitations which scrupulously reproduce the gestures, not the spirit, of a John Sartoris. However much they feel themselves committed to the family tradition, such imitation cannot help but be a violation of their own integrity. The young Bayard of *Sartoris* refuses, however, to admit that there is a conflict, though he feels himself being destroyed by it.

Young Bayard's pursuit of death seems romantic and insufficiently motivated because the family myth is continually interposing itself between him and his experience. Thus, it is impossible for him to reconcile the two wars, one glamorous and significant, the other terrifying and incomprehensible. The way he should conduct himself as a soldier has been established by Colonel John Sartoris' brother whose brief career, evoked by Miss Jenny, "swept like a shooting star across the dark plain of their mutual remembering and suffering, lighting it with a transient glare like a soundless thunder-clap, leaving a sort of radiance when it died." (18) Life is carelessly tossed aside and not even for a cause since "neither Jeb Stuart nor Bayard Sartoris, as their actions clearly showed, had any political convictions involved at all." (10) A jar of anchovies is the stake for which they gambled and lost. Four generations later, young John has no difficulty in carrying on the tradition despite the absence of swords, lace, and horses. Bayard remembers that " 'Then he thumbed his nose at me like he was always doing and flipped his hand at the Hun and kicked his machine out of the way and jumped.' " (252)

These examples make Bayard grimly determined to prove himself a Sartoris, but his own nature interferes. There is a tenseness each time he takes a chance and risks his life that is foreign to Johnny's casualness. For him the war was not an opportunity for displaying reckless gallantry or for making dramatic gestures. His dominant and recurrent memory is one of "old terror" when "momentarily, the world was laid away and he was a trapped beast in the high blue, mad for life, trapped in the very cunning fabric that had betrayed him who had dared chance too much." (203) But no Sartoris can admit to feeling like "a trapped beast," nor can he admit to a "mad desire for life." The result is an impasse: the memory of his brother and of his fear are equally inescapable, equally compelling, but to submit to one would be to deny the other. It is clearly an impossible choice. The untamed horse, the speeding car, the untested plane: each is a propitiatory ritual performed on the altar of the two John Sartorises.

The conflict between Bayard's inherited tradition and his

personal experience of the war is indicated even more strongly
by his differing accounts of the war. After sharing a bottle with
MacCallum, his description echoes Miss Jenny's of the first
Bayard's career. The actual fighting is forgotten as he talks "of
a life peopled by young men like fallen angels" whose lot is
simultaneously "doomed immortality and immortal doom."
(126) Even the qualities of the similes are the same: "the
shooting star" and "the soundless thunder-clap" in Miss Jenny's
story correspond to the "meteoric violence" and the "fallen
angels" of Bayard's account. But thrown offguard by his nightmare, he reveals a quite contradictory memory of senseless
violence and brutality to Narcissa. Bayard's references to his
brother are marked by similar shifts in attitude, for he alternates
between glorifying and deriding his brother's final exploit. His
love for Johnny, however, weighs the balance so that he is not
only prepared to glorify the foolishness but to make of it a
touchstone for his own behavior. Thus, while establishing a
pattern and model for Bayard, Johnny destroys in him any
possibility of responding to life in his own terms. No experience
is allowed to make its own impression or establish its own
values.

And like the Colonel's, Johnny's death is an even more potent
influence on Bayard than his living presence had been. He feels
a mixture of violent regret, responsibility, and envy which
pervades his every action. The thought that he had been
turned back by a spatter of bullets across the nose of his plane,
that he had put his own safety before that of his brother, returns to haunt him. The more recent death of his grandfather,
in which he is also implicated, intensifies his feeling of concern
for Johnny's death until it culminates in a semi-hysterical denial
of responsibility. At the same time his own escape from death
merely compounds his guilt and instead of freeing him from
the past serves to confirm his bondage. But no amount of will
or determination can capture Johnny's elusive spirit, for he is a
Sartoris not by choice but by virtue of his own nature. Bayard,
on the other hand, forces himself to become one in despite of
his, through his relentless pursuit of violence.

Nor can the now rigid pattern of Bayard's life be modified.
He marries Caroline and sleeps with her while thinking of
Johnny, more real because of his absence than she can ever be
through her presence. Any possible significance that love or
marriage might have is overshadowed. His second marriage

holds the past in abeyance for but a brief moment. All Narcissa's serenity proves an insufficient bulwark and soon she, like Caroline, finds herself ignored and rejected. There is no way of establishing any human relationship, however transitory, as long as Bayard feels compelled to act out the role of the Sartoris to its bitter conclusion. Even the land cannot hold him, for days of labor are followed by days of rest as the earth lies fallow, and when its need of him is over, he cannot wait with it for the new quickening and the new harvest.

Yet it is his desire to terminate his involvement in the Sartoris legend that leads to his marrying Narcissa. Her aloof but steadying presence during his convalescences establishes her in his mind as part of, yet a bulwark against, his own violence. In this, Bayard sees a possible means of resolving his conflicts. She could fulfill Johnny's role, sharing with him the same spirit, while directing it to a different conclusion. Or if not that, she could at least minister with sympathy while he gropes for comprehension in his mental chaos. But Narcissa's presence as a witness to his various accidents is a matter of chance. The violence he deliberately seeks out is completely alien to her nature and past. Consequently, she cannot give him the comprehension he desires and her inability to do so is only intensified by her total lack of imagination and her essential self-centeredness.

Narcissa's motives for accepting Bayard seem every bit as devious and cross-grained as his. Her reason appears to be similar to that of Margaret Powers, for both identify a dead man with a living one who seems to need their care. But what is made quite clear in *Soldiers' Pay* is here presented only by implication. Narcissa's love for Johnny has not been declared, perhaps not even admitted to herself. Yet the only time her mind ranges over the past it singles out not Bayard but Johnny. Once more she sees him outlined against the sky on his trapeze bar while all breath leaves her and she stands watching as if hypnotized. There is no such imaginative absorption present in her account of how, soon after, Bayard had swung himself by a rope from the top of a building to a pool. The fact that Bayard's escapades after Johnny's death evoke the same response is the basis of her resentment of, yet attraction to, him. She is outraged, not because Bayard risks his life, but because he does it in her presence and so reminds her of Johnny.

Bayard most fully imposes his own identity on Narcissa during his convalescence after his first major accident. She feels pity for his physical and mental suffering and expresses sufficient concern to exact his promise to behave with more discretion. But it is not to this chastened and reformed Bayard that she surrenders. After his sudden burst of speed on one of their drives, she meets his violence with an unexpected, explosive emotion of her own which is an echo of her response to Johnny's balloon flight.

By her marriage to Bayard, Narcissa pits her own serenity and the Benbow pattern of life against the Sartoris violence and brooding awareness of the past. For though a Francis Benbow is mentioned as bringing a lantana plant from the Barbados to Jefferson in '71, the Benbows have no strong family traditions such as have been established and maintained by the Sartorises. The lone exception is Horace's law practice to which he returns out of a sense of familial obligation. But the very nature of law, its concern with the more broadly social rather than the familial forms of behavior, militates against the formation of a restrictive and isolating tradition. Both Horace and Narcissa are thus free to shape their own lives and to respond to experience without inhibiting preconceptions. But since they too choose to live by illusion, the original contrast between Benbow and Sartoris is at least partially obscured. The only difference is that the Benbow myths are personal rather than familial. Horace's takes the form of an exaltation and treasuring of beauty. Thus, having served overseas in the Y.M.C.A., he brings home from France not a memory of suffering and death but a recollection of a fragile loveliness wrested from the inferno of the cave. The agony and the evil in life remain peripheral to his vision until he is forced through the purgative experience of *Sanctuary*.

Narcissa's blindness, on the other hand, pertains only to herself and to her belief that she is indeed, to use Horace's phrase, the unblemished, the inviolate "bride of quietness." (182) This illusion of her own innocence persists despite her clear vision of and active engagement in a fallen world. Accordingly, she can accuse Belle of having a backstairs nature and express her abhorrence of Horace's relationship with Belle, even as she holds the latest letter from Byron Snopes in her hand. Her sense of moral superiority is fostered by her conviction that nothing has actually happened. As long as the words in the letter remain words, unaccompanied by overt action on either her or Snopes' part, they are harmless. She can even use them to stimulate Miss Jenny's belief in her virtue and unprotected innocence.

Narcissa is, of course, deluding herself since her continued acceptance of fresh letters and her treasuring of them constitute definite though secret acts which make her doubly vulnerable. First, they initiate a chain of events which ultimately involves not only herself, her child, and Miss Jenny but even a complete outsider and stranger, a Yankee detective. Secondly, the existence of the letters constitutes an ever present threat to that image of herself which she is determined to preserve. Self-deception imperceptibly merges into hypocrisy as she lies to Miss Jenny. And an excessive concern with appearances takes the place of any genuine sense of ethics, though it takes the crises of "There Was a Queen" and *Sanctuary* to reveal all the implications of this substitution.

Unlike Narcissa, Horace is aware of his own limitations and of the nature of his illusions. Yet eagerly he withdraws to his bedroom where he can lose himself in a world created by his imagination, "where unicorns filled the neighing air with galloping, or grazed or lay supine in golden-hoofed repose." (179) This imagination colors and eventually distorts reality and conditions his own reactions to it. At the same time Belle, consciously or not, can also use the magic of imagination and, being a woman, she uses it for very practical ends. She creates a romantic situation with herself as heroine to which Horace responds even though intellectually he realizes her pettiness, selfishness, and crudity:

They sat thus for some time while the light faded, Belle in another temporary vacuum of discontent, building for herself a world in which she moved romantically, finely, and a little tragically, with Horace sitting beside her and watching both Belle in her self-imposed and tragic rôle, and himself performing his part like the old actor whose hair is thin and whose profile is escaping him via his chin, but who can play to any cue at a moment's notice while the younger men chew their bitter thumbs in the wings. (194)

Horace's mistake is that he responds to one cue too many. The play acting has very real consequences, especially since one cannot decline the role and walk off the stage once the play is in progress. This juxtaposition of the play and reality actually telescopes the whole theme of *Sartoris*. The Sartorises are also moving romantically, finely, and a little tragically in self-imposed roles. And like Horace, they find that they cannot stop playing no matter how disastrous the consequences are. The only difference is that they lack Horace's ironic self-consciousness which enables him to recognize that it is an illusion to which he is responding and even to admit his own share of responsibility.

Of all the characters, only Miss Jenny appears able to make an effective compromise between past and present and between illusion and reality. Without denying the superior attractions of the former, she is still capable of acting to meet the demands of the latter. Although she is a Sartoris, she is also a woman with a woman's instinctive ability to adapt herself to circumstances and to do whatever is required of her. Memories of her romantic past do not prevent her from being the first to go for a ride in Bayard's car. The Civil War Sartorises have, however, taught her to accept and even anticipate a certain form of behavior in their heirs. Eventually this expectation becomes so strong that she is outraged by the manner of old Bayard's death. But coupled with her conviction that a violent death is *noblesse oblige* for any Sartoris is her woman's practicality and common sense which picks up the pieces and re-establishes order after each new act of folly. She makes old Bayard change his wet shoes, keep out of drafts, and see the specialist about the wen on his face. Similarly, she tucks young Bayard into bed with a glass of milk. Yet always she is waiting for the news that one or both of them have fulfilled their obligation to their name and ancestors by departing life in fittingly dramatic fashion. Actually, by her semi-humorous carping on the inevitable end of each Sartoris, she contributes to that end by admitting the closed nature of the pattern of life they have embraced.

The two sides of Miss Jenny enable her to recognize simultaneously both the power and the emptiness of the Sartoris dream and tradition. On the one hand, she weaves a legend about the name of the first Bayard Sartoris, making a significant focal point for the whole Civil War out of a reckless and useless gesture. On the other hand, she is the first to deflate not only young Bayard's actions but the whole tradition which, in fact, she has helped to establish. Her willingness to criticize as well as admire and to modify as well as preserve reveals a flexibility lacking in the male Sartorises. In one of the last scenes in the book, Miss Jenny visits the graveyard and provides a final evaluation of the Sartoris myth. There she traces the tradition of what she calls "humorless and fustian vainglory" (374) to Colonel John Sartoris and his defiance of time and change. She does not need to inspect the individual headstones to know that they will be repetitions of the Colonel's. Nor does she need to recollect specific incidents to know that the individual lives of his descendants present equally faithful copies of the Colonel's life since "she knew what it would be, what with the virus, the inspiration and example of that one which dominated them all." (374-75)

Imagination imperceptibly transforms the crude, chaotic stuff of experience by moulding it into a recognizable formal pattern. Whether it be one of romantic love, chivalric adventure, or primitive simplicity, it has value as a symbol of human potentiality. It also has all the high excitement and meaningfulness of drama. The danger arises when the individual first seeks a certain preconceived pattern and then, not finding it, forces it upon his experience. The designs created and preserved by legend and tradition cannot be faked or bought by cheap imitations. Only that man who is driven to the re-enactment of a legend by the necessity of his own nature does no violence to himself or his humanity. The appeal and the danger inherent in legend is underscored in the choric passage at the end of the novel:

The music went on in the dusk softly; the dusk was peopled with ghosts of glamorous and old disastrous things. And if they were just glamorous enough, there was sure to be a Sartoris in them, and then they were sure to be disastrous. Pawns. But the Player, and the game He plays . . . He must have a name for His pawns, though. But perhaps Sartoris is the game itself—a game outmoded and played with pawns shaped too late and to an old dead pattern, and of which the Player Himself is a little wearied. For there is death in the sound of it, and a glamorous fatality, like silver pennons downrushing at sunset, or a dying fall of horns along the road to Roncevaux. (380)

The Sartorises chose to act in terms of legend instead of history. Out of "the dusk peopled with ghosts of glamorous and old disastrous things," out of the stories of Charlemagne and Roland, the feats of gallant knights and the panoply of ancient battles, they created a legend of Sartoris and the Civil War in which disaster was made glamorous. But as this legend developed, it replaced history and itself assumed the validity of a historical pattern. Each of the Sartorises seeks to re-enact this pattern in his own life because he believes that only in this way can he fulfill his obligations to the past and perpetuate his traditions. At this point the myth created and controlled by the Sartorises asserts its control over them. Miss Jenny enriches and embellishes her account of Bayard Sartoris' death until she herself cannot distinguish between what actually happened and her dramatized version. The legend and not the facts of history sends young Bayard on his search for death. The irony attendant upon those who play the game of "Sartoris" is that their lives are, in fact, most determined at the very moment they most strongly assert their independence from all compulsions. By their worship of the glamorous and old disastrous things they have put the sound of death and fatality into the name of Sartoris. At this point they are themselves made into pawns, powerless and expendable, in a game whose rules they formulated for their own destruction.

3 : WORLDS IN COUNTERPOINT

The Sound and the Fury

The Sound and the Fury was the first of Faulkner's novels to make the question of form and technique an unavoidable critical issue. In any discussion of its structure the controlling assumption should be that there are plausible reasons for the particular arrangement of the four sections and for the use of the stream of consciousness technique in the first three and not in the fourth. Jean-Paul Sartre's comment that the moment the reader attempts to isolate the plot content "he notices that he is telling another story" indicates the need for such an assumption, not only for any light that may be thrown on *The Sound and the Fury* but for any insight that may emerge concerning Faulkner's method and achievement.

The structure of the novel is clearly reflected in the organization of the events of the evening on which Damuddy dies. These events reveal the typical gestures and reactions of the four children to each other and to the mysterious advent of death. They chart the range and kind of each of their responses to a new experience. In this way the evening partakes of the dual nature of the novel: primarily it is an objective, dramatic scene revealing the relations and tensions which exist among the children, but at the same time it is a study in perspective. Between the fact of Damuddy's death and the reader stands not only the primitive mind of the narrator, Benjy, but the diverse attitudes of the other children and the deliberate uncommunicativeness of the adults.

Within the novel as a whole it is Caddy's surrender to

Dalton Ames which serves both as the source of dramatic tension and as the focal point for the various perspectives. This is evident in the fact that the sequence of events is not caused by her act—which could be responded to in very different ways —but by the significance which each of her brothers actually attributes to it. As a result, the four sections appear quite unrelated even though they repeat certain incidents and are concerned with the same problem, namely Caddy and her loss of virginity. Although there is a progressive revelation or rather clarification of the plot, each of the sections is itself static. The consciousness of each character becomes the actual agent illuminating and being illuminated by the central situation. Everything is immobilized in this pattern; there is no development of either character or plot in the traditional manner. This impression is reinforced not only by the shortness of time directly involved in each section but by the absence of any shifts in style of the kind that, for example, accompany the growing maturity of Cash Bundren in *As I Lay Dying*.

By fixing the structure while leaving the central situation ambiguous, Faulkner forces the reader to reconstruct the story and to apprehend its significance for himself. Consequently, the reader recovers the story at the same time as he grasps the relation of Benjy, Quentin, and Jason to it. This, in turn, is dependent on his comprehension of the relation between the present and the past events with which each of the first three sections deals. As he proceeds from one section to the next, there is a gradual clarification of events, a rounding out of the fragments of scenes and conversations which Benjy reports. Thus, with respect to the plot the four sections are inextricably connected, but with respect to the central situation they are quite distinct and self-sufficient. As related to the central focus, each of the first three sections presents a version of the same facts which is at once the truth and a complete distortion of the truth. It would appear, then, that the theme of *The Sound and the Fury*, as revealed by the structure, is the relation between the act and man's apprehension of the act, between the event and the interpretation. The relation is by no means a rigid or inelastic thing but is a matter of shifting perspective, for, in a sense, each man creates his own truth. This does not mean that truth does not exist or that it is fragmentary or that it is unknowable; it only insists that truth is a matter of the heart's response as well as the mind's logic.

In keeping with this theme each of the first three sections presents a well demarcated and quite isolated world built around one of these splinters of truth. The fact that Benjy is dumb is symbolic of the closed nature of these worlds; communication is impossible when Caddy who is central to all three means something different to each. For Benjy she is the smell of trees; for Quentin, honor; and for Jason, money or at least the means of obtaining it. Yet these intense private dramas are taking place in a public world primarily concerned with observable behavior. Accordingly, in the fourth section we are shown what an interested but unimplicated observer would see of the Compsons. For the first time we realize that Benjy has blue eyes, that Mrs. Compson habitually wears black dressing gowns, and that Jason looks somewhat like a caricature of a bartender. Moreover, since we are prevented from sharing in the consciousness and memories of the characters, Caddy is no longer an immediate center. Nevertheless, through the conflict between Jason and Miss Quentin the final repercussions of her affair penetrate into the life of Jefferson and even Mottson. And out of the Compson house, itself a symbol of isolation, one person, Dilsey, emerges to grasp the truth which must be felt as well as stated.

Out of the relation that Benjy, Quentin, and Jason bear to Caddy yet another pattern emerges: a gradual progression from the completely closed and private world of the first section to the completely public world of the fourth. The latter, in a sense, both reverses and repeats the former: in the one Benjy is restricted by his retarded mind to immediate facts and sensations, in the other the reader is similarly limited. But Benjy's subjectivity has been replaced presumably by the reader's objectivity. Quentin's section is very close to Benjy's, for although he performs the gestures expected of him by other people, his world is essentially as isolated and irrational as his brother's. Jason, on the other hand, moves nearer to the public world of the fourth section insofar as he is able to act effectively, if unethically, in a social situation.

Moreover, each of these shifts from the private to the public world is accompanied by a corresponding shift in the form of apprehension. With Benjy we are restricted entirely to sensation which cannot be communicated; quite appropriately therefore Benjy is unable to speak. The closed world which he builds for himself out of various sensations becomes at once the least and the most distorted account of experience. He merely presents snatches of dialogue, bits of scenes exactly as they took place. Such reproduction is not necessarily synonymous with the truth. Benjy, however, makes it his truth and his ethics, for it is in terms of sensation that he imposes a very definite order on his experience. Despite the apparent chaos of fragments, Benjy himself lives in a world which is inflexible and rigid. The extent of its inflexibility is indicated by his bellows of protest whether over a wrong turn taken by Luster, Caddy's use of perfume, or her sexual promiscuity.

Quentin's world is almost as isolated and inflexible as Benjy's, but its order is based on abstractions rather than sensations. While Benjy can comprehend only the physical aspects of his experience, Quentin sees the physical only as a manifestation of ideas. Thus, his section is filled with echoes, both literary and Biblical, phrases, names quoted out of context but falling neatly into the pattern of his thought. These echoes assume the quality of a ritual by which he attempts to conjure experience into conformity with his wishes. When Caddy's behavior disarranges his world, his protest partakes of Benjy's outrage and agony. He stands despairing before the abyss which has suddenly separated experience and his conception of what experience ought to be, and when all his efforts to coerce experience with a word, "incest," fail, he chooses death which alone can terminate his unwilling involvement in circumstance.

The third section shows a greater degree of clarity though not of objectivity. The reason for this is that Jason operates in terms of a logic which forms the basis of social communication. We may not approve the direction in which his logic takes him, but that his actions are the results of clear, orderly thinking in terms of cause and effect cannot be disputed. The steps in his reasoning follow one another naturally: since it was because of Caddy that he was deprived not only of his inheritance but of his promised job, his recompense must come from Caddy; and since Miss Quentin was the actual cause of Herbert's displeasure, it is through her that he simultaneously gains his wealth and his revenge. It is part of the general satiric intent of this section that Jason's obvious distortion of Caddy should be associated with logic and reason, for it throws a new perspective not only on the actions of the Compsons but on Jason, the representative of the "rational" man.

The objective nature of the fourth section precludes the use of any single level of apprehension, and accordingly it provokes the most complex response. Dilsey, almost as inarticulate as Benjy, becomes through her actions alone the embodiment of the truth of the heart which is synonymous with morality. The acceptance of whatever time brings, the absence of questioning and petty protests, enables her to create order out of circumstance rather than in defiance of it, and in so doing she gains both dignity and significance for her life. In a sense, Dilsey represents a final perspective directed toward the past and the Compsons, but it is also the reader's perspective for which Dilsey merely provides the vantage point. This fact suggests another reason for the objective narration in this section: to use Dilsey as a point of view character would be to destroy her efficacy as the ethical norm, for that would give us but one more splinter of the truth confined and conditioned by the mind which grasped it.

Our first impression of the Benjy section is that it presents a state of utter chaos for which the only possible justification is the fact that Benjy is an idiot and therefore has the right to be confused. But out of this disorder two patterns emerge: the one, completely independent of public perspective, constitutes Benjy's world, the other serves as the author's guide for enabling the reader to grasp the fragments as a comprehensible order. With respect to the latter, critics have pointed out both Faulkner's use of italics to indicate shifts in time and the fact that the reason for such shifts occurring are easily recognizable. An object, a sound, an incident may propel the mind toward some point in the past where a similar experience took place.

Equally important is the fact that there are actually very few scenes involved despite the length of time covered. The events of 7 April 1928 are easily identified because of the prominence given to Luster in them. His dogged and somewhat querulous search for the lost quarter and his single-minded preoccupation with the show run like an identifying motif in a difficult composition. Otherwise, there are but three extended episodes: one taking place some time in 1898, the day Damuddy died; the second occurring on the evening Benjy received his new name; and the last consisting of the scene of Caddy's wedding. Each of these episodes has its own principle of organization. Benjy's other recollections create the impression of a mind confused and undiscriminating, but they are for the most part short, self-sufficient vignettes. At times these unit-episodes interlock as when Benjy's intrusion into Miss Quentin's privacy on the swing recalls a similar scene involving Caddy. In this case the recollected event is completed before we are returned to the present scene of Miss Quentin's anger and her friend's perverse humor.

The organization of the fragments in the first main episode is more complex but none the less comprehensible. Large sections of the time between 1898 and 1928 are marked off by the succession of Benjy's nurses and thus some sort of relative chronology can be established as we shift from Versh to T.P. to Luster. But more important is the fact that the pieces forming the scene beginning at the Branch and ending with the children's reactions to Damuddy's death are only interrupted by other pieces and not themselves dislocated in time. If it were possible to blot out these intrusive scenes, we would have the events of that day in a chronological order. Yet since there can be a double shift in one of the interrupting passages, both of which are indicated by italics, the continuity of the single day has to be established by other means.

Accordingly, we have a succession of verbal clues which show that the interruption is over. For example, a train of recollection begins when Luster allows Benjy to play in the water and Benjy remembers the earlier scene when all the Compson children were playing at the Branch under the somewhat uncertain supervision of Versh: *"and Roskus came and said to come to supper and Caddy said, It's not supper time yet."* (37) Just when he remembers Caddy promising not to run away, Luster breaks in with his impatient scolding, and this is immediately followed by the verbal echo: "Roskus came and said to come to supper and Caddy said it wasn't supper time yet." (39) A number of the scenes from the day of Damuddy's death are identified by references to the buzzards who have "undressed" Nancy or to the bottle of lightning bugs which Benjy carries. But again paired sentences are used to indicate resumption of the episode. "Versh took me up and we went on around the kitchen" (56) is picked up by "We stopped under the tree by the parlor window. Versh set me down in the wet grass." (57) This careful interweaving of the fragments, evident throughout the whole episode, is supported and its efficacy increased by the fact that most of the interrupting passages are too short to interfere with our recognition of the linking phrase.

The scattered pieces of the wedding scene are identified

mainly by T.P.'s inebriated antics and his prowess with "sass-prilluh" but also, of course, by Caddy's "long veil like shining wind." These provide sufficient clues since we are concerned with a single scene rather than a succession of events. The evening on which Maury is renamed Benjy gains its unity through the use of repeated sensations rather than echo words. Each fragment of the evening is marked by some reference to the sound of rain or the presence of the fire. Eventually the mirror, which by itself is not a sufficient clue since it is also associated with Caddy's wedding, becomes a secondary means of identification as Benjy watches all the actions of the Compsons reflected in its surface. A somewhat similar use of sensations is found in the episode which begins with Benjy's waiting for Caddy and ends with their visit to Mrs. Patterson. Here the sign is a reference either to the coldness of the weather or to Benjy's propensity for getting his hands frozen.

With consummate skill the repetitions and identifying sensations which are used to guide the reader are also used as the basis of Benjy's own ordering of experience. Benjy's mind works not by association which is dependent, to some extent, on an ability to discriminate as well as compare but by mechanical identification. Thus, being caught on the fence while walking with Luster does not recall an associated feeling or fact but the exact replica of the incident. More important is the fact that the three deaths in the family, which Benjy senses are repetitions of each other, provoke an identical response. What he reacts to is the fact of death or the fact of being caught on the fence. To differentiate in terms of time and circumstance is a logical matter and therefore beyond Benjy's range of apprehension.

This is further illustrated by his inflexible identification of one word with one object. Very seldom, for example, is the name of a speaker replaced by a pronoun in his section. Each person is freed from the multiplicity of descriptive relations which make him at once man and brother, father, Negro or white. For Benjy, he is forever fixed as simply Jason, Quentin, or Luster. In the one scene where Benjy is brought into contact with Luster's friends, parts of the dialogue are consistently attributed to Luster, but the answers appear to come out of the air. Benjy does not know the names of these strangers and to give them an identity in terms of description is beyond his power. His literalism finds its sharpest illustration in the scene where the cries of the golfers are heard. "Caddy" can mean only one thing and elicit only one response.

Benjy both orders and evaluates his experience with this same rigidity. The objects he has learned to recognize constitute an inflexible pattern which he defends against novelty or change with every bellow in his overgrown body. At what time or under what circumstances the small mound of earth which Dilsey calls his graveyard was formed and marked with two empty bottles of blue glass holding withered stalks of jimson weed is unimportant. But that this arrangement, once established, should remain unchanged in the slightest detail is of the utmost importance. When Luster removes one of the bottles, Benjy is momentarily shocked into a silence which is immediately succeeded by a roar of protest. It is not that the bottle has any intrinsic value for Benjy, but merely that it forms part of the pattern which must not be disturbed. The fixed route to the graveyard is also sacred; Benjy is overwhelmed with horror and agony when Luster takes the wrong turn only to subside the minute the mistake is corrected.

Within this rigid world Caddy is at once the focus of order and the instrument of its destruction. The pasture, the fire, and sleep, the three things Benjy loves most, are associated with her, as is illustrated by the recurrent phrase "Caddy smelled like trees," his refusal to go to sleep without her, and his memory of her during the rainy evening when for a brief moment everything in his world was in its proper place. Caddy both realizes and respects his fear of change: while playing at the Branch she is quick to reassure him that she is not really going to run away; later, she washes off her perfume and gives the rest of it to Dilsey in order to reassure him. Even when she has accepted the inevitability of change for herself and is preparing to marry Herbert, she tries to bind Quentin to a promise of seeing that Benjy's life is not further disordered by his being committed to a mental institution. Yet what Benjy most expects of Caddy is the one thing she cannot give him, for his expectation is based on his complete indifference to or rather ignorance of time. As long as Caddy is in time, she cannot free either herself or his world from change. His dependence on her physical presence, her scent of trees, is subject to constant threats which he fends off to the best of his ability. The intensity of his reaction is caused by the fact that any alteration in Caddy makes her not-Caddy. Thus, Caddy, as in the Quentin section, is at once identified with the rigid order of Benjy's private world and with the disorder of actual experience. Depending on which of the two is dominant at the moment, Benjy moans or smiles serenely.

Since Benjy is concerned with preserving the pattern rather than any single one of its parts, there is little that he can lose. Even Caddy has no existence for him except as she forms part of that pattern. As with the blue bottle which Luster snatches from its place so with Caddy, he is reminded by the small depression in the earth or by the sound of her name that something is missing, but what it is he misses, he scarcely knows himself. Despite his moans Benjy suffers less than any other person in the book because even pain is something external to himself and because one pattern can be replaced with another. If the "bright shapes" of the fire are shut off from him, he can still look into the mirror and see there an endless panorama of shape and color reflecting reality but confining it within a frame so that it is no longer a threat but an amusement.

The parallels between the Quentin and Benjy sections are very strong despite the widely different impression each conveys. Quentin too has constructed for himself a private world to which Caddy is essential, a world which is threatened and finally destroyed by her involvement in circumstance. His hopeless and endless brooding is but Benjy's moan become articulate though not rational. His order, however, is based on emotions rather than sensations, on concepts rather than physical objects. And whereas Benjy is saved by being outside time, Quentin is destroyed by his excessive awareness of it. For the former, both the pattern and its disordering are eternally present as his alternation between moaning and smiling demonstrates; for the latter, the pattern has become a part of the past and contentment has been replaced by despair. Quentin can neither accept nor reconcile himself to that change or to the possibility that a further change may make even his despair a thing of the past, and so he chooses death as a means of escaping the situation.

The structure of the section with its two sets of events, one past and the other present, reflects Quentin's problem. Throughout the day he can proceed quite mechanically with such chores as getting dressed, packing, writing letters, and generally tidying up the loose ends of his life at Harvard. To a large extent he can even make the appropriate gestures and speak the proper words expected of him by others. Meanwhile, his mind is occupied with echoes of the past which make themselves felt with increasing intensity until they threaten to prevent even a mechanical attention to the details of living through that final day. Quentin cannot escape either his memories of the past or his involvement in the present. The Italian child who is connected with his thoughts of Sister Caddy stops him by her very presence from concentrating solely on Caddy.

His fights with Julio, the outraged brother, and with Bland constitute the two points at which past and present, the private and public worlds, collide. In the first case, the present asserts its power, once more involving him in a situation not of his making. The irony of the scene lies not only in the fact that Quentin should be blamed for doing the one thing which it would be impossible for him to do, but that chance should involve him in a present which he has already rejected by choosing death. In the incident with Bland the past breaks into the present as Quentin's memory of Dalton Ames becomes stronger than the routine responses he is forced to make to Mrs. Bland and her guests. Significantly, in neither case does Quentin offer any resistance to the blows he receives.

The order which Quentin had once built around Caddy is as rigid and inflexible as Benjy's and it shares Benjy's fear of change and his expectation that all experience should conform to his pattern. The cause of his ineffectuality and his ultimate destruction is the fact that his system antecedes his experience and eventually is held in defiance of experience. His is an ethical order based on words, on "fine, dead sounds," the meaning of which he has yet to learn. He has, in short, separated ethics from the total context of humanity. Insofar as virginity is a concept, associated with virtue and honor, it becomes the center of Quentin's world, and since it is also physically present in Caddy, it forms a precarious link between his world and that of experience. Mr. Compson remarks that virginity is merely a transient physical state which has been given its ethical significance by men. What they have chosen to make it mean is something which is a defiance of nature, an artificial isolation of the woman. Caddy, who seems almost a symbol of the blind forces of nature, is an unstable guardian for that "concept of Compson honor precariously and . . . only temporarily supported by the minute fragile membrane of her maidenhead." (9)

Quentin can only try to buttress it with more words, with "some presbyterian concept of . . . eternal punishment." (9) Since his emotional responses center on these concepts, Quentin is quite incapable of love for any human being, even Caddy. Despite his feverish preoccupation with ethics, he is unable to perform any ethical actions himself; even his death is not so much a protest as it is simply a withdrawal. Thus, it is not the time that is out of joint but Quentin's relation to time.

Whereas Benjy had selected odd fragments of his actual experience to form a pattern which he endowed with expectations of eternity, Quentin attempts to coerce experience into conformity with his system. Having rejected the life around him as insufficiently meaningful, he invents instead his own play, which he regards as reality, and peoples it with creatures of his own fantasy. He begins grooming Caddy for her role from the outset, insisting on her conformity to his conception of her. At the Branch he slaps her for disregarding his orders, and periodically after that he reasserts his control, scouring her head in the grass for kissing boys and smearing her with mud for not being concerned with his behavior. But his main intention is not simply to punish her for forgetting her part but to make her understand the significance of her role as the guardian of Compson honor. Hence his pique when she refuses to bother herself about his games with Natalie.

Quentin's desire to convert Caddy's promiscuity into an act of incest is another instance of his attempt to trick experience into conformity with his pattern. In the long sweep of time Caddy's affair is but one more event, seemingly without reason or significance, providing one more illustration of transience and change in human life. She herself places little importance on the actual Ames affair, although she is concerned with its effect on Quentin, Benjy, and her father. For Quentin, however, it means the complete collapse of his careful ethical structure which he had tried to hold beyond time. Like Benjy's, his reaction is a moan of pain and outrage which expects no answer.

His solution is to make Caddy admit that they have committed incest. In this way he hopes to make Compson honor a thing of importance and momentous significance even as he destroys it. This gesture is in contrast to Caddy's promiscuity which merely slights the honor. Moreover, incest can be used to affirm the validity of his ethical pattern. Quentin has already, in a sense, usurped the role of God by creating a paradise for himself and Caddy isolated from the world through the fact of sexual innocence. Through incest he can convert this paradise into hell, thereby maintaining the same order but in reverse. Sin instead of virtue, punishment instead of bliss, will be made everlasting. The isolation through innocence can become isolation through sin. The incest, however, is as unreal a center for Quentin's hell as his sister's sexual purity was for his paradise. It is significant that he refuses to commit the actual act. Committing incest would destroy his order completely by involving him in the terrible reality of experience. But through a lie he can circumvent experience; like the boys discussing the money they would have received and spent had they caught the fish, he makes "of unreality a possibility, then a probability, then an incontrovertible fact, as people will when their desires become words." (136) Yet his ritualistic chant of "Father, I have committed incest" has no power over "the sequence of natural events and their causes which shadows every mans [sic] brow." (195)

The greatest enemy of Quentin's ethical system is time, the whole long diminishing parade of moments whose beginning and ending we cannot conceive. His very concern with time takes place in time. Accordingly, the inexorable passing of one moment after another gives an emotional and dramatic intensity to his brooding since we know that each instant brings him that much closer to death. His act of breaking the watch merely increases his and our awareness of time; the chiming of bells, the lengthening shadows, his own hunger, all insist that night is approaching. And irrespective of any act of his, even suicide, time will continue whether or not it is being marked off by hands on a dial or the sound of bells. Man's efforts to control even his own allotted time can only result in a mockery, as Quentin realizes when he looks in the shop window. By becoming conscious of time man puts himself in opposition to it only to find that his victories are illusions. Yet Quentin's every effort is bent toward circumventing time and achieving permanence by somehow arresting that steady succession of events which reduces everything, even sorrow and disappointment, to points in time. He would like to believe that Caddy's one act is so monstrous that it has instantaneously made of him an old man whose involvement in experience is at an end. He attempts to make first Caddy's purity and then her "sinning" everlasting, and when both attempts fail, he chooses death not so much to terminate time as to arrest it forever at one point.

Nonetheless, Quentin cannot sever his relation to time or "the sequence of natural events and their causes." Each day weaves its own pattern of chance and circumstance, flouting his will and desire. The battle against time cannot even be fought since defeat is inevitable and victory "an illusion of philosophers and fools." (95) Ignoring the plans and dreams of one man or all men, time, working through circumstance, forms a pattern of its own in which men are only pawns. That is the fact most difficult for Quentin to accept and live with. It is especially difficult in view of Quentin's youth which tends to invest even trifles with tragic profundity. Rather than face the certainty of further change, even change toward happiness, he takes his own life.

Quentin's desire for death is, of course, bound up with his consciousness of time and more specifically of memory. Only that has reality which has made an impression on human minds and is preserved in human memory. It is by emphasizing his role as the recording spectator that he makes one last desperate effort to bring experience into alignment with his dream. In a sense, the whole history of Caddy lies in his memory and when he ceases to be, so does her betrayal of Compson honor. By declining all further participation in life, he can isolate himself and his memory of Caddy from the "loud world."

The symbols and recurrent phrases that run through Quentin's section both intensify the emotional impact and reinforce the meaning. Such names as Jesus, St. Francis, Moses, Washington, and Byron not only add a richness of historical and literary allusion but convey the nature of Quentin's world. Into that world Benjy is admitted as "Benjamin the child of mine old age held hostage into Egypt" and Caddy as Eve or Little Sister Death. Mr. Compson forces an entry not as father or friend but as a voice which can juggle words and ideas while insisting on their emptiness. As for Quentin, he sees himself as the hero of the family drama, the "bitter prophet and inflexible corruptless judge." (10) Part of his outrage and frustration in connection with Caddy is that neither her husband nor her lover seems worthy, in his eyes, of assuming a role in his world: Herbert is obviously despicable and Ames refuses to act in terms of Quentin's preconceptions.

The heavy, choking fragrance of honeysuckle dramatizes the conflict between his order and the blind forces of nature which constantly threaten to destroy it. Honeysuckle is the rife animality of sex, the incomprehensible and hateful world for which Caddy has abandoned his paradise, and hence it is also the symbol of his defeat. Yet honeysuckle is only a sensation, just as Caddy's affair with Ames is simply a natural event. It is Quentin who makes of the one a symbol of "night and unrest" and of the other the unforgivable sin. The references to roses have a similar function in that they too are associated with sex, but they are identified with a single scene, that of Caddy's wedding. Therefore, they are at once the symbol of the world he fears and of his irrevocable betrayal by that world. Roses are Caddy's sex, her promiscuity and her "sin" made socially respectable. The validity of his world is challenged and defeated by a counter system: "Roses. Cunning and serene." (96)

There is a parallel as well as a contrast in the symbolic value attached to scents in the first and second sections. Both Benjy and Quentin associate disorder and a threat to themselves with a particular fragrance. The difference lies in the fact that Benjy resents either the inexplicable absence of the smell of trees which belongs to Caddy or the change of one scent for another, the substitution of perfume for the tree scent. Quentin, on the other hand, resents a change in the scent itself whereby the honeysuckle which he once liked becomes something oppressive and hateful. The scent which had enveloped his games with Caddy also envelops Caddy and Ames in quite a different game. Everything seems the same, yet there has been an agonizing change which makes each familiar object or sensation a mockery of itself.

The constant references to the shadows and the mirror emphasize the barrier between Quentin and reality. It is not only Benjy but also Quentin who sees Caddy's wedding reflected in the mirror. Caddy, however, cannot be confined to its surface; she runs out of the mirror and out of his and Benjy's world. Similarly, Quentin sees her and Ames not as people but as silhouettes distorted against the sky. He is lost amid these shadows, feeling that they falsify the objects they pretend to reflect, yet unable to reach out beyond them. It is significant that he sees only those aspects of Caddy as shadows which he cannot incorporate into his world: it is her love affair and her marriage which he finds perverse, mocking, denying the significance they should have affirmed. The same feeling of mockery is present in his insistence that he has tricked his shadow. A man who is dead needs no shadow, but still his accompanies him throughout the day as if it were mirroring reality when in truth it is but aping another illusion.

The number of times that the shadow images are fused with images of water indicates that death by water is Quentin's way of reconciling his two worlds, of merging shadow and reality and tempering their conflict. Whatever suggestion of purification may be present, water is primarily a symbol of oblivion for Quentin. Both Quentin and Caddy run to the Branch to surrender themselves to its hypnotic rhythm which, like sleep, soothes the mind into unconsciousness, blurring thought and emotion, eliminating the necessity for acting. It is in the hope of making this peace eternal that Quentin surrenders his body to the water where the hard knots of circumstance will be untangled and the roof of wind will stand forever between him and the loud world.

With Jason's section we enter a world far different from Benjy's or Quentin's yet related to theirs through Caddy. It represents a third possible way of reacting to experience, as distorted yet as "true" as the former two. Since Jason reacts logically rather than emotionally, his section offers no barriers to comprehension. His particular method of ordering and explaining his actions in terms of cause and effect, profit and loss, is all too familiar. Yet logic, presumably the basis of human communication and hence of society, isolates Jason as effectively as the moral abstractions of Quentin or the complete dependence on sensations of Benjy. In the midst of Jefferson or even his family, he is by necessity as well as by choice alone. And instead of being concerned, he glories in his self-sufficiency, "since to him all the rest of the town and the world and the human race too except himself were Compsons, inexplicable yet quite predictable in that they were in no sense whatever to be trusted." (17)

One of Jason's dominant characteristics, and the main source of humor, is his pride that he has no illusions about his family or himself. The humor, however, arises not from the situation but from the way in which Jason talks about it. Where Quentin sees Caddy's behavior and his own relation to it in terms of tragedy, Jason assumes the role of comic hero. He sees himself as a modern Sancho Panza who could never mistake a windmill for an army, but who has no objections to others doing so, especially if he can turn it to his own advantage. This tolerance or rather non-interference even extends to allowing Mrs. Compson to go on supporting Uncle Maury and protecting Miss Quentin against any real discipline, although he accepts as fact that the former is a wastrel and the latter a bitch.

The conviction that he alone has a firm grasp on reality results in a literalism untouched by any hint of qualification in Jason's thinking. Through it we get a new and welcome perspective on the Compsons, but it is just a perspective and not the final word that Jason makes it out to be. It is his very insistence on facing facts that causes his distorted view of Caddy, his family, and the whole human race. He cannot imagine that there might be other facts, other aspects of the situation, than the ones that directly affect him; as a result, he sees certain things so clearly that all others escape him. In the process logic replaces truth, and law, justice. Caddy's affair with Ames does result in Herbert's eventual rejection of all the Compsons and that, in its turn, in his double loss since he was deprived at one stroke of both his inheritance and his job. In this reasoning the human beings involved are quite irrelevant. He is not concerned with either Caddy or her daughter except as they enter into the pattern of loss and recompense and finally loss again. In short, his is a world reduced to calculation in which no subjective claims are tolerated and no margin for error allowed.

This calculating approach to experience pervades his every act, no matter how trivial. He offers Luster a ticket for five cents and burns it rather than give it away. His promise to Caddy to allow her to see her baby is a bargain that he fulfills to the letter but no further. He never permits himself or Earl to overstep the terms of their agreement of so much work for so much pay. Even where sincere affection is apparently involved, his relationship with Lorraine gives the impression of a contract duly notarized. Two days are devoted to keeping house in a most serious and even uxorious fashion; the other five are devoted to business and into that part of his life Lorraine must not intrude by so much as a phone call at the risk of terminating their "contract." All these arrangements constitute Jason's way of protecting himself from any intrusion of the irrational. It is his method of assuming control over experience by preventing himself from becoming involved in circumstances he has not foreseen.

His control over the Compson house reveals the same tendency to think in terms of contracts. He fulfills his filial duties by supporting his mother and even her servants in much the same condition as before Mr. Compson's death. But the way in which he sacrifices "what pleasures might have been the right and just due and even the necessity of a thirty-year-old bachelor" (17) travesties his obligations. Nevertheless, he expects to receive full value in return, not only in services but in subservience. In his own home he insists that dinner be served on time to all the members of the family even though such familial repasts become grotesque parodies of conviviality and family life. Special attention is directed to Miss Quentin, who must be made not good but discreet; Jason disclaims all concern for what she does, providing appearances are not flouted. This preoccupation with social form partakes of the nature of a ritual with which Jason would charm away disorder and placate the Player, but it is destructive of the very significance it should affirm.

Jason's concern with forms of action rather than with the actions themselves is reflected in his legalistic view of society and especially of ethics. It is on this view that the double irony of Miss Quentin's theft of his thieving hinges. He has retrieved his losses, suffered because of Caddy, at the expense of Caddy's daughter without actually breaking any law. Caddy is sending money for her daughter's support and the daughter is being supported. Mrs. Compson retains the pleasure of tearing up and burning cheques even while her account at the bank grows. Meanwhile, Jason recovers what he considers to be his own money in a legal though unethical fashion. But with her one unpremeditated act Miss Quentin destroys the work of years; more important, she is as safe from prosecution despite her heedlessness as Jason was because of all his care. Legally, she has only stolen what already belonged to her. When Jason demands an endorsement of his just indignation from the sheriff, the latter refuses to help on the basis of the very letter of the law Jason had so carefully observed. Thus, he is effectively hoisted with his own petard and fairly defeated with his own weapons.

During his frantic pursuit of Miss Quentin the nature of

the conflict in which Jason is involved becomes explicit. He realizes that his enemy is not his niece or even the man with the red tie; rather it is "the sequence of natural events and their causes which shadows every mans [sic] brow." (195) From the first he had distrusted everything which he could not himself control. Unlike Quentin for whom reality lay in ethical concepts, Jason had learned to believe in whatever he could hold in his hands or keep in his pocket. That alone could be protected from chance and change. The money placed in a strong box, hidden in a closet, kept in a locked room is the symbol of Jason's world. Yet even that is vulnerable to circumstance, to the accidental juxtaposition in place and time of a girl's whim and a man's red tie. Hence his outrage that Miss Quentin should have taken the money more or less on impulse; had her act been deliberate, calculated, he could have foreseen it and so guarded against it. The red tie becomes for him the symbol of the irrational, the antithesis of his own careful logic.

With the car speeding toward Mottson, Jason surveys the available courses of action. But he is not able to foresee and arrange for all the possibilities; the pattern of circumstance begins to close in. The fact that he has forgotten his camphor and that there is none mislaid in the car gives the first indication of his helplessness. The main setback, however, is that Miss Quentin and the man should not be where he expected to find them. Jason is not only forced into letting the recovery of his money rest on chance but even that chance is suddenly denied him. A similar surprise awaits him in the old man whose responses he calculates quite dispassionately. He finds himself caught in an unforeseen and uncontrollable situation: the unexpected occurs and he is overwhelmed by the "fatal, furious little old man" (325) whose strength he had so confidently discounted.

Jason is thoroughly defeated by the "rear guards of Circumstance" (322) which he had challenged by his trip to Mottson. The contents of his inviolate strong box and Miss Quentin, together the symbol of his revenge and frustration, disappear from Jefferson, yet his world does not collapse as Quentin's does. Like Benjy, he violently protests his loss, but, also like Benjy's, his order remains intact despite the loss of certain elements. Always the practical man, Jason cuts his losses and continues in exactly the same way, discharging his obligations to the letter, slowly accumulating money for another strong box, neither asking for nor giving more than the law requires. In a sense, the final and irrevocable loss of the money is even somewhat of a relief, for it spells the end of his involvement with Caddy, who has always, even in her absence, represented the threat of the irrational and incalculable.

Still isolated and unrepentant, Jason survives while Quentin is destroyed by the events he can neither accept nor control. On the other hand, that survival is itself futile, for Jason is the last of the Compson line and a childless bachelor. That very childlessness is another indication of his deliberate rejection of any relationship which he cannot control, especially one in which emotions dominate logic and trust replaces contracts. Insofar as Jason flourishes in a world in which Quentin, a more sensitive individual, perishes, a certain amount of satire and irony is involved. But it is by no means restricted to the South or the contemporary scene. The tendency to identify logic with truth and law with justice is not limited to twentieth century America; the Jasons of the world have been claiming an eye for an eye long before Jesus began speaking of love and forgiveness and pity and sacrifice. Furthermore, even in Snopes-infested Jefferson, Jason stands alone; he is rejected by Earl, the sheriff, and even old Job, whose Negro wisdom sums up Jason's philosophy and its flaws: " 'You's too smart fer me. Aint a man in dis town kin keep up wid you fer smartness. You fools a man whut so smart he cant even keep up wid hisself. . . . Dat's Mr Jason Compson.' " (267)

In the last section we finally emerge from the closed world of the Compson Mile into the public world as represented by Jefferson. No longer colored by the subjectivity of a single point of view, the outward manifestations of appearance and behavior assume a new importance. We are still permitted occasional glimpses of Jason's mind but only as he reacts to experience and not as he attempts to control it. The primary result is that the whole history of the Compsons is given a wider reference. Absence and time have erased Caddy and Quentin from the scene, even if the promiscuity of the one and the suicide of the other originally had an impact beyond the family. And Caddy, at any rate, never existed in the novel except in the minds and memories of those whom she had affected. In this larger context the sound and the fury of the family signifies very little if anything.

Certain individuals such as the sheriff and Earl sense some-

46

thing of the situation and this influences their actions with regard to Jason. Others such as the furious, little old man and the show's manager simply react to what they see of Jason, without knowing or caring what his reasons or provocation might have been. Beyond these few people who are caught up in the last reverberations of the events set in motion by Caddy's act, larger numbers remain untouched and indifferent except for mild curiosity. Only Benjy continues to make some impression and that simply because his idiocy has its external manifestations which cannot be ignored. The Negroes are excited by his presence, especially the children who watch him "with the covertness of nocturnal animals." (307) The whites regard him as a problem: since he is obviously white, they frown on his attendance at a Negro church, but since he is as obviously an idiot, they are unwilling to receive him into theirs. Somehow in the process, the additional fact that he is a human being is forgotten by all except Dilsey.

In this section Dilsey emerges not only as a Negro servant in the Compson household but as a human being. With nothing to judge but her actions, with no prolonged ethical or religious polemics, her very presence enables the reader to achieve a final perspective on the lives of the Compsons. Mrs. Compson's nagging self-pity, Jason's carping exactions, Miss Quentin's thoughtlessness gain a dramatic actuality lacking while they were being filtered through an individual consciousness. Various contrasts between Dilsey and the others are delineated with striking clarity. The contrast becomes actual conflict where Dilsey and Jason are concerned. It is not only that Dilsey "survives," because, for that matter, so does Jason, but that her endurance has strength to suffer without rancor as well as to resist, to accept as well as to protest. She is the only one who challenges his word in the household, who defends the absent Caddy, Miss Quentin, Benjy, and even Luster from his anger. But more important, she challenges the validity and efficacy of his world by a passive and irrational resistance to which he has no counter. That someone should work without pay is so foreign to his system that he is helpless in the face of it.

There is no doubt but that Dilsey is meant to represent the ethical norm, the realizing and acting out of one's humanity; it is from this that the Compsons have deviated, each into his separate world. The mother and her two elder sons have abandoned their humanity for the sake of pride or vanity or self-pity. Both

Benjy and Caddy are tests of the family's humanity, he simply because he is not fully human and she because her conduct creates a socio-moral hiatus between the family and Jefferson. Benjy's behavior is a constant trial to the family and to this extent counterpoints Caddy's lone disgracing act. Both challenge the family's capacity for understanding and forgiveness and the family fails both. Quite appropriately, the Compson Mile exists in an atmosphere not only of disintegration but of constriction. The property shrinks as the town begins "to encroach and then nibble at and into it." (7) The only room which seems to be lived in is Dilsey's kitchen; the others are so many private mausoleums. While each of the Compsons to some extent attempts to coerce experience and to deny his involvement in the sequence of natural events and their causes, Dilsey accepts whatever time brings. She alone never suffers that moment of rejection which is equated with death.

By working with circumstance instead of against it she creates order out of disorder; by accommodating herself to change she manages to keep the Compson household in some semblance of decency. While occupied with getting breakfast, she is yet able to start the fire in Luster's inexplicable absence, provide a hot water bottle for Mrs. Compson, see to Benjy's needs, and soothe various ruffled tempers. All this despite the constant interruptions of Luster's perverseness, Benjy's moaning, Mrs. Compson's complaints, and even Jason's maniacal fury. The same calmness is evident with regard to Caddy's affair, Quentin's suicide, and the arrival of Caddy's baby. As she herself states, she has brought up Caddy and can do the same for Miss Quentin. And if it so happens that their conduct mocks all her care and love, then it is time to find another order in the subsequent confusion. Dilsey's attitude, as she lives it, is formed by her instinctive feeling that whatever happens must be met with courage and dignity in which there is no room for passivity or pessimism.

Her ability to stand steadfast without faltering in the face of circumstance finds further expression in her patient preoccupation with the present, which is the only possible way of living with time. This does not imply that Dilsey is cut off from the past but only that she deals with it as it is caught up in the present without attempting to perpetuate a part of it as Quentin does, or to circumvent it as Jason tries to do. In a sense, she is a living record of all that has happened to the Compsons made significant by her own strength and courage. It is a record of pain and suffering and change but also of endurance and permanence in change.

In describing Dilsey as an ethical norm it should be stressed that she propounds no system, no code of behavior or belief, and this despite the emphasis on the Easter service which she attends. Neither in her attitude nor in the service itself is there any reference to sin and punishment but only to suffering and its surcease. At no time does Dilsey judge any of the Compsons, not even Jason, though she does object at one point to those who frown on Benjy's presence in a Negro church. But her presence enables the reader to judge not systems but actions and hence to grasp the truth instinctively: "They [Negroes] come into white people's lives like that in sudden sharp black trickles that isolate white facts for an instant in unarguable truth like under a microscope." (189) And though she does not judge, Dilsey is never deceived; her comprehension of the relations between Caddy and the rest of the family is unerring.

Dilsey's participation in the Easter service is the one meaningful ritual in the book. As she proceeds sedately from house to church, acknowledging greetings with proper reserve and dignity, she is still conscious of being, in some sense, a member of the Compson household with a certain prestige and obligations. With each member of the congregation similarly conscious of his own distinctive position in society, the Reverend Shegog begins using the magic of his voice. When he concludes, communication has been replaced by communion in which each member loses his identity but finds his humanity and the knowledge that all men are equal and brothers in their suffering.

Out of Dilsey's actions and her participation in the Easter service arise once more the simple verities of human life, which Faulkner's Stockholm address describes as "the old universal truths lacking which any story is ephemeral and doomed—love and honor and pity and pride and compassion and sacrifice." It is these truths which throw the final illumination not only on Caddy and the whole sequence of events that started with her affair but also on what each of the Compsons believed her to be. The splinters of truth presented in the first three sections reverberate with the sound and the fury signifying nothing. But out of those same events, the same disorder and confusion, come Dilsey's triumph and her peace, lending significance not only to her own life but to the book as a whole.

4 : THE DIMENSIONS OF CONSCIOUSNESS

As I Lay Dying

As I Lay Dying possesses basically the same structure as *The Sound and the Fury* but in a more complex form. Instead of four main sections, three of which are dominated by the consciousness of a single character, there are some sixty short sections apportioned among fifteen characters. Each of these brief chapters describes some part either of the funeral preparations or of the procession itself, even as it explores and defines the mind of the observer from whose point of view the action is described. Accordingly, the clear sweep of the narrative is paralleled by a developing psychological drama of whose tensions and compulsions the characters themselves are only half-aware. The need to co-operate during the journey merely disguises the essential isolation of each of the Bundrens and postpones the inevitable conflict between them. For the Bundrens, no less than the Compsons, are living each in a private world whose nature is gauged in relation to Addie and to the actual events of the journey to Jefferson. The larger frame of reference, provided in *The Sound and the Fury* by the impersonal, third person narration of the fourth section, is here conveyed dramatically through eight different characters who comment on some aspect of the funeral in which they themselves are not immediately involved. Their diverse reactions to and judgments of the Bundrens chart the range of social responses, passing from friendliness to indifference to outraged indignation.

As in *The Sound and the Fury*, each private world manifests a fixed and distinctive way of reacting to and ordering experience.

Words, action, and contemplation constitute the possible modes of response, while sensation, reason, and intuition form the levels of consciousness. All of these combine to establish a total relationship between the individual and his experience; for certain of the characters in *As I Lay Dying*, however, this relationship is fragmented and distorted. Anse, for example, is always the bystander, contemplating events and reducing the richness of experience to a few threadbare clichés. In contrast, Darl, the most complex of the characters, owes his complexity and his madness to the fact that he encompasses all possible modes of response and awareness without being able to effect their integration. It is Cash, the oldest brother, who ultimately achieves maturity and understanding by integrating these modes into one distinctively human response which fuses words and action, reason and intuition. In short, the Bundren family provides a locus for the exploration of the human psyche in all its complexity without in the least impairing the immediate reality of character and action.

The different levels of consciousness are rendered by Faulkner through variations in style ranging from the dialect of actual speech to the intricate imagery and poetic rhythms of the unconscious. When the characters are engaged in conversation or concerned with concrete objects, the vocabulary used is limited and repetitious and the style is realistic and colloquial. These same qualities, though to a lesser extent, characterize the expression of conscious thought, for whatever a person is aware of, he articulates in his habitual way, which in a number of instances involves a groping for words. There is, however, some loss of immediacy and vividness since on this level language strives to achieve the impersonal order and clarity of reason rather than the concreteness of sensation. With the unconscious or intuitive, the personal element is at once restored and transcended. Making its appeal to emotion and imagination, the language of the unconscious relies heavily on symbols with their power to evoke rather than to define reality. Thus, Faulkner is able to indicate the particular combination of sensation, reason, and intuition possessed by each of his characters as well as their range of awareness through a subtle manipulation of language and style.

Quite naturally, the three modes of response to experience—words, action, and contemplation—are implemented not by the style but by the series of events with which the characters are confronted. Each of the Bundrens is concerned with Addie's death and with her funeral, events which are by no means identical. As Doctor Peabody suggests, the former is a personal and private matter: "I can remember how when I was young I believed death to be a phenomenon of the body; now I know it to be merely a function of the mind—and that of the minds of the ones who suffer the bereavement." (368) Thus, it is Addie not as a mother, corpse, or promise but as an element in the blood of her children who dominates and shapes their complex psychological reactions. Their motivation lies within her life, for she is the source of the tension and latent violence which each of them feels within himself and expresses in his contacts with the rest of the family. Obsessed by their own relationships to Addie, they can resolve that tension only when they have come to terms with her as a person and with what she signifies in their own consciousness.

In contrast to her death, her funeral is a public affair, participated in and, indeed, supervised by the neighbors as well as the family. On this level she is simply the corpse which must be disposed of in accordance with a long established ritual of interment. While the neighbors prepare themselves to comfort the bereaved, the Bundrens are expected to assume the traditional role of mourners, a role which carries with it unspoken rules of propriety and decorum. Only Anse, for whom Addie never existed as an individual, finds such a role congenial. His face tragic and composed, he easily makes the proper responses to condolences and recites his litany of grief, though somewhat marred by his irrepressible egotism. There is even a sense in which Anse thoroughly enjoys the situation since as chief mourner he is, for once in his life, a person of importance. It is not, however, that simple for Addie's sons, who find that the conventions of mourning and burial can neither channel nor contain their grief. Thus, Cora Tull, the self-appointed champion and arbiter of propriety, finds that each of them fails, at some point, to behave in a fitting manner.

Because the agonizing journey to Jefferson does fulfill the promise to Addie, because it does reunite her in death with her family, some critics have seen in it an inspiring gesture of humanity or a heroic act of traditional morality. In reality, however, the journey from beginning to end is a travesty of the ritual of interment. Any ritual, as Addie herself suggests, can become a travesty, even though it has been ordained and sanctioned in its fixed order from the beginning of time. Since there is no virtue attached simply to the meticulous repetition of its words and gestures, it is the individual who must give meaning and life to ritual by recognizing its symbolic function. But the spirit which should give meaning to Addie's funeral is either absent, as in Anse and Dewey Dell, or in conflict with it, as in Cash and Darl. As this becomes clear, the series of catastrophes that befall the Bundrens becomes a source of macabre humor, for it is only when the ritual is disengaged from its symbolic function that the comic aspect becomes apparent.

Awareness of the difference between empty and significant ritual, framed in terms of the word and the act, dominates Addie Bundren's dying thoughts. She concludes that any experience— love, marriage, motherhood, bereavement—can be either an intensely felt reality or a mere conventional form of speech and behavior. The ritual of the word attempts to impose an order and a significance on experience, while the ritual of the act allows them to emerge from it. While Anse talks about his trials and his grief, Cash, Darl, and Jewel, each in his own way, express the meaning of love and bereavement through their actions which frequently come in conflict with accepted and acceptable forms of behavior. This contrast, sustained throughout the funeral journey, is a confirmation of Addie's perception of "how words go straight up in a thin line, quick and harmless, and how terribly doing goes along the earth, clinging to it, so that after a while the two lines are too far apart for the same person to straddle from one to the other." (465) Words need not, however, be empty providing they are grounded in non-verbal experience. It is when this condition is not met that they tend to be separated from and ultimately to replace the act. There are, as Addie realizes, both "the words [that] are the deeds, and the other words that are not deeds, that are just the gaps in peoples' lacks." (466)

Addie and Anse themselves represent the two polar opposites of action and words which must be meshed if their relationship is to be meaningful. The word by itself leads to a paralysis of the ability to feel and act; the act by itself results in excessive and uncontrolled responses to various stimuli both internal and external. Addie and Anse, however, are not able to effect this fusion of word and act. Because they are "husband" and "wife," Anse feels no need to establish a personal relationship which would give significance to those words and to the ritual of marriage. He is completely blind to Addie's intense desire for life and to her conviction that language is a grotesque tautology which prevents any real communication.

The birth of Cash confirms her feeling that words are irrelevant and that only physical experience has reality and significance. Through the act of giving birth she becomes part of the endless cycle of creation and destruction, discovering that, for the first time, her "aloneness had been violated and then made whole again by the violation." (464) Yet accepting Cash as the sign of her own passionate involvement in experience implies a total rejection of Anse who is now father as well as husband in name only. Because Addie accepts the fact that she and Anse live in different worlds, her second child, Darl, comes as the ultimate and unforgivable outrage. Addie, however, quickly disowns the thought of Anse as the deliberate agent of her betrayal; they have both been "tricked by words older than Anse or love." (464) Precisely what these words are is not clear, but what they signify for Addie is quite apparent. Primarily, she realizes that the ritual of the word does have its repercussions in the world of experience, and on this basis she is able to distinguish between the empty words of Anse and the words which are deeds.

Her sudden and brief affair with Whitfield constitutes Addie's attempt to explore this new relationship between words and acts, for it encompasses even as it differentiates between two quite distinct conceptions of sin. As a word, sin is the opposite of virtue and leads inevitably to damnation. It is this aspect which Addie stresses when she thinks of sin as garments which she and Whitfield wear in the face of the world and which they remove "in order to shape and coerce the terrible blood to the forlorn echo of the dead word high in the air." (466) But as an act, sin may be a step toward salvation. Accordingly, Whitfield becomes "the instrument ordained by God who created the sin, to sanctify that sin He had created." (466) The adultery thus becomes a moral act, not, of course, in the sense of "good" or "virtuous," but in the sense that it re-establishes the reality of moral conduct and of the relationship between God and man. This reality is neither linguistic nor factual in character; instead, it consists of the possible, the hypothetical, the conceivable, all, in short, that follows from the capacity for unrestricted choice. Significantly, Addie sees in Jewel, the child of her sin, a sign of grace: " 'He is my cross and he will be my salvation. He will save me from the water and from the fire. Even though I have laid down my life, he will save me.' " (460) Through sin Addie seeks to find and enact her own humanity, and if her solution seems extreme, so is her provocation. For the alternative, as she sees it, is the moral

54

myopia of those who live by words "because people to whom sin is just a matter of words, to them salvation is just words too." (468)

After her desperate effort to explore and encompass the potentialities of life in one intensely felt act, she is ready to set her house in order. She consciously and deliberately gives Anse Dewey Dell to "negative" Jewel and Vardaman to replace him. Yet in a deep and profound sense, Anse can never claim or share in the lives of any of his children and this gives her a final moment of exhilarated realization: "My children were of me alone, of the wild blood boiling along the earth, of me and of all that lived; of none and of all." (467) Through her, life itself has effected its own continuance and in that process the mother-child relationship has its roots. Two of the children, however, are hers in an additional sense, for she has chosen them for a relationship that is personal as well as maternal. There is an unspoken understanding between herself and Cash. The same understanding, though no longer peaceful, exists between her and Jewel. In both cases the relationship is simple and direct, uninterrupted by conventional expressions of familial sentiments.

The circumstances of the birth of her children establish the level of their awareness of Addie and the mode of their response to and participation in her burial. Through an unconscious identification with her, they faithfully reproduce, though in varying degree, her very moods as well as her attitude to the external world. Jewel comes closest to recreating one aspect of her character, while Dewey Dell and Vardaman, the children reserved for Anse, seem least directly involved with her as a person. The structure of *As I Lay Dying* in which the progression is centrifugal as well as linear implements this pattern. Centrifugally, each section establishes the relationship between Addie and the character whose thoughts and observations are being recorded. Linearly, each section contributes to the sequence of actions and events which constitutes the plot. Furthermore, the separation of word and deed which Addie had recounted is dramatized in the journey to Jefferson. Anse undertakes a moral pilgrimage but solely on the verbal level. Inarticulate except when he is cursing, it is Jewel who rushes into action each time there is a new barrier to be overcome or a new catastrophe to be countered. The rest of the family move between these two extremes.

Because Anse lives by words alone, Addie has no influence over him except when she ironically exacts a promise which is a word but which will compel him to act. All that saves him from equating the deed with the word and the intention with the achievement of it is his own desire for new teeth and Jewel's savage determination to perform the promised act. At the first sign of difficulty he falls back on his inexhaustible stock of moral platitudes to isolate himself effectively from the horrors of the journey, to avoid any exertion on his part, and to maneuver others into acting for him. Incapable of formulating any plan or initiating any action, he depends on his sons to overcome each new obstacle. If they fail, there are always the neighbors to come to his rescue. Certainly the neighbors can do nothing but help when confronted by his covert pleas couched in the language of forbearance: " 'I ain't asking you to risk your mule. It ain't your dead; I am not blaming you.' " (436) His words create an image of himself as the meek and magnanimous victim forgiving a cruel and heartless world. To refuse him help after this is to admit the validity of his remarks and therefore, by implication, their own hardheartedness. They see through his verbal camouflage, but since it is based on emotional and moral clichés to which the response is predetermined, they are helpless before it.

From the beginning the distance between what Anse says and what he does is ironically and humorously emphasized. The irony is, however, most apparent in the scene of Addie's burial. Having had his promise to her fulfilled for him, he makes a short funeral oration. His words and his sentiments as he expresses his grief, though a trifle marred by self-pity, are appropriate to the occasion and to his role as chief mourner: " 'The somebody you was young with and you growed old in her and she growed old in you, seeing the old coming on and it was the one somebody you could hear say it don't matter and know it was the truth outen the hard world and all a man's grief and trials. You all don't know.' " (511) But it is simply a verbal sincerity, unrelated to the act and therefore to the kind of truth that arises out of and touches the heart directly and immediately. Lacking these, his words, like his expression, constitute "a monstrous burlesque of all bereavement." (394) The lament for Addie is followed by his unwillingness to buy a shovel for digging her grave; and even before her body has been placed in it, he has found a new wife to reassure him in his old age. These ironic incongruities are profoundly in keeping with Anse's character. Cushioned by words and conventional sentiments against the harsh impact of reality, he is the only one of the Bundrens completely unchanged by Addie's death or by the funeral journey. The horrors which drive Darl into insanity and leave their mark on the others pass him by so that he avoids agony and insight alike.

In contrast to his father, Cash undergoes certain very clear and definite changes as a result of Addie's death and funeral. Apparently reflecting Addie's rejection of words at the time of his birth, Cash begins by being silent, absorbed in his work, and curiously remote from the tensions and violence of the rest of the family. It is only after something concrete has been accomplished that he speaks. As a carpenter, Cash is concerned with working with his hands and building well; as Addie's son, he uses those hands and that skill to express what she means to him. Thus, the construction of the coffin becomes an act of love, understood as such by Addie, in which emotion tempered by reason is manifested in a concrete form. The sense of proportion which guides his hands also distinguishes his behavior and makes him the inevitable peacemaker in the family. Yet admirable as these characteristics are, Cash is, at the outset, a curiously stiff and one-sided figure. By devoting all his energy to and expressing his emotions through his work, he leaves no room for the cultivation of imaginative or linguistic potentialities. If Anse represents words without action, Cash is action in search of a word. Accordingly, a whole realm of human awareness and response is closed to him.

Cash does, however, develop a more comprehensive understanding of himself and his world. His exclusive preoccupation with concrete tangible objects yields to a more flexible, imaginative vision. The violence he suffers is, if not the cause, then the means of this profound transformation. The twice broken leg and the pain which he accepts without protest, as Addie had accepted the violence of his birth, pave the way for the extension of his range of awareness and for his increased sensitivity both to events and to people. The process is accelerated by the fact that his traditional mode of response, constructive action, is suddenly denied him. Lying helplessly on the coffin, his leg encased in cement and jarred by every turn of the wheel, he is forced to seek new forms of expression.

The increasing range of Cash's awareness is suggested by his growing sympathy with Darl. Facing the flooded river, they "look at one another with long probing looks, looks that plunge unimpeded through one another's eyes and into the ultimate secret place." (439) In that moment crossing the river becomes more than a problem of finding ways and means; Cash begins to realize that the prolonged journey is, in effect, destroying the significance it should affirm. During their stay at the Gillespies', Cash and Darl once more share the same revulsion and repudiation of the family's obsession with fulfilling the letter of the promise to Addie. Although it is Darl who sets fire to the barn, Cash accepts the responsibility as his own because he is the elder and because he too had contemplated the same violent act. Accepting this responsibility is one more step in his recognition of the complexity of those moral and emotional qualities which inhere in men's actions. Accordingly, he alone comprehends that the judgment of Darl's attempt to destroy the coffin and of Jewel's grim efforts to saves it must depend upon whether the body is viewed realistically or symbolically. Darl's action issues from his conviction that the corpse has long since become an offense to God and man, Jewel's from the equally strong emotional conviction that the coffin contains his mother. Combined with his own firm foundation in action and the concrete details of his trade, this increase of sensitivity and imaginative perception makes Cash the one character in the novel who achieves his full humanity in which reason and intuition, words and action merge into a single though complex response.

Darl, the second son and the most complicated of the Bundrens, faithfully reflects and dramatizes Addie's attitude at the time of his birth. She had believed, a belief later qualified, that reality lay only in physical experience and that the word and the act were polar opposites. Feeling Darl to be an outrage, she had denied him a place in her affections and in her world. Consequently, Darl's is a world of consciousness exclusively, and this, of course, renders his connection with the external world increasingly precarious and insecure. He exists in a kind of limbo where the firm, defining shape of objects and of people is continually dissolving. Only by a painful process of reasoning can he establish the physical existence of himself, his mother, and the loaded wagon: "Yet the wagon *is*, because when the wagon is *was*, Addie Bundren will not be. And Jewel *is*, so Addie Bundren must be. And then I must be, or I could not empty myself for sleep in a strange room." (396) This attempt to define objective reality is an index of Darl's separation from it.

But the same absence of defining and limiting outline permits Darl to penetrate the minds of others and to intuit those secret thoughts of which they themselves are scarcely aware. Twice, while he himself is absent, he apprehends the actions of Cash, Anse, and Dewey Dell as they cluster around the dying Addie and describes them with startling vividness. And at every moment he is able to expose, with merciless accuracy, the secret thoughts and motives of others. He knows that Jewel is the son of Addie's sin, a fact with which he repeatedly taunts the latter by asking, "Who is your father, Jewel?" More important, he knows that the horse Jewel caresses and curses is a surrogate for Addie. Similarly, he is aware of Dewey Dell's pregnancy. In both cases his knowledge forces them to face certain facts about themselves and their world. Unwilling to do so, Jewel relieves his mounting frustration in the violence of curses, while Dewey Dell finds temporary release in a fantasy of murder. Both join in the vicious physical attack on Darl when they arrive in Jefferson. Addie's rejection of him is thus repeated: with the exception of Vardaman, who is too young to know what is happening, each of the Bundrens contributes to the decision to send Darl to Jackson. As Cash's final, unacrimonious assessment suggests, the rejection is inevitable: "This world is not his world; this life his life." (532)

As Darl loses contact with the external world and with objective reality, his resemblance to Vardaman becomes more pronounced. When the wagon reaches the Gillespies', their sections are juxtaposed five times. The two of them have reached an understanding which is beyond logic and reason. Just before the fire their attitudes toward Addie become identical: as Vardaman states in one scene and Darl repeats in the next, Addie is stirring in her coffin. Darl's own intention becomes clear as he informs Vardaman that she is asking God " 'to hide her away from the sight of man. . . . So she can lay down her life.' " (495) Their shared delusion suggests that for both of them the world of fantasy has become as real as the concrete facts which we call reality.

Yet Darl's delusion is grounded in the conviction that the funeral has become an unbearable travesty of filial piety. Addie's imagined but not unreasonable request prompts him to abandon his usual role as spectator. Thought and action are fused, though in a particularly violent way. Depending on one's point of view, his action becomes a sign either of a deranged mind or of an acute moral sensibility, an ambiguity recognized by Cash who reflects: "Sometimes I ain't so sho who's got ere a right to say when a man is crazy and when he ain't. Sometimes I think it ain't none of us pure crazy and ain't none of us pure sane until the balance of us talks him that-a-way." (510) Action, the basis of individual moral conduct, is subject to social judgments and these are implemented through language. Hence, though Cash understands and is sympathetic to Darl's gesture of protest, he is forced to conclude that society's judgment is the only possible one.

Although Jewel is the most closely connected with Addie and the most active during the journey, only one section is devoted to his stream of consciousness. The reason for this is that his world is least accessible to public scrutiny since it consists of a welter of emotions, centering on Addie, which cannot be communicated. These emotions are not subjected to the control of reason but are translated immediately into actions which, unlike Cash's carefully planned moves, are the products of spontaneous reflexes. Whether the results of such actions are destructive or constructive in any given instance is a matter of chance. Thus, his is the blame for perpetuating the horrors of the journey and his the credit for forcing it to a successful conclusion. It is significant that when the stimulus to action is removed, when Addie's corpse is buried and Darl committed to an insane asylum, Jewel's fury subsides except for brief spasms of irritation caused by some word or gesture of Anse's.

Because Jewel is himself largely unconscious of his own motives and emotional compulsions, it is Darl who expresses them. As Darl keeps reiterating, Jewel has no father. Addie, then, becomes the sole center of his emotional life. There is, however, no way in which Jewel's violent feelings can be channelled into socially acceptable rituals. Seeing, as usual, only the surface meaning of actions, Cora Tull mistakes his despair for indifference. But when Jewel's own thoughts are revealed, they are seen to be devoted entirely to Addie. He imagines the two of them defiantly and violently isolated from the world and its interference. Most of Jewel's subsequent actions are, in effect, attempts to make this fantasy a reality and so to claim exclusive possession of Addie. Dewey Dell, Vardaman, and Anse, he simply ignores; but each time he meets Cash it is to override the latter's caution with his own impetuous activity. As for the neighbors, they are kept at a distance by his coldness and his deliberate insults. Even the genuinely helpful and sympathetic Tull is repulsed. Only Darl cannot be excluded from his private world and he is finally eliminated by being sent to Jackson.

This process of exclusion merely intensifies Jewel's emotional attachment to Addie without providing a release for it. The latter he finds in the wild horse which he tames and on which he can lavish his love and inflict his hatred. Because the horse is actually his possession, he can and does isolate himself and it from all contact with others. No one except himself is permitted to feed, care for, or even touch it. In a sense, the horse perpetuates Addie's emotional relationship with Jewel. Because of this identification, Jewel insists on bringing the horse with him despite Anse's protests and Darl's oblique taunts. And when he finally sells it to pay for a new team, the full intensity of his feeling reverts to Addie. This explains why he is almost prevented by his concern for the horse from rescuing Addie's coffin out of the river, whereas during the fire all his energies are directed solely toward saving it.

In sharp contrast to Jewel, Dewey Dell seems the least concerned with Addie's death and funeral. Addie, however, had revealed the same impersonal and unemotional attitude toward Dewey Dell when she stated that she had given Dewey Dell to Anse in order to "negative" Jewel. In a way, Dewey Dell has no need of Addie because she herself is recreating Addie's past and discovering that pregnancy is both a state of mind and a physical fact, both a word and an action. But unlike Addie, she is determined, if possible, to effect their separation. Thus, she will not name her condition even to herself because to do so would be to transfer her pregnancy from her private world of awareness to the public world of fact.

Yet it is only by admitting the physical reality of her pregnancy and by making it, at least to some extent, public that she can do anything to terminate it. The problem is focussed for her by the presence of Peabody. By destroying the physical evidence of her pregnancy, Peabody would become a witness to its reality, a reality which would be perpetuated in his consciousness. She avoids telling Peabody, but Darl, unfortunately, already knows. Her desire to destroy Darl and with him his knowledge is first expressed in fantasy: "I rose and took the knife from the streaming fish still hissing and I killed Darl." (423) This is followed by her savage physical attack on him and by her determination to have him sent to Jackson. Darl's departure does not, of course, solve anything for Dewey Dell, but it does postpone the need for immediate decision and action. Because there is no one present who knows of her pregnancy, she can act, for the time being, as if it did not exist. As she sits on the wagon, placidly munching a banana, her mind relapses into its normal state, that of the minimal level of conscious thought.

The limitations of Vardaman's mind are of a different order; they are those of the youngest child, who is bewildered by a phenomenon completely new to him. Out of the various sensations that he experiences and the facts that he observes while Addie is dying, he attempts to define for himself the meaning of death. He can do this only by constructing analogies to what he already knows or remembers. But because Vardaman is limited largely to sensations, he is not able to pass from the concrete to the general and abstract. What begins as an analogy ends as an identification. Addie and the fish are linked by death and therefore, according to his own particular logic, what happens to one happens to the other: "Then it wasn't and she was, and now it is and she wasn't. And tomorrow it will be cooked and et and she will be him and pa and Cash and Dewey Dell and there won't be anything in the box and so she can breathe." (386) Eventually the dead fish and the dead mother fuse into a single thought: "My mother is a fish." Knowing that he himself is the cause and instrument of the fish's death, Vardaman seeks to find the agent responsible for Addie's death. Selecting Doctor Peabody, he gains his revenge by mistreating the doctor's horses.

Still arguing from analogy, Vardaman remembers the lack of air in the corn crib and assumes that his mother, now confined in the coffin, must feel a similar lack. Drilling holes in the coffin thus becomes a reasonable and humane act, an expression of his concern for his mother. Though certain of Vardaman's acts seem to border on the insane, he himself is not. He is a child, sensitive and even intelligent, who is exposed to a tremendous shock. And in meeting it, he has neither precedent nor advice to guide him. It is, therefore, almost inevitable that he should arrive at a distorted conception of death and that his actions, having their source in that concept, should appear grotesque and incongruous. Certainly Vardaman suffers from a delusion but an understandable one since it permits him to dissociate his mother from the horrors of physical death and decay: "*My mother is not in the box. My mother does not smell like that. My mother is a fish.*" (483)

Through the interaction of the characters the complexity of the central situation is evoked, and through an understanding of those complexities, the motivation and hence the credibility of the characters is established. At the end, we see them in terms of their relationship to Addie and to each other, "sitting bolt upright in [their] nakedness, staring at one another and saying 'Now is the truth.'" (433) The private world of each of the Bundrens has been exposed, partly by their own actions and partly by Darl's constant probing. With his departure and the burial of Addie's corpse, the period of tension ends. The new wife, the gramophone, the memory of the toy trains, and the bananas do not replace Addie, but they do indicate a shift in the family's focus of consciousness. It is through the inception of such new patterns that the characters seek to avoid too close, protracted, and painful a scrutiny of the meaning of life and death.

Addie's death and her funeral are construed in terms of the family's varied levels and modes of consciousness, but they also possess a wider frame of reference, for the actions of the Bundrens project both death and funeral into the public world. It is in this capacity of responding to the Bundrens and their funeral procession that Faulkner introduces his eight reverberators. Mosely and MacGowan reveal two contrasting attitudes to Dewey Dell's pregnancy. The former responds to her request for pills with self-righteous moral indignation; the latter unhesitatingly takes advantage of what he conceives to be an essentially comic situation. Between them they indicate the range of possible social reactions to and judgments of her condition. Quite obviously, neither Mosely nor MacGowan is concerned with Dewey Dell as a person; they respond only to the fact that she is clearly somewhat stupid, pregnant, and unmarried.

In Samson, Armstid, and Tull, the purely social and moral judgment is tempered by personal knowledge of the Bundrens. They are, in fact, themselves implicated to some extent in the funeral. There is a kind of humorous despair in their frustrating knowledge that Anse has and will continue to take advantage of their neighborliness. Tull, for example, remarks: "Like most folks around here, I done holp him so much already I can't quit now." (360) Each of these men describes a stage in the journey to Jefferson in terms of his contribution to it. Significantly, as individuals, they are appalled by the horrifying physical aspects of Addie's decaying body; but as neighbors, they feel obligated to offer their help in continuing the journey. With the burning of Gillespie's barn, however, the limits of neighborliness are reached.

In contrast to the three men, Cora Tull and Whitfield see the Bundrens solely in terms of their own ethical systems. It is fitting, therefore, that Addie's soliloquy, with its emphasis on the separation of the word and the act, should be flanked by their moralizing and empty rhetoric. Fearing that he will be forced at last to face Anse, Whitfield is intent upon finding the right words for framing his confession. Yet the moment he learns that Addie has not betrayed their secret, all thoughts of confession leave his mind. He is once more free to act as if he had never violated the moral code of his community since the public world is still unaware of his guilt. As for the sin against God, a verbal apology is sufficient: "He will accept the will for the deed, Who knew that when I framed the words of my confession it was to Anse I spoke them, even though he was not there." (469) Confession, repentance, and even penance are carried out in his mind, thereby obviating any necessity of embracing them in an act. Anse's own formula of verbal evasion is thus, ironically, turned against him.

Whitfield's account of his relationship with Addie is rendered wholly in terms of ethical and religious clichés from which all human passion and meaning has been carefully deleted. Similarly, everything about Addie, her family, and her death is but another moral lesson to be interpreted by Cora Tull as she elbows her way to heaven. Having learned her ethics by rote, Cora has no difficulty in affixing praise and blame or in predicting salvation or damnation for all whom she meets. Though she consigns Addie and her family to the latter category, she is consistently and determinedly helpful. Her help, however, is offered in the name of duty not love, and it is meant, whether she realizes it or not, to be one more step in establishing her own virtue and her own right to salvation. Kindness such as Cora's is essentially selfish, debasing both the giver and the recipient and destroying the possibility of any personal relationship between them. In her eyes even family ties are moral rather than emotional. As a result, Cora is totally unaware, in any real sense, of those agonizing and exalting human experiences which stand outside her rigid system of ethics, resisting and disrupting its smooth simplification of existence.

Of all the characters who observe and comment on the actions of the Bundrens, Doctor Peabody is the most judicious. Although Tull's remarks often contain shrewd assessments of specific events, it is Peabody who grasps their broader significance. His insight is the result of long and varied experience with people compelled to face the realities of pain, suffering, and death. Thus, when he makes separate evaluations of life, love, and death, his statements serve as a general guide for interpreting the actions of the family. His is the compassionate but detached vision of the country doctor-cum-philosopher. Yet when he is suddenly confronted with the Bundrens in Jefferson, he loses his philosophic objectivity. Overwhelmed by the massing of concrete horrors and sensations, he reacts with bitter indignation.

While acting as reverberator for the actions of the Bundrens, these eight characters offer release from the tension through humorous or ironic remarks. Because only the actions of the Bundrens and not their thoughts and emotions are perceived, they become grotesques. What is horror and pain for the family becomes farce for those who are not themselves involved and who merely observe with the physical eye. For the Bundrens, the journey seethes with unresolved tensions; for the townspeople of Mottson, it is only a ridiculous or macabre spectacle. This intermingling of humor and horror, which is part of the very texture of *As I Lay Dying*, issues out of the Bundrens' conviction that their actions are eminently reasonable and out of the spectators' conviction that the Bundrens and their coffin have long since passed beyond the realm of reason, logic, or even commonsense. The juxtaposition of the two views gives rise to a complicated and ambivalent feeling of hilarity and despair. Confronted with the irrational, the rational mind finds itself bewildered and uneasy, indignant and outraged, or simply wryly amused. As the funeral journey is prolonged, all these attitudes are exhibited.

The interplay of seriousness which reaches toward tragedy and of humor which is practically farce is part of the complete success of *As I Lay Dying*. In a sense, it reinforces the theme of the separation of words and acts by insisting on at least these two modes of response to the same set of characters and events. At the same time, it precludes any easy generalizations about the funeral journey itself. Any event or series of events elicits various and, at times, contradictory responses. The meaning of an experience as distinct from a word exists in the consciousness of the individual observer. Accordingly, it is only when one becomes conscious of the mingling of humor and pathos, of the relation of the Bundrens to Addie, and of the observers to the action that the full complexity of *As I Lay Dying* is plumbed and Faulkner's easy mastery of it recognized.

5: THE SHADOW AND THE MIRROR

Light in August

Despite Faulkner's use of a clearly defined plot, *Light in August* is by no means a return to the traditional novel. Rather it constitutes his attempt to integrate certain experimental features of his earlier novels into a conventional narrative frame, thereby carrying one step further his use of structure to clarify theme. In both *The Sound and the Fury* and *As I Lay Dying* the public world serves merely as a frame for events which the reader is engaged in seeing from different perspectives. In *Light in August*, however, we are no longer concerned with examining the particular nature and limits of the individual consciousness but rather with its relation to other minds and to the public world of events, statements, and mass responses.

Because of the interpenetration and interdependence of the private and public worlds, each character is multidimensional. He is at once subject and object, observer and observed, creator and created. Thus, Joe Christmas as well as the Reverend Hightower and Joanna Burden are both self-crucified and crucified by others, both villain and victim. The interplay of these polar aspects of the human being produces much of the dramatic tension and the grotesque quality in the novel. There is a continual movement from one world to another, each with its own kind and degree of distortion. Depending upon who is acting as observer, this distortion provides a mirror image of the particular world of the observer or of the public world as represented by the town of Jefferson. In a sense, the individual and the community are obverse reflections of each other. Yet because the reflection is obverse, each fails to recognize himself, and so reacts with instinctive fear and anger which ultimately lead him to destroy his own image. In short, each is the victim of the other.

The nature of the private world and its relation to others is indicated by a threefold pattern of interlocking imagery—the circle, the shadow, and the mirror. All the main characters in *Light in August* are strangers to Jefferson and they remain strangers no matter how long their stay or how deep their roots. Their isolation is suggested by the image of the circle which achieves its clearest expression and greatest significance in the episode of Joe Christmas' flight and his sudden realization: "It had been a paved street, where going should be fast. It had made a circle and he is still inside of it. . . . 'And yet I have been farther in these seven days than in all the thirty years,' he thinks. 'But I have never got outside that circle.'" (296) In the midst of that jostling, noisy intercourse which is society and to which all men contribute, each is alone, unable to break through the circumference of his own circle or to admit anyone into it. Because of the solipsistic quality of the private world, each individual sees others and is himself seen as a shadow, ghostlike and unreal. Walking the streets of Jefferson, Joe Christmas, for example, looks like "a phantom, a spirit, strayed out of its own world, and lost." (99) The images of the circle and the shadow are linked in the description of Byron Bunch and Brown, passing "one another as though on opposite orbits and with an effect as of phantoms or apparitions." (386) It is Hightower, however, who extends the insight provided by these images with his recognition that other people are simply "mirrors in which he watches himself." (427)

Yet no matter how isolated and impenetrable the private world of an individual, he still has a physical and social existence in the public world which makes its demands of him. His comfort, if not his life, depends on his accepting and exemplifying in his own life those stereotypes which represent society's vision of itself and its past. And since withdrawal or rebellion are as much public acts as is affirmation, no one can escape. Society has myths not only of the hero but also of the antagonist, and it has evolved rituals to deal with each. Collectively, Jefferson is Southern, White, and Elect, qualities which have meaning only within a context which recognizes something or someone as Northern or Black or Damned. This antithesis is periodically affirmed through the sacrifice of a scapegoat who represents, in fact or popular conviction, those qualities which must be rejected if Jefferson is to maintain its self-defined character.

Miss Burden, Hightower, and Christmas serve as such scapegoats and serve willingly, almost eagerly, since they too have accepted the absolute necessity and validity of the dichotomies in whose name they are destroyed. Thus, Miss Burden, despite her birth in Jefferson, is a "Northerner" in the eyes of the town, and hence she is automatically aligned with the "Negro" and the "Damned." Hightower, on the other hand, offends not by being a Northerner but by refusing to play the role of "Reverend" in the manner established by custom and tradition. He becomes "Gail Hightower Done Damned in Jefferson." (52) This judgment is then in part justified and in part explained by the town's accusation of Hightower's unnatural relationship with a Negress. Out of this judgment his ritualistic punishment by masked men and his ostracism follow inevitably. Joe Christmas, of course, represents the third category, that of the Negro, and it is this assumption that predetermines the manner of his pursuit and lynching. But at the same time he constitutes an omnipresent threat to all categories: he cannot say with certainty whether he is Negro or white; he is a Southerner with too many Northern ideas; and he seems quite indifferent to salvation or damnation.

Accordingly, Christmas has a dual function in the novel. As an individual, he explores his own relation to the myth of the Negro, while as a part of society, he is identified with the myth. Through his oscillation between repudiation and affirmation of his black blood, he reveals his own uncertainty and his need to resolve the dilemma posed to him by the old Negro gardener: " 'You dont know what you are. And more than that, you wont never know. You'll live and you'll die and you wont never know.' " (336) He is obsessed with the idea that he must choose, yet his every action emphasizes his inability to do so. In the world of Jefferson, however, after Brown's accusation has taken root, he is treated as if he were in actual fact a Negro. The varying responses, ranging from Gavin Stevens' cool, impersonal analysis to Gail Hightower's anguished sympathy to the mob's violence, are directed at the concept of the Negro with which he is identified. Inescapably Joe is forced into the ritual of pursuit and lynching performed almost casually by a society which has been elaborating it for generations.

The basis of this pattern is Jefferson's conviction that the individual can only become a member of society by permitting himself to be classified according to race, color, geographic origin, and so on. Created by man, these categories become creators of man insofar as they establish social identification as the necessary prerequisite to human existence. The sheer weight of generations, each in its turn conforming to and therefore affirming this process of public labelling, establishes the labels not only as a matter of tradition but as a kind of revealed truth. What starts as a verbal pattern of classification thus becomes a social order not to be challenged or changed. And what starts as a category becomes a myth, for certainly the word "Negro" is a compressed myth just as the stock response to that word is a compressed ritual. The result is that men like Joe Christmas or Velery Bon, who can neither fit nor be fitted into these categories, are either sacrificed to or driven out of the society whose cherished beliefs they threaten.

Certainly there is no one set of categories which can claim Christmas or be claimed by him. He is indeed the "disaccommodated man," with "something definitely rootless about him, as though no town nor city was his, no street, no walls, no square of earth his home." (27) Yet he cannot ignore the concept of race which assigns men to one of two separate worlds, each with its traditions and modes of thinking and acting. The irony of Joe's position is that what seems to be a choice is in reality a delusion: Negro or white—to choose one is to affirm the existence of the other. His awareness of this dichotomy makes him take up the role of antagonist in all situations. In the presence of whites he becomes Negro; among Negroes he feels himself to be white. The result is that series of tensions and conflicts for which he himself is at least partly responsible. The Joe Christmas who is finally lynched as "Negro" is the joint creation of his private world and of the larger public universe.

In this respect Mrs. Hines's account of his birth becomes significant, for it reveals that Joe is born into a myth created for him by others. Since Millie's pregnancy is considered an unforgivable sin by Hines, he looks for a scapegoat who will bear the guilt and punishment. By calling her lover a "nigger," he can transform a commonplace seduction into the horror of miscegenation. That is his justification, moral and religious, for the brutally inhuman treatment of his daughter, her lover, and her child. His reasons for regarding Christmas with malevolence and hatred remain personal, but his actions and statements help formulate that confused and violent myth which is Joe's particular agony. His brooding watchfulness having isolated Joe from the other children at the orphanage, Hines then provides the three year old with an explanation: " 'Why dont you play with them other children like you used to? . . . Is it because they call you nigger?' " (335) The awareness of something strange or different about Joe is thus simultaneously impressed on Joe and on others.

The identification of Joe with Negro receives additional and unexpected support from the dietitian. Surprised in the midst of her clandestine love affair, she lashes out at Joe calling him a "little rat" and a "little nigger bastard." In the days of frenzied uncertainty and fear which follow, she links the carelessly spoken invective with Hines's attitude and with the meaningless taunts of the children. Though she had never considered Joe to be a Negro, "she believed that she had, had known it all the while, because it seemed so right: he would not only be removed; he would be punished for having given her terror and worry." (113) At cross purposes, each speaking a strange, private language, and each motivated by personal reasons, the dietitian and Hines, nevertheless, combine to extend and intensify Joe's awareness of himself as a different kind of being and to force the matron to act on the assumption that he is indeed a Negro.

Although the "taint" of Negro blood is never revealed to McEachern, Joe himself is imbued with its possibility. For a time, however, it lies quiescent in his consciousness while he endeavors to assimilate yet another aspect of his life. To the social pattern of black and white, the implications of which he is yet to realize, is added the religious pattern of the elect and the damned. His vague, emotional response to God is replaced by the creed and discipline of a particular church. And the spiritual relationship of father and son is submerged in an intricate and deadly game of good and evil, reward and punishment. McEachern's religious discipline is accepted eagerly by Joe because it makes his life completely predictable, relieving him of the necessity for self-judgment and responsibility. Accordingly, he rejects Mrs. McEachern's awkward and uncertain attempts to establish a more purely human relationship with him.

Ultimately, however, he seeks and finds such a relationship in his love for Bobbie, the waitress. It is this love which prompts him to rebel against McEachern's Calvinistic ritual of confession and penance and to resist the customary punishment which

McEachern seeks to inflict on him at the dance. But this achievement is short-lived, for Bobbie's later shrieks of rage signal the destruction of the last of Joe's natural, spontaneous emotions. Her betrayal, which impels him into the long, lonely street of his life, is not only sexual but religious and racial, for all three are involved in the idea of miscegenation into which their affair is suddenly transformed. So long as their affair proves satisfactory and trouble free, Bobbie simply ignores Joe's confession that "'I think I got some nigger blood in me.'" (171) In a moment of crisis, however, and in order to save herself, she, like the dietitian, finds it convenient not only to believe but to act upon that belief. All blame, all possible punishment is shifted to Joe as "Negro" who significantly enough has himself provided the material for this accusation. Suddenly conscious of her white blood, Bobbie has no compunctions about abandoning a "nigger" whom she had naïvely mistaken for a white man nor about watching that "nigger" beaten senseless by her friends.

The beating establishes the antithesis of black and white in Joe's own physical experience and thereby intensifies his awareness of it. His life becomes a series of episodes in which he provokes racial violence from Negro and white alike, a violence which constitutes an almost joyful affirmation of the Negrowhite pattern in which both Joe and his opponents are trapped. That someone could simply ignore that pattern fills him with an indignant amazement and outrage. He beats the prostitute who refuses to be horrified by his Negro blood, thus forcing her to initiate that ritual of violence which he expects. His reaction is understandable, for her indifference challenges the validity of the premise on which he has built his whole life. Whether or not he himself is a Negro may remain in doubt, but that there is something called Negro which demands certain attitudes and actions on the part of all white people must not be denied.

During his relationship with Joanna Burden, Joe's preoccupation with such categories becomes especially acute since he recognizes the same obsession in her. In fact, her concern with racial, geographical, and religious myths serves as a complement and antithesis to his own. Not even their frenzied and insatiable love-making can destroy their ingrained awareness of what each believes the other to represent. While her body surrenders completely to his, Joanna still mutters "Negro! Negro! Negro!" And Joe, on his way to her bedroom, still pauses to smash the dishes of food prepared by the white woman and left for him in the kitchen. Thus, even miscegenation is powerless to erase their concern with racial differences and indeed serves only to intensify it.

Joe's wild hope, as he holds her letter in his hand, that they can escape from their own preconceptions into a world where " 'She is still she and I am still I' " (238) is doomed from its very inception. For what he visualizes is a return to the natural world where the only meaningful categories are male and female and the only meaningful relationship is sexual. But Joanna, her physical need for him exhausted, demands of him that choice which he has spent his whole life evading. She insists that he ignore his uncertainty and accept once and for all the role of Negro as modified by the North together with that of repentant sinner. The violence between them is inevitable, but significantly it is both impersonal and unimpassioned. Joanna's act of raising the pistol and Joe's use of the razor are both projected as shadows against the wall—phantom weapons directed at phantom opponents. For each sees embodied in the other that racial myth which has dominated their lives and which they must destroy if they are to be free.

Yet in the very act of gaining his freedom, Joe loses it. The act of murder leaves him vulnerable to society's judgments and actions. The fire at Miss Burden's and her decapitated body generate a tension in the milling crowd which needs only the proper spark to explode it into violence. That spark is supplied by Brown, a man whose parentage is as obscure as Joe's own. The pattern made familiar by Hines, the dietitian, and Bobbie is repeated as the cry of "Negro" and the suggestion of miscegenation channel the restless and undirected energy of the observers away from the accuser. Three times Brown repeats " 'Accuse the white man and let the nigger go free' " until the crowd grasps the significance of that contrast and prepares itself for action. Once he pronounces the word "Negro," the actual guilt of Joe Christmas, the circumstances, and the motivation, all become irrelevant, for the connection between "Negro" and "murder" is part of the public myth. At the same time Joanna Burden loses all individuality, becoming simply a white woman and hence an innocent victim who must be avenged. Accusation, conviction, and punishment constitute a single, simultaneous belief-act as "Joe, the son of Joe" becomes Joe, the son of a Negro.

The compelling nature of the pattern evoked by Brown is

indicated by the fact that no one thinks to question his premise. The mob is, of course, wholly absorbed in the idea of revenge, but even those who sympathize with Joe never doubt that he is a Negro. Though he has ample evidence of Brown's character, Byron still takes his word and in his turn convinces Hightower. The intense shock felt by the latter is occasioned by his sickening realization that a public myth is once more demanding its victim, that the ritualistic sequence of the chase, the pursuit, and the final immolation is now inevitable. Even the cosmopolitan Gavin Stevens, with his Harvard and Heidelberg studies behind him, is not able to see Joe Christmas except through a filter of preconceptions. Though he recognizes that Hines is quite mad, he, nevertheless, accepts his contention that Joe's father was actually a Negro. More important: despite his disinterested rationalism and objectivity, he assigns definite though arbitrary moral values to black and white blood, claiming that it was the former which made Joe strike Hightower and the latter which enabled him to die heroically.

As these stock reactions and attitudes crystallize in Jefferson, Joe Christmas himself is able if only temporarily to escape their coercive pressure. At the outset he is still sufficiently obsessed with the fictions he has spent his life affirming through endless challenges to pause in a Negro church. Standing in the pulpit and cursing God, he assumes, possibly in his own mind and certainly in the minds of the congregation, the terrifying form of anti-Christ. But the body's need for food and rest erases all the illusions that the mind creates and perpetuates. The stage beyond, where even food becomes unnecessary, gives to Christmas the human dignity all his violence could not seize. For the first time, he sees his life not in terms of "black" and "white" but simply of the human race. Inevitably his new found awareness of himself as man causes him to be rejected by both the Negroes and the whites. Negro fear is balanced by white outrage at the fact that " 'He never acted like either a nigger or a white man. That was it. That was what made the folks so mad.' " (306)

Ironically, as Christmas transcends the categories of black and white and of good and evil, thus resolving his own personal dilemma, he is once more forced to exemplify them in the sequence of flight and pursuit, capture and death, begun by his own act of murder but given shape by Brown's accusation of "nigger." Dazedly he half-comprehends that he has given himself up to the public world by his act and that he can no longer refuse the role it has given him to play. Since he is a "nigger" murderer, each gesture, even each emotion which he is permitted to feel, is already established. Sardonically he reflects on his unsuccessful attempts to give himself up: " 'Like there is a rule to catch me by, and to capture me that way would not be like the rule says.' " (294) As Christmas recognizes the inevitability of this pattern and of his own part in it, he visualizes himself sinking "at last into the black abyss which had been waiting, trying, for thirty years to drown him and into which now and at last he had actually entered, bearing now upon his ankles the definite and ineradicable gauge of its upward moving." (289) Significantly, he becomes aware of the borrowed shoes as a symbol of his acceptance of "the black abyss" only when he is in the wagon on his way to Mottstown to give himself up and thus to assume the role of Negro which Jefferson has prepared for him.

It is, then, as "Negro" that Christmas is lynched in a scene that echoes and intensifies all the earlier acts of his life. In the "cloistral dimness" of Hightower's house Christmas resembles "a vengeful and furious god pronouncing a doom" (406) on the men whose "faces seemed to glare with bodiless suspension as though from haloes." (405) Saints and sinners, the elect and the damned, the victim and the persecutors become strangely confused with one another. Through Percy Grimm, the "young priest" of the occasion, the elect and white of Jefferson castrate and slay the Negro according to ancient custom, but instead of purification, they are left with a sense of their own guilt and self-doubt. Through his castration, Christmas finally does escape society's categories. Having made him a "Negro" in order to crucify him, society, by its own passion for affirming the reality of its myths in actual living experience, in the end explodes both those myths and the categories out of which they were evolved. It is no longer the Negro murderer or even Joe Christmas but simply "the man" who rises "soaring into their memories forever and ever." (407)

In the moment of Christmas' death, then, there occurs a final violent fusion of the public and private myths of the "Negro," a fusion developing out of the interaction of these myths as charted in the actual chronological sequence of the novel. Moreover, in the process of unfolding this interaction the chronological sequence has shown the gradual identification of the individual, Joe Christmas, with this public myth. Through Joanna Burden and Gail Hightower that identification is given historical per-

Light in August

spective, not only because they themselves are conscious of the
historical origins of the particular myths which dominate Joe
Christmas and themselves alike, but because they have virtually
stopped living in the public world where their beliefs might be
modified by further interaction. At the same time they represent
the two remaining categories, one geographical and the other
religious, in terms of which the South establishes its identity.
The Negro, the Yankee, the Apostate—these are the key figures
in a society which defines itself by exclusion.

Like Joe Christmas, Joanna Burden presents an obverse reflection of one aspect of the South. For though she is excluded from
the community as a Northerner, she too is obsessed with the
myth of the Negro. Despite the apparently irreconcilable opposition of their attitudes which led them to actual war, both North
and South are concerned with the problem of the Negro, a concern which gives form and substance to a concept but which
takes no cognizance of individuals as individuals. In both, this
concept, bolstered by the legends of history as seen from their
own particular perspective, engenders a set pattern of beliefs and
actions. Eventually, these acts and beliefs involving the "Negro"
are transformed into a kind of religion, a distorted version of
Calvinism in which black and white replace or are identified with
evil and good. Each holding this extreme view, Joanna Burden,
the scion of New England, is scarcely distinguishable from
McEachern or even Hines.

Joanna's increasing awareness of this myth parallels Joe's,
though without his tormenting uncertainty as to his own relationship to it. As a child, she simply accepts the fact that certain
people have darker skins than her own. But this innocence or
naïveté is not permitted to continue. Her father, Nathaniel
Burden, slowly transforms the physical black and white she sees
into a moral and religious order. She is made aware of "Negro"
" 'not as people, but as a thing, a shadow in which [she] lived, we
lived, all white people, all other people.' " (221) The shadow
becomes a "black cross" to which she is a martyr, a phantom
priestess immolating herself on a phantom altar. Consequently,
her whole life is devoted to perpetuating and giving substance to
a metaphor: " 'You must struggle, rise. But in order to rise, you
must raise the shadow with you.' " (222)

To this belief in her martyrdom, Joanna Burden sacrifices all
her natural impulses, thereby creating a bifurcated individual.
Thus, Joe sees her as "a dual personality: the one the woman at

75

first sight of whom in the lifted candle . . . there had opened before him, instantaneous as a landscape in a lightningflash, a horizon of physical security and adultery if not pleasure; the other the mantrained muscles and the mantrained habit of thinking born of heritage and environment with which he had to fight up to the final instant." (205) His entrance into her life signals an overt conflict between these two aspects of her being. The sex-starved body conquers for a time "the mantrained habit of thinking" and expresses itself in a desperate and imperious need to experience every possible sensation and every possible emotion that physical love can suggest. Acting out of a world of fantasies, she quickly passes "through every avatar of a woman in love": (226) the lover's pursuit, secret trysts, baseless accusations and jealousy, seduction, and even rape.

Yet even in the midst of these exaggerated manifestations of her long suppressed desires, she is not entirely free of her intellectual heritage. She can only seek to postpone its mastery over her: " 'Don't make me have to pray yet. Dear God, let me be damned a little longer, a little while.' " (231) The implicit identification of sex with sin prepares the way for the corruption of her relationship with Joe and for her own final perversion in which he ceases to be the means of satisfying her physical demands and comes to symbolize the sexual superstitions associated with the Negro. In this last phase, she is not having intercourse with a man but with an image of her own creation, with the idea of "Negro" for which she has given up her life. Accordingly, she emerges from the affair with her instincts once more subdued and with her obsessions once more crystallized and intensified.

No longer driven by her desire to sin, Joanna is left free to brood over the fact that she has sinned. In retrospect she naturally sees all the facets of her relationship with Christmas in the light of her old "mantrained habits of thinking" and the result is a reaffirmation of Calvinism and rededication of herself to the black cross. Nor can she leave Christmas alone, for he is the Negro, the symbol of her responsibility, her sin and damnation, and most important, her salvation. Her pleading, bribes, and threats are her attempt to make him translate into living flesh and act her concept of the Negro. He is to ignore his own uncertainty, admit his black blood, his sinfulness, and his dependence for salvation on her and her God. Joe's refusal to submit himself to that formula threatens that myth for the sake of which she has continued to draw breath. She reacts to his recalcitrance, as the mob does later, by resorting to violence. Ironically the transformation of Joe Christmas into a Negro which she does not accomplish in her life is effected through her death.

Gail Hightower is, of course, rejected by Jefferson because he has proved himself unworthy of directing its religious, spiritual life. Like Joe Christmas and Joanna Burden, he is an impure element of which society must purge itself; and like them, he too mirrors yet another aspect of the South: its preoccupation with the legends of its own past. The exploits of the gallant Confederate forces are part of the inheritance of every Southern boy as well as an article in the belief of every Southern community. Such legends, provided they are accepted as legends, remain as valuable and harmless as the stories of Charlemagne. Hightower, however, sees a kind of revealed truth in the vision of his grandfather, compounded of an old Negress' storytelling and his own boyish imagination. The imagination is given full scope because there is nothing and no one to contradict his fictions. With an equal opportunity for deifying his father who also had a share in the glorious war, young Gail is unable to place the mantle of heroism on his shoulders. Thus, the dead grandfather becomes the symbol of "that fine shape of eternal youth and virginal desire which makes heroes," (423) while the living father evokes only the grim brutality and carnage of battle.

Eventually the legends of the past become the only truth and the only reality for Hightower, rendering his connection with the public world precarious at best. For unlike his father, he cannot function as "two separate and complete people, one of whom dwelled by serene rules in a world where reality did not exist." (415) And since nothing can compare with his vision, the people he meets and the tasks he is forced to perform become annoying interruptions of the commonplace and trivial. What destroys Hightower is not the fact that he has a dream, but that for the sake of the dream, he becomes insensitive and indifferent to the quality of his actual experience. Thus, he ignores his wife and her needs because the affection due her has already been preempted by her counterpart so that "when he did see her he did not see her at all because of the face which he had already created in his mind." (420) Dominated by his vision, he stands in the pulpit, fusing religion, the galloping cavalry, and his dead grandfather into one incoherent rhapsody, while he remains sublimely indifferent to the growing uneasiness of his parish and to the suicide of his wife.

As if recognizing that he has no place in Jefferson, that indeed his dream-world is threatened by it, Hightower deliberately provokes the violence which will ensure his isolation. For he can only justify and safeguard his withdrawal by "making it appear that he was being driven, uncomplaining, into that which he did not even then admit had been his desire since before he entered the seminary." (428) Each of his actions becomes a defiance, a calculated incentive to public outrage and retribution. Thus he, like Christmas, is at least partially responsible for his own isolation and for the violence he suffers. In his self-chosen role of antagonist, he experiences a fierce exultation, momentarily revealed by his demonic grin hidden by the prayer book. As passive victim, he suffers the threats and beating by the K.K.K. "with that patient and voluptuous ego of the martyr," (429) since it merely confirms his contemptuous judgment of society.

Safe at last in his lonely house, unvisited and undisturbed, Hightower yet retains one tenuous connection with the external world in the person of Byron Bunch. And it is Byron who ultimately forces him to re-examine his world and his life. Compelled by Byron to attend the birth of Lena's child, he becomes for the occasion a participant in rather than a spectator of life. But more important, through the birth he is initiated into the world of nature and discovers that life itself is a source of human value. Reversing his former opinion of Lena, he sees her as a symbol of life and a new paradise: *That will be her life, her destiny. The good stock peopling in tranquil obedience to it the good earth.*" (356)

Byron's plea that he at least attempt to save Joe Christmas is much more difficult to deal with. For though Hightower is willing to accept the natural world, he is not prepared to re-enter the social world. From the moment he hears of Christmas' Negro blood and of the murder, he knows beyond any doubt the sequence of events which must culminate in violence and death. He knows because he himself had been caught in a similar pattern. And though he feels pity, compassion, even horror, he waits passively for the mob to turn once more "with insult and violence upon those who like them were created by the same God and were driven by them to do that which they now turn and rend them for having done it." (319–20) To interfere with the beliefs and rituals of society would be to admit his responsibility for that society. It would, in effect, expose the futility of a life devoted solely to the worship of a dream and to a world "intact and on all sides complete and inviolable, like a classic and serene vase, where the spirit could be born anew sheltered from the harsh gale of living." (419)

Nevertheless, when the escaped and fleeing Christmas rushes into his house, Hightower does make the one gesture which could give substance to his vision. Ironically, this one fumbling but heroic attempt to save Christmas at the risk of his own life, this one act which so far transcends practical considerations that it contains the germ of another legend, is nullified by a younger version of himself. Percy Grimm, engrossed in his own vision of military gallantry which has been fostered by a more recent war, sees nothing in Hightower's words but another example of the degrading crudeness of the non-military world. Too much has happened to Hightower and to Jefferson since the day he abandoned his chosen calling for him to be able to sway or influence the lynch-mob in any way. The past is irremediable.

Jarred out of his complacency and self-righteousness by Joe's death, Hightower sees his past with a new clarity. The image of the great wheel, which gives form to his memories, echoes and passes judgment on all the other solitary circles that have collided violently without ever establishing contact with one another. What he finally comes to recognize is the interdependence of the individual and society, of the private and public worlds, and, more important, the interdependence of individuals within the public world. He, Joe Christmas, and Joanna Burden have all been self-created martyrs to an idea and to that idea they have sacrificed others beyond themselves. Society, no less deluded, attacks and sacrifices them in the name of the same ideas. Their personal histories, like the history of Jefferson, consist of a perpetual denial of life for the sake of empty rituals, each of which enshrines some abstraction. Hightower has the intelligence to attain this bitter self-knowledge and to realize that the responsibility rests with the individual, but he does not have the strength to live with it. As his head falls to the window sill, he hears once again the thunderous cavalry charge peopling Jefferson with the old insubstantial phantoms.

Compared with the embattled lives and specter-haunted thoughts of Hightower, Christmas, and Miss Burden, the calm journey of Lena Grove with a willing Byron Bunch in her wake seems almost an impertinence. Yet it is through her presence that we achieve a final perspective on the action. Into the schematic world of Jefferson she introduces, by virtue of her own intellectual limitations and her pregnancy, the world of nature with its total indifference to both moral and social categories. This provides a significant contrast to Joe Christmas' painful initiation and absorption into society. Both are strangers to Jefferson; but while Joe comes bearing death for himself and others, Lena comes bearing life. The ritual in which she involves others is the natural one of pregnancy and birth. Thus, while the one crystallizes the obsessions of society, the other dispels them. The same almost anonymous figures who attach the label of Negro to Christmas in order to lynch him also forget the social stigma of Lena's pregnancy in order to help her.

Like Joe Christmas, Lena herself is a center for the actions and reactions of various characters and the object of a clearly defined public attitude. Each person she meets sees not her but an image of what he believes her to be, and that image is at least partly predetermined by the convention that identifies virginity with virtue. For Mrs. Armstid she is the fallen woman; for the men at the store, a foolish virgin to be treated with mingled pity and scorn; and for Byron, who loves her, she is the innocent victim of a scoundrel. Each of these images, grounded in a concern with Lena's unmarried state, conveys more information about the observers and their society than they do about her, for unlike Christmas, she does not mirror or share the preconceptions of the community. From the moment we see her delicately licking the sardine oil from her fingers, she is wholly absorbed in the new sensations with which her leisurely travels provide her. Even her search for a father for her child is more a matter of instinct than of morality. What she is looking for is security not respectability. Once Byron assumes this responsibility, she shows no great haste to marry and so to remove the social stigma from herself and her child.

Though Lena is judged harshly, she is consistently treated with kindness. The reason is that she offends against the mores of society without challenging its very foundations as Joe Christmas does. In a sense, the community's convictions and actions operate independently. Mrs. Armstid or the men who offer Lena a ride preserve the myth of virginity in which they share by revealing their contempt for the unmarried Lena, but at the same time they respond to her needs as a woman about to give birth to a child. Here the pressing demands of nature take precedence over social convention.

Thus Lena's arrival signals the breaking up of the old compulsive patterns which match action to judgment. Mrs. Armstid's tight-lipped offer of food, shelter, and money prepares us for Byron's quick abandonment of his routine of overtime work and weekly trips to the country church when Lena appears. He too acts "contrary to all the tradition of his austere and jealous country raising which demands in the object physical inviolability." (42) It is not, however, until Mrs. Hines calls him to the cabin where Lena is in labor that he fully realizes and admits to himself that she is not a virgin. Hightower, despite his distrust of Lena and his fear for Byron, disrupts the pattern of his life and leaves his sanctuary to attend the birth of her child. The sheriff, momentarily overlooking the letter of the law, recognizes her need and therefore her right to use Miss Burden's cottage. Even the anonymous truck driver is trapped into kindness towards Lena and gives up his bed, though not the right to grumble about it.

In each of these cases, the separation of judgment and action is made possible by Lena's own indifference to the former. The relationship between society and the individual is reciprocal as the lives of Hightower, Miss Burden, and Christmas amply illustrate. But Lena refuses or rather is incapable of acting in the light of society's preconception of her. Accordingly, where Joe Christmas intensifies, she destroys the barriers between herself and others; where he forever threatens life with extinction, she becomes the means of its renewal and continuance. This difference is made explicit by the incidents involving food. Lena herself is indifferent to the spirit in which it is offered so long as it sustains her and her child. And her acceptance of it invariably fosters a more personal, human relationship with the giver. Christmas, on the other hand, is forever rejecting the food offered him because of his abnormal sensitivity to the thoughts and attitudes of the giver. He is able to share food with Bobbie, believing that she loves him, but he consistently rejects meals offered by Mrs. McEachern, Byron Bunch, or Miss Burden. The food which sustains Lena in her world of physical experience proves poisonous to Christmas, who lives largely in a world of obsessive ideas which he projects, rightly or wrongly, into every situation. Joe and Lena thus present two contrasting attitudes to experience and to society, and these in turn evoke sharply different responses from society.

Both make a claim on Byron Bunch, the one uncommitted character in the novel, since he has isolated himself from both nature and society. But it is his love for Lena and his sudden and unexpected initiation into the world of nature which she represents that makes Byron willing and eager to help Christmas. Her needs destroy those protective barriers of meaningless routine which he has built around himself. As Hightower points out, Byron, by loving her, becomes vulnerable, for he has allowed himself to be caught up in a chain of events and circumstances over which he can exercise no control. At the same time, however, he has gained in some measure a self-respect, a dignity, and a courage which was lacking in his isolated safety and which gives promise of being a sufficient shield against whatever catastrophes he may encounter. His romantic desire to protect Lena, to convert Hightower, and to save Christmas appear, at first sight, exaggerated reactions to his former passivity and belief in non-interference. But the important thing is that he does not rest in these attitudes or treat his vision of Lena as immutable. He is still necessarily the creator of his own world, but now he is willing to recognize when he has built awry and to reshape it with an eye to reality.

His ability to do so is dependent, to a large extent, on his eventual discovery of the resources of humor. His love for Lena, itself an irrational act, makes him realize the comic aspect of his own behavior. By laughing at his own follies and gullibility, he is able to continue acting irrationally which, in this case, is also humanely; for laughter is one means of re-examining the shibboleths of society and of placing the individual and his world once more in perspective. Though Byron is still sustained by illusions, he is no longer blindly ruled by them. Instead he endeavors through them to establish his kinship with other men. Though he continues to believe in Lena's chastity, Hightower's wisdom, and Joe's black blood, nevertheless, he arranges for the confinement, argues for the first time with Hightower, and does what little he can to help Joe. His illusions are thus more nearly centered on humanity and grounded in the immediacy of living experience. It is man's nature to dream and dreams by their very essence are both distortions of reality and desires for a new shape to experience.

Certainly, the real Lena, more than slightly stupid and more than slightly selfish, and the real Confederate Hightower, who found an inglorious death in a chickencoop, are both unworthy of the dreams and the devotion they inspire. The responsibility, however, lies not with them but with the Byron Bunches and Gail Hightowers who can be moved to save or to deny Joe Christmas because of their dreams. Reason and imagination can prove an integrative force, identifying the interests of the individual with those of the community and establishing a link between the private and public worlds. They can also be destructive insofar as they enable man to invent infinitely various excuses which permit him to live while ignoring life itself. Rationally conceived categories and myths may render morality simpler and clearer by providing formulas of universal applicability, but in the process they destroy those essential motives for morality which must be found by the individual in life itself. This is the truth that Hightower could only know; it is also the truth which Byron, in fumbling and often farcically inadequate fashion, seeks to live.

6 : THE IDOLS OF THE SOUTH

Absalom, Absalom!

Absalom, Absalom! continues Faulkner's attempt to make technique and structure focus the meaning of the novel. It is most closely linked to *The Sound and the Fury* whose structure it elaborates and enriches. Like Caddy Compson, Thomas Sutpen is never presented directly, and like her, he becomes a tremendously vital as well as an enigmatic figure by being the object of intense concern for a number of characters. The difference, and it is a large one, is that Sutpen, unlike Caddy, provides a dynamic rather than a static center. The perspectives are no longer self-contained and self-illuminating; as a result, we have a kaleidoscope instead of a juxtaposition of views. Each successive account of Sutpen is constantly being merged with its predecessors. At every moment, there falls into place yet another pattern which disavows some parts of the earlier interpretations but never discards them. Rosa's story of Sutpen makes its own impression and despite later qualifications and objections, it contributes to and influences Mr. Compson's narrative. Both of these are, in turn, caught up in Quentin's and Shreve's version. Rosa's "demonizing" is still evident in the final reconstruction, though altered considerably by Shreve's mocking tone. This means that our final picture of Sutpen results from a fusion of at least three accounts, each of which belongs to a different generation and reflects a different personal bias.

These successive accounts once more map out the relationship between truth and fact and between legend and history. For what we have in *Absalom, Absalom!* is the creation of the kind of legends that have already crystallized about the figure of Colonel John Sartoris in *Sartoris*. At the core are the facts of Sutpen's career—the dates of his birth, marriage, and death, the building of the plantation house, and so forth. This biographical data is inert and incapable of stirring either the imagination or the emotions. But there are also certain acts and gestures, such as Sutpen's arrival in Jefferson, Henry's and Bon's abrupt departure from the plantation, the shot echoing at the gates, each of which seems to contain within itself the whole meaning of the past, if only read aright. But to grasp this elusive meaning is rendered difficult, if not impossible, by the number of interpretations that any event can encompass. Conflicting voices, each claiming truth, converge upon every act of Sutpen. His refusal to reveal his reasons for coming to Jefferson or for leaving it provokes speculations about hidden loot, robbery, and even murder. And though these are later disproved, they are not entirely forgotten. Thus, not only do these submerged tales contribute to the legend of Sutpen, but they prevent any of the major narrators from circumscribing Sutpen for the reader. The element of ambiguity is sustained to the very end of the book.

This method of converging accounts and multiple perspectives reveals the creation of truth inherent in the attempt to find it. Whereas in *The Sound and the Fury* Faulkner's concern was with the relation of the individual to truth and reality, here he is interested in the contribution both of the individual and of time to a growing and expanding legend which may be called the public truth about Sutpen. Certain facts, as distinct from interpretations, are available from the beginning; others are either added by successive narrators or discovered by them. Mr. Compson, for example, reveals that Sutpen's wagonload of wild Negroes included a woman, a fact Miss Rosa either did not know or chose to ignore. Since there are not enough of these indisputable facts to "explain" Sutpen, the next step is to make facts out of convictions. Rosa feels that the only explanation needed for Sutpen's refusal to sanction Judith's marriage to Bon is his perverse, demonic nature. Mr. Compson offers as an alternative Sutpen's disapproval of Bon's New Orleans mistress. Quentin adds the "fact" of Eulalia Bon's Negro blood, and at this point, everything appears to fall into a logical and convincing pattern. But even this final revelation is open to question. There is no doubt that Quentin himself is convinced of the truth of his interpretation, but so is Miss Rosa of the truth of her "demonizing." Nor is there any doubt that in the light of it Sutpen's actions become more comprehensible, but the same is true of the disproved "fact" of his exploits as a highwayman.

The number of alternative explanations and unresolved ambiguities in the three accounts of Sutpen suggest the immense difficulties attendant upon the effort to arrive at truth. Adding to this difficulty is the fact that truth must eventually be fixed by words, which by their very nature falsify the things they are meant to represent. This distortion inherent in language is the reason for the tortuous style of *Absalom, Absalom!* The characters themselves are engaged in the frustrating attempt to capture truth and then to communicate it. Quentin tries to convey a look on Clytie's face and quickly eliminates "shock," "fear," and "triumph" without finding a word to satisfy him. The clearest example, however, is Miss Rosa's account of what was happening at the moment when Clytie stopped her at the head of the stairs. She qualifies, adds, masses analogies, similes, and metaphors, and goes over the same points incessantly as if the repetition would suddenly make everything comprehensible not only to Quentin but to herself. In the final effort to explain Clytie's action and her own reaction, she is forced to reiterate her entire history, her childhood, her dreams, and her disappointments. The qualities evident in Miss Rosa's description of a single incident are also found in the style as a whole. Whoever the speaker, the long sentences bristle with qualifications and alternatives beneath which the syntax is almost lost. And what is true of the sentence is true also of the paragraph, of the chapter, indeed of the total structure. Hence the style is more closely related to the creation of the legend of Sutpen and to the common effort to fix reality and formulate truth than it is to the characters who retell the story.

All the narrators are sincerely trying to be truthful, correcting and contradicting themselves as they reconstruct the past, and all have certain unique qualifications for the task. Miss Rosa obviously has the advantage of having lived through the events and of a close personal knowledge of Sutpen, while Mr. Compson has his carefully guarded objectivity, and Quentin and Shreve the uncluttered perspective afforded by the passage of time. Yet it is plain that the result of their efforts is not the truth about Sutpen but rather three quite distinct legends which reveal as much about the narrators as about Sutpen. The element of distortion most evident in Miss Rosa's version is, nevertheless, present in all three. For in accordance with his own experience and bias, each of them works the available facts into what is essentially an aesthetic form. Consequently, Sutpen takes the main role in Miss Rosa's Gothic thriller and in Mr. Compson's classical drama which is forever verging on satire. But in the story told by Quentin and Shreve, he recedes into the background as love becomes the dominant interest and chivalric romance the dominant form. Moreover, through the three successive accounts, history moves from the factual to the mythic, leaving Quentin and Shreve free to interpret, imagine, and invent so long as they remain true to what they believe is the spirit of the past.

Though Miss Rosa knew Sutpen most intimately, her account of him is the most distorted, revealing only her own obsession, the narrowness of her experience, and the grim inflexibility of her responses. Her "demonizing" is, however, natural and inevitable in view of her lifelong isolation. Born between two generations, the one destroyed by the Civil War and the other engaged in reconstruction, she can find no place for herself in either. Her youth with its ardent desire for experience is nullified by the old age of her parents, her culture, and her tradition with their insistence on living in memories of the past.

That isolation which leaves Miss Rosa forever watching other people's lives unfold while hers remains unchanged gives unlimited scope to her fantasies compounded of religion and romance. Without being put to the test of reality, the world becomes a matter of masks "interchangeable not only from scene to scene, but from actor to actor and behind which the events and occasions [take] place without chronology or sequence." (62) In her childhood Sutpen has been the demon-ogre who had carried Ellen to his "grim ogre-bourne" to produce "two half-phantom children." In her old age she merely adds a few new words and similes to embellish the childhood concept and to give it a religious overtone: *"He was the light-blinded bat-like image of his own torment cast by the fierce demoniac lantern up from beneath the earth's crust."* (171) The other people she sees or even hears about are similarly drawn into her fantasies: Ellen becomes the captive maiden, Clytie is *"the cold Cerberus of his* [Sutpen's] *private hell,"* (136) while Judith and Charles Bon enact a fairy tale of love and courtship.

Only complete withdrawal from the world can preserve such fantasies as these from the impact of reality. Rosa, however, rushes forth in the conviction that her fantasies actually correspond to the people she encounters only to find, inevitably, her illusions of herself and others shattered. Her humble effort to provide Judith with a trousseau and so to share vicariously the role of bride is met with peals of laughter from Ellen, who has already betrayed her by acting like a lady of the manor rather than a captive in "Bluebeard's den." She rushes out to "save" Judith and Henry from Sutpen after Ellen's death only to find that neither of them will permit her to do any saving. Ready to weep with the widowed bride, she finds that Judith remains stone-faced and silent at the news of Bon's death. Perhaps her greatest surprise occurs in connection with Sutpen. The complete separation of her vision of Sutpen from the man himself is indicated by the ease with which she replaces the *"ogre of my childhood"* with *"a shape which rode away beneath a flag."* (167) The demon is slain by the hero who returns to claim a virgin bride. But this pleasant charade dissolves when Sutpen muffs his lines and destroys her image not only of him but of herself. His crude proposition forces Rosa to choose between her fantasy and an experience that is brutally shorn of all romantic illusion. The outrage to her sensibility as well as her moral principles simply intensifies her obsessions and completes her retreat into a world where nothing and no one can challenge her vision of Sutpen as the essence of all evil.

It is little wonder, then, that Miss Rosa's account of Sutpen and of the past in general is rank melodrama and that all the characters in it are exaggerated, distorted phantoms. The fine touch of the Civil War maiden-poetess, untouched by the brutalities of combat and so free to write of gallantry and honor and aesthetically placed wounds, is evident throughout. What she does is create a pattern which some have applied to the book as a whole—the Gothic novel with its gloomy castles, dark, evil villains, and innocent victims. As motive for and explanation of all the Gothic horror and violence that she evokes, she posits a mysterious curse, though she is curiously unable to decide whether it was incurred by Sutpen, her family, or the South. In any event, Sutpen is, for Miss Rosa, both curse and accursed. In the nightmare world of her imagination, his evil assumes such gigantic proportions that it threatens both social and cosmic orders.

The antithesis and antidote to Rosa's hallucinatory view of Sutpen is Mr. Compson's account. For him, Sutpen and the past provide scope for interesting speculations and a number of broad generalizations. His is the deliberately rational, impersonal approach which allows him not only to weave patterns and to posit hypotheses but also to doubt his own conclusions. The irony which pervades his section is as much directed at himself as raconteur as it is at the story he is telling. Yet in establishing his own impersonality, in attempting to abstract all emotional bias from his account, Mr. Compson also abstracts much of the human quality of the past. As a result, the pattern that he presents lacks even that artificial "demonic" vitality with which Rosa infuses her narrative. He is incapable of recreating the agony of a situation or of evoking the interplay of human emotions which give substance and reality to the words which he, like Miss Rosa, must use. The tension between Henry and Bon is explained as the meeting of the puritan provincial with the weary amoralist, each of whom has his own concept of honor and love. Judith's care of Etienne is pictured in terms of a conflict between her love for him and her awareness of his Negro blood. The rational has, in some way, submerged the imaginative power;· deduction has taken the place of intuitive understanding. Accordingly, what he describes is a battle of ideas or concepts and not a conflict of people.

Mr. Compson's impersonality, however, enables him to make one contribution to the legend which is not in the power of either Rosa or Quentin. His age, experience, and temperament make him more aware of the characters in relation to society and time. The attention of Quentin and Shreve is directed toward the tensions of love rather than of society. For Rosa, Jefferson, like Sutpen's Hundred, is an "ogre-world" in which she has no place. So it is Mr. Compson who describes the interaction of Sutpen and Jefferson. He shows the town's curiosity, suspicion, indignation, and finally, its slow and unwilling acceptance of Sutpen. He shows Sutpen surrounded by his Negroes or by visitors from Jefferson during the building of the house. His account of Sutpen's courtship and wedding reveals the "intruder" in a better light than the town which seeks to reject him. Levelling his irony simultaneously at the follies of Sutpen and at the pettiness and cruelty of the old South, Mr. Compson is able to preserve his own detachment while exercising his bent for satire.

But the larger pattern in terms of which Mr. Compson reconstructs and evaluates the past is neither social nor ideological. Still less is it historical. If Miss Rosa's account of Sutpen can be described as Gothic thriller, then Mr. Compson's constitutes a classical tragedy. His habitual reading of the classics as well as his identification of Clytie with Cassandra indicate at least a predisposition to this particular literary form. Accordingly, his section of the narrative is filled with references to staging, to actors and the drama. It is he who presents the Sutpen family as actors each playing a role while "Fate, destiny, retribution, irony —the stage manager, call him what you will—was already striking the set and dragging on the synthetic and spurious shadows and shapes of the next one." (72–73) Miss Rosa's "ogre-world" is thus transformed into a heroic drama in which the characters are larger than life, not because they are demonic, but because their conflict is itself writ large and placed against the backdrop of eternity. They become " 'victims of a different circumstance, simpler and therefore, integer for integer, larger, more heroic and the figures therefore more heroic too, not dwarfed and involved but distinct, uncomplex who had the gift of loving once or dying once instead of being diffused and scattered creatures.' " (89) In this drama Sutpen is the protagonist, pitting himself not only against men and their society but against fate and eternity. Heroically he struggles against his own doom and his own extinction, trying to establish his dynasty in defiance of the gods. And like the heroes of Greek tragedy, he is doomed to defeat. Miss Rosa's vague unspecified curse becomes the family curse of the House of Sutpen working itself out in successive generations.

In contrast to Mr. Compson's and Miss Rosa's, the recreation of the past by Quentin and Shreve is the product of their youth and romantic imagination. These enable them to overcome geographical and cultural differences so that it is almost impossible to tell where the Southerner leaves off and the Canadian begins the reconstruction of the Sutpen legend. Both are able to anticipate the thoughts and words of the other and both are able to identify themselves with Henry Sutpen and Charles Bon simply because that identification is not one of individuals but of similar states of mind. It does not matter "what faces and what names they called themselves and were called by so long as the blood coursed—the blood, the immortal brief recent intransient blood which could hold honor above slothy unregret and love above fat and easy shame." (295)

The vividness with which they see and endow the past has its source in romantic rather than historical imagination. Thus, the eighty odd years which separate them from the events they seek to recreate allow them a kind of poetic license in arranging the scenes and characters. Charles carries a wounded Henry from the battlefield, knowing that Henry will prevent him from marrying Judith. Later he substitutes the octoroon's portrait for Judith's as a means of saving Judith tears and Henry her condemnation. Both these romantic gestures are contradicted by the earlier evidence of Miss Rosa and General Compson; nevertheless, they are true to the spirit of Shreve's account in a way that the prosaic "facts" could not be. Shreve can even insist that there must have been an embittered, vengeful mother living in dusty, baroque splendor and a Dickensian lawyer carefully entering Sutpen's assets in a ledger while he waited for Bon to grow up. All these creations or inventions are poetically true even as Mr. Compson's heroic simplifications and Miss Rosa's "demonizing" are true for their respective narratives. But in each case it is a truth far removed from the historian's concern with facts, evidence, and careful documentation.

Quentin and Shreve clearly remove from their actual social and historical context those parts of the Sutpen story which deal with love. Facts are preserved or discarded as they "fit the preconceived," revealing the moment of love, "where there might be paradox and inconsistency but nothing fault nor false." (316) This world of love is treated as pure legend and romance, possessing its own language and logic. As a result, the South becomes an atmospheric background providing even in the gloom of a Mississippi winter the correct mixture of magnolias and moonlight for the lovers, Judith and Charles. Miss Rosa's curse becomes "a glamorous fatality" which ennobles those it destroys. Against this background an intense drama of passion, courage, and self-sacrifice is played out.

Since it is a drama of love, it is understandable that it should evoke poetic echoes. Certainly it is in this final section that the greatest number of literary allusions occur. And in many instances it is impossible to determine whether poetry provides the pattern into which the events are fitted or whether the events recall the poetry. Henry's contemplation of incest, for example, is inextricably fused with the story of Duke John of Lorraine. Charles is the "silken and tragic Lancelot nearing thirty," (320) Henry "an academic Hamlet waked from some trancement." (174) At times such allusions become ironic as when Rosa and Sutpen are likened first to Agamemnon and Cassandra and then to "an ancient stiff-jointed Pyramus" and an "eager though untried Thisbe." (177) Consistently Quentin and Shreve interpret the past and frame their narrative in terms of literature, for it is in it that they find those eternal values of youth which can be confined to no one place or time.

Yet only Shreve recognizes that the story they have jointly created is only poetically true and that its function is the symbolic one of embodying love, courage, and loyalty in a single form without exhausting them. Quentin, on the other hand, is unable to maintain aesthetic distance or to distinguish the symbolic from the literal. For he, like Henry Sutpen, is obsessed with the idea of incest and with his own responsibility for his sister. And since Henry's gesture in killing Bon is identified with "honor vindicated" and virginity protected, Quentin feels that only by repeating the gesture (which he attempts in *The Sound and the Fury*) can he defend Compson honor. Equally important to Quentin's confused and ambivalent reaction to the Sutpen story is the element of miscegenation he himself has introduced. That word, more terrible even than incest, alone has the power to destroy the world of love, to make Henry Sutpen kill the person he loved more than his father or sister. Quentin is thus forced into a decision the consequences of which have already been delineated in *The Sound and the Fury*. He has the choice of viewing the past symbolically or literally and of affirming or denying its "design." With his passionate reiteration that he does not hate the South, Quentin reveals his decision to perpetuate the design he has found in the past.

In this last respect, Quentin is related to the Sutpen story in which, shorn of the wealth of interpretive comment, one fact is clear. Each of the events discussed and rediscussed by the narrators represents a moment of decision for the characters in the story. Time is constantly weaving a pattern in opposition to the "design," whether inherited or self-created, that the individual seeks to live by. Even the most carefully considered act can have outrageous results simply because once committed, it becomes part of the sequence of natural events which no man can control. It is in these moments of crisis that the individual or the community is forced to re-examine its shibboleths. Since the Sutpen legend is part of the South, it follows that the conflict and the choice are rendered in Southern terms. The narrators see each of the characters in the legend as confronted by a human being who is also a Negro. This confrontation occurs, moreover, in a situation and at a moment in their lives when they feel compelled to deny either the man or the Negro. In essence, they are seen as being forced to choose between mutually exclusive alternatives, between personal and social relationships, between the individual and tradition.

Sutpen himself is a mirror image of the South, for his career in Jefferson merely repeats in a foreshortened form the rise of many families whose longer tenure of the land has given them respectability. Through his single-minded preoccupation with the "design," he effects consciously and in the span of a few years what other Southern families accomplished over a period of generations. But whereas he is far from being a special case, he is definitely an anachronism: he is the ruthless and purposeful founding father of a dynasty who lives in a time of consolidation rather than of expansion. Time proves his worst enemy, for not only has it established the social hierarchy of the Sartorises and Compsons, but it has limited the time he can devote to creating even the rudiments of a similar structure for his family. Because he lacks a past while recreating the past of the South, the townspeople regard him with distrust, then hatred, and finally with an exacted tolerance.

Nevertheless, Sutpen becomes the staunchest defender of the idols of the South at a time when they most need defending. At no point in any of the Yoknapatawpha novels or stories is Sutpen accused of failing the South during the four long years of agonizing combat. Not once does he place his property or the safety of himself or his family above that duty which he has assumed along with the Sartorises and Compsons. Even Rosa does not deny him courage and gallantry on the battlefield. Like the South as a whole, Sutpen refuses to admit defeat or the changes that it inevitably brought about. He attempts to rebuild his plantation and to set his family in order as if the war had never occurred, an attempt that is very much like Colonel Sartoris' defiant rebuilding of his mansion on a grander scale than before. For better or worse, Sutpen does reflect both the virtues and the vices of the South, but he does it without any of the social graces, the courtly gestures of the Sartorises.

It is through a deliberate choice involving the repudiation of his past that Sutpen becomes an image of the South. However lacking in elegance, his mountain home had stressed certain fundamental human values—the man rather than his possessions—"Because where he lived the land belonged to anybody and everybody and so the man who would go to the trouble and work to fence off a piece of it and say 'This is mine' was crazy." (221) But as he and his family journey into the valley, all the familiar and comprehensible beliefs and manners give way to a strange, nightmare world which has no place for them. As they pass from hamlet to hamlet, the Negroes become the focus of their bewilderment. That bewilderment is channelled into resentment by the poor whites who find relief in hating the Negro as a symbol of and foundation for an economic and social system in which the land is "all divided and fixed and neat with a people living on it all divided and fixed and neat because of what color their skins happened to be and what they happened to own." (221)

Sutpen feels the full force of this pattern of exclusion and its application to himself when the "monkey-nigger" orders him to the back door of the plantation house. In that brief moment the central symbol of *Absalom, Absalom!* is established —the boy seeking admittance and being turned away in the name of the social code. What makes it even more disastrous for the young Sutpen is that nothing in his past has prepared him for such a moment. Nothing or no one can help him either to understand or to accept it. The rifle analogy will not hold, and so there is no way that he can integrate this new experience into the old. Consequently, for the first time, he is forced to think, to employ a logic which culminates in his formulation and adoption of the "design." His instinctive reaction is to believe that the behavior of the plantation owner as expressed through the Negro is wrong and inhuman. Yet his final decision betrays that instinctive reaction and he exchanges individual integrity for a handful of social concepts and conventions. His acceptance of circumstance or "luck" as the controlling factor in man's life is replaced by his worship of a man-made pattern; his primitive mountain ethics give way to what he believes to be the code of the South.

The germ of Sutpen's design is simply his determination to create by his own shrewdness, courage, and will that pattern which he sees, rightly or wrongly, in Southern society and to conduct his life strictly in terms of its ethical code. Both designs, Sutpen's and the South's, are based on concepts which deny human values in a large area of conduct and on social rather than natural definitions of the individual. The security of a long family line and of an undisputed position allows a Bayard Sartoris to chat with Will Falls on terms of intimacy and to permit his old Negro servant certain liberties. Sutpen, on the other hand, never deviates from the design, never allows himself to forget the letter of that law by which he has chosen to regulate his own behavior. Since his position must be achieved rather than simply maintained, he cannot afford any such relaxation of principle.

Nor does this rigid attitude provoke any tensions or conflicts in his own mind. During his agonizing stay in the cave, Sutpen had made an irrevocable decision; consequently, his succeeding choices involve no apparent agonies on either a personal or a moral level. He is presumably bound to Eulalia Bon by ties of marriage, children, and daily companionship. Yet in the "just" divorce that follows, he gives up all these without hesitation in order to conform to the South's worship of pure blood and its horror of miscegenation, though as Quentin points out, " 'he could have closed his eyes and, if not fooled the rest of the world as they had fooled him, at least have frightened any man out of speaking the secret aloud.' " (266) Sutpen's "innocence" is manifest: it consists not only of his unquestioning belief in the value of all the idols of the South but in his belief that the structure, the design, is itself the secret of its strength and its perpetuation, that he need only follow its ritual to grasp its substance and that he can do so with the same blunt honesty which was part of his mountain heritage. On the contrary, it quickly becomes evident that each betrayal of humanity betrays its agent as well as the victim. Sutpen's rejection of his wife and son constitutes a rejection of himself as husband and father.

A new attempt to create his counterpart of the South's design takes Sutpen to Jefferson. He is once more the outsider, but at least he knows the passwords—wealth and power. Lack of a respectable past remains a disadvantage, but the grandest mansion with the most magnificent furnishings in Jefferson helps to compensate. Moreover, Ellen Coldfield is bought to complete the picture and to provide him with those roots in Jefferson which he can never obtain through his own efforts. Despite her tears at the wedding, interpreted in quite different ways by Miss Rosa and Mr. Compson, Ellen rapidly learns to play the lady of the manor to Sutpen's lord. She develops into the social butterfly, "gracious and assured and talking the most complete nonsense, speaking her bright set meaningless phrases out of the part which she had written for herself, of the duchess peripatetic with property soups and medicines among a soilless and uncompelled peasantry." (69) Ultimately she becomes not only the instrument of Sutpen's design by bearing his children but his partner, for she it is who seeks to acquire the elegant Charles Bon as the final, graceful complement to the manor.

In the complex tensions existing between Sutpen and his children, particularly Charles Bon, the boy symbol and the rejection are repeated under different circumstances. The most striking instance, of course, is Charles's arrival at Sutpen's Hundred and his unspoken demand for recognition. The boy is no longer barefoot and tattered, but he too is seeking acceptance on his own merit. It is denied him, as it was to his father, for the sake of the design. Time has once more produced a situation in which Sutpen must choose between his adherence to the concept of pure blood and his own and his son's humanity. His refusal to acknowledge Charles goes far toward destroying the very design it was intended to protect. Just as the unconscious action of his boyhood insulter had driven Sutpen to violate the *status quo*, so his own rejection of Charles marks the beginning of another eruption in which Charles challenges the moral *status quo*. Like his father, Charles eventually forces an indirect recognition, though at the cost of his own life.

The death of Charles, the subsequent flight of Henry, and the self-imposed withdrawal of Judith forces Sutpen to one more effort at coercing circumstance to fit his design. Judith cannot give him the grandchildren he needs, and even if she were to do so, they would still be on the distaff side and hence a compromise with the Southern notion of male hierarchy and primogeniture. Henry, unfortunately, has negated his own potential contributions at the moment of destroying his brother and friend. And Sutpen's own ability to put matters right through a new wife and a new heir is limited, if not rendered impossible, by the approach of old age. He turns, therefore, to Rosa, the poor dependent relation, and with the same simple logic that permitted him to disown his first wife, proposes that Rosa prove her ability to further his design. The crudeness of the proposal shocks "the little dream woman" completely out of her fairy tale world in which a Sutpen in love becomes softened and mellowed by her presence. With a single phrase Sutpen destroys her illusion both of him and of herself. It is an insult she cannot forgive, if only because it denies her the opportunity of either saving or annihilating the demon of her childhood in some fittingly dramatic fashion.

Only one more trial faces Sutpen and with it he comes full circle. In denying Milly, he once more rejects the claims of a wife and a child because they do not conform to his pattern. The fact that Milly is the granddaughter of his own retainer, that she is probably both ignorant and inelegant, shows the extent to which Sutpen has been forced to compromise. But he still holds firm to the central core of his design—the male heir who will possess and perpetuate his name and property through all time. In rejecting Milly, Sutpen also destroys the admiration, which is almost hero-worship, of Wash Jones. In a sense, the aging Jones is closely akin to the young Sutpen, for he too stands bewildered before a world that posits and flaunts inequality. But he seeks to enter the privileged circle through Milly's marriage and Sutpen's benevolence rather than his own efforts. And though he had been able to countenance Millie's seduction and even to see in it a mark of favor, the brutality of Sutpen's rejection of her and her child rouses him to an awareness of his own humanity. His violent and fatal attack on Sutpen is but the most extreme protest against the design in that series which begins with Sutpen's own hurt bewilderment.

The necessity of choosing between social patterns and the individual is not restricted to Sutpen alone. Each new generation and every individual in it faces the same problem. The only difference is that Charles Bon, Henry, and Judith go through an emotional struggle which is rendered in vividly dramatic terms by the sympathy of Quentin and Shreve. In contrast, all of Sutpen's agony is compressed into the single incident of his lonely vigil in the cave and even that is lacking in the kind of dramatic immediacy that would make it imaginatively compelling. Sutpen's children all learn that the demands of circumstance frequently run counter to the dictates of their heredity, training, and principles. Temporarily, Judith and Henry both become rebels for the sake of love: the former is willing to marry Charles Bon without parental consent, the latter actually gives the lie to his father and renounces his patrimony in order to accompany his friend. For them, the conflict at first is simply between love and filial duty with its implicit obedience to authority. Their youth and idealism prompt them to choose the former.

The crucial test, however, is one that neither Judith nor Henry nor Bon can meet. At the core of Sutpen's design and of the social structure of the South is the concept of the "Negro" as an inferior being or social pariah. The drop of black blood effectively prevents the recognition of certain individuals as human beings with human needs and desires. To accept the man behind the mask of the Negro simply as a man would necessitate a denial of the precepts rendered sacred by years of unquestioning obedience. Bon, believing himself to be white, treats his octoroon wife with more courtesy and perhaps more kindness than is attributed to Sutpen's treatment of Eulalia, if only because the octoroon represents a costly investment. There is even a certain kind of honor evident in his behavior since he assumes responsibilities toward her that he has no intention of abrogating. But one thing he cannot give her is a place in society equal to his own. Neither he nor the octoroon question the "justice" of this, nor is it questioned by any other member of his class. There is no moral stigma attached to Bon's treatment of his mistress as there would have been had he actually claimed her as his wife. Consequently, there is no conflict; that comes when Bon is himself forced to battle for the recognition denied him, ironically enough, on the grounds of blood.

The choice Henry has to make is a much more agonizing one. For him, Bon represents all that is admirable, fine, and noble in a man. The faint suggestion of homosexuality and Henry's ardent hero-worship create unusually strong bonds of love and affection, so strong indeed that Henry does not hesitate in choosing between father and friend. So compelling is his emotional commitment that, after a self-torturing struggle, Henry is even willing to countenance Bon's incestuous marriage with Judith. Such a sin, involving, as it would, *"the irrevocable repudiation of the old heredity and training and the acceptance of eternal damnation,"* (347) would only be a further proof and affirmation of a love which will not be restricted. But there is still one more test, one more aspect of his heredity and training which is stronger than love itself. It is *"the miscegenation, not the incest, which [he] cant bear."* (356) The shadow of the Negro effectively separates brother from brother, son from father, lover from beloved. The emotional pressure exerted on Henry is revealed by the juxtaposition of the two short sentences which state the nature of the choice he is faced with: *"—You are my brother.—No I'm not. I'm the nigger that's going to sleep with your sister. Unless you stop me, Henry."* (357–58) By his shot at the gate of Sutpen's Hundred, Henry commits himself and his sister to an affirmation of Sutpen's design. The lives of Charles Bon, of Judith, and of Henry are sacrificed to an abstract principle and a social tradition that proves stronger than the moral or religious.

Although Judith is not a party to Henry's decision, she, nevertheless, condones it by her own subsequent action. Charles Etienne, the white-skinned Negro, the nephew to both her and Clytie, is brought to Sutpen's Hundred by her direction. Whether the two women ever realize that he is their nephew is one of the unresolved ambiguities of *Absalom, Absalom!* but that they know him to be the son of an octoroon is beyond dispute. With his appearance the boy symbol recurs in the third generation. Etienne's youth, his dependence, his complete vulnerability arouse a certain maternal love and affection in both Judith and Clytie, but in neither of them is it allowed to express itself freely and naturally. His claims on their love are balanced by his Negro blood, a situation that is dramatically rendered by the sleeping arrangements made for him midway between Judith's bed and Clytie's pallet.

Judith finally makes her decision, the one already made by her father, brother, lover, and the whole South. The frail youth is not allowed to be simply Charles Etienne St. Velery Bon. To the name must be added the label and the stigma of "Negro." Thus, in her relation with Etienne, Judith repeats almost exactly the action of her father in connection with Eulalia Bon. She too need only have closed her eyes to have "fooled the rest of the world"; she too chooses to assert principle at whatever cost to her own and the boy's emotions. But having revealed the taint of Negro blood, Judith is herself horrified by what she has done and urges him to hide the very thing she has impressed upon his consciousness: "What ever you are, once you are among strangers, people who dont know you, you can be whatever you will." (204) No change of scene can, however, restore Etienne's world of innocence "where pigmentation had no more moral value than the silk walls and the scent" (199) or erase his own awareness of that concept of Negro which he can neither ignore, accept, nor reject. Judith's subsequent behavior, nursing the stricken Etienne and scrimping to pay for his tombstone, is her way of expressing penitence, a penitence that is perhaps also implied in Henry's painful return to and concealment in Sutpen's Hundred.

Within the design, whether Sutpen's or the South's, only

the Jim Bonds have the possibility of surviving. This half-mocking conclusion of Shreve's refers to Bond's survival both as "Negro" and as idiot. Lacking reason, this last descendant of Sutpen is incapable of realizing that he is colored or that there are social conventions which define his position with respect to other men. The information that he was a Negro's son would have "vanished from what you (not he) would have had to call his mind long before it could have set up any reaction at all, either of pride or pleasure, anger or grief." (215) Whatever feelings and emotions he may have arise out of his needs for the essentials of human existence rather than for social status. It is because the South cannot control him that he can outlast the South. The full irony of Shreve's remark thus becomes apparent: the only one who is not forced to decide between the claims of humanity and society, the only one who is not destroyed by the very necessity of choosing is the idiot who possesses nothing which can be destroyed. He alone escapes all social categories, he alone has perfect freedom and scope to be himself, and all he can be is an idiot.

But insofar as Shreve's statement also implies the survival of Jim Bond as Negro, another factor is involved. It is the Negroes who are fighting to be recognized as human beings, and it is a fight in which victory must ultimately be theirs, if only because the whites destroy their own integrity and humanity each time they succeed in reasserting their position. In this respect, Bond's projected triumph constitutes a warning of the possibility of a doom which may yet be avoided. The choice confronting the Sutpens is a recurrent one and therefore there is always the hope that someone, some time will open the doors of the plantation, thus reversing Sutpen's decision, ignoring all categories, racial and economic, and altering the course of history itself.

The fact that the Sutpen story is framed in terms of a choice between one's responsibility to man and to social tradition suggests that the narrators are related to the story they tell in yet another way. Miss Rosa, Mr. Compson, and Quentin, each exemplify, though in different ways, the abdication of responsibility to man. Each is free to interpret the past and to accept it or to modify it according to his own emotions and his awareness of the demands of a living present. Rosa, however, uses the past to justify her moral judgments, which have been formulated in advance of the situations she feels called upon to judge. More important, she uses it as the justification for her withdrawal from the world of present experience. With the grim air of a vengeful Cassandra, she waits for all those who have provoked her censure to " 'prove not only to themselves but to everybody else that she had been right.' " (176) She is, in a sense, the perfect defender of the idols of the South, for she is never tempted either to question or to deny them.

While Rosa's attitude is explained by her self-delusion, Mr. Compson has no such excuse. He appears to see the nature of man's struggle with himself and with time; he formulates the conflict betwen instinct and precept with commendable clarity; and he even recognizes the responsibility of the individual. But, whatever his reason, he has rejected the gambit of life for the sake of sitting on the sidelines and playing the role of ironic commentator. His refusal to concern himself with the Sutpen legend, his careful avoidance of choosing sides makes his section a quiet interlude between Rosa's fury and Quentin's passion, but it also makes him less of a man. His intellectualism may be a little more refined, a little more subtle than Sutpen's halting logic, but it serves just as efficiently to isolate him from humanity. In so doing, it replaces a " 'single simple Yes and a single simple No as instantaneous and complete and unthinking as the snapping on and off of electricity' " (272) with a deliberate weighing of ideas which precludes any action. By default, Mr. Compson contributes to the perpetuation of a system whose vices and follies he sees all too clearly.

The intense absorption of Quentin in the Sutpen story is accounted for by the fact that his decision is yet to be made; meanwhile, his relation to Caddy adds urgency to the problem. In *The Sound and the Fury* Caddy's promiscuity challenges his identification of "virginity" with Compson "honor" by placing her immersion in life and the present against his abstractions and preoccupation with the past. His despairing cry at the end of *Absalom, Absalom!* reveals Quentin's decision and his solution to the problem of his dual self. He commits himself to the past, denying the Quentin preparing to enter Harvard and to participate in life for the sake of the Quentin "who was still too young to deserve yet to be a ghost, but nevertheless having to be one for all that." (9) He insists on the reality of his concepts and on the validity of the past the character of which he himself has helped to establish. And when he cannot recreate in his own life the principles and gestures which he admires in Henry, he commits suicide.

Absalom, Absalom! is an extension not only of the structure but also of the theme of *The Sound and the Fury*. The relation of the narrators to the center once more points out the essential ambiguity of fact and the multiplicity of "subjective" truths to which it can give rise. The later novel also examines the relation of time to the center: with successive generations the diverse versions coalesce, the inconsistencies are ironed out, and the legend assumes an independent existence. The legend, in its turn, becomes a motivating factor for those individuals who inherit it. Once the contributions of individual narrators, their deductions, speculations, and inventions, are forgotten, the legend, which embodies a poetic truth, tends once more to become identified with fact. Accordingly, it becomes a motivating force for those who inherit it. Quentin, whose "very body was an empty hall echoing with sonorous defeated names," (12) represents all those who are dedicated to serving the past, to preserving and perpetuating in their own lives those myths and rituals enshrined by their tradition. Neither the tradition nor the dedication is necessarily bad; but when they are used simply for self-perpetuation, and when they resist all change and alteration demanded by the exigencies of the present, they become a destructive or at best a stultifying force. The Golden Age of necessity exists in the past, while its return can be envisaged only as of the future. And just as necessarily man's position is confined essentially to the present. To recognize this is to accept the truth of the legend without becoming helplessly paralyzed by its form.

As in *The Sound and the Fury*, inherited traditional concepts of the Old South are contrasted with the eternal virtues and truth which cannot be confined to a single historical period. In *Absalom, Absalom!* the choice between them is not only rendered dramatically in each of the Sutpens but is extended to the present in the figure of Quentin. Consequently, the decision is formulated in terms of the whole South rather than a single family. Sutpen's design is and can be no other than a microcosm of the South; his values are its values. To make Sutpen the scapegoat as Rosa does or to isolate him from Jefferson in a kind of moral quarantine as Quentin tends to do distorts the meaning of what is perhaps Faulkner's finest novel. For it is when a Sutpen makes a travesty of "principles" by a too meticulous observance, when a Charles Etienne destroys his life, or a Henry his love, that a re-examination of the tradition and the past becomes imperative for characters and readers alike.

7 : CRIME AND PUNISHMENT

Sanctuary
and *Requiem for a Nun*

Sanctuary and *Requiem for a Nun* are related by more than
continuity of plot and character, for the latter is not so much a
sequel as a restatement and commentary on some of the ideas
which were overshadowed by the bizarre and exaggerated brutality of the events in the former. Actually both books are concerned with violence, though in *Requiem for a Nun* it takes the
form of a completed act which is talked about while in *Sanctuary*
it is part of the developing action, provoking an immediate and
often unformulated response. In both, violence is stressed not for
its sensationalism but because it has the curious power to initiate
two parallel and contradictory modes of response, one social and
conventional, the other distinctively personal and exploratory.
Thus it both confirms and disorders familiar patterns of thought
and action, and in so doing, it forces a re-evaluation of self and
society together with a subsequent readjustment of one to the
other. In short, violence administers a shock not only to the
nervous system but to the moral intelligence as well.

In both books an act of murder signals an exploration of crime
and punishment in its social, moral, and legal aspects. Justice
with its attendant problems of guilt and innocence, responsibility
and punishment is probed from various points of view. Temple's
rape is merely a prelude to Tommy's murder which in turn starts
Horace on his quest for justice. The concluding scene in which
Horace discovers that justice and law have scarcely a nodding
acquaintance echoes the opening scene of *Requiem for a Nun*
in which Nancy's punishment is determined by the law whose

jurisdiction she has already transcended. Through Gavin Stevens, the concern with the legal aspects of the situation, the terminal point of *Sanctuary*, is quickly subordinated to a preoccupation with divine justice which, in the last analysis, is simply human justice aware of its own divinity. The prose interchapters recount chronologically the history of Yoknapatawpha while exploring the process by which justice has become abstracted and conceptualized, housed in and symbolized by a courthouse, a jail, and a "gilded dome." At this point justice ceases to be a living reality in the heart of man and becomes a set of laws and precedents of the kind that defeat Benbow. Thus, *Sanctuary* and the two parts of *Requiem for a Nun* explore the same problem but by radically different approaches and techniques.

Lacking the historical perspective of *Requiem for a Nun*, *Sanctuary* is concerned not with the manner in which concepts of law and justice are established but with the way in which they function at one particular time and place. The result is a dramatic enactment of those ideas which are presented discursively in the later book. Temple's rape and Tommy's murder invoke certain social and legal rituals of justice which are more interested in completing the pattern of crime and punishment than in understanding its moral complexity. Violence is thus countered with violence whether in the form of a legally prescribed and exacted death sentence or a lynching performed by an infuriated mob. It is the act of murder that is being punished and the final grotesque and ironic proof of this is that the wrong man dies, his death satisfying the ritual of justice even as it reveals its ultimate injustice. In the process, Goodwin's self-elected executioners break the law, kill an innocent man, and debase their own moral nature, all in the name of justice and morality.

Even as this pattern crystallizes, Horace Benbow is forced to re-evaluate it in the light of his own growing knowledge about the murder and his moral sense. As a product of his culture and tradition, he begins by assuming that society is the repository of human values and that it will act humanely and rationally even though individuals within it may fail to do so. He ends by uttering some of the bitterest condemnations of Jefferson's moral complacency, hypocrisy, and heartlessness to be found in any of Faulkner's novels. Disillusioned by his society, he yet has faith in the power of truth and the unimpassioned due process of law, but he finds that the court too lends itself to the horrifying travesty of justice based on prejudice and emotional appeals. Even religion proves hollow as the church turns viciously on Ruby while God, whom Horace believed to be "a gentleman," remains genteelly indifferent to the subversion of his divine laws by human ones. What reduces Horace to a state of shock is the discovery not of evil but of the shoddy foundations of his vision of a moral and rational universe, supported and sustained by the institutions of the church, the state, and the law.

All the groups with which Horace comes in contact during his desperate effort to make truth and justice prevail fall short, though in different ways, of his harmonious vision. Jefferson's respect for law and social morality manifests itself in self-righteousness and unconscious hypocrisy while its preoccupation with social values leads to an indifference to personal values. Thus, Ruby is first branded a whore, an adulteress, and a murderess, and then harried from one shelter to another in the name of decency and respectability. Horace himself becomes the subject of gossip and condemnation simply because he refuses to accept the public judgment of her or to treat her inhumanely. In contrast to Jefferson's concern with social morality, Goodwin and Ruby do realize certain personal values in their love for each other, in their child, and in their care for Tommy and the old blind man. Similarly, Miss Reba shows a very real if maudlin love for the departed Mr. Binford and is able to sympathize with Ruby whom she does not know. On the other hand, both Goodwin's and Miss Reba's households exist in defiance of law and the rules of society. Each group thus lacks some quality essential to Horace's ideal of man in society enacting his own moral nature.

Furthermore, each group, marked by its own distinctive attitude and code of behavior, is both exclusive and excluded. The result is an uneasy antagonism flaring into violence whenever a member of one group intrudes into another. This pattern of intrusion and consequent violence is presented in its mildest form by the town boys gathering outside the college to watch the dance. The students become louder and more self-assertive, while the town boys scrawl lewd remarks about coeds on lavatory walls and strew the road with broken glass. More central is the arrival of Popeye at the Old Frenchman place. Indifferent to personal and social values alike, and therefore as much an intruder at Goodwin's as he is at Miss Reba's, Popeye by his very presence is a source of latent violence over which Goodwin manages to maintain a precarious control until two more intruders, Temple and Gowan, introduce a new and explosive element into his house.

By attempting to impose their code on a group and in a situation where that code is not only meaningless but dangerous, Temple and Gowan generate the violence which overwhelms them. Gowan's adolescent conviction that the honor of a Virginia gentleman is measured by his ability to drink every man under the table determines his behavior both with the town boys and later at Goodwin's. For him, the social and moral criterion is simply one's capacity for liquor. He actually seems to believe that by outdrinking Van he can establish his own standards of behavior and hence his control of a situation long since out of hand. Appropriately, he can only judge the events in which he and Temple have become involved and his own responsibility for them in terms of that same sorry code. He thinks not of what might have happened to Temple but of her returning among people who know him to reveal that he has committed the "unforgivable sin"—not holding his liquor—which makes him forever an outcast in decent Virginia society. Gowan's abject despair over his folly and his hope that the extent of that folly will never be revealed indicate not so much his youth and stupidity, though that is also present, as his inability either to act or to think in any but the ways established by his group. His obsessive concern with social values has atrophied his every moral and human instinct. In him conformity has been carried to an extreme at once ludicrous and tragic.

Like Gowan, Temple seems to be dominated by campus mores but as they bear upon sex rather than liquor. At seventeen she already fits easily into the artificiality of campus life, a life of discreet promiscuity and irresponsibility. Thus, while she apportions her favors between the college and the town boys, she herself remains inviolate and unmoved, "her eyes blankly right and left looking, cool, predatory and discreet." (32) But the responses she provokes anticipate those of the men at Goodwin's. Gowan, enraged by Doc, one of the town boys, truculently accuses Temple of denying him while playing "around all week with any badger-trimmed hick that owns a ford." (43) Doc, in his turn, becomes progressively more belligerent with Gowan and more resentful of Temple's retreat as he mimics her constant reminder that her father is a judge. The degree of her promiscuity is not at issue. What is important is that she has sought excitement by arousing desire while reserving the right to retreat into the sanctuary of her family. This pattern is, of course, repeated when the presence of her family in the courtroom enables her to evade moral action, this time at the cost of a human life.

Yet like Gowan, she clings to her customs in the presence of an alien group. Temple can never quite rid herself of the unnatural flirtatiousness and the arch provocativeness which had served her well at Ole Miss because the young men also knew their role in the *pas de deux* of sexual teasing. The men at the Old Frenchman place, however, do not know the rules of her game and have no intention of permitting her to establish them. For them, the only relationship between a man and a woman is sexual; and crude and violent though it may be, it still possesses a vitality and forcefulness which at once repels and attracts Temple.

Caught between her longing for the safety of her own world and her desire to share in the "adventure" of this new one into which she has stumbled, Temple reaches a state of semi-hysteria. She attempts to persuade herself that the two worlds are identical, or if not, that hers has the power of control. Her family, the guardians of public morality, the representatives of the forces of law and order—a judge, two lawyers, and a newspaper man— should certainly be sufficient to intimidate a Goodwin, a Van, or a Popeye. But her wish not to be protected reveals itself in the constant advance and retreat, provocation and cringing withdrawal, that mark her behavior throughout her stay at Goodwin's. She forces herself on the attention of all the men including Popeye whose callous aloofness is not easily invaded and whose sexual desires are certainly not easily aroused. Temple's provocativeness, like Gowan's cavalier use of the bottle, are natural or at least accepted forms of social behavior in their world. At Goodwin's they become grotesque in their inappropriateness and highly dangerous once they are translated into the language of the Old Frenchman place. The flirtatiousness is construed as an open invitation and the drunkenness as indifference to what may happen.

Time and again Temple is given the opportunity to leave; time and again Ruby warns her to be quiet, to stop running, to stop impressing her fear and desire on the men. But she persists, half-fascinated by the idea of her own rape and half-dreading the actual experience. She can never quite make up her mind to flee either at Goodwin's, the filling station, or Miss Reba's. It is not her fear of encountering greater evils or dangers but her fascination with the idea of violence that holds her immobile. For only by becoming the victim of violence can she participate in Ruby's world without losing her position in her own. Since she does not will her rape, but only passively suffers it, she is freed of responsibility for it, thus enabling her to preserve her social innocence no matter what physical or moral degradation she experiences. In Ruby's spare room, her fear almost forgotten in her excitement and anticipation, Temple goes through a self-conscious ritual of preparing for her victimization and self-sacrifice. She combs her hair, renews her makeup, glances at her watch repeatedly, and lies down to wait, "her hands crossed on her breast and her legs straight and close and decorous, like an effigy on an ancient tomb." (84)

In Temple's later account of the night she spent "in comparative inviolation," the alternation between fear and desire is obvious. Her wish to evade the coming rape is expressed by her fantasies: her vision of herself as somehow physically sealed against contact, as dead, as a matronly schoolteacher, and finally as an old man with a long white beard. But this is balanced by her repeated cries of "Touch me! You're a coward if you dont." And at the very moment of her rape, Temple's scream is one of mingled protest and exultation: " 'Something is happening to me!' " (122) At last even the naive and inexperienced Horace realizes that the self-confessed "victim" is "recounting the experience with actual pride, a sort of naive and impersonal vanity." (259)

At Miss Reba's Temple gives full scope to her inclinations while still playing the role of "victim-prisoner." The door which she carefully locks not only keeps Popeye out but herself within. Certainly when she desires to leave, neither the door nor the servant-wardress stand in her way. During her stay she becomes completely corrupted, not because she is kept in a whore house, not even because she has accepted a gangster for a bed-mate, but because her capacity for moral commitments and responsibilities has steadily and persistently declined until in the underworld it is wholly atrophied. She has absolutely no interest in Red, her lover, as a human being. At the moment of his greatest danger, her one thought is to obtain just one more second of sexual gratification; and later she does not regret or mourn his death but only that "it will never be again." In short, Temple eagerly abandons all the social values of her group without accepting the personal values which, however minimal, lend significance to the lives of Ruby and Goodwin.

Temple's excursion into the underworld is paralleled by Ruby's forced sojourn in Jefferson. With her practical common sense or suspiciousness, Ruby not only accepts but jealously guards the isolation of her world, " 'asking nothing of anyone except to be let alone, trying to make something out of her life.' " (139) Hence, she furiously resents Temple, the intruder who threatens her security. But she is also aware that she herself is the intruder in Jefferson and calmly accepts its intolerance and cruelty. She moves without protest from the Benbow house to the Hotel to the lean-to shed room in ironic repetition of Temple's flight from room to room at Goodwin's. But even in the shack Ruby is not safe from Narcissa who feels that her world has been threatened by her brother's interest in a woman who is not his kind. Though Narcissa consistently reveals a complete indifference to the moral qualities of any act including her own, she is intensely concerned with the interpretation that may be placed on these acts by people she knows. As she carefully explains to Horace, " 'I dont care where else you go nor what you do. I dont care how many women you have nor who they are. But I cannot have my brother mixed up with a woman people are talking about.' " (220) It is with and through Narcissa that Jefferson rises to protect public morality, to speak in defense of an " 'odorous and omnipotent sanctity' " (221) in the eyes of which Ruby and Goodwin are murderers, adulterers, and polluters of " 'the free Democratico-Protestant atmosphere of Yoknapatawpha county.' " (151)

Narcissa is coolly indifferent to the methods she uses as long as they succeed in bringing her brother, who refuses to conform to Jefferson's preconceptions and prejudgments, back into the fold. She points out that while he has been babbling about truth, justice, and responsibility, he has succeeded in offending social decorum past the point of forgiveness by taking another man's wife and then abandoning her, and finally, by sheltering a "streetwalker," "a murderer's woman" in his apartment. She attempts to frighten him with public opinion, shame him by an appeal to the Benbow past and tradition, bribe him with an offer of a better criminal lawyer than he is for Goodwin's defense, and when all these fail, to disillusion him about Ruby's motives and her needs. Her final step is to deny even lip service to truth and justice: " 'I dont see that it makes any difference who did it. The question is, are you going to stay mixed up with it?' " (221) Horace, of course, refuses to be swayed; but while he is savoring his indignation and exploring the possibilities of action, Narcissa acts expediently and effectively to thwart justice with law and to return a humbled Horace to Belle.

Society, concerned with its own preservation, is thus as intolerant of the saint as of the sinner, of Horace as of Popeye. Strangely enough, there are certain startling similarities between these two morally antithetical figures. Both are primarily spectators rather than participants in life. Popeye's fear of nature, his terror when he senses the swooping owl, is matched by Horace's inability to remember the name of the bird whose call he hears and by his desire to escape from the rich fertility of the land. Moreover, Popeye's rapt and unnatural absorption in watching Temple and Red perform an act in which he can never share is echoed by Horace's painful exclusion from the grape arbor where Little Belle casually experiments with sex. Both are conscious of their isolation and attempt to break out of it, the one through violence, the other through fantasy and hallucination which are themselves a form of violence. Popeye's brutal act fuses with Horace's thoughts and culminates in the nightmare vision of the rape of a composite Temple-Little Belle.

The separation from the world of nature also implies a separation from the nature of man, characterized by a capacity for good and evil. Both Horace and Popeye are therefore incomplete human beings—figures symbolic of good and evil, unintegrated into the human world. Significantly, Popeye is seen only through his actions, violent, reflexive, destructive; in contrast, Horace is all thought, sensitivity, and perception but without the ability to act effectively. The difference between them, and it is, of course, an overwhelming one, is that the latter is isolated by his dream of moral perfection, the former by his total indifference to all moral values. Consequently, they represent two possible aberrations from the social norm represented by Jefferson as well as the two possible alternatives between which society itself must choose. For only by sharing Horace's dream while recognizing it as a dream can society re-examine its conduct and make it once more a living expression of man's aspirations.

Unlike Horace who discovers the force of human relationships even as he is rejected and threatened with lynching by society, Popeye continues to live in complete and utter isolation. The hereditary syphilis and insanity stress his inability to make any kind of meaningful contact, either physical or social, with other people. From his birth he is alone and his survival depends on accentuating that aloneness. The doctor warns that " 'he will never be a man, properly speaking. With care, he will live some time longer.' " (369) Only by eschewing life can Popeye prolong his existence, and only by affirming the reality of death can he, by implication, affirm that existence. His killing the various animals is more than precocious sadism: it is his attempt to gain a fleeting and illusory sense of life through the very act of destroying it. Oddly enough, the same motive is present in his attachment to his half-crazed mother. Since he is rejected by all the groups with which he comes in contact, she is his only link with the human world, the source and therefore the living proof of his own existence.

Into this sterile, circumscribed world of Popeye's, Temple introduces lust, herself desiring that violation of which she suspects Goodwin to be capable and which she later admires so greatly in Red. But all that Popeye can offer is the mechanical violence of a corncob—a horrifying but futile protest against both his impotence and his isolation. His vicarious participation in sex terminated by Temple's revolt, his murder of Red proven an empty gesture, he chooses death out of sheer boredom and the realization that, quite literally, he has never lived. Once having chosen death, he finds it unimportant whether it comes as punishment for killing Tommy, Red, and indirectly Goodwin, or for slaying a policeman in a town he has never visited. It is, after all, the last joke that life will ever play on him and he makes no effort to counter this final gambit.

In contrast to Popeye, Horace wills his own isolation. His desire to escape from Kinston is caused initially by his disillusionment in those relationships which give meaning to a man's life. Experience mocks the poetic ideal as marriage settles into the routine of fetching shrimp from the station and locking doors, and love becomes identified with the grape arbor frequented by a multitude of young men. Narcissa, the "still unravished bride of quietness" proves to be a stupid, self-centered, and shallow woman. And even the fragile beauty of the fairy Titania is tarnished by too much handling so that he sees in Little Belle's portrait "a face suddenly older in sin than he would ever be, a face more blurred than sweet, . . . eyes more secret than soft." (200) The world of beauty, symbolized by the glass-blowers' cave in *Sartoris*, has been completely destroyed.

But though the beauty he worshipped is denied by experience, Horace yet has faith in goodness. As he travels from Kinston to the Old Frenchman place, Jefferson, the campus of Ole Miss, and finally Miss Reba's whore house, that ideal too is put to the test of reality. For wherever he goes, he carries with him his vision of a world peopled by gentlemen and benevolently ordered by a God who may be " 'foolish at times, but at least He's a gentleman.' " (337) As an ideal, his dream is a noble one; as a description of reality, it is hopelessly inadequate. The crudity of actual life and the intermingling of good and evil in the very texture of experience leave him bewildered and helpless. The very ideals which make him an unerring judge of his society render him incapable of fighting that society.

All of Horace's actions are thus marked by a curious bifocal vision. As he becomes actively involved in helping Goodwin and Ruby, he sees various events and relationships with increasing clarity. But this is dependent on his intuitive comprehension of certain complex situations and their moral quality. Consciously, he cannot help but see through the eyes of a forty-three year old gentleman lawyer, scholar, and poet. He consistently forces the material of his perceptions into a pattern of abstractions which reduce irrationality and complexity to a simple order. He is, in short, hampered by the same kind of innocence and naive faith in reason that plagues Sutpen. Reason and his legal training mediate between Horace's responses and his actions with the result that he finds himself conducting a mock battle with a phantom opponent: armed with Truth, Honor, and Justice, he assails Evil. The battle of abstractions continues while beneath it the intensely human drama of experience is played out to its bitter conclusion.

The source of Horace's frustration is his discovery that his concepts of justice and honor have no coercive power or even influence over either experience or people. When driven to it, Narcissa is prepared to admit that the possibility of a miscarriage of justice is far less important than her position in Jefferson. Senator Snopes and Eustace Graham are concerned only with advancing themselves in the name of justice; both are willing to attribute justice to the side which pays most. Horace cannot even convince Ruby and Goodwin, who have the most to lose, of the importance of truth. Goodwin decides simply to take his chances with the law while Ruby prepares to pay Horace for undertaking Goodwin's defense in the only way she can. The final and complete subversion of Horace's ethical system comes when he sees the Jefferson mob, acting in the name of the very justice he has defended, kill Goodwin.

It is increasingly borne in upon Horace that he will have to stand and act alone. Though for a while he is strengthened by a stubborn courage, he is, nevertheless, doomed to fail. Because he himself is unsure of his ability to take control of a situation, he still relies for support on words and phrases. He offers Goodwin the protection of " 'law, justice, civilization' " (156) against the concrete menace of Popeye's gun, and talks to Ruby about " 'a thing called obstructing justice' " (158) as a counterweight to her concern for her husband's safety. While he talks to Temple about the importance of truth and justice, Miss Reba cuts through his abstract verbiage with " 'They're going to hang him for something he never done . . . And she wont have nuttin, nobody. And you with diamonds, and her with that poor little kid.' " (256) The sharp contrast between his generalizations and Miss Reba's concrete statement of the human issues is underscored by Miss Jenny, who points out that his moral indignation and championing of the right is purely verbal and that he is spending his time making speeches instead of doing something. Horace's answer is to go off on another tirade in which he threatens to legislate evil out of existence: " 'I'm going to have a law passed making it obligatory upon everyone to shoot any man less than fifty years old that makes, buys, sells or thinks whisky.' " (199) Presumably his statement is intended ironically, but even so it reveals his habit of thought: one additional law will finally either regenerate or frighten men into living in accordance with virtue, decency, and the moral law.

Even though Horace finds that justice no longer lives in the hearts of men, he still retains his faith in the power of truth—if only all the facts are made available, then innocence and guilt, the victim and the murderer will be unmasked. Truth must prove itself independent of and stronger than individual prejudices and distortions. With Ruby's unwilling help he learns of Temple's presence at the Old Frenchman place; with Snopes's information he tracks her down. With dawning horror he realizes, however, that victim though she may be, Temple is also the cause of her victimization. The responsibility for the rape and hence for Tommy's murder is as much Temple's who provoked it as it is Goodwin's who did not act to prevent it or Popeye's who actually committed it. Gowan Stevens is also involved in the guilt, and even Ruby, who anticipated it and yet walked away, is not without blame.

Horrified as he is by his discovery that good and evil do not live in separate compartments, Horace yet risks a final throw of the dice. He presents his facts to the judge and jury and waits confidently for the only possible verdict. In the courthouse, if no other place, justice and truth must be living realities. Yet they are not—he is defeated and not by deliberate, conscious evil but by self-interest and respectability. Horace's collapse is complete and inevitably so. For through most of his conversations with Ruby and Goodwin one refrain had been dominant, that of "Good God. What kind of people have you lived with?" To find that the evil he abhors is in his own backyard, in Narcissa, in his wife and her daughter, in Temple and her respected father-judge, is too much. The enormity of fighting it becomes the impossibility of even challenging it, and Horace who anticipated total victory submits to total defeat. He returns meekly to Belle and the routine of his life with her. Murmuring " 'Night is hard on old people. . . . Something should be done about it. A law,' " (359) he appears to shrink, to lose stature as he stands alone, gazing at the fragments of the Grecian Urn in whose aesthetic and abstract image he had built his life.

The pathos of this scene arises from the fact that Horace's sanctuary, his imaginative world of moral and aesthetic perfection, has been violated and destroyed by his one excursion into the world of concrete experience. For it is only in the verbal universe, whether philosophic, legal, or poetic, that evil can be isolated as the antithesis of good. In experience evil is a necessary condition of existence which cannot be destroyed without destroying life itself. That Horace contemplates such a destruction, though only in fantasy, suggests that he is not yet ready to live in terms of his painfully acquired knowledge of the real world. Because of his search, the separation of justice and law, truth and belief, dream and reality is recognized; but the task of reuniting them, which is the necessary prerequisite to the salvation of man and his society, is beyond his powers.

*

Requiem for a Nun continues to probe those concepts of law and justice which Horace Benbow had explored tentatively. Faulkner, however, uses a very different method from the one employed in the earlier book. The group morality so central to *Sanctuary* is presented in the prose sections, while the drama is confined to three or possibly four individuals. In addition, the violence is even more rigidly controlled than in the earlier novel. Not only is the act of murder and Temple's new descent into the underworld presented as past, but Gavin Stevens constantly reminds us that this past violence is unimportant and directs our attention to the immediate moral problem. Stevens' concern is to re-establish justice as a moral and personal concept instead of merely a legal and social precept. In order to concentrate on this single, all important task, dramatic suspense is reduced to a minimum. For despite Temple's persistent self-deception, there is no question of Nancy's being saved from death; and even the struggle between Temple and Gavin, which provides an unfolding plot containing the expected climax and resolution, is conducted on the rhetorical level of words rather than the dramatic plane of actions.

Since Stevens' attempt to return justice to man is also an attempt to reverse the course of history, clearly the drama proper is intimately related to the prose interchapters. The latter recapitulate and extend the theme of *Sanctuary* by presenting history as a record of man's furious efforts to establish a collective identity, to delegate his moral responsibility, and to find security within a system of laws. The present is quite obviously the product of that history, for as Gavin Stevens remarks, "the past is never dead. It's not even past." (92) Nothing is ever finished, done, forgotten. Each decision, whether personal or communal, initiates a sequence of cause and effect which weaves a pattern of retribution independent of man's will or desire. Each man thus helps to mold the fate that finally overtakes him. But, paradoxically, man is free to act in the present and by those actions to shape history and therefore the future. This is so because despite all the accidents and permutations of history human nature is essentially changeless. And perennially it exhibits the capacity for love and hate, suffering and joy, self-sacrifice and selfishness. These are eternal and universal, these make "you know again now that there is no time: no space: no distance." (261) Because he is capable of such antithetical emotions and actions, at any given moment he can reverse the pattern of his life and so, in greater or lesser measure, of history itself. This interrelation of past, present, and future is rendered by the very structure of the book. Thus, the three prose sections recount one more moment of decision and the subsequent course of action which finally creates the dramatic situation in which Temple, Nancy, and Gavin Stevens find themselves.

In the historical process, delineated in the interchapters, the ideal of justice as man's inner moral force is blurred to such an extent that ethics are reduced to a legalistic formula. The building of the Jefferson courthouse is undertaken by a few individuals to relieve themselves of the responsibility for the loss of Uncle Sam's lock. This it proceeds to do with a thoroughness and a ruthless efficiency far beyond the hopes or fears of these founding fathers. The voice of the individual, fleetingly represented by Ratcliffe, is silenced by the mighty thunder of collectivism. Built in order to evade a law and the threat of punishment, the courthouse becomes in its turn a battleground where justice can be defeated by law, where a Goodwin can be condemned to death and a Temple offered the sympathies of the Court. " 'How can we corrupt an ethical man?' " (26) asks Peabody and the answer is the courthouse. That the corruption assumes the magnitude of a tidal wave is unforeseen but not unpredictable.

Thus, from its inception there is a moral contradiction involved in the courthouse. It is at once the symbol of man's dream of moral perfection and the cause of its destruction. Having housed their hopes and aspirations not only decently but magnificently, men freed themselves of responsibility for making their dreams a reality. The subsequent confusion of morality and legality was inevitable; appropriately, the temple of justice serves as the guardian of all the old, accumulated legal documents, which are a constant reminder of legalized injustice, of men's exploitation of the land and other men. Symbol of law and order, of progress and civilization, the courthouse dominates Jefferson, asserting that "the whole race of man, as long as it endured, [had] forever and irrevocably fifteen dollars deficit, fifteen dollars in the red." (36) The degree to which ethics is confused with law is ironically revealed by the moral deficit's being computed in terms of legal tender.

In 1903 the State Capitol was completed, bigger, brighter, higher than the Jefferson courthouse and even further removed from the life of the individual. It was not, however, a new creation but simply one of the results of that first town meeting and its decision. This second edifice now relieves the individual of his right to determine his own actions. The human duty and privilege of exercising self-government is replaced by the social duty and privilege of being governed. The result ultimately is a closed and regimented society with rules and regulations covering every aspect of behavior and with a duly constituted police force to implement these rules. The undeniable gain in security is, however, balanced by the attendant loss of human dignity and freedom. A perpetual affirmation of the belief that "profit plus regimen equals security," (104) the Golden Dome embodies the final victory of the "Idea" over concrete living individuals. Mississippi is no longer a place where people are born and live and die; it is "a state, a commonwealth; triumvirate in legislative, judiciary, executive." (105) Beyond it is "the United States," a "towering frantic edifice poised like a card-house over the abyss of the mortgaged generations," (247) the biggest, the most inclusive of the "Ideas" and hence the most dangerous.

While the courthouse and the capitol suggest the fusion and confusion of ethics with law and the surrender of individual responsibility, the jail serves at once as an extension of and a departure from this position. In a sense, punishment has become as abstract and arbitrary as the law it purports to implement. For one thing, the jail is a visible symbol of the assumption that the virtuous can be separated from the wicked and that the latter can be purged of their wickedness by a specific kind and degree of punishment. The result is complete chaos in which public morality is confused with virtue, legal immunity with innocence, and legal punishment with penitence. There is no responsibility attached to sin save as it impinges on the legal system. This arbitrary punishment, whether it be imprisonment or death, for breaking arbitrary rules takes the place of conscience, in short, of self-judgment and self-punishment.

Paradoxically, however, the jail is also the one place which isolates the individual from the masses, thereby returning him to self-awareness, stripping him of all pretense and leaving him at last face to face with his own humanity. Thus, it is in this building that the continuity of human nature through all change and vicissitude is stressed. It is on its window that a scrawl suddenly brings to life the old dead loves and fears and hopes of a time long past. The jail is the record of the town, "filled not only with its mutation and change from a halting-place: to a community: to a settlement: to a village: to a town, but with the shapes and motions, the gestures of passion and hope and travail and endurance, of the men and women and children in their successive overlapping generations." (214) The changes of history and the permanence of humanity are significantly juxtaposed. In his enforced solitude, the prisoner receives his last and perhaps his only chance to recognize his share in that humanity and to make his peace not with society but with himself and his God. He can, in short, transcend the laws which confine him and so recover his moral nature, to stand once more "erect and lift his battered and indomitable head." (247)

Each of the prose sections functions as a preface to the drama in that the courthouse, the state capitol, and the jail form both the subject matter of the three narrative histories and the setting for each of the three acts. Gavin Stevens' rhetoric serves as a modern commentary on these histories even as it goads Temple and Gowan into self-awareness and self-judgment. Relentlessly he forces Temple out of each of her sanctuaries—law, authority, scepticism—and at the same time he insists that she herself take each successive step on the long journey of redemption in which the whole process of history with its sorry betrayal of the individual is retraced even as it is reversed and transcended. While she is rediscovering her humanity, which was almost destroyed by her own acts and those of her forebears, Stevens takes up the task, begun by Horace Benbow, of making truth and justice prevail. By making Temple and Gowan arrive at their own conclusions and by forcing them to accept responsibility for their own actions, he transcends his own office and function—the lawyer is replaced by the attendant priest whose duty is simply to guide his people to self-knowledge and understanding of God. Simultaneously, the three symbolic edifices of social justice—the courthouse, the state capitol, and the jail—are also transcended.

Unlike Horace Benbow, Stevens has something much stronger than words with which to coerce Temple and that is his simple and unflinching expectation of her rising to the occasion. Nancy's life has already been forfeited to law and society, but her death must be given significance by Temple's coming to understand both Nancy and herself. The bereaved mother and the childless murderess are inextricably linked from the very beginning. Temple had originally hired Nancy because their pasts were complementary: both are ex-whores, the one with a past addiction to dope and the other to gin. Nancy has suffered a life of "being beaten by some man or cutting or being cut by his wife or his other sweetheart"; (50) Temple has provoked and suffered rape, caused and witnessed murder. Because of their common experiences, they can at least speak honestly to each other. Only in Nancy's company is Temple relieved of the oppressive necessity of pretending that nothing had ever happened and that "Mrs. Gowan Stevens" is quite distinct from "Miss Temple Drake."

Nancy accepts her past as part of her continuing personal history and so manages to live with it. Temple, on the other hand, can establish no such easy relationship with time. Instead she seeks to preserve her past while keeping it quite distinct and separate from the present. Through her conversations with Nancy she relives her experiences and savors their explosive violence; through her position as Mrs. Gowan Stevens she denies that such experiences ever existed. This uneasy balance is disturbed by Pete, who, like Red or Goodwin, possesses a vitality which mocks the secure artificiality of her kind. Once more she turns to sex, crude, violent, even dangerous, but capable of making an impression. Pete is, in comparison with Gowan, "a man so single, so hard and ruthless, so impeccable in amorality, as to have a kind of integrity." (171) And this time she makes no effort to ensure her own safe return to society; instead she prepares herself for a final and deliberate break with her family and her group.

With intuitive understanding and sympathy, Nancy is aware of the social, moral, and human implications of Temple's choice between Gowan and Pete. Her act of murdering the child is certainly not an effort to reclaim Temple to respectability by making it impossible for her to leave her husband, for she realizes the sterility of such social respectability as well as does Temple. Nor is her decisive and violent action meant simply to shock her into a sense of guilt. Rather it is Nancy's attempt to make Temple see that the solution does not lie in escape, that her only hope is to accept and endure and by so doing find not happiness but peace. Having tried argument and threat to no avail, she, in desperation, sacrifices her own and the life of the child in the belief that pain and suffering may at last prove strong enough to break through Temple's egotism.

There is, however, another and more important motive which Nancy only half grasps but which Temple herself articulates: "Oh yes, I know that answer too; that was brought out here to-night too: that a little child shall not suffer in order to come unto Me. So good can come out of evil." (208) Somewhere a stop must be made in the continual process, initiated by the building of the courthouse, of mortgaging future generations.

Somewhere each must take a stand when confronted by good and evil since the consequences of one's deeds are never confined to one's own life. Since every act has future implications which man can neither foresee nor prevent, all he can do is attempt to make restitution, to render payment, in his own person without involving the innocence of children in the inevitable pattern of retribution: "He dont tell you not to sin, he just asks you not to. And He dont tell you to suffer. But He gives you the chance." (278) Expiation and suffering also can be written into the record of history, thereby changing, no matter how slightly, the shape of things to come.

This knowledge which Temple has to struggle to attain, Nancy possesses intuitively. She accepts full responsibility for her violent act without attempting to minimize or justify it. Rightly or wrongly, she has done what she felt was necessary and she is ready to pay for it both to the sovereign State of Mississippi and to God. However horrifying her action, she has stopped Temple from starting yet another pattern of evil to be paid for not only by herself but by her children and perhaps even her children's children. With her clear admission of "guilty, Lord" Nancy is not only "disrupting and confounding and dispersing and flinging back two thousand years, the whole edifice of corpus juris and rules of evidence we have been working to make stand up by itself ever since Caesar," (200) she is reaffirming her own moral nature, her own responsibility not only to the law but to herself and to God.

The courtroom scene with which *Sanctuary* concluded is echoed briefly at the beginning of *Requiem for a Nun*. Once more Temple is legally absolved of any guilt and once more she prepares to escape by travel. It is at this juncture that Gavin Stevens becomes the moral gadfly forcing Temple to examine her past and her conscience honestly. Since Temple balks at every turn, rushes into every shelter provided by her self-delusions, it is a long and painful process. With mounting desperation, she utilizes every possible trick to ward off Stevens and her own conscience which is not quite so dormant as she pretends. In *Sanctuary* Temple had assumed the role of "victim," and now she again tries to evade responsibility by playing the bereaved mother. The sacred words "mother" and "bereaved" should produce the same automatic response as "womanhood" and "rape" did in the earlier book. Stevens, however, is not to be put off by this barefaced plea for sympathy; he offers her a handkerchief, commenting "It's all right. It's dry too." (56) Perhaps because he himself is a man of words, Gavin seems fully aware of their subtle power to distort reality and to command man's actions. He refuses to treat her as a "victim" with its further meaning of "wronged innocent." Driven out of this first retreat, Temple assumes indifference. This callousness is, however, as much a pretense as her plea of bereavement: both are attempts at verbal evasion.

Temple's return to Jefferson is an admission that she herself is definitely involved in Nancy's act, an admission which she transforms into another defense: "So Nancy must be saved. So you send for me, or you and Bucky between you, or anyway here you are and here I am." (79) If it is simply a matter of saving Nancy's life, she can continue protecting herself; both can be accomplished in a variety of ways. She offers to write a note from Mrs. Gowan Stevens, the bereaved mother, seeking clemency for her former servant. As Stevens rejects this proposal, she tries frantically to keep the issue within the legal framework, insisting that a cerificate of insanity will accomplish more than a revelation of her own past. This too is exposed and rejected by Stevens; Temple cannot use her social position or his knowledge of the law to save Nancy because saving Nancy is not the point. Nancy's crime has been judged and her punishment determined—that part at least has been irrevocably settled: "We're not concerned with death. That's nothing: any handful of petty facts and sworn documents can cope with that. That's all finished now; we can forget it." (88)

Even when Temple is forced to admit that it is her own salvation she must be concerned with, she still clings to the pretense that the Governor might be persuaded to pardon Nancy, that that is her reason for finally admitting her share in the guilt and the responsibility for the death of her child. Sincerely desiring at last to tell and face the truth, she discovers that she has practically forgotten how. She postures, pretends, exaggerates, becoming bitter and flippant by turns. Cynically she questions the value of what she is forcing herself to do, describing it as "just anguish for the sake of anguish." (133) Her last feeble but tenacious defense is to describe Temple Drake from the point of view of Mrs. Gowan Stevens, hoping that such detachment will preserve her from further moral anatomy. She deliberately blackens the character of the Temple of eight years ago, eliminating whatever decency, dignity, and capacity to love and suffer had been present. It is for this reason that Stevens interrupts her with "Wait. Let me play too." (126)

As she finishes her story, Temple's eyes are still tearless; she still keeps an ironic distance between herself and her story, still maintains the pretense that she is concerned solely with saving Nancy. It is only when Gowan takes the Governor's place that Temple's play-acting collapses. Thus, Gowan's eavesdropping, plant though it may be, is a necessary method of forcing her to take the final step to self-knowledge. His presence destroys the carefully guarded objectivity with which Temple has related her past, it also fuses irrevocably the past and the present, Temple Drake and Mrs. Gowan Stevens. Simultaneously, Gowan is himself made aware of his share of guilt and the pattern it wove over eight years. This confession, then, serves to force both to admit the other's suffering, guilt, and responsibility at the same moment that they admit their own. Some form of communication, perhaps even of understanding, has arisen between them.

The Governor's symbolic abdication of the seat of judgment has, of course, other implications. Even more than Nancy's calm "Guilty, Lord" it hurls back the years of blind confusion of justice and law, the years of irresponsible dependence on abstract authority. In one moment, it shatters the three symbolic edifices of the prose chapters and the whole intricate system of delegating responsibility that they represented. All the Governor can do is determine legal guilt to which neither Temple nor Gowan are subject. He can prescribe no punishment and no absolution for them because they have not sinned against the State or its law but against each other, against their children, and their own humanity. Whether they recognize this and prepare to pay for those sins is something they must decide for themselves. In any case, the chance to do so is always present.

Although Temple has been forced to confront as well as to tell the truth, her submission is a grudging one, for she is still confused and bewildered by intellectual doubts and scepticism. Her redemption is far from certain and Nancy, who seems to hold the key, can only use it to effect her own entry into knowledge and quietude. She cannot erase Temple's uncertainty nor answer her questions except by her own calm conviction. When Temple contemplates the future with its successive tomorrows, she doubts her own understanding of how to achieve her goal. The desire for some token, some visible sign represents the last fragment of Temple's resistance to accepting full and complete responsibility for her life. She refuses to see that the only guide man needs is the truth of his own heart and the divinity of his own soul. For that, he does not need intellectual conviction, only faith. If heaven and even God are simply figments of man's imagination, he must still act as if both are indisputable since man's ethical responsibility is a necessity and not a contingency.

It is this necessity which accounts at once for the relentlessness of the argument and for the rigid formality of the structure in *Requiem for a Nun.* To point out the flaws in the dramatic sections is perhaps inevitable, but it also impedes our realizing that we are dealing not with a drama, in the accepted sense of the word, but with a Socratic dialogue possessing stage directions. If man has become so blinded by language and reason that even violence is powerless to strip him of all pretense and to force him into self-knowledge, then a new method of attack must be used. The rhetoric of evasion must be countered by the rhetoric of persuasion. Language can be manoeuvered into exposing its own limitations. Thus, Gavin Stevens, the "Sage of Yoknapatawpha," becomes a Socratic midwife presiding over the moral dialectic which focusses on Temple Drake. Like Plato's greater creation, his one saving grace in a thankless job is his awareness that he must humble himself to learn as well as to teach, to be led as well as to lead. It is in this spirit that he seeks to arrive at some definition of Truth, Justice, and Goodness. When their usual identification with Society, Law, and Authority has been elaborately analyzed, disproven, and discarded, he and the rational intellect have fulfilled their function of preparing the individual for the ultimate turning round and facing of "the brightest blaze of being." Stevens is silent as the inarticulate, uneducated Nancy says simply "Believe." Nancy is herself the visible sign which Temple had sought, the concrete illustration of what is meant by "Believe." With this the stage is set for the individual to exercise his function—to recognize the sign, to engage in the moral dialectic and to make a living reality out of what has been too long merely a word.

8 : INITIATION AND IDENTITY

Go Down, Moses
and Intruder in the Dust

Go Down, Moses and *Intruder in the Dust* are complementary studies of that state of mind, first explored in *Light in August,* which is engendered in white and colored people alike by the myth of the Negro. The one examines this state of mind through a temporal, the other through a spatial sequence. *Go Down, Moses* covers not only some six generations of the complicated McCaslin family, both white and black, but also Isaac McCaslin's midnight conversation with Cass Edmonds which places the family in the historical perspective of a world caught up in time as well as in the religious perspective of man's fall and expulsion from Paradise. Throughout, the Negroes act as catalysts for the white man's history and in so doing they point up its moral significance. In *Intruder in the Dust,* on the other hand, the action is restricted to a few short days during which Chick Mallison is continually moving, without pause for sleep or even food. Through his travels he discovers the social geography of his land, a discovery which Gavin Stevens uses as the basis for his own particular brand of geopolitics. In the process, the attitudes of various groups toward Lucas Beauchamp, the Negro, are carefully probed and evaluated.

All the stories in *Go Down, Moses* have certain unifying features which give the book the character of a loosely constructed novel. Structurally, the framework of each individual story is a ritual hunt. Isaac's pursuit of the magnificent buck and then of Old Ben is simply the clearest and finest example of this hunt motif, but the breathless chase of Tomey's Turl, the lynching of

Rider, the determined search for gold by Lucas, and Gavin Stevens' aborted search for Samuel Beauchamp are all variations of the same theme. In each case, the hunt illuminates some facet of the relationship between whites and Negroes, whether personal or social. At the same time a number of suggested parallels indicate that the significance of the ritual of the hunt is determined by the nature of the hunted as well as of the hunters. Only the best hunters and dogs are worthy of Old Ben. The difference between this and Boon's obsessive concern with a tree full of squirrels or Roth Edmonds' irresponsible slaughter of does needs no elaboration. Equally clear is the distinction between the spirited pursuit of Tomey's Turl, the love-stricken Negro, and the grim, relentless tracking down of Rider, the human quarry marked for a violent death, or the impersonal execution of Samuel Beauchamp, "the slain wolf."

In addition to this recurrent hunt motif, the stories are further related through their connection with the plantation. For even when the characters travel, their excursions either carry the sense of plantation life with them or else produce certain repercussions within it. With the sense of place, the self-contained McCaslin-Edmonds-Beauchamp world, so firmly established, Faulkner is able to range freely in time. The stories do, however, fall into a roughly chronological sequence beginning with the second generation of McCaslins in "Was" and ending with the fifth generation of Beauchamps in "Go Down, Moses." Accordingly, they chart the shifts and changes in the life of a culture. As the wilderness steadily retreats before the slow pressure of roads and neatly fenced farms, the plantation world also begins to crumble. The autocratic control of Carothers McCaslin gives way to the firmness of Cass Edmonds and finally to the harried fussing of Roth, while the Negroes who were once locked in the big unfinished house for the night scatter to Arkansas and Chicago and Indianapolis.

Most of the episodes in the book thus have a twofold function. Primarily they contribute to the total picture of the changing history of the South, but more important, they are the means by which various characters are initiated into the life of the plantation world and their own role in it. That world is the creation of Carothers McCaslin, the pioneer settler in a virgin land who, out of the land grants, transfers, patents, and deeds which he collected, instituted a way of life that was ultimately to prove a cage for his descendants. In a sense, he usurped God's authority by presuming to replace His order with a code of his own, arbitrarily ordained and demanding unquestioning obedience. Thus, he "knowing better, could raise his children, his descendants and heirs, to believe the land was his to hold and bequeath since the strong and ruthless man has a cynical foreknowledge of his own vanity and pride and strength and a contempt for all his get." (254–55) His free choice becomes their necessity, his actions become their pattern. And the essence of that pattern is found by Isaac McCaslin in the horrifying vision of the white man ordering his Negro daughter into his bed.

In the first story, "Was," Uncle Buck and Uncle Buddy, representing the second generation of McCaslins, stand midway between old Carothers and young Isaac. They free whichever of the slaves will accept freedom, but they still make the gestures expected of a McCaslin by Jefferson and perhaps by the very Negroes themselves. The ritual obtaining between master and slave persists even though slavery itself is repudiated. As observed by the McCaslin twins, the ritual becomes literally a game. Solemnly they count the two dozen black men, herd them into the unfinished house, and drive a home-made nail into the front door. The gesture is made and "neither of the white men would go around behind the house and look at the back door, provided that all the negroes were behind the front one when the brother who drove it drew out the nail again at daybreak." (263) Tomey's Turl continually escapes and is pursued in a wild game of hide-and-seek, complete with hunting horns and baying dogs. His pursuit and recovery forms a highly amusing parody of Liza's flight over the ice floes in *Uncle Tom's Cabin*.

Although the point of the ritual is lost, the pursuit of Tomey's Turl is conducted with all the ceremony, all the determination, and earnestness of Major De Spain's company stalking their quarry. The hunters and the hunted know the rules and abide by them. There is, of course, a vast difference in tone: the hunt in the wilderness alone has overtones of religious solemnity and self-dedication in keeping with its culmination which is the sacrificial spilling of blood. Death for any of the participants in the hunt for Tomey's Turl is not even a remote possibility and the only approximation to sacrificial blood is Uncle Buck's unfortunate accident with his pocket flask of whisky. Yet even this hunt, this playful and antiquated bit of folklore, is an initiation. The only reason for having the story told from the point of view of the child, Cass Edmonds, is that he is being initiated into the plantation world with its various duties, responsibilities, and adventures. Whatever he learns will be reflected when he, in his turn, becomes the social mentor for the young Isaac and the guardian of the McCaslin tradition, now somewhat reduced and modified by what Uncle Buck and Uncle Buddy have made of it.

"The Fire and the Hearth" takes us two generations further in time as Lucas Beauchamp and his son Henry are pitted against Zack Edmonds and his son Roth. The two men, Lucas and Zack, facing each other in the white man's bedroom, and the two boys, Henry and Roth, for the first time not sharing a bed, test that identification between race and manhood which is both the fate and nemesis of every Southerner, black or white. While carrying out the dominant theme of initiation, both these episodes are casually introduced into a story of Lucas' dogged search for gold. This search, like the hunt for Tomey's Turl, has its own humorously ritualistic features. The mechanical box, serving as both compass and chalice, is carried reverently by Lucas "as if it were some object symbolical and sanctified for a ceremony, a ritual" (87) while the other Negroes watch and wait for the box to perform its miracle. Aunt Molly, however, fears that this particular ritual may destroy not only Lucas but the young George Freeman, for to take what is consigned to God's earth is an impious act capable of provoking God's curse. Lucas' absorption in his search coupled with Aunt Molly's warning illuminates one of the main themes of Go Down, Moses. Rituals have no value in themselves; they provoke praise or censure to the degree in which they affirm or deny the sacred order upon which all moral behavior is dependent for its efficacy. Money and success have their own profane myths and rituals, and by engaging in these, Lucas almost destroys his relationship with Molly just as, in The Hamlet, Bookwright, Armstid, and Ratliff almost destroy themselves.

Lucas is able to save himself from the fate of Armstid because his approach to the legend of buried gold is exploratory, not compulsive. Even during the frenzied nights of digging, he yet retains some measure of critical detachment, enough in any event to turn the tables on the salesman at the crucial moment. This same detachment serves to preserve his integrity when he is forced into certain ritual patterns of social behavior. Thus, when it is necessary or convenient, he can assume, without compromising his essential nature, the mask of the anonymous "nigger," "not secret so much as impenetrable, not servile and not effacing, but enveloping himself in an aura of timeless and stupid impassivity almost like a smell." (60) Yet he can also assert his white McCaslin blood and half reveal his contemptuous conviction that the sheriff is only "a redneck without any reason for pride in his forbears nor hope for it in his descendants." (43) It is because he is able to fuse the white and black blood with their divergent myths and rituals that he becomes self-progenitive, as old Carothers was, and establishes rules instead of blindly following those already formed. As a black Carothers McCaslin, Lucas creates his own world, his own modes of action and belief. The result is a mirror image which reflects the plantation world grounded in patriarchy and possessions. Lucas is the man in his house, the head of his family, the lawgiver to his wife and children. In this there is not simply a Negro's imitation of white ways but a calm and measured assertion that the moral and social principles of the South are equally applicable to both Negroes and whites.

By casually assuming intimacy with Molly, Zack· Edmonds challenges Lucas' right to make this assertion. That identification of a man's honor with his wife's chastity which Zack would be the first to support within his own circle has no place in the relationship between Negroes and whites. The fire on the hearth, symbol of the sanctity of the home, is to be held sacred only by other Negroes. Thus Carothers McCaslin's casual seduction of his Negro daughter, Tomey, is repeated into the third generation, though with certain significant differences. Zack's affair with Molly is not incestuous though it does cut across family connections, and in addition it no longer remains unchallenged. Lucas insists, even at the risk of his own and Zack's life, that Zack recognize the extension of the white code into Lucas' world. "Thou shalt not covet thy neighbor's wife" must make Molly interdict for Zack, the white man, as well as for Negroes. Facing a man who is no longer a white man and his master but his rival, Lucas asserts his manhood and through it his equality with any man.

For both men, this violent confrontation with its test of strength and courage provides an initiation into a bitter kind of knowledge. While Zack is forced to recognize the hollowness of those conventions which separate him socially from Lucas, Lucas in his turn is forced to recognize their power. The child, Roth, senses that something has happened to make the relationship between Zack and Lucas other than that obtaining between a white man and a Negro and that Zack has somehow lost both authority and prestige. Lucas, on the other hand, finds that his is a limited victory and dependent on his never questioning what it is he has won. The contest between Zack and Lucas, the two individuals, has been settled and within the personal world of human relationships, Lucas has achieved a lasting triumph. Yet insofar as both men are inextricably involved in society and tradition, the problem of racial double standards remains unsolved. Within that larger world of a society inhabited by the two races, Lucas is still faced with the issue which he himself has raised. The most that can be expected in such a situation is a stalemate and that is exactly what Zack and Lucas achieve.

Nevertheless, in that fleeting moment when the two men grapple for the gun, the shibboleths of caste and color are forgotten. Roth's affirmation of these same shibboleths ironically reverses that movement. He, unthinkingly, follows the old established mode of initiation into manhood and society only to discover too late that they are not identical. As children, he and Henry enjoy together the perfect freedom and innocence in which the raw material of experience is explored but not forced into any ethical or social code. Both accept, as did their parents in their childhood, the interchangeability of homes, beds, kitchens, and even parents. However, when Roth relegates Henry to the pallet, himself claiming solitary possession of the bed, he exchanges spontaneity for calculation and affections for principles. For the first time, his movements are planned in advance. There is deliberation in the way he paces his walking so that the Negro boy never quite catches up with him and in the way he times his undressing to allow Henry to lie down on the pallet so he can take solitary possession of the bed.

Roth's gesture of repudiation signifies his acceptance of "the old curse of his fathers, the old haughty ancestral pride based not on any value but on an accident of geography, stemmed not from courage and honor but from wrong and shame, descended to him." (111) At the same time, it implies his irrevocable loss of innocence, which must be followed by expulsion from Eden. Once he has taken this step, there can be no retreat. Roth wants to pretend that everything has remained unchanged, but this pretense failing, he is prepared to express his grief and shame over the course events have taken. In this mood he comes to Lucas' cabin, but there he is no longer permitted to share in that ceremonial meal which establishes kinship among its partakers. The old familial kitchen is vacated and the table is set for one. For Roth, the platter of fried chicken, eaten alone, becomes the "bitter fruit" of his shame and his repentance. By leaving the room, Lucas and Henry repeat his own ritual of exclusion so that once more Negro behavior becomes an obverse and mocking reflection of the white man's.

"Delta Autumn" presents the formal gesture of repudiation in yet another context. Roth disowns the woman who loves him and bears his child not for lack of love on his part but because it is a gesture expected of him even by old Isaac McCaslin and sanctioned by all the unwritten laws of Southern tradition. Example and precedent have been established by old Carothers McCaslin himself. Significantly, the girl is the grand-daughter of James Beauchamp and therefore a direct descendant of Tomey as well as her most recent avatar. Roth's own uneasiness at his betrayal of the girl, which repeats his earlier rejection of Molly, his Negro nurse, is revealed not only by his conscience-payment to her but also by his cynical evaluation of all human nature including his own. His killing the doe relieves his own tension even as it underlines his contempt for himself. From Molly, Roth had learned honor, courtesy, and magnanimity. With the quadroon, he had shared that moment of love which Isaac calls divinity. He fails both women for the sake of his ideological heritage. Since the tradition he rationally accepts and affirms is the object of his emotional revulsion, he is continually torn between conscience and principle and between emotion and reason. Such a conflict presents a significant and hopeful change from old Carothers McCaslin's self-possession and callous indifference to the moral qualities of his action.

Roth's initiation into society and its modes of thinking, presented in "The Fire and the Hearth," is counterpoised against Isaac's initiation into the wilderness of nature and its modes of action as set forth in "The Old People" and "The Bear." Of central importance here is the significance of Isaac's renunciation. On one side of him is Cass Edmonds representing the plantation world and its tradition. On the other is Sam Fathers, scion of a "vanished and forgotten people," (182) who is linked to the plantation only through that drop of blood which had been the blood of slaves. For Isaac, it is scarcely a matter of choosing between the two traditions as represented by Sam and Cass. His long midnight conversation with Cass in the commissary represents his effort to explain a decision already made inevitable by and encompassed in the ritual of the hunt. Significantly enough, his explanation consists of juxtaposing the McCaslin ledger, symbol of the history of the South, against the Bible and its expression of the eternal verities of the heart.

Isaac's interpretation of history is biblical and, more specifically, Miltonic in its poetic emphasis on the hierarchy and the contractual agreement between man and God: " 'He made the earth first and peopled it with dumb creatures, and then He created man to be His overseer on the earth and to hold suzerainty over the earth and the animals on it in His name.' " (257) Man's happiness consists in recognizing the greatness and the limitations of his position in the divine order. By forgetting, even momentarily, that he is at once the ruler and the ruled, man destroys that order and with it his proper relationship to God and to nature. Nor does it matter whether he sinks below or attempts to rise above his divinely ordained position. Since animal and demi-god are both foreign to his nature, both constitute a threat to his distinctive humanity. It is only by recognizing and accepting his place in the hierarchy that man fully realizes his moral nature.

The fact that men will destroy the hierarchy and deny God is foreknown thought not foredoomed: " 'I will give him his chance. I will give him warning and foreknowledge too, along with the desire to follow and the power to slay.' " (349) Since man is created sufficient to stand, though free to fall, the responsibility for the destruction of the moral order and the consequent corruption of his own nature must be his alone. His sin is pride and the lust for power, the one perverting his relationship to God, the other to nature and other men. In either case, the overseer becomes the tyrant, seeing himself as the measure of all things and replacing God's laws with his own. His punishment is increasing blindness to his own corruption until the game he hunts and kills becomes human.

The original sin, repeated by each successive generation, spreads through time and place. Even the new world with its promise of a new beginning serves only to confirm the old error. Out of it, however, there slowly emerges the reverse pattern of redemption. The actual enslavement of man by man marks the final horrifying destruction of the moral order. But ironically, his bondage prevents the Negro from learning how to forget God. Barred from possessing land or exercising authority over other men, he is forced into " 'the communal anonymity of brotherhood' " where he pays God's fee of " 'pity and humility and sufferance and endurance and the sweat of his face for bread.' " (257) In his chains lies the assurance of his salvation. And he is not alone. In the midst of the fallen world there is still the individual who can resist the way of the world and say " '*I am just against the weak because they are niggers being held in bondage by the strong just because they are white.*' " (285) This gesture of protest prepares the way for Isaac's repudiation of his patrimony and the more active engagement of Chick Mallison. That such gestures are made indicates God's continued presence in the fallen world and gives earnest of His final forgiveness. Each is a preparation for and an anticipation of the triumph of Christ as a man. Thus, what begins as an explanation of Isaac's decision to relinquish the land becomes an impassioned poetic effort "to justify God's ways to man."

Isaac's repudiation of the wrong and the shame, symbolized for him by Eunice's suicide, is made possible by the fact that Sam Fathers has provided him with the wilderness and the code of the hunter as an alternative to the plantation world. In the forest Isaac can be one of a group of men "not white nor black nor red but men, hunters, with the will and hardihood to endure and the humility and skill to survive." (191) From this vantage point Isaac can examine the history of his people and although he cannot change it, he can at least refuse to condone it and to contribute to it. The gesture of protest too can become part of recorded time. His rejection of the McCaslin tradition and his subsequent life together constitute a transcendence of public morality. But the significance of that rejection depends on whether it is juxtaposed against the wilderness or the tamed land. Isaac's moral and spiritual stature is not only derived from but, in a sense, dependent on the existence of the wilderness and the ritual of the hunt. He becomes literally one of the "Old People" who have vanished and been forgotten by invoking the past until "those old times would cease to be old times and would become a part of the boy's present, not only as if they had happened yesterday but as if they were still happening." (171) What is an annual vacation for Major De Spain and his friends becomes Isaac's life.

This pastoral form of existence in which the hunter and the hunted share immortality and eternal youth constitutes Isaac's dream of escape from the McCaslin world. Because it is an escape and a desire to find personal salvation, his gesture of relinquishment is only superficially an atonement for the sin of his forefathers. He shows his own awareness of this when he calls himself " 'an Isaac born into a later life than Abraham's and repudiating immolation: fatherless and therefore safe declining the altar because maybe this time the exasperated Hand might not supply the kid.' " (283) Accordingly, Isaac's withdrawal is in reality an attempt to evade both the guilt of his forefathers and his own responsibilities. Thus, while his daily life is a humble imitation of Christ's, it also denies the spirit of Christ who did not hesitate to share in the life of men, to accept guilt, and to suffer immolation. In rejecting sin, Isaac also rejects humanity. Significantly, he holds himself aloof from close human ties; though he is uncle to half the county, he is father to no-one and husband solely to the wilderness. Having confused the wilderness with the Garden of Eden, he not only dedicates but sacrifices his life to it. Man must leave the Garden in order to discover his humanity and whatever the reason, Isaac does not do so; his knowledge stops just short of the paradox of the fortunate fall.

When he is outside the wilderness, Isaac is virtuous but ineffective. His is essentially "a fugitive and cloistered virtue, unexercised and unbreathed." The measure of this lies in the fact that nothing happens to him between his twenty-first and seventieth year. We know that he married and that his wife failed to draw him back into history, failed even to give him a son who might have provided the crucial test of his withdrawal from life. And we know that he retreated into his dream while excluding his wife from it. The magnificent ritual of the hunt holds a promise which is never fulfilled by Isaac's life. The significance of any ritual must lie in its power to create order and to establish a sense of continuity with the past for the individual. Isaac, however, confuses the ritual with the life it orders. The qualities he learned under the tutelage of Sam Fathers, the fyce, and Old Ben should have been asserted within the context of civilization, whereas he forever applies them solely to the hunt itself, until he finally presides over a group of city vacationers who find sport in slaying a doe. Thus, as the wilderness retreats and shrinks in size, Isaac seems to lose stature even as his gesture of dissent loses significance.

"Delta Autumn" with its poignant account of an Isaac grown too old to participate in the hunt throws the final perspective on his life. There is scarcely any change in his talk; much of what he says to Roth Edmonds might have been said to Cass fifty years earlier. But when he meets Roth's castoff mistress, he does not have the courage to repudiate the McCaslin code in Roth's name. What he could not forgive in Carothers McCaslin, he accepts without hesitation in Roth Edmonds. Even in nature and the wilderness man can be corrupted, if only by age and its instinctive conservatism. He denies what he himself called the divinity of love because the man is white and the woman colored. Wistfully he suggests that in a thousand or two thousand years, time will perhaps sanction the divinity of love in such cases. He is not wilfully blind to the real and immediate suffering of the girl, but he seems to have lost courage and to have forgotten his own youthful insistence that the time for protest is the present. Nor can Isaac even maintain his moral vantage point on the verbal level. When he urges her to marry a man of her own race for the sake of revenge, he himself is unimpressed by the justice of his argument. Isaac's whole life has exalted the *choice* of perfection rather than the *creation* of it out of those intractable and intransigent materials which confront man on every hand from the moment of birth. Shorn of the splendor of youth and the wilderness and seen from the perspective of the "tamed land" he has renounced, Isaac is a figure of pathos who knows there is no answer to the girl's bitter question: " 'Old man . . . have you lived so long and forgotten so much that you dont remember anything you ever knew or felt or even heard about love?' " (363) It is only in his own chosen setting, role, and time that Isaac McCaslin can be considered a hero. Going into the wilderness as a young man was part of the hero's quest; remaining there as an aged hermit betrays a myopic view of that pattern which the "chosen man" must realize in his life.

*

Intruder in the Dust is next in the sequence of Faulkner's novels though separated from *Go Down, Moses* by seven years. It affords a further perspective on the problem raised by an individual's repudiation of or dissociation from his tradition. Chick Mallison, like Isaac in "The Bear," is a sensitive young adolescent faced with the necessity of reconciling the traditions of his people with his own impulses and of establishing his own identity in relation to certain social categories. At the outset, despite the sincerity of his friendship for Aleck Sander, Chick accepts, without question, the complex of social categories which govern and define it.

It is Lucas Beauchamp who reveals to him the implications of that acceptance. His first reaction is guilt, followed by resentment and frustration. That Chick finally outgrows these reactions is due to the continued, though unknowing, influence of Lucas who educates him into virtue and human relationships. In this respect, Lucas parallels Sam Fathers. Fulfilling a role analogous to that of Cass Edmonds for Isaac, Gavin Stevens concerns himself with fostering Chick's intellectual comprehension of public morality and social relationships. Chick's venture into Beat Four to open a Gowrie grave, despite his knowledge that even his uncle would not understand or approve, constitutes his excursion into the wilderness. On his return, he, like Isaac, is ready to repudiate society and to isolate himself from it. Because of Stevens' efforts, he does not do so; he returns into history and time, a step that Isaac never took. In so doing he fuses the divergent initiatory traditions of Isaac and Roth and establishes once more the identification of the individual's interests with those of his community even as he affirms the responsibility of the individual not only for his own conduct but for the conduct of all men.

The novel as a whole encompasses two themes for both of which Lucas provides a focus. As in *Light in August,* the public world of Jefferson and its modes of thought and action are explored in relation to the individual who is out of step with the community. As the book progresses, the two lines of thinking diverge until there seems to be no possibility of reconciling Chick Mallison with Jefferson. From the moment Lucas is caught standing near the dead body with a gun in his possession, more and more individuals are gradually absorbed into the mob which prepares to enact the ceremony of a lynching which simultaneously confirms and perpetuates the myth of color. Chick Mallison, on the other hand, leaves Jefferson and the mob, both literally and symbolically. He defies the already clarified and accepted racial and social judgment of Lucas together with the pattern of action it releases and strikes out on his own. It is the reconciliation of Chick's search for and discovery of truth with Jefferson's unmoved faith in its own dogmas that marks Chick's attainment of personal and social maturity.

Lucas Beauchamp provokes both patterns of conduct since he is at once the "nigger" who is to be lynched by the mob and the man who must be saved by Chick and his two companions. Effectively isolated by his imprisonment and prevented from acting, Lucas yet gains a tremendous vitality simply by being the object of other people's concern. He is able to function as a significant focus for the novel in part because of that inactivity but to a greater degree because of his opaqueness. There is no way of penetrating the mere eccentricities of his clothes and behavior—the worn, handmade beaver hat, the gold watchchain and toothpick, and the upright carriage of head and body. The imposing façade does not permit anyone to probe, define, and label the man behind it. This becomes a cause of frustration for everyone who encounters Lucas; all find that the intractable old man will not be fitted into the social pattern based on race and position. And because he refuses to be labelled, his very presence constitutes a threat to a society which thrives on the multiplicity of labels.

Intruder in the Dust is, in a sense, a novel of manners, of formalized social attitudes and speeches to which Lucas himself provides one of the few exceptions. By accepting both his white and black blood as a matter of course, he establishes a personal identity, independent of race, and the world he creates for himself has a similar uniqueness. Within that world, symbolized by the lonely isolation of his house in the midst of the Edmonds' plantation, Molly is not permitted to wear a headrag, nor is Chick allowed to pay for his lunch. Lucas himself emerges from it only on rare occasions when he visits Jefferson. Even then he carefully avoids the weekends "as if he refused, declined to accept even that little of the pattern not only of Negro but of country Negro behavior." (24)

Although Lucas is willing to ignore Jefferson, the town cannot afford to make the same gesture. His mere presence is a trial to white patience and tolerance, for it constitutes a threat to the neat stratification of society and the formalization of conduct. The town would be willing to permit eccentricities in his private life, provided first that Lucas allowed himself to be labelled and filed: "*We got to make him be a nigger first. He's got to admit he's a nigger. Then maybe we will accept him as he seems to intend to be accepted.*" (18) The final blow to Jefferson's pride lies in the fact that they are unable to ostracize Lucas, while at the same time they themselves are excluded from his world. They are the ones who bear the stigma of alienation and squirm under the unfamiliar sensation of being tolerated.

His possession of a gun and his presence at the scene of the murder leave Lucas vulnerable for the first time. This situation gives the whites a reason, though not a justification, for forcing him to be a "nigger" at least once in his life. He is assumed to be part of the pattern of "nigger-murder-lynching" which makes any consideration of individual cases unnecessary and provokes the identification of the traditional social pattern of behavior with the moral pattern of judgment. Accordingly, Lucas is judged, sentenced, and executed the moment he is found near the body. Mr. Lilley, temporary representative of Jefferson, provides a picture in miniature of the blending of social and ethical patterns: " 'All he requires is that they act like niggers. Which is exactly what Lucas is doing: blew his top and murdered a white man—which Mr. Lilley is probably convinced all Negroes want to do—and now the white people will take him out and burn him, all regular and in order and themselves acting exactly as he is convinced Lucas would wish them to act: like white folks; both of them observing implicitly the rules: the nigger acting like a nigger and the white folks acting like white folks and no real hard feelings on either side.' " (48–49)

The subsequent actions and reactions have all the precision and order of a ritual dance. There is no confusion, no haste, because the performers know their roles as well as the inexorably increasing tempo that will culminate in the violence of the Negro's death. The sheriff takes Lucas into custody and Will Legate guards him because the forms of legal justice must be maintained. Similarly, Gavin Stevens, more than half expecting to lose his client at any moment, is present strictly as "the lawyer for the defense." He views Lucas' problems in legal terms so that even before he asks Lucas what has happened, he is plotting his course of action—the plea of guilty of manslaughter, the request for clemency, and even the possibility of parole for good behavior providing Lucas survives that long. Although probably futile, these are no idle gestures calculated merely to satisfy appearances. The three men occupy a position midway between Chick's moral and the mob's social compulsiveness, just as the legal framework through which they operate is midway between the two different kinds of disregard for law exhibited by Chick and the mob.

Even before Lucas is deposited in the precarious safety of the jail, no Negroes are to be found in or around the town. As long as the tension lasts, Jefferson, to all intents and purposes, is inhabited only by white men in whose midst is one black murderer. Aleck Sander, the precocious spokesman for his race, voices the Negro attitude toward Lucas and, oddly enough, it echoes that of the whites: " 'It's the ones like Lucas makes trouble for everybody.' " (85) In a sense, he is quite right. In a static society which has formalized its structure and its code of behavior, anyone who establishes a private and independent mode of existence constitutes a threat as a potential source of unrest and violence. The South has room for both whites and Negroes, but it cannot tolerate that phenomenon represented by Lucas who is neither one nor the other though his origins are in both.

While the Negroes remove themselves from the path of violence, Beat Four marshals its forces. Again, despite the latent explosiveness of their power, there is no disorder. The Gowries must give the signal which will release the violence—theirs the victim, theirs the vengeance. In fact, the discipline of Beat Four is more rigid and more severely enforced than in Jefferson simply because it is the discipline of a patriarchal society, a stage that Jefferson has already passed. With all its members interlocked and intermarried, Beat Four constitutes a tribe based on blood relationship and governed by a single code. In a sense, it is a prehistoric survival of Jefferson, not too far different from the self-contained and autocratic plantation world of old Carothers McCaslin. Both constitute primitive units of social organization based on a rigid system of paternal discipline and familial ethics. McCaslin ordering his Negro daughter to his bed exerts the same unquestioned authority as old Gowrie pronouncing judgment and sentence on his son.

Lucas Beauchamp, Negro and murderer, acts as a cohesive force with respect to Beat Four and Jefferson. He is the outsider, the non-Gowrie, who has caused the death of one member of the clan. That loss inflicted by an outsider makes them acutely conscious of familial duty and unity. He is also a Negro, a fact which binds together Beat Four and Jefferson through a consciousness of their racial unity. The lynching becomes an expression of this clan and racial cohesion and an affirmation of its honor. However, when Lucas is cleared and Crawford Gowrie implicated, the reverse process occurs. For by his act of fratricide, Crawford has denied the very basis of human relationships—blood kinship. The respect for life simply because it is life is a relatively sophisticated concept, while respect for the sanctity of blood kinship is the very basis, almost the original source, of society. Crawford

138

Gowrie's action becomes, then, not only a crime but sacrilege and his punishment is, appropriately enough, not only death but familial and communal repudiation. Just as the murder of a Gowrie by a Negro served to unite the mob, so the killing of a Gowrie by a Gowrie serves to disperse it, leaving Crawford in lonely pariahhood.

Since the people of Jefferson are concerned with Vinson's death only by reason of their color and not their family ties, they assume the traditional role of spectator and judge, while leaving the actual enactment of the ritual of lynching to the Gowries. As the size of the crowd increases, its individual members suffer a complete loss of identity as well as of the power to act and think independently. Faced with the problem of a Negro found near a murdered white man, the community speaks in accents in which the voice of reason and the voice of custom have become one. Stevens is simply the most articulate spokesman for this mass reaction to Lucas. The man in the barbershop and Mr. Lilley use almost the identical words: " 'It aint their fault it's Sunday. That sonofabitch ought to thought of that before he taken to killing white men on a Saturday afternoon.' " (48) Even stranger is the fact that confronted with "suppose Lucas didn't do it" Gavin Stevens, lawyer and cosmopolite, makes the same retort as Aleck Sander, a Negro child. It appears that not only a man's reactions but also his very thoughts are determined by the customs of his land and even Harvard and Heidelberg are powerless to counteract them.

Isolated from these clichés and stock responses, Chick Mallison, Miss Habersham, and a reluctant Aleck Sander take it upon themselves to act not only independently but in actual defiance of Jefferson. Unlike Chick, who is motivated by an inner compulsion, Aleck Sander is simply maneuvered into the expedition by Chick's and Miss Habersham's calm assumption that there is nothing else he can do. There is no question in his mind of Lucas' guilt and no doubt about what his own reaction and attitude should be. All his instincts and training prompt him to join the anonymous black figures huddled in their darkened homes. Instead, he becomes, like the solitary Negro plowing the earth, an exception to his race. Despite logic and an awareness of what is racially and socially permissible for him, Aleck Sander becomes one of the three who leave Jefferson to find truth and justice.

Similarly, Miss Habersham becomes the exception to her class and sex. The Habersham name, the thirty dollar shoes, the expensive gloves, all link her to the tradition of the Southern lady. From the moment Lucas found himself convicted without trial on the evidence of a gun and a dead body, her responses should have been predetermined by her blood, her class, and her sex. She should have remained in the house, unimplicated and uninvolved. Yet Miss Habersham ignores the apparent "facts" and rejects Stevens' neat analysis of Lucas' situation and its legal consequences, for she is moved by something more compelling than logic and propriety. Lucas may be *"an arrogant insufferable old nigger who got the whole county upset trying to pretend he murdered a white man,"* (189) but he is also Molly's husband. The division of race and color is annihilated by Miss Habersham's recognition of kinship. She refuses to repudiate or forget the past and the fact that she and Molly grew up together "almost inextricably like sisters, like twins." (87) Despite Gavin's arguments, the human relationships and obligations take precedence over the social ties, and basic intuitions over logic and the stock rationalizations of the community. Even Chick vacillates between belief and disbelief in Lucas' innocence and finally compromises by simply repeating " 'He said it wasn't his pistol.' " (87) Miss Habersham's conviction, however, is instantaneous: " 'So he didn't do it,' she said, rapid still and with something even more than urgency in her voice now." (87)

More important than the deviation from the norm by Aleck Sander and Miss Habersham is that of Chick Mallison who instigates the expedition to save Lucas not because he is convinced of Lucas' innocence but because he cannot take the risk of not believing it. And Lucas himself prepares him for this crucial action. The first step in Chick's education parallels that of Roth Edmonds'. Casually, Chick, like Roth, accepts the black world as part of his environment just as he accepts the fact that Aleck Sander is colored while he himself is white. He notes without surprise or any attempt at evaluation that there are certain differences between his and the Negro's world. There is, for example, the "nigger food . . . accepted and then dismissed also because it was exactly what he had expected, it was what Negroes ate, obviously because it was what they liked." (13) Lulled into false security by such familiar features, Chick accepts food, shelter, and warmth from Lucas. But when he offers payment for the meal, he perverts the relationship of host and guest into that of Negro and white. Only after the gesture has been made does Chick, again like Roth, realize its full implications and consequences. Both boys find that their attempt to exclude the Negro boomerangs and results in their own exclusion. Both find that once they have entered upon their "bitter heritage" there is no escaping it. The only justification for his rudeness that Chick can envisage consists in making Lucas admit that he is "a nigger." With mounting fury he attempts to cancel his obligation to Lucas while making Lucas obligated to him. But Lucas counters each of the successive "gifts" with one of his own until Chick finally admits the impasse: "whatever would or could set him free was beyond not merely his reach but even his ken; he could only wait for it if it came and do without it if it didn't." (23)

When Lucas, after being imprisoned, offers him this opportunity, Chick is once more forced to choose between social conformity and individual moral responsibility, between his race and his own distinctive manhood. His first instinctive feeling is that the choice does not have to be made or that at least it can be postponed. Physical absence can preserve his freedom from implication in Lucas' death and the violence of the mob. Like Isaac, Chick keeps repeating "I am free." For both, it is a mere physical freedom: Isaac can retreat to the wilderness; Chick can saddle Highboy and keep riding away from Jefferson. Such a removal in space cannot, however, bring moral freedom. Realizing this, Chick contemplates another kind of retreat, that represented by his home. But the child must leave the safety of his home and the protectiveness of his mother if he is to achieve the stature of a man. Chick makes one more effort to evade the problem by shifting it onto his uncle. Even as he speaks to Gavin, he is conscious that if the expedition is to be made, he will have to do it because Gavin's excessively rational approach blinds him to the human and moral issues.

While Chick's mind is occupied with all these possible dodges, his body is already moving out of the security of his uncle's office and his home, calling Aleck Sander, catching Highboy, and preparing for the trip. The wild race through the night into the wilderness of Beat Four and the various dangers which he faces with a courage that still leaves room for fear constitute his trial and initiation into manhood. The distance Chick has travelled and the tasks he has performed give him a new perspective on the society of which he is a member. He becomes the stern, inflexible judge of the customs and manners of his people. The resultant moral judgment of what is essentially a social tradition is devastating in its condemnation. Like Isaac McCaslin, Chick can see only the incredible disparity between his vision of man and the tawdry reality which debases even his own personal actions. He, Miss Habersham, and Aleck Sander return to Jefferson bearing truth and seeking justice. Not expecting reward or praise, Chick still had not anticipated that the result of their action would be "not a life saved from death nor even a death saved from shame and indignity nor even the suspension of a sentence but merely the grudging pretermission of a date." (193–94) In a sense, this is Chick's repudiation of Jefferson and its ledgers, of the South and its history. And that repudiation is dangerously close to being moral and spiritual withdrawal. He is prepared at this point to follow Isaac's example in "repudiating immolation" and "declining the altar."

It is Gavin Stevens who leads Chick back into the society he so bitterly denounces. Stevens' long orations constitute his attempt to re-evaluate the whole problem of Lucas Beauchamp in the light of the new evidence supplied by Chick. His new interpretation of the South is enlarged to include the action of Chick and his two friends and as such it differs materially from his earlier explanations. Chick does not so much accept all Gavin's ideas as he occasions their transmutation into an acceptable form which can encompass both their angles of vision, the idealist and the realist. Stevens, indeed, confesses his own shortcomings, principally his reliance on talk when action is needed. Suddenly distrustful of all words and conscious of his new-found power to act, Chick, a little self-righteously, questions the sincerity of his uncle's shift in position and his "abnegant and rhetorical self-lacerating." (133) Time and again Chick taunts Stevens with the phrase "You're a lawyer" thereby implying that it is a lawyer's business to talk convincingly on either side of an issue, to defend or prosecute as the case demands and to make logic do the work of ethics.

Stevens' argument, with its tendency to identify explanation with justification, is continually short-circuited by Chick's indignant refusal to see anything but the moral bankruptcy of his tradition and his people. For a time the two of them stand as polar opposites insofar as Chick's moral vision runs counter to Stevens' social and historical dialectics. Approval of the former, however, does not demand an outright and total rejection of the latter. The reconciliation of the ideas of uncle and nephew comes when each admits the justice and cogency of the other's position. Chick learns that his moral impulses must be exercised within the social framework. He must repudiate the shame, the dishonor, and the injustice but not by running away " 'because you escape nothing, you flee nothing; the pursuer is what is doing the running and tomorrow night is nothing but one long sleepless wrestle with yesterday's omissions and regrets.' " (195) Stevens, on the other hand, is forced to recognize that his defense of the South rests necessarily on the actions of Chick, Miss Habersham, and Aleck Sander all of whom have defied and so transcended and revivified the social norm.

It is on the basis of this belief that the moral instinct must operate within a specific social context that Stevens argues for the homogeneity of the South and against the interference of the North. The South, like Beat Four, is an idea with physical boundaries and as such it cannot be conquered or legislated. Just as a Negro murderer unites all Jefferson in consciousness of its race, so interference from the North unites men in their consciousness of being Southerners. Thus, it is within the physical boundaries of Beat Four, Yoknapatawpha County, and the South that the Chick Mallisons and Miss Habershams must save the individual Lucases so infusing morality into the social structure and preparing the way for that time when no Lucas will need to be saved.

Stevens provides a verbal pattern large enough to encompass the action of the mob and of Chick and Miss Habersham. But it is Chick who actually manages to fuse the two into a single, emotional acceptance of his land. He returns from the wilderness to the "tamed land," thereby admitting his share in and responsibility to the South and its history. He returns to "stand with them unalterable and impregnable: one shame if shame must be, one expiation since expiation must surely be but above all one unalterable durable impregnable one: one people one heart one land." (209–210) He brings with him the capacity for repudiating and rejecting, acquired on his excursion out of Jefferson, and for conforming and accepting, a harder lesson learned from his uncle. In his recognition of the common interests shared by the individual and his community, by ethics and convention, lies whatever hope there is for the future. Even as he himself has been shaped by his history and his land, so he, in his turn, can exercise his "one anonymous chance too to perform something passionate and brave and austere not just in but into man's enduring chronicle." (193) The future is determined by the past, but it is the present actions of the individual which form that past.

The vitality and importance of these actions are dramatically emphasized in *Intruder in the Dust* and *Go Down, Moses* (most heavily in "The Bear") by their being enveloped in a maze of words, a complicated polemic. Furthermore, a great many similar points are made by Isaac McCaslin and Gavin Stevens not only about the process of history but about the nature and potentialities of man. Their words, however, are juxtaposed against the simple and direct actions of the young Isaac and Chick, momentarily poised between childhood and maturity. To some extent, the talk provides a verbal equivalent to the action. At the same time, that action exposes the ineffectuality of talk and poses in compelling terms the question with which Isaac confronts Cass Edmonds: " 'what distance back to truth must they traverse whom truth could only reach by word-of-mouth?' " (260–61) Gavin Stevens' circumlocutions suffer in comparison with Chick's actions. Similarly, Isaac McCaslin, philosopher of the commissary, does not have the compelling magic of the young hunter rendered speechless by his first vision of the magnificent buck or of Old Ben.

In short, Faulkner in these two novels is attempting to bridge the gap between words and deeds by sustaining the parallel between them. By themselves, the words are facile, glib, almost meaningless; they achieve their power and effectiveness only in concert with those actions which provoke them. Words cease to be mere verbal counters when the individual restores meaning to them out of and by his own experience. The problem of the child emerging into manhood is, in a sense, a verbal one, for he is compelled to reconcile language with experience and in the light of their significant interaction to accept, reject, or redefine his tradition. In such a situation there is room not only for the revivifying action of Chick but for the verbal readjustments of Gavin Stevens.

9 : A NEW WORLD FOLKLORE

Pylon

Written within a year of each other, *Absalom, Absalom!* and *Pylon* are concerned with the growth of a legend which can and does encompass alternative or even mutually exclusive interpretations of the same events and characters until it achieves its final form. But this inherent design is obscured in the latter by the fact that the events and the legend which they sustain are temporally as well as spatially juxtaposed. Reality and symbol are so intermingled that each pulls against the other. At the same time, the Reporter, himself involved in the action, is forced to assume two contradictory roles, that of the reporter and the myth-maker. As a newspaper man, his sole duty is to write " 'an accurate account of everything that occurs . . . that creates any reaction excitement or irritation on any human retina.' " (51) Moving freely from New Valois to the airfield and the hangar, himself not integrally a part of any of these worlds, he is in a position to record impartially the peculiarities of each.

From the beginning, however, his objectivity is threatened by imagination. Description yields to interpretation which, however faulty, is a living and developing thing. Initially he sees Roger, Jack, and Laverne as creatures of science fiction: strange, mechanical robots from another world who provoke his curiosity. While they continue in this guise for the gaping spectators, his view of them undergoes a dramatic reversal. Gradually he recognizes himself as the robot in a dead world and them as the only beings still possessing life. And gradually he comes to see the hangar as a symbol of a new world emerging out of a society that has lost its sense of time and place. As the Reporter moves from curiosity to comprehension and from the merely factual to the symbolic and legendary, his responses to situations and people become deeper and more complex. For by discovering the humanity of others, he is able to recover his own and hence to perceive the significance of those aspects of experience which he had formerly regarded as simply sensations.

It is thus only in retrospect that the Reporter understands the meaning of his own images as they relate to the world of the pilots and to New Valois. The latter is a City of the Dead. In it one is conscious of continual mechanical motion and the presence of people, but no actions are being performed and no human beings emerge out of the mass. As the ghostly crowds flow endlessly through the streets in antic procession, T. S. Eliot's Unreal City, reflecting the spiritual barrenness of the Wastelanders, is recreated. The Reporter is himself a symbol of the city he seeks to escape. No matter how far he travels, he can still see "the glare of it, no further away," until he realizes that "he was not escaping it; symbolic and encompassing, it outlay all gasolinespanned distances." (283) In effect, he carries the Waste Land with him, but his recognition of this fact is the first step to self-knowledge.

Though relying heavily on Eliot's images for his description of New Valois, Faulkner introduces his own symbols of sterility in the clock, the newspaper, and the Mardi Gras itself. Significantly enough, *Pylon* has more references to specific hours of the day and night than any other of his novels. Although none of the characters are concerned with the problem of time, they are all obsessed with the minutiae of time's record, with examining the position of the hands on a dial. Seasonal and diurnal rhythms are forgotten and the natural tempo of human life is reduced to a routine or an elaborately worked out schedule. In the process, man becomes a robot controlled by his own invention as if he and "the red light worked on the same clock." (176)

Where the hands of the clock make their repeated circles of the dial, directing man's activities, the newspapers methodically make a record of that time and direct man's emotional responses. In the papers the complexity of truth and life is first reduced to a handful of facts and then translated into the formulas confidently expected by a million subscribers and advertisers. Lieutenant Burnham's death, for example, becomes meaningless at the precise moment it becomes a news item, shrieked aloud by the newsboys, "apparently as oblivious to the moment's significance as birds are aware yet oblivious to the human doings which their wings brush and their droppings fall upon." (55) It is simply one more fact, one more piece of information to be recorded and forgotten except for the brief moment when it provides the reader with a synthetic thrill.

The third and most important insight into New Valois is gained through the Mardi Gras which apparently has ceased to have any religious or even social significance. The merry-making has become a confused mass of tinsel and traffic to which the human spectators are more or less irrelevant. And lest the floats prove insufficient entertainment, there is the air circus, courtesy of H. I. Feinman and the Sewage Board. But though the air circus is regarded as simply entertainment, properly understood it is also the culmination of the Mardi Gras, offering two ritual deaths. Both death by fire and death by water are, however, rendered empty and meaningless, for though the ritual remains, its significance has long been forgotten. Accordingly, the crowds of people no longer share in the sacrificial death. Feeling neither guilt nor purification, they merely observe and derive from it a delusory sense of life insofar as they themselves have escaped this particular instance of destruction. In short, death becomes a fortuitous event provoking curiosity rather than a vision of the cyclic nature of existence. With over-ingenious irony, the recurrent phrase "Momus' Nilebarge clatterfalque," compressing love and death into a single symbol and linking it to the god of ridicule, emphasizes the absence of any genuine human or religious feeling. As observed in New Valois, the Mardi Gras represents an exhausted tradition which mocks both its Christian and its pagan sources.

"Raised up and Created out of the Waste Land" (14) for the further glorification of H. I. Feinman, the airport provides a point of meeting, though not of communication, between New Valois and the hangar. Itself an expression of man's mastery over earth, it also enshrines on the walls of the mausoleum "the furious, still, and legendary tale of what man has come to call his conquering of the infinite and impervious air." (37-38) That legend, re-enacted by the pilots of the air circus, is interpreted for the spectators by the Voice, sourceless but omnipresent, drowning out the sounds of people and planes alike. Scarcely able to see the tiny racing planes, the audience stares passively upwards and waits for the Voice to create a verbal equivalent to the air drama. It is to the words not the events that they respond. Death itself is thus made into a source of profit for Feinman and a spectacle and entertainment for the audience, thereby completing the travesty of the Mardi Gras.

Paradoxically, it is within the hangar, built to house the trim, vicious planes, that the mechanical routine of New Valois, symbolized by the newspapers and the clocks, is transcended. The machine is, of course, central to both worlds, for it is a new but already integral part of man's environment. But though man can not reject his environment, he is free to determine his attitude to it. The attempt to master the planes is the new world equivalent of man's ageless struggle to dominate his environment and to assert, under whatever conditions, human dignity and values. All of the pilots' ingenuity, patience, and courage are marshalled against the machine, which waits for the momentary faltering, the one slight misstep which would make "the irreparable difference between motion and mere matter." (19) Significantly, the planes are not inert metal; they are described as "a species of esoteric and fatal animals," as a "maddog," and as "the half-eaten carcass of a deer." Even the phlegmatic Shumann attributes to them a life and will of their own, saying " 'They will kill you if you dont watch them.' " (155) Whether man pits himself against the plane or the wilderness, whether he pursues Old Ben or races against time, the meaning of the .ritual remains the same. Both offer a test of man's courage, of the will to endure and the skill to survive.

The difference between the ritual of the wilderness and that of the air—and it is a considerable one—is that the former has been sanctified by time and tradition. All the material for a new legend is to be found on the airfield; only the poet capable of giving it form is needed. The Reporter is the first, fumbling precursor and his effort is only partially successful. His initial account of Roger, Jack, and Laverne is conditioned by the fact that he is a member, however ghostly, of New Valois, which does not easily tolerate change or accept new forms of conduct. He can, therefore, scarcely be blamed for not recognizing that the pilots, jumpers, mechanics, and their women have broken their ties with the old settled earth in order to form a new kind of society in which the unit is no longer the family but the group required to care for one plane. Each of its members knows in advance what his contribution must be; consequently, "they worked quiet and fast, like a circus team, with the trained team's economy of motion, while the woman passed them the tools as needed; they did not even have to speak to her, to name the tool." (130) Moreover, each time the planes with their particular teams converge on an airfield, a larger social unit is temporarily created. The accident of birth into a specific geographical and historical position is no longer the basis for human society. It is their particular way of living that unites the various teams and makes their members practically indistinguishable. In the lobby of the Terrebonne hotel they are a species unto themselves, sitting "in blue serge cut apparently not only from the same bolt but folded at the same crease on the same shelf." (61) This unmistakable stamp is on them whether they come from Iowa, Ohio, or California. "Sober and silent because they cannot drink tonight and fly tomorrow and have never learned to talk at any time," (61) the pilots offer a striking contrast to the meretricious glitter and noise of New Valois.

Unconscious of the irony, the ghostlike Reporter, the "etherized patient in a charity ward, escaped into the living world," (20) denies life to the pilots: " 'Because they aint human like us; they couldn't turn those pylons like they do if they had human blood and senses and they wouldn't want to or dare to if they just had human brains.' " (45) Then he proceeds to elaborate his myth of the mechanical men sharing the mechanical woman whose child was " 'dropped already running like a colt or a calf from the fuselage of an airplane.' " (48) The very elaborateness of this interpretation of the pilots reveals the Reporter's own failings in sympathy and the shortcomings of his humanity. With brutal frankness, Hagood, the editor, suggests that the Reporter write up his account and then burn it, for he has communicated only his own attitude and not the reality of the pilots.

But the story, at first so clear and dogmatic, which the Reporter outlines for Hagood, begins to lose shape and elude him as he becomes personally involved in the pilots' world. Significantly, his attitude changes only when Shumann's crew enters New Valois. Away from the familiar environment of the hangar, the fliers' façade of controlled self-sufficiency is shattered. They are simply four tired people denied the money which would procure them needed food and rest and surrounded by callously indifferent Mardi Gras merrymakers. The juxtaposition causes the Reporter to make a drastic re-evaluation of himself and his world as well as to modify his first interpretation of the airfield. It is as representative and defender of New Valois that he tries to get justice for them from the officials and when that fails, to obtain help from Hagood. The latter's refusal to help and his dismissal of the Reporter clinches the newsman's emotional identification with the group.

With increasing conviction, the Reporter sees the world of the pilots as the sole remaining sanctuary of human life and values. In explaining his love for Laverne to Roger, he completely reverses his former position, emphasizing that it is himself and New Valois that are dead and mechanical. Hence his longing to become an actual part of the group takes the form of a frustrated desire for Laverne, who in his fevered imagination becomes the symbol of fertility and renewal. It is as if he recognizes that his only chance to escape New Valois and the barren routine of his own life is through the woman. But though it is their emotional life which the Reporter wants and needs to share, that life is in turn dependent on the nature of their work and their world, and these he can neither share nor even fully understand.

Accordingly, despite the best of intentions and a genuine desire to help, his actions result in one catastrophe after another. Wishing to find beds for them, he keeps them up half the night. The gallon jug of New Valois absinthe results in Jigg's drunkenness, the half-checked plane, and Roger's first accident. But despite Hagood's warning, the Reporter persists. In a sense, he attempts to take over Roger's position as head of the group, providing for their wants and managing their activities. This, however, becomes disastrous once they are at the airfield where he is and must necessarily be a stranger. He does not know about Laverne's pregnancy and therefore the desperate need for money, nor does he know about the incessant fierce battle of wills between the plane and the pilot. Since Shumann has now become a hero, invincible and indestructible, to the Reporter, he thinks of his ingenious plan for getting Ord's plane as the perfect solution, thus precipitating the final catastrophe of Roger's death.

At no point after that death does the Reporter refer to the pilots as inhuman or mechanical. They have paid for their humanity with the price of blood and suffering. Significantly, while the other reporters speculate about the dead Roger and about Jack and Laverne, employing familiar clichés and barnyard jokes, the Reporter sits silently. The epitaph for Roger comes not from him but from the second reporter who refuses to countenance the ghoulish enjoyment of the human "scavengers": " 'They were trying to do what they had to do, with what they had to do it with, the same as all of us only maybe a little better than us. At least without squealing and belly-aching.' " (290) The Reporter's despairing lethargy is broken only by the facile prediction that Laverne will leave the child with the Shumanns. With this he realizes that Laverne and his one chance for life have escaped him. Whether or not he had anticipated Shumann's death, he had not foreseen the disintegration of the group: " 'I just thought they were all going. I dont know where, but I thought that all three of them, that maybe the hundred and seventy-five would be enough until Holmes could . . . and that then he would be big enough and I would be there.' " (301) Consequently, his final shock is to discover that not the woman but the pilot had held the little group together.

Yet through his active involvement in a world not his own, the Reporter gains some measure of self-knowledge as well as a deepening perception of others. Obviously his various responses to and interpretations of the aviators are still subjective, perhaps excessively so. But the multiplicity of conflicting, subjective accounts is Faulkner's way of forcing the reader to recognize the complexity of experience at the very moment that he intuitively apprehends its truth. This explains, in part at least, the ghostlike quality and the namelessness of the Reporter. A name and a personal identity presuppose a certain consistency of attitude, whereas the Reporter exists solely as a reverberator who can and does articulate a series of disconnected and, at times, contradictory interpretations of the New World. He is not and was not meant to be a realistic character; it is in and through his legends that he finds a surrogate form of life. And in order to sustain the Reporter's vision, the pilots must remain opaque and impregnable. The molding of a legend must not be interfered with by its heroes. They remain static while the Reporter's attitude toward and therefore his story about them changes; they act while he attempts to translate their actions into symbols. It is this relationship that gives rise to the sense of ambiguity which pervades the novel.

The particular aspect of the air world which most baffles and intrigues the Reporter is the three-sided relationship between Roger, Laverne, and Jack. He could understand it if Laverne were simply a whore, but obviously she is not. He could understand and accept her deceiving her husband, but she does not even pretend to do so. There is precedent for adultery in New Valois and also a way of dealing with it, but the behavior of Laverne and her two men flouts these accepted rules and conventions. Initially the Reporter can only make sense of this by postulating their inhumanity and amorality: " 'It aint adultery; you can't anymore imagine two of them making love than you can two of them airplanes back in the corner of the hangar, coupled.' " (231) This explanation is entirely plausible to the outsider, to the New Valoisian who sees only the surface of the relationship. But Roger, Jack, and Laverne are also, and more basically, members of a new society that is slowly emerging out of the "Waste Land." In it, the team is the social unit and the sexual relationship of the three is simply a tacit admission of this fact. The paternity of the child is irrelevant since he is born into and becomes the responsibility of the whole group. However incomprehensible it may be to New Valois, this group is capable of commanding all the loyalty, responsibility, love, and self-sacrifice that the more conventional social unit, the family, habitually regards as its prerogatives.

Nevertheless, only the child, Jackie, who is born into the group, takes all its arrangements for granted. The others have deliberately chosen this new way of life and as a result can never rid themselves of their memories of the world they have abandoned. In consequence, there is a conflict of loyalties in each of them. Jiggs, the half-accepted extra member of the group, cannot resist the dazzling riding boots, thereby violating the unspoken rule that the earnings of each member belong to the group as a whole. Yet he sacrifices the very same boots for a strange assortment of parting gifts for Laverne and the boy. Jack wavers between acceptance and bitter repudiation of his position. In a sense, the situation is much easier for Roger whose relationship with Laverne is accepted not only within the group but also within New Valois. Consequently, it is Jack who is most sensitive to the three-way affair and its implications. By calling Roger a cuckold and a pimp, he thereby tortures himself with the knowledge of his own status of tolerated intruder. His sensitivity is further irritated by the Reporter's attentions to Laverne since he feels that his own honor and pride are dependent upon Laverne's sexual fidelity to himself and Roger. As a result any suggestion of her yielding to an outsider is met with outraged indignation.

Yet it is Laverne who suffers and perhaps sacrifices the most for the sake of the new air world. Whether Roger and Jack made a conscious choice or whether they had to do it, both men accept the conditions of their nomadic life. Laverne, on the other hand, had accepted that life originally because of her connection with Roger. Hers, therefore, is the task of adjusting the human relationships of which she is the basis to that world which she can only enter through the men. In order to do so, she gives up her hope for permanence and security. At the same time she must accept Jackie's anomalous position for which she herself is, in part, responsible. But most difficult for her to accept is the knowledge that each day she must risk separation and death all over again. Her life with Jack and Roger depends on the existence of the plane which each day offers a new threat to that life. Only once does Laverne make a despairing and foredoomed attempt to rebel. She climbs back into the cockpit with an expression on her face that Roger "was later to realise was not at all fear of death but on the contrary a wild and now mindless repudiation of bereavement as if it were he who was the one about to die and not she." (194-95) After that she takes her place with the other women waiting passively and fatalistically for the planes to return the hostages.

It is Laverne's second and as yet unborn child that threatens to destroy the precarious balance of her life with Roger and Jack. Their common acknowledgement that the child is Jack's once more introduces the concept of the family. Both Jack and Laverne are caught between two loyalties: one, to the old traditional family from which Roger is excluded since the second child is not his; the other, to the new way of living of which Roger is the head, the organizer, and the pilot. Significantly, Laverne resists Jack's assumption of the role of husband, refusing to yield to him in the matter of taking money from the Reporter and preventing him from carrying the sleeping child. Only through Roger, exerting the leader's powers of command and cajolerie, is the group held together. He manages to effect an uneasy peace between Jack and Laverne, to take care of the battered Jiggs, and even to listen patiently to the Reporter's maudlin confessions. But more important, he risks and loses his life in an attempt to provide the group with the money necessary to its continuance. He has accepted full responsibility for the child which is not his own and in so doing he makes it his own. For a few brief moments he pits his skill against the plane and its perverse antics, fighting to preserve the world it has made possible. Roger is, in a sense, a sacrifice to the plane-dominated world, but that sacrifice also asserts the capacity for love, loyalty, and self-sacrifice within that world.

At the same time out of Roger's death and his own suffering and sense of guilt, the Reporter creates the reality and the legend of the airfield. In order to do so, he has had to make his transit through fire, leaving the safety of New Valois for the inexplicable fury of the airfield, and then returning to the city once more, his face "altered from that of one brightly and peacefully dead to that of one coming back from, or looking out of, hell itelf." (138) But he also has to terminate his involvement with the pilots in order to write about them. His two accounts of Shumann's death juxtapose the facts against the dramatized legend. The second account is also a vicious parody of the journalist's reliance on facts, impregnated with the Reporter's own sense of frustration and bitterness against a society which is not worthy of comprehending the sacrifice of the modern Mardi Gras. The specific time and place of Roger's death, the precise description of the planes, the reference to the "six year old son," and the grandparent's home in Ohio: these are the details that place Roger Shumann's death in a historical and geographical context.

In the first account the facts are detached from their roots in space and time. Though Roger Shumann is still called by name, he has become generalized, a symbol of "man against the sky." Lieutenant Burnham's name could be substituted for Shumann's with no loss of aesthetic truth or effectiveness. The Reporter has in some measure found the proper aesthetic mold for the historical facts in sentences and paragraphs which are "not only news but the beginning of literature." (314) In it Shumann assumes a heroic role, sentimentalized perhaps but no more so than the first Bayard Sartoris' raid on the Yankee camp. The important thing is that Roger's death has made an impression on the Reporter which can be preserved in spite of space and time. For to retain its memory is to continue to cling to the vision of a new world whose folklore reveals unmistakably that courage and integrity are twin aspects of a single awe inspiring capacity and that together they underlie all truly human conduct.

THE ODYSSEY OF TIME

The Wild *Palms*

The interlocking narratives of *The* Wild *Palms,* whatever else
may be said of them, do reveal yet another facet of Faulkner's
interest in formal and technical experimentation. For the total
meaning of the book is derived from a recognition of the three
possible ways in which the stories are related. Regarded as
parallel, each is concerned with the relationship between the
individual, society, and nature, and between freedom and
order. In both, the same pattern of confinement, flight, and
capture is developed though in diffcrent contexts. Juxtaposed,
the two narratives obviously modify and influence the reader's
interpretation of either one. A too facile admiration of the
noble savage in the "Old Man" is prevented by a recognition
of the greater sensitivity and potentialities of the lovers in
"Wild Palms," with the result that the literary shibboleths of
primitivism and romanticism are both placed in a truer perspective. And finally, taken together, the two stories transcend
the peculiarities of a specific time and place as described in
each and depict that cyclic movement of culture which Faulkner has explored from various points of view in all his major
works. The emphasis is shifted from the individual and his
personal history to man and history in general.

In both sections the tension between man's desire for freedom and for security is suggested through two pairs of contrasting symbols—confinement and flight, earth and water. The
first pair illuminates the relationship between the individual
and society. It is clear that both Parchman prison in which the

tall convict is serving his sentence and the hospital where
Harry Wilbourne is an interne are microcosmic images of
society which must of necessity impose limitations on personal
freedom for the sake of order. That complex of laws, judicial,
social, and moral, which gives society its distinctive character
is binding on all its members. But as his freedom becomes
more and more restricted, the individual's only hope for preserving his distinctive humanity is to escape from or challenge
those patterns which have become moribund. Confinement
itself generates a new awareness of and desire for freedom.
Fortunately the irrational in both nature and man provides a
balance to any excessive regimentation. The flood destroys all
familiar landmarks just as Harry's and Charlotte's passion
sweeps away the customs and conventions of the established
social order. Society, however, relentlessly reasserts itself and
its own power by rebuilding the dams and levees, returning the
convict to prison, and punishing Harry for his defiance of law
and morality. Its triumph over the individual is, nevertheless,
only temporary since change and the gesture of protest are as
much a part of the record of history as tradition and conformity.

The second pair of symbols, earth and water, develop the
contrast between society and nature. In the midst of the city
or in landbound Utah, Charlotte and Harry think of earth
as a prison or a wasteland, barren of feeling and devoid of
values, in which they are trapped. The city itself becomes a
symbol of the culture which men " 'have worked and suffered
and died shrieking and cursing in rage and impotence and
terror for two thousand years to create and perfect in man's
own image.' " (136) Water alone remains indifferent and impervious to his plans, the last remaining part of nature which
he has not subdued and corrupted. Ironically, the experiences
of the convict reverse the value though not the meaning of the
symbols. Water is still the world of nature but a world from
which the convict tries desperately to escape. Earth and the
security of its familiar routines becomes infinitely desirable.
And the prison itself is transformed into a vision of an ideal
society, "the place where he had lived almost since childhood,
his friends of years whose ways he knew and who knew his
ways, the familiar fields where he did work he had learned to
do well and to like. . . . But most of all, his own character
. . . his good name, his responsibility not only toward those
who were responsible toward him but to himself, his own

honor in the doing of what was asked of him, his pride in being able to do it, no matter what it was." (165–66)

The lovers and the convict thus both have a vision of the ideal relationship between the individual, society, and nature. So perfect a balance is, however, necessarily a dream, for it is continually being disrupted by the dominance of one of its elements. Temporarily the flood asserts its power over man and society alike, blotting their achievements from the face of the earth and threatening their very existence. Just as the convict recovers the balance between man and nature in the Cajun community, society once more establishes its control by blowing up the levee and removing him by force from the island. Its desire for order, which is shared by the convict, slowly yields to regimentation and coercion. Once more society becomes a prison so that *"you are born submerged in anonymous lockstep with the teeming anonymous myriads of your time and generation; you get out of step once, falter once, and you are trampled to death."* (54) Under such conditions the revolt of a Charlotte and Harry is both inevitable and essential. For their repudiation of society and their obsessive concern with the individual, however romantic, does constitute a necessary and valuable effort to restore the balance between man and society.

The two stories are, then, part of one never-ending cycle. The order for which the convict yearns in the midst of the flood becomes the oppressive routine from which the lovers try to escape. Their journeys, linked to a specific time and place, are matched by the greater odyssey of the human race which gradually emerges out of chaos into order and then into regimentation only to find chaos come again. The flood is therefore a twofold symbol. In its unchecked fury, it is the Biblical flood of punishment and purification. Relentlessly it obliterates all those purely human achievements which are embodied in the tamed land. The cities and towns, the neatly fenced farms and houses disappear beneath the flood and the sheets of never ending rain. The stability of place and time, of people and their routines, is abrogated and the rational or at least predictable order of society gives way to the irrational forces of nature.

The flood, however, not only destroys, it also projects us back into the creative genesis of man. The impression of a world still inchoate is furthered by the apparent confusion of the very elements themselves. Thus, water seems actually to feed the flames of the burning plantation house. The convict feels himself "being toyed with by a current of water going nowhere, beneath a day which would wane toward no evening." (147) But as the land emerges out of the waters, time begins and night and day separate themselves from the universal greyness. Clinging to that land, a man, a woman, and a new born child form a group which is not so much a family as a biological unit. Both adults are instinctive, intuitive creatures who suggest an almost pre-conscious state of existence. Thus, the convict senses when the course of the flood is about to turn and so is able to meet its challenge. By the same token, with no overt or conscious knowledge of the technique, he nevertheless knows how to make a paddle, utilizing fire as his only tool. The woman, too, relies on instinct even to the extent of acting as her own midwife when the necessity arises.

The next stage in man's development is represented by the Cajun settlement, a primitive form of society which provides a precarious and merely temporary equilibrium between the individual, the community, and nature. No longer wholly absorbed in the struggle to ensure his own physical survival, the convict takes pride in pitting "his will and strength against the sauric protagonist of a land, a region, which he had not asked to be projected into." (270) Significantly, he does not use a rifle to kill the crocodiles. The skins he hands over to the Cajun, knowing that he will eventually receive half the profit though there has been no formal agreement, written or even verbal. Individual integrity and mutual trust are the basis of human association in the Cajun settlement. Gradually, however, a more sophisticated society emerges to destroy its predecessor, scattering the Cajuns and blowing up their home. As the convict discovers, the wilderness must give way to the city and the lone hunter of crocodiles to "social" man.

But just as the meaning of man is not exhausted by his biological function or his relationship to nature, so it is not fully realized through his position in an organized society. For in the process of becoming civilized, man repudiates his own roots in nature. Eagerly he separates himself as far as possible from the animal, deliberately atrophying his natural senses, denying instinct and intuition, and relying solely on his reason. And eagerly he surrenders his freedom and his destiny to society. But though society is man's highest achievement and the source of his richest values, it is also a Frankenstein monster which can and does enslave its creator. As its power increases, man's emotions are channeled into the institutions of marriage and the family, his religious impulses into the church or radio sermon, and his social and moral instincts into unquestioning conformity. The transformation of man into a robot is complete. Having succeeded only too well in imposing his design on experience, nothing is left for him but " 'to conform to the pattern of human life which has now evolved to do without love—to conform, or die.' " (140)

This slow emergence of society is reflected in the convict himself and in his attitude to language. At the beginning he and the woman simply respond to each new crisis as it appears, for they are unable either to anticipate or predict the course of events. On this simple level, language can be dispensed with; both of them are almost completely inarticulate. In the Cajun settlement the convict assumes some measure of control over his own life and establishes certain more purely social relationships with other people. But so long as those relationships are grounded in mutual trust and a mutual concern with the concrete necessities of life, language is still relatively unimportant. A combination of gestures and intuition is enough to ensure the necessary minimum of comprehension. It is only when he is back in Parchman prison, when his life is once more ordered for him, that he feels both the need and the ability to use words: "Then, suddenly and quietly, something—the inarticulateness, the innate and inherited reluctance for speech, dissolved and he found himself, listened to himself, telling it quietly, the words coming not fast but easily to the tongue as he required them." (332) Obviously, language is no longer simply an instrument for communicating needs and directing action. However unskilled and uncertain he may be, the convict is attempting to find a verbal equivalent for his experience which will make it collectively accessible. In this respect, language becomes the foundation of society and of literature, while the convict takes on certain aspects of the civilized man. As he tells his story, there are continual references to the change in his appearance. Through his clean clothes, fresh haircut and shave, and through his new command of language he takes his place in society and separates himself from the man on the river whose story he is telling.

As this change suggests, for both the convict and Harry

Wilbourne, the journey is one of discovery and exploration of themselves and their potentialities. The exhausting demands of a medical training had prevented Harry from discovering either the purely physical world with its exciting contact of human bodies or the emotional world of love. His youth had been wasted in "a constant battle as ruthless as any in a Wall Street skyscraper as he balanced his dwindling bank account against the turned pages of his text books." (32) Similarly, the convict had spent two years absorbed in his paper-backs and his scientific method of "reading and rereading them, memorising them, comparing and weighing story and method against story and method, taking the good from each and discarding the dross as his workable plan emerged." (24) Both consider this textbook knowledge as a way of entering society and proving that they too were best at their "chosen gambit in the living and fluid world of [their] time." (25) The doctor and the robber both constitute forms of behavior recognized by society though the one is sanctioned and the other condemned. In either case the result is the same. The convict is confined to a prison for having broken the law; Harry enters the hospital with its barracks-like rooms furnished with army cots and filled with men who have traded life for a career.

Having spent the years of discovery and experiment under arbitrary and limiting conditions in a purely masculine and authoritarian environment, both Harry and the convict are unqualified to cope with an experience not rendered familiar by the strict routine of Parchman prison or the New Orleans hospital. The difference between them is that the convict has an instinctive ability to adapt himself to new conditions, and this is due, at least in part, to his total lack of self consciousness and imagination. Though he feels hunger and accepts pain, he does not visualize himself as either starving or dying. Nor does he anticipate and worry about what will happen if he does not get the pregnant woman to land quickly enough. Thus while he weathers the flood by accepting it as a purely physical phenomenon which demands certain physical responses, Harry nearly goes insane as he calculates the number of cans left in the cupboard, which represent the sole bulwark against starvation. He walks into interviews, foreseeing and accepting his rejection and defeat. At every moment Harry is fighting not only circumstances but himself and his own imagination. It is this introspective quality that makes Harry's story a tragedy, while the convict's is essentially a comedy. The former is continually struggling against his environment and himself, challenging the gods and anticipating his defeat; the latter simply adapts himself to each new situation as it arises, whether it be the flood, the Cajuns, the pregnant woman, or the prison.

Yet simple and uncomplicated as he is, the convict is not "natural" man. He is unmistakably a product of Parchman prison and his behavior is conditioned by its code. Most of his actions and decisions conform to the rules he has been taught to obey. The woman and her unborn child, for example, are essentially an obligation which he fulfills to the letter. He enters the world of the flood with the deputy's order fixed firmly in his mind, and that order becomes the thread which finally draws him back to the dock at Vicksburg. He has been delegated responsibility for the woman whose swollen body insists on the prosaic nature of that responsibility by obliterating all suggestion of whatever maidens he had "dreamed of rescuing from what craggy pinnacle or dragoned keep." (149) She and later the child are in his charge, jointly inflicted on him by the deputy and the flood which prevents him from getting rid of her. Consequently, he is as solicitous for her safety as for the boat's—no more and no less. The fact that he does save her indicates the power of the code he has learned, for it takes precedence over personal inclination.

Her pregnancy, however, is a different matter. The simple masculine code of behavior learned at Parchman has not taught him how to cope with childbirth. Nor is it a problem that Jesse James or Diamond Dick ever had to deal with. Like the flood, the pregnancy is a natural force that cannot be controlled; it is "a separate demanding threatening inert yet living mass of which both he and she were equally victims." (154) It is this pregnancy and not the woman herself that forms the antithesis "to that monastic existence of shotguns and shackles" (153) where he is free from involvement in circumstance. He can accept with equanimity the fury of the flood because "when it was done with him it would spew him back into the comparatively safe world he had been snatched violently out of." (147) It does not really threaten the familiar pattern of his life. But deliberately to ally himself with the woman passively waiting to give birth would be to recognize the limited and moribund character of his prison world. He can accept nature in its destructive aspect but not in its creative opulence;

and though he is eminently fitted to live in nature, he prefers the familiarity and dependability of society. Significantly, the convict has no qualms about seducing someone's wife while he is on land. There his act becomes a social one, enabling him to know the risks he is taking and the punishment he may receive. The affair, the outraged husband, and the convict's "trouble" follow in familiar and predictable succession.

Charlotte and Harry, on the other hand, never attain that easy passivity which sustains the convict during his nightmare journey. They are continually active, continually anticipating the need for action. As a result, their travels are a series of sudden, jerky flights and uneasy settlings. New Orleans, Chicago, Utah, Texas, and Mississippi—in each they pause only long enough to gain strength for a new departure. The convict husbands his strength by travelling with the current: they squander theirs by a never ending conflict with their environment. In battling both nature and society—the cold and the corruption of society are juxtaposed in Utah—they are, in fact, attempting to create a world whose identity is dependent on its opposition to the world they have rejected. This involves them in a deliberate search for uniqueness since neither of them can be sure of the genuineness of their emotions unless those emotions have previously been condemned by society.

Their mistake lies not in placing an excessive value on love but in forgetting "that love no more exists just at one spot and in one moment and in one body out of all the earth and all time and all the teeming breathed, than sunlight does." (43) In their intense reaction to a world without love, they seek to create a world, quite independent of their environment, devoted solely to love. At each of their successive stops, Charlotte looks for a room where *"it's only incidental that there is a place to sleep and cook food. She chose a place not to hold us but to hold love."* (84) Whenever their environment begins to intrude, whenever they find themselves developing conflicting interests, they start looking for a new place or a new climate where their love will be safe. Hence they leave Chicago because the city and the winter are sapping their energies and distracting their attention from each other. But as was to be expected, they find that each new place merely repeats the one they have left. The isolated mining camp in Utah is only another version of Chicago.

Charlotte and Harry's love thus becomes a divisive and

isolative factor. For its sake, they deliberately separate themselves from society and nature alike, fleeing both the city and the idyllic lake. It is, of course, perfectly obvious that their behavior defies social convention and that moral code which considers the institutions of marriage and the family as sacred. But no less significant is their constant termination of close human relationships because they happen to be in a social context. Rat, for example, is not only Charlotte's husband but a man of whom she is genuinely fond. And McCord is not only a man who transforms their apartment into a social club but an unselfish friend. In their revulsion at society's restrictions and dictatorial power, the lovers also reject some of its enduring values.

Equally obsessive is their desire to be completely free of nature. By her refusal to bear a child, Charlotte makes one supreme effort to circumvent nature and her own biological function. Her insistence that Harry perform an abortion is her last desperate defiance of natural as well as social law. A technique perfected in and by society is to be used to thwart nature, thus cancelling out each other. Ironically, however, the lovers are not destroyed by either of the forces they feared; it is the love for the sake of which they risked life itself that makes Harry a bungler. And with Charlotte's death and Harry's imprisonment nature and society signal their inevitable victory over the aspirations of the individual. For by choosing to isolate love, Charlotte and Harry destroyed the balance between man, society, and nature. As an assertion of human values in a dead society, their conduct is admirable; as a way of life it is ultimately self-defeating. For it creates an imbalance in the individual, developing one of his capacities at the expense of all others.

Though the individual's journey ends in a prison, this does not entail a total defeat. In one sense, the convict and Harry are both victorious, for the convict has met the physical challenge of the flood and Harry has risen to the emotional challenge of Charlotte's love. Yet the meaning of imprisonment is far different for Harry than for the convict. The primary difference is that the former knows where he has been and what he has done and he carries that knowledge to prison with him. The brief moments of his passion, already part of his past, constitute his only reality; the bars, like his body, are simply something he has to accept and endure in order to keep on remembering. The convict, on the other hand, finds a reassuring and familiar reality in the solidity of the prison which separates him from the nightmare journey and divorces him from the story he is finally able to tell. Both have been changed by their experience, but only Harry knows that he has been changed.

Harry's complete indifference to the physical fact of imprisonment stems from his recognition of the relationship between the individual consciousness and time. For though man is, in one sense, subject to time, in another sense he is its master: "'You know: *I was not.* Then *I am,* and time begins, retroactive, is was and will be. Then *I was* and so I am not and so time never existed.'" (137) The past can exist only in memory, the present only in man's consciousness, and the future in his hopes and desires. On the basis of this conviction, Harry chooses to live, not because the present has any meaning or the future any hope, but because only through his life and memory can Charlotte and love exist or even prove that they have existed: "*So it is the old meat after all, no matter how old. Because if memory exists outside of the flesh it wont be memory because it wont know what it remembers so when she became not then half of memory became not and if I become not then all of remembering will cease to be.— Yes,* he thought, *between grief and nothing I will take grief.*" (324) Harry's decision to endure the present for the sake of his memory of the past is a triumphal gesture, asserting the dignity, honor, and pride of man who has been strong enough finally to risk the defeat he has already foreseen and foresuffered. The wild palms, swaying yet resisting, become a symbol of the lovers and of mankind.

It is against this background that Harry's discussion of time with McCord suggests the larger unity of *The Wild Palms.* All its characters are caught in a double trap set by time. Thus, both Harry and Charlotte are conscious of being confined within the circle of human life. They have only a limited number of years before death plunges them into oblivion. The structure of their section of the novel repeats this circle, for it both begins and ends in the small Mississippi town and also follows their departure from and return to New Orleans. Similarly, in "Old Man," Parchman prison is both the narrative and geographical beginning and end for the convict. This pathetically brief individual odyssey is caught up in that larger time which continues irrespective of the loss of an individual or a nation. The world of the flood is succeeded by the world of civilization and the choices made at one stage affect all succeeding ones. Society is the goal of the convict and the point of departure for Charlotte and Harry. Born into a specific time and place, into a world already shaped by the past, the individual must ensure his integrity as a human being by preserving that part of his heritage which sustains life and rejecting that which destroys it. The balance between man, nature, and society, between reason and emotion, between an excess of order and chaos, is a precarious one, but it alone ensures man's freedom and dignity. To be sure, this is a complex theme, and one that Faulkner perhaps handles with a more compelling power in the discursive passages of "The Bear" and *Requiem for a Nun*, but certainly it demands and gains for *The Wild Palms* a place in the main current of its author's works.

The Hamlet, The Town,
and *The Mansion*

Some sense of narrative continuity, however loose, gives to *The Hamlet* the character of a novel. But the meaning of the book is established not by the plot but in and through the successive tales of barter and stories of love. This simple device of repetition with variation, anticipating the structure of *Go Down, Moses*, becomes in Faulkner's hands an astonishingly effective means for suggesting the quiddity of experience as well as the continuity of certain traditions in the midst of change. His choice of the love story and the tale of barter as frames for the actions of his characters is directed by the fact that sex and economics involve the two primary modes of human survival, the one natural and the other social. Hence they constitute the dominant concerns of man, finding their expression in his literature, his history, and his daily life. Balancing the realistic present against the legendary past and the current form against the perennial archetype by means of style and allusion, Faulkner makes of *The Hamlet* a study in metamorphosis.

The significant difference between man's sexual and economic activity is that the former is necessary and eternal whereas the latter is contingent and historical. The one is an integral part of human nature, the other simply a pattern of behavior sanctified by custom and tradition. As the reluctance of Houston, Mink, and Labove amply illustrates, the lover neither chooses his role nor the object of his love. He is driven by his own nature to enact the ritual of sexual pursuit even though it means the surrender of his cherished masculine freedom, his engrained beliefs, and his personal plans and ambitions. Compelled by that natural force which he both acknowledges and resists in the woman, he is transformed into the lover whose sole objective is to achieve union with the beloved. The triumph of emotion and desire over reason, ethics, and society itself is inevitable. In the process, men are reduced to a common denominator—the male. For the idiot Ike and the scholar Labove, the victim Houston and the murderer Mink, all share the same identity as lover and all become part of the natural and timeless world of love.

Unlike love, economic activity, once it is dissociated from the simple necessities of life, is not a matter of compulsion though it can and often does become obsessive. It assumes this obsessive quality only when it ceases to answer an actual human need and introduces its own standards and values. At its best it provides an opportunity for exercising an intellectual skill against a worthy opponent for the sake of honor or even for the sheer pleasure of the game. At its worst the same skill is used ruthlessly and efficiently to amass wealth and to acquire power over other men. In both cases, the result is a destruction of human relationships as based on mutual trust, for such honor and wealth must inevitably be gained at someone else's expense. Yet ignoring these moral implications, society makes of wealth a positive value, of self-interest an acceptable motive, and of the shrewd trader a folk hero. Flem Snopes, the master trader, does nothing to change the essential pattern of Frenchman's Bend; he merely redistributes its wealth and power. Accordingly, even as he disrupts the established order of the village, he acts in terms of one of its oldest traditions and accepts some of its oldest values. But by isolating these values, refusing to temper reason with emotion or self-interest with sympathy, he becomes an economic monster repudiated by that society whose creation he is.

The economic tradition of which Flem Snopes is the culmination is suggested not only by the various horse trades but by the successive owners of the original plantation house at Frenchman's Bend. The nameless foreigner, an almost legendary figure who built the enormous house, serves as the archetype for his successors, each of whom, however, introduces his own particular variations. Thus Will Varner continues to own much more than he can ever put to use and to occupy a position roughly analogous to that of the Frenchman and his vanished breed. For though exercised more indirectly, his power is every bit as real and as extensive as that of a plantation owner. Significantly, his is the only household to employ Negro servants, a superfluous vestige of plantation life since neither he nor Mrs. Varner need or even want their services. The final touch contributing to the vision of Varner as a bucolic Sartoris is the barrel chair, made to Will's order and reserved for his sole use—a mock throne from which he surveys his domain and, according to the villagers, contemplates old foreclosures and new mortgages.

The parody implicit in this presentation of Will Varner becomes quite explicit and highly comic in the case of Flem Snopes. As he usurps the barrel throne, the bystanders gleefully note each new evidence of his plagiarism while he establishes "his own particular soiling groove" in a "life and milieu already channelled to compulsions and customs fixed long before his advent." (58) To the smallest detail, he patterns himself and his behavior on that of Jody and Will Varner. Like Jody's succession of identical suits worn until they disintegrate, Flem's shirts are cut from one bolt of cloth and display the same sunbrowned streaks on each fold. His black tie is a copy of Will's, the only other man in Frenchman's Bend to possess so extravagant and useless a piece of apparel. Together the white shirt and black tie give him "Jody Varner's look of ceremonial heterodoxy raised to its tenth power." (66) Having appropriated the dress, Flem next takes over the Varner gestures and mannerisms. He enters the store "jerking his head at the men on the gallery exactly as Will Varner himself would do" (102) and his secretiveness imitates even as it parodies Will's bland inscrutability. Completing and extending this parody, Flem even provides himself with his own set of imitators, for as each new Snopes arrives, he is seen to be a slightly blurred carbon copy of the preceding one.

While contributing greatly to the comedy of *The Hamlet,* the deliberate repetition of mannerisms and details of dress indicates that Flem is merely following certain established patterns. In this he is a comic version of Thomas Sutpen forcing his way into an ordered and hierarchical society and confronting it with its own mirror images. Both, to some extent, share the same innocence which consists of acting in terms of a design, the one social and the other economic, from which all vital instincts and feelings have been eliminated. Thus through Flem's exclusive preoccupation with business, the nature and limitations of the economic man and of the ethics of business are demonstrated. For Flem, and this can scarcely be overemphasized, does have ethics, but they are ethics concerned with a ledger rather than with people. Though he may exploit Varner's customers, at no point does he cheat them. It is Jody Varner, not Flem, who miscalculates accounts usually in his own favor. Flem, on the other hand, has an uncompromising integrity with respect to his books which leaves the villagers, accustomed to Jody's good-humored dishonesty, vaguely uneasy. Not even Will Varner can corrupt him: with inflexible determination he exacts payment for the five cent plug of tobacco taken by Will. Confronted by the devil himself, Flem resists all bribes, claiming that *" 'he dont want no more and no less than his legal interest according to what the banking and the civil laws states in black and white is hisn.' "* (172)

This legalism, acceptable and even necessary in the world of business, is extended by Flem to cover human relationships as well. Where Will Varner successfully combines a ruthless control over the economic life of Frenchman's Bend with a sympathetic paternalism towards its people and where Jody is quick to extend credit though not without exacting interest, Flem eschews all personal relationships and moral obligations in favor of contracts. Unlike the Varners, he is unable to serve God and Mammon too. In his eyes, people are simply economic agents; therefore it does not matter whether he refuses credit to a stranger or to Will Varner, whether he makes a profit out of Jody or the impoverished Armstid or even his own idiot cousin and ward. And if he has no friends, neither does he consider any man his enemy. The carefully contrived treasure-bait is not directed at Ratliff, his self-appointed challenger. Always he remains dispassionate and imperturbable where business is concerned whether he is confronted with Ratliff's challenge, Mink's threat, or even Eula's seductiveness. It is a relatively easy matter to be indifferent to other people; Flem, however, manages to be wholly indifferent to himself. In effect, his attitude embodies the economic principle around which his life revolves; he has no emotions and no imagination because economics has none.

Not one of the other Snopes is able to emulate Flem's attitude of impersonal detachment with malice to none which reduces all experience to factors in an economic equation. Ike, the idiot, is totally unaware of the economics of existence. Since he is indiscriminately herbivorous, eating anything except certain kinds of soil and old plaster, he is not even subject to the economic necessity of working for a living. And Eck, a man "whose intentions were good and who was accomodating and unfailingly pleasant and even generous" (75) is certainly kin to Flem in name only. In contrast to Eck and Ike, who have neither the desire nor the ability to follow in Flem's footsteps, Lump and I.O. are enthusiastic if imperfect disciples. Neither of them is capable of initiating or even understanding any action which is not directly conducive to gain. Misinterpreting Mink's reluctance, Lump patiently explains to him that sharing the murdered Houston's money is " 'just a matter of pure and simple principle. . . . If I had my way, I'd keep all of it myself, the same as you would.' " (281) I.O. attempts to be a little more subtle, using ethics instead of logic as a means of persuasion when he maneuvers Eck into paying the major share for Houston's cow. The readiness of Lump and I.O. to take advantage of their relatives clearly indicates that they acknowledge only economic relationships between men and are motivated only by self-interest. But neither of them have the objectivity or shrewdness necessary for success. Their verbal logic is simply a burlesque of Flem's dispassionate calculations and their very eagerness and greed dooms them to be the opportunists and scavengers following in Flem's triumphant wake.

The last of the Snopeses, Ab and Mink, share Flem's excessive concern with economics but not his ability to exclude all other considerations. Both of them show an almost pathological determination to preserve their honor and integrity. This dual concern with economics and honor leads to a dangerous confusion of moral and economic values. Certainly Ab finds in his conflict with De Spain over the cost of the ruined carpet a moral principle which he defends with the weapon of arson. And in the three dollar pound fee which he is forced to pay to Houston, Mink sees not an arbitrary fine but a moral outrage, an affront to his pride, of such dimensions that only a death can erase it. Violence for both Mink and Ab is at once a form of moral retribution and a protest against their own economic failure. The burning of the barn and the murder of Houston are ritual acts intended to preserve a minimal kind of integrity and to effect a crude kind of justice. These assertions of human values translated into economic terms result in the grotesque absurdity of balancing a barn against a personal slight and a pound fee against a human life.

The spaced arrival and the similarity in appearance of the Snopeses suggest a burlesque of the progress of the economic man through the pages of history, while their differences illuminate various aspects of man in the economic world, ranging from Ike's almost complete freedom from it to Flem's as complete enslavement to it. The nature of that world is clarified by the successive trades or scenes of barter in *The Hamlet*. In the elaborate swapping of horses and mules by Ab Snopes and Pat Stamper not profit but the sportsman's pride is the issue. Related by Ratliff, the whole episode is hilariously funny and it is funny precisely because it is a story. As such, it presents the horse trade in its purest form, a contest of wits between two more or less evenly matched individuals in which the winner is more interested in glory than in gain and the loser loses nothing but his self-esteem which can be recouped in the next encounter. Since it is essentially a game, the most outrageous deceit and trickery is taken as a sign of commendable shrewdness. Admiration is reserved for the one who proves himself most adept at the confidence game, while laughter is the punishment for the defeated. It is simply taken for granted that moral judgments are not to be applied to Pat Stamper or to the horse trades in which he is involved.

But in actual practice, the individual is and must be held morally responsible for his actions. Significantly, it is a Varner who refuses to accept this responsibility, thus both providing an opportunity and setting an example for Flem. Though he could well afford to be fair if not generous, Jody does not hesitate to undertake a plan that would deprive Ab Snopes of his earnings and his family of their very food and shelter. Gleefully he anticipates the profit he can make out of Ab's reputation for burning barns and the pleasure he can derive from his own shrewdness. Yet he himself introduces a moral note in his half-mocking piety when he says that " 'Burning barns aint right. And a man that's got habits that way will just have to suffer the disadvantages of them.' " (13) Jody is himself forced to suffer the disadvantages of his habits since there is nothing so deadly as a trap set by oneself. The contract which was to be a source of unexpected profit becomes instead the source of seemingly endless losses. Intimidated by

Ab and outmaneuvered by Flem, he watches the consequences of his opening gambit pass from the absurd to the monstrous.

In the episode of the Texas ponies, Flem Snopes, after a long and profitable apprenticeship, shows that he can not only emulate but surpass Jody Varner in a total indifference to any but economic motives. Not only Flem, however, but all of Frenchman's Bend is being tested as the choice between personal and economic values is placed before them. Eck, for example, is sorely tried as he alternates between a harried concern for little Wallstreet Panic and a determination to capture his gift horse, doubly valuable because it cost him nothing. He compromises by warning his son to stay near him and to run when told to. Little Wallstreet, however, is already infected with the virus of ownership and not to be daunted by any personal hazards. Armstid, on the other hand, does not share Eck's divided loyalty. The entreaties of his wife and the needs of his children are ignored as reason and conscience desert him. It is a madman who pursues the elusive horses and then turns savagely on his wife, beating her with a rope for not heading them off.

In her desperate need Mrs. Armstid becomes the focus for various reactions, ranging from the humane to the brutal. The Texan, despite the fact that he is Flem Snopes' agent, cannot hold to the impersonal, contractual quality of the bargaining. It is Armstid himself who insists on the sacred nature of a bargain by forcing her to give up the money. His attitude is, of course, supported by Flem Snopes for whom the sale is a legal transaction to which the misery of Mrs. Armstid is quite irrelevant. Keeping the five dollars, he offers her a nickel's worth of "sweetening for the chaps," (362) suggesting perhaps Flem's awareness of how far beyond the norm tolerated by traders he has gone. Meanwhile, the bystanders watch everything that occurs "in attitudes gravely inattentive, almost oblivious." (332) That this is not indifference is indicated by their willingness to help the Armstids with their plowing or to extend their sympathy after the horse-trading is completed. While it is actually going on, however, a different set of rules obtains than the one to which they ordinarily adhere. The cardinal injunction of non-interference in another man's trade must be obeyed though every human instinct and every principle is flouted. The separation of economic from personal ethics, suggested in Ratliff's account of Ab Snopes and Pat Stamper and wholly accepted by Flem, is here extended to include all of Frenchman's Bend.

That separation is confirmed and buttressed in the trial scene. The sympathies not only of the crowd but of the Judge are with Mrs. Armstid, yet he is forced to render his judgment not in terms of morality and truth but of law and evidence. On this basis he makes two judgments, though only one of them is enunciated. The one, personal and moral, condemns Flem Snopes, the human being; the other, impersonal and legal, exonerates him as an economic agent. The latter judgment, insofar as it sanctions Flem's behavior, implicates the community. The irony is clear: Frenchman's Bend is impotent to deal with Flem because it too has a double standard of judgment. Though the villagers repudiate him as a person and condemn his heartlessness, they, nevertheless, continue to admire his shrewdness, his machine-like efficiency, and above all his success.

If Flem represents the culmination of an economic tradition established long before his time and is himself but the most recent avatar of the nameless Frenchman, Ratliff, his self-appointed antagonist, embodies the humanistic tradition. Appropriately, then, he is characterized by an active interest in people, a large tolerance for all aspects of life, and a just sense of proportion with respect to his own attitudes and behavior. Hence, though he is fascinated by the phenomenon of human energy directed to a single goal, he is himself as incapable of the romantic excesses of the lover as he is of the obsessive greed of the economic man. Each facet of his character is kept in check by another. Thus his emotions are consistently tempered by reason and his sympathetic response to individuals by his recognition of the claims of society. Similarly, his habitual reflectiveness delays impulsive action until he formulates a plan which has already considered and rejected all but one alternative. But most important is the fact that even his moral sense is subject to the restraint of his own ironic sense of humor and his compassionate understanding. The result is a sane and balanced vision which can only be called human and which achieves its finest expression in his management of the problem presented by Ike and the cow.

What makes Ratliff a suitable opponent for Flem, however, is that he too is adept at "the science and pastime of skullduggery" (94) which passes for honest shrewdness in trading.

But though he does not deny the material world and its values, he does keep them firmly subordinated to his other more purely human interests. Barter is for him at once a source of profit, an exciting game, and a way of extending and cementing personal relationships. While he engages in complicated though modest financial maneuvers, he travels from house to house, satisfying his own curiosity about people, serving as a messenger, and providing the county with a walking newspaper complete with editorials. Because Ratliff's view of life encompasses Flem's, only he can challenge Flem on his own ground and with his own weapons. No one else has the necessary skill with the possible exception of Will Varner who is eliminated as a moral antagonist by virtue of his approval of Jody's vicious scheme to exploit the Snopes family.

The conflict between Ratliff and the Snopeses cannot be reduced to a simple antithesis of good and evil or matter and spirit. For Ratliff is not so much bent on the destruction of materialism as he is on transforming it by providing it with new ends. Carefully, then, he elaborates a plan whereby Flem will be tricked into buying the goats and thus indirectly into assuming the obligations of kinship towards Mink and Ike. But though he does maneuver Flem into buying the goats and exchanging them for Mink's note, it is at best a pyrrhic victory; he himself destroys Ike's note and leaves a message for Will Varner confessing a stalemate. The same sense of only partial victory is evident in his encounter with a far less redoubtable opponent, I.O. For though he blackmails I.O. into ending Ike's relationship with the cow, it is actually Eck who pays for the animal and makes the spontaneous humane gesture of providing Ike with a wooden image of his beloved.

Not only are Ratliff's efforts to make good come out of evil frustrated, but he himself suffers a resounding defeat at Flem's hands. He not only falls into the same kind of trap he baited for Flem but persuades Bookwright and Armstid to accompany him. Eagerly they hand over both money and property for the privilege of digging holes on the old Frenchman's place. The fact that is is Ratliff who takes Flem's carefully contrived lure is accidental but not surprising. Confronted with an opportunity to gain a fortune at Flem's expense, his humanistic discipline fails him. Reason, judgment, humor, even commonsense yield to self-interest and a consuming greed. Temporarily at least Ratliff's world shrinks to precisely the scope of Flem's.

As the digging for treasure becomes more frantic, he and his friends become rivals if not enemies engaged in a fierce competition with one another. It is only when Ratliff discovers that they have been duped that he recovers his perspective and with it his sense of humor. The crippled Armstid, however, refuses to be turned from his search or freed from his obsession. Our last glimpse of Frenchman's Bend appropriately juxtaposes Armstid and Flem, victim and conqueror, both consumed by the same disease, themselves inhuman and indifferent to the humanity of others.

If the various horse tales in *The Hamlet* illuminate the world of economics and the economic man, the love stories serve a similar function for the world of love and the lover. Strangely enough, despite their manifest differences, there are certain parallels between these two worlds. To begin with, both represent deviations from the humanistic norm represented by Ratliff and the social norm represented by Frenchman's Bend itself. Accordingly, each has a kind of hierarchy gauged by the degree of deviation from these norms. From Ike to Flem Snopes there is obviously a rapidly increasing preoccupation with economics and conversely, a rapidly decreasing regard for all other values. Between these two extremes lies the area of conflict in which opposing and at times mutually exclusive values clamor for the individual's recognition. In the world of love the positions of Ike and Flem are ironically reversed. It is the former who is at the apex of the hierarchy and the latter who is completely excluded. No extraneous consideration, practical, ethical, or social, distracts him from or qualifies his absorption in his love. Even the cow's resistance, euphemistically described as coyness or maidenly shyness, proves no barrier since he is content simply to love and to serve without demanding love in return. In this Ike is the perfect lover just as Flem is the perfect economic man.

The others involved in the various love affairs are lovers *manqué,* hopelessly torn between the desire to possess and the will to be free. But as they become progressively more absorbed by their love, they are forced to choose between it and other conflicting values. Labove fights his attraction to Eula as a threat not only to his freedom but to his dignity and self-respect. Yet not even his precious academic degree, his driving ambition, or his engrained asceticism can prevent him from being "drawn back into the radius and impact of an eleven-year-old girl." (128) And neither distance, time, nor another woman can keep Houston from returning to Lucy Pate. But even when he does marry her, he still has certain reservations, albeit unconscious. The wild stallion, ostensibly a wedding present to Lucy, is an attempt to preserve in some form "that polygamous and bitless masculinity which he had relinquished." (246) While Labove surrenders his ambition and Houston his freedom, Mink Snopes makes the greatest sacrifice. For he can never forget the moral precepts which he defies to marry a nymphomaniac, knowing he will have to compete for her love with "the ghostly embraces of thirty or forty men." (272)

Thus there is in the stories of love, as in those of barter, a double conflict, one within the lover himself and the other between the sexes. Because her attraction deprives him of the freedom of choice and of rational control over his own actions, the woman is regarded as the natural enemy of man. Looking at Eula, Ratliff reflects that she is beautiful and adds "but then, so did the highwayman's daggers and pistols make a pretty shine on him." (171) Labove is even more explicit as he welcomes Eula's unexpectedly vigorous resistance: " 'Fight it. Fight it. That's what it is: a man and a woman fighting each other.' " (138) But whereas the competitive struggle between men is destructive or at best stultifying, the battle between the sexes is ultimately creative. Of course in both cases the individual loses sight of propriety and exceeds the bounds of Ratliff's humanistic vision. But the excessive preoccupation with economics reduces the world to the dimensions of the ego and denies social values. The compulsiveness of love, on the other hand, results in a transcendence of self and society, adding a new dimension to life which finds its expression in the romantic tradition. The seemingly unlimited world discovered by Ike in pursuit of his beloved is in sharp contrast to the circumscribed existence of Flem.

The range and quality of both kinds of obsession are indicated by examining them from the naturalistic, realistic, and poetic points of view. With respect to the first of these, it is a critical commonplace to point out that the Snopeses are, by and large, associated with animal imagery. Yet while Flem himself is a whole menagerie—a dog, a small hawk, a frog, and a bulbous spider—Ike and Eck do not have animal characteristics attributed to them. Obviously this is reserved only for those who accept Flem's values and thus fall below the level of recognizably human behavior. The animal imagery is, however, also extended into the world of the lovers. Mink, whose very name is significant in this respect, answers his summons to the bedroom of his future wife to find that he has entered "the fierce simple cave of a lioness." (273) Houston is himself the wild stallion or "the beast, prime solitary and sufficient out of the wild fields." (246) Eula's admirers are compared to a swarm of bees or wasps and a stampede of wild cattle. As their rivalry becomes keener, they are caught up in "a leashed turmoil of lust like so many lowering dogs after a scarce-fledged and apparently unawares bitch." (149) This unflattering description of Eula's effect on men is repeated by the enraged Jody and seconded by Will Varner himself. And, of course, it scarcely needs to be mentioned that Ike's beloved is still very much a cow. Apparently, then, not only Flem but the lovers fall below what is considered to be the proper conduct for man.

Regarded realistically, all the love affairs and all the horse trade incidents are a source of comedy. This humor is dependent on a close attention to concrete detail and a concern with the characters and their actions apart from moral or social judgment. Divorced from the symbolic weight which actions carry, Flem Snopes is an absurd and laughable figure attempting to make a fortune out of a flock of goats and the interest on five dollars loaned to a Negro. Similarly, when the emphasis is on action rather than emotion, the lovers are seen from a comic perspective. There is, for example, Lucy Pate, prim, demure, but absolutely implacable in her determination to get Houston through school. Or there is Mink's wife, "the confident lord of a harem," (272) ordering the convicts to her bed made by hand of six-inch unplaned timbers cross-braced with steel cables, all of which cannot prevent it from advancing across the floor in short skidding jerks. The element of humor in the courtship of Eula whether by Labove or McCarron and in Ike's honeymoon with his seductive cow is unmistakable.

Ike as a lover is absurd, but there is no absurdity in his love. Similarly, Houston's method of grieving for his wife by banishing all females except the cow from his farm is ludicrous but not the depth and intensity of that grieving. By virtue of these emotions, the lovers give expression to all that is most permanent in human nature. Regarded from the poetic point of view, they are projected beyond the world of space and time to the timeless world of legend that is recreated by the use of rhetoric and allusion. Houston and Lucy re-enact an old fertility ritual, exposing themselves to the full moon of April. Mink finds in his wife a kind of goddess of love who initiates him into erotic knowledge and claims him for her own. And to the vision of love, the cow is indeed Io, the heifer-maid, who attracted Zeus himself. A barnyard joke is thus transformed into a poetic idyll in which Ike and the cow lose their particular identity and become simply lover and beloved wandering through an enchanted land far removed from Frenchman's Bend and Yoknapatawpha County.

A similar transformation takes place in Eula who is a jiggling, undulating mass of flesh, giving off the odor of a bitch in heat, but who as an object of love or desire suggests "some symbology out of the old Dionysic times—honey in sunlight and bursting grapes, the writhen bleeding of the crushed fecundated vine beneath the hard rapacious trampling goat-hoof." (107) Whatever she touches is transformed, even "the cold potato which at recess she would sit on the sunny steps and eat like one of the unchaste and perhaps even anonymously pregnant immortals eating bread of Paradise on a sunwise slope of Olympus." (140) Even Flem Snopes is drawn into this poetic or legendary world, becoming a "crippled Vulcan to that Venus." His marriage to Eula becomes a kind of abduction of Proserpine since, as Labove anticipates, he can never "possess her but merely own her by the single strength which power gave." (135) From these instances it is clear that in each case the tone and rhetoric of the rhapsodes reflect the extent to which love awakens man poetically and imaginatively.

At the same time the tremendous weight of symbolism which Eula and Ike's cow carry, their identification with Olympian deities, and the highly extravagant rhetoric also point up the excesses of the romantic view. It is only through the realistic and naturalistic views of the same experience that these excesses are brought back into perspective. In like manner, the vision of Flem as the invincible conqueror of Frenchman's Bend who is capable of outwitting the devil himself is deflated by the presence of the real man sporting his absurd black tie in imitation of Will Varner. The relationship between legend and reality, each providing an implicit satire of the other, becomes apparent. From the point of view of the legend and tradition, whether economic or romantic, Flem and Ike Snopes represent a complete degeneration. But confronted with the reality of these two characters, it is the purple rhetoric of the romantic tradition and the heroic trappings of conquest that are suddenly exposed as false or inflated.

By itself either tradition isolates the individual from the rest of humanity, and though a choice may be made between Flem and Ike, neither is capable of encompassing the total needs and desires of mankind. The necessity of mediating between the two is indirectly suggested by Houston's inability to do so. One of the few characters in *The Hamlet* who plays a part in both the world of love and of economics, he is confronted with two Snopeses and his response to both is equally uncontrolled. His quarrel with Mink has its roots in the concept of private property and legal ownership. Both completely lose their sense of proportion in the petty bickering over the cow which eventually leads to Houston's murder and Mink's imprisonment. A similar absence of restraint is evident in Houston's attitude toward Ike. Like the nameless farmer whose barn is raided, he is initially moved by "impotent wrath at the moral outrage, the crass violation of private property." (218) Since neither law nor force nor bribery can divert Ike from his love, Houston suddenly surrenders his own claims. In effect he recognizes that the love Ike feels transcends questions of moral or social propriety. It is left to Ratliff to make the much harder decision, to sympathize with Ike, to recognize the validity of his emotion, and yet to terminate what the men gathered around the fence see and what I.O. describes as "stock diddling."

Clearly the sexual as well as the economic drive is liable to ignore the social dicta of good taste, moderation, and reasonableness, the qualities which promote stability and peace in society. Ike and Flem both offend the sensibility of Frenchman's Bend, the one by his choice of a love, the other by his fanatical zeal for economics which involves an attendant indifference to love. But the object of Ike's passion is destroyed, albeit reluctantly, while Flem is permitted to continue his career of rapaciousness, protected by the laws of the community from the community itself. Thus if Flem and Ike may be said to represent power and love, self-interest and selflessness, then two possible alternatives confront mankind. It may occupy itself exclusively with power or love, or it may, like Ratliff, attempt to balance the two. The tremendous importance of making the effort to reconcile what appears to be two antithetical concepts is suggested by the uncontrolled excesses of each taken by itself. Ratliff's defeat at Flem's hands points up the difficulty of maintaining such a moral equilibrium. Yet the consequences of that defeat make it abundantly clear that the alternative is the destruction of all those qualities of character and all those values which are embodied in the humanistic tradition as represented and defined by Ratliff himself.

*

The two worlds of economic and sexual activity explored in *The Hamlet* receive broader definition in *The Town* in as much as Flem Snopes and Eula Varner transcend their relatively restricted roles in the earlier book to represent two constant, warring elements in man and his society—the conscious and the subconscious, the civilized form and the primitive urge, the drive to conform and the desire to rebel. The one realizes itself in social power and order, the other in the potency of the individual. In his transition from a rural agricultural economy to an urban business economy Flem recognizes that society itself is a source of power. Hence he redefines his goal to include respectability and achieves it by a scrupulous attention to propriety in all his observable actions. Gradually he is absorbed by and into the social and economic patterns of Jefferson. Eula, on the other hand, belongs to the natural world, whether it be called timeless or simply primitive, the submerged world of impulses and desires which the civilized man has either eliminated, suppressed, or channeled into socially innocuous undertakings. In their pure form the principles embodied by Flem and Eula are necessarily inimical, a fact made abundantly clear by Flem's impotence, which makes him as alien to Eula's world as she is to his. Accordingly, each is an ever present danger to the other. His concern with appearances and public morality is continually threatened by her indifference to them simply because she is a "woman who shapes, fits herself to no environment, scorns the fixitude of environment and all the behavior patterns which had been mutually agreed on as being best for the greatest number." (284)

The attitude of society toward the values implicit in this

conflict is indicated by one of the dominant patterns of *The Town*. For while Eula and her affair with De Spain are at first not only tolerated but abetted by the community, she is eventually rejected. Conversely Flem overcomes his initial exclusion to win from society at least a partial acceptance. The reason is simple: Flem regulates his behavior by those conventions which Eula ignores and causes others to question. Though every man in Jefferson responds to Eula, feeling "a kind of shock of gratitude just for being alive and being male at the same instant with her in space and time," (6) they also recognize in her that principle of disorder which threatens their individual and communal security. It is, therefore, with fear as well as longing that they regard Eula's vibrant, amoral world of the senses, of the physical life, which they have lost and to which they can return only surreptitiously. Secretly the whole town is accessory to the cuckolding of Flem, enjoying vicariously through Eula and De Spain "the divinity of simple unadulterated uninhibited immortal lust which they represented." (15) But the moment the relationship is in danger of being exposed, the lovers become sinners liable to punishment and retribution. The conscious moral life of the community triumphs over the instinctual life of its individuals. And in the repudiation of Eula as a sinner, Jefferson also repudiates its own roots in the physical and emotional world which is the source of its strength. Even though social forms and conventions have a very real value in regulating behavior, the healthy society is the one that dares to flout its own prescriptions. Hence Flem's victory and Gavin's despairing anguish at the end of the novel mark not only the death of Eula but also the illness of human society.

The new dimension given to the theme is at least partially the result of increasing the number of narrators, who reverse the communal judgment of Flem and Eula without, however, being able to nullify it. Essentially they afford a moral perspective on morality. In addition each has an essential function in contributing something of himself to what Gavin calls "our folklore, or Snopeslore, if you like." (146) Ratliff, of course, establishes the continuity of *The Hamlet* and *The Town* by virtue of his presence and his ironic though humane perspective. More important, he makes available those past events in Frenchman's Bend which will enable Gavin and his nephew Charles Mallison to understand the phenomenon of Snopesism. As chronicler of Yoknapatawpha County he can quickly summarize such incidents as Flem's conspicuous absence at Mink's murder trial or Eula's romantic indiscretions whenever they become relevant. Moreover, because his love of paradox and humor is established, certain though by no means all of the discrepancies in detail between the two books can be attributed to his poetic license rather than Faulkner's carelessness.

Though Ratliff continues to transform what he sees and guesses into highly amusing anecdotes and though his intense interest in Flem, Eula, and Snopesism in general continues unabated, at no time does he step out of his role as observer and interpreter. Even while Gavin is in Europe, he merely acts as a central clearing house of information, keeping track of the various Snopeses but not interfering with them save for his loaning money to Wallstreet on one occasion. It is as if he recognizes that Flem has passed out of his own particular orbit —barter between two presumably more or less evenly matched individuals. The absence in Jefferson of such an uncomplicated form of economic exploitation makes it obvious that Flem must be challenged by a different kind of antagonist.

It is therefore to Gavin that Ratliff relinquishes this role. In consequence Gavin becomes the pivotal character in *The Town,* at once a participant in the action and a narrator of a story that happens to include himself. Moreover, in his reactions to Flem and Eula he is both an individual and a public figure: defender of the old established order by virtue of his family background and champion of civic morality by virtue of his office. This dual role is reflected in his character which combines elements of the poet and the lawyer, the romantic and the conventional moralist, the rebel and the conformist. Inevitably the one conflicts with the other, complicating motives and thwarting action. It is, of course, as an individual that he surrenders to Eula. Yet he refuses to enter her world surreptitiously as De Spain does, but instead by using his sister's influence he attempts to persuade or coerce Jefferson into accepting her. The paradox of his position is indicated by his readiness to fight De Spain in order to defend Eula's nonexistent honor and by his concern with appearances when he sends her flowers or receives her alone in his office. In other words, he attempts to make Eula respectable, failing to recognize that social respectability could only be gained at the expense of her potency and uniqueness as a human being.

In contrast Gavin's conflict with Flem is premised on his

position as a public figure. But his effectiveness as an antagonist to Flem is diminished by his own inability to eliminate the human element. Significantly, his abortive attempt to prosecute Flem for theft is motivated as much by his rivalry with De Spain as concern with law or justice. And it is terminated by Eula's mute appeal. From that point on his attacks on Flem are purely verbal. Gavin is caught in the obviously impossible situation of wanting to save Jefferson from Flem and to save Eula from Jefferson. His significance, however, does not depend on the issue since his defeat is perhaps as inevitable as Ratliff's was. What is important is that he embraces the disorder that Eula introduces into his life and on that basis is willing to re-examine his own habits of thought as well as the conventions of his society.

To Charles Mallison, the third narrator, falls the task of mediating between Gavin's ambivalent views and Ratliff's ironic and occasionally cryptic comments. That a great deal of what he relates is based on admittedly faulty information obtained from his cousin Gowan and that he is made the recipient at an incredibly early age of confidences and reflections from both Gavin and Ratliff suggest that he is both the vehicle for the preservation of a legend and a stage in its promulgation. Thus Ratliff, Gavin, and Charles together convey the completed past, the developing present, and the incipient future of the legend of Flem and Eula. The growth of this legend is also indicated by yet another pattern. For while Gavin is restricted by his own participation in the action, Ratliff's view encompasses him as well. In his turn Charles broadens the canvas to include his observation of both the other narrators.

At the same time because of his receptivity and the absence of a recognizable bias, Charles represents the collective consciousness of Jefferson, claiming "when I say 'we' and 'we thought' what I mean is Jefferson and what Jefferson thought." (3) But as the book progresses, he does develop an identity of his own until at the end he becomes a precocious critic of that society which has repudiated Eula and accepted Flem, thus anticipating his even more active role in *Intruder in the Dust*. Ratliff makes his mission clear: " 'So you might just as well start listening now . . . whether you aint but five or not. You're going to have to hear a heap of it before you get old enough or big enough to resist.' " (112) That resistance, keeping a society strong and healthy, is a sacred task assumed in succession by Ratliff, Gavin, and young Charles.

The three narrators thus become part of that archetypal pattern which Faulkner sees in society and its history. Knowing that their victories are at best temporary and their ultimate defeat inevitable, they yet offer that same resistance to society in the name of human values that was found in Horace Benbow, Isaac McCaslin, or the Christ-like Corporal of *A Fable.* Theirs is the voice of protest which keeps society from becoming moribund. Conversely Flem, in his repudiation of human values, is in a direct line of descent from Sutpen, old Carothers McCaslin, and the Marshal, all of whom are instrumental in the destruction of one of their children. It is as if power and success can only be attained through a ritual sacrifice of a human being. From this point of view Eula's death is not fortuitous; it is at once the final test of Flem's ruthlessness and the signal of his victory.

Since Flem is seeking a place in society, he does not challenge its forms as Eula does. On the contrary, he accepts them at face value with that same "innocence" which was attributed to Sutpen. Thus in Frenchman's Bend he patterned himself after Will Varner, leaving the old man "wild with rage and frustration at the same man who had not only out-briganded him in brigandage but since then had even out-usury-ed him in sedentary usury." (328) In Jefferson it is De Spain who both provides Flem with a new model and reveals that first fatal flaw which gives him his opportunity. His example turns the inscrutable Flem of Frenchman's Bend into the hypocritical Flem of *The Town.* For what Flem learns is that respectability is not necessarily identical with morality, that the popular ex-mayor, the president of a bank, the warden of the Episcopal church can also be an adulterer without losing his position in the town. Moreover, Jefferson itself is willing to compound the sin, "supporting the sinners' security for the sake of De Spain's bank." (308)

Accordingly, Flem methodically begins to acquire those outward signs of success and respectability which he feels to be the source of De Spain's power. As he rises from restaurant keeper to president of the Sartoris bank, his dress changes slightly but significantly. In addition to the black tie once worn in imitation of Will Varner, there is a soft, black felt hat of the kind worn by county preachers and politicians. But an even more accurate index of the stages in his success story is provided by the changes in his quarters. The tent behind the restaurant yields to the rented house on the outskirts of town. When he becomes vice-president, the house is bought and then furnished, with the help of a saleswoman, to reflect his new status. In his final step Flem manages to maneuver De Spain not only out of the bank but out of his home as well, thus providing himself with the outward signs of a tradition which he does not possess in his own right. That no mistake may be made, the house is remodelled into an ante-bellum Southern mansion "like in the photographs where the Confedrit sweetheart in a hoop skirt and a magnolia is saying good-bye to her Confedrit beau jest before he rides off to finish tending to General Grant." (352) All that is lacking is a respectable connection with the Civil War. And though Flem disclaims any such intention, a hint that this too can be managed eventually appears in the reference to the original Ab Snopes as "the (depending on where you stand) patriot horse raider or simple horse thief who had been hanged . . . while a member of the cavalry command of old Colonel Sartoris." (41)

Concomitant with this steady accretion of the outward signs of respectability is what Flem would like to have regarded as his social regeneration. Quite naturally, this too is a matter of externals, a fact made abundantly clear by the contrast between Flem and Wallstreet Panic Snopes, honest Eck's honest son, who is himself engaged in a grim ritual of purification. Inheriting courage, generosity, and a sense of honor from his father, Wall is further influenced first by his teacher and then by his wife, who doesn't want him to change his name, only " 'to live it down. She aint trying to drag him by the hair out of Snopes, to escape from Snopes. She's got to purify Snopes itself. She's got to beat Snopes from the inside.' " (149–50) Each action of Wall's shows him to possess that moral integrity which wins the admiration of the town. Indeed, so strong is his integrity that Ratliff is driven to speculate about the chastity of his grandmother as the only possible explanation of this deviation from the Snopes line and heritage.

Flem, on the other hand, is totally unconcerned with the moral qualities of his own behavior except as it impinges on public opinion. Once the incident of the stolen brass is behind him, his public conduct is impeccable. As vice-president of the Sartoris bank, he is absolutely trustworthy, a fact that Gavin, fretfully anticipating further Snopes looting, is forced to conccde. Matching De Spain's position in the Episcopal church, he becomes a deacon in the Baptist church. Bit by bit, Flem successfully establishes a public personality, buttressed by the strongest of all communal institutions—the church and the bank. Gavin's bitter acknowledgment of defeat is Flem's accolade, the sign of his triumph: "let us then give, relinquish Jefferson to Snopeses, banker mayor aldermen church and all, so that, in defending themselves from Snopeses, Snopeses must of necessity defend and shield us, their vassals and chattels." (44)

This very defence of Jefferson by Flem from the hordes of relatives who as usual have followed in his wake is one of the major sources of comedy in *The Town.* No matter how irreproachable his own conduct, Flem is continually being embarrassed by his kinsmen who are still content to sacrifice respectability for profit and who have no desire to become deacons in the Baptist church. Byron is a bank embezzler on a small scale, I.O. a petty insurance swindler, and Montgomery Ward a moderately successful purveyor of pornography with visions of branching out into blackmail. These along with Mink and Lump are, of course, part of the legend of the Snopes invasion of Yoknapatawpha County related with so much relish by Ratliff. But though Flem cannot change the past, he can at least fumigate the present in the name of civic virtue. Ab, the barn burner, who now grows watermelons to entice boys within gunshot range, is relatively harmless so that he is relegated to the status of the town eccentric. Montgomery Ward is dispatched to prison by Flem's benevolent manipulation of evidence; Byron's own act forces him to flee; and I.O. is partly bribed and partly threatened into leaving what can now be called Flem's town. Though the mass evacuation of embarrassing Snopeses seems complete, Flem's position is once more threatened by the sudden eruption of yet another generation of Snopeses, the nameless and vicious progeny of Byron and an Indian squaw. With their enforced return to Texas, however, Ratliff can confidently predict the end of an era: " 'the last and final end of Snopes out-and-out unvarnished behavior in Jefferson.' " (370)

After disposing of his relatives, Flem still has the problem of doing something about his immediate family, Eula and Linda. Both of them have served him well as hostages, giving him a hold not only over Will Varner but Manfred de Spain and Gavin Stevens as well. Both also have a personal integrity, a basic honesty which, he sees, is a very real danger. Certainly he does not object to Eula's relationship with De Spain or to Linda's illegitimacy on any moral grounds. What he fears is that being women, they cannot be trusted to play the parts he has created for them. It is with the skill of a master that Flem then proceeds to clean his house by manipulating each person's strength and weakness. Efficiently, after his very generous bribes fail, he maneuvers Linda into a declaration of affection by allowing her that freedom of action which makes further rebellion impossible. But he can only fit Eula, with her steady indifference to public opinion, into his design by destroying her. Pitting Varner's bullheadedness against De Spain's pride, he creates that situation which forces Eula to take her own life in order to protect her daughter from an open scandal.

In a series of moves pregnant with irony, Flem gains revenge on Eula's lovers, both successful and unsuccessful, by forcing them to compound his own hypocrisy. By publicly acting as if nothing had happened to involve him personally in Eula's death, De Spain betrays their eighteen years of mutual love, devotion, and faithfulness, relinquishing to Flem the role of the bereaved husband. Gavin, meanwhile, sees to it that she is "buried all right and proper and decorous and respectable, without no uproarious elements making a unseemly spectacle in the business." (348) He also supervises the sculpting of Eula's monument which, at Flem's instigation, bears the inscription "A Virtuous Wife is a Crown to Her Husband." (355) As his contemptuous gesture of spitting by her grave indicates, this conventional testimonial to his wife's chastity is a calculated reproach to Eula. But more important, it is a calculated defiance of Jefferson based on his knowledge that the town cannot refute the inscription's claim without exposing its own eighteen years of hypocrisy. The gamble succeeds and Flem takes his position in the community as president of the Sartoris bank, grieving widower, and loving father by a tacit agreement with Jefferson that the truth which is known by all will be spoken by none.

The unspoken truth as it bears on Eula rather than Flem takes two different forms, the one social and the other poetic. Both are to some extent distortions since that life which Eula represents largely ignores the conscious attitude or judgment, whether moral or romantic. As she tells Gavin, " 'You just are, and you need, and you must, and so you do. That's all.' " (94) But while the social view regards her sexual behavior as a sin, the poetic view glorifies it as a love which transcends moral judgment and is its own justification. The former is concerned with preserving order through its conventions, the latter with unfettering man's emotional responses and with exalting the individual whose life is replete with that potency supplied by a totally uninhibited and therefore infinite and incalculable capacity for responding to experience.

The social force of convention is explored in terms of the various efforts first to fit Eula into the social order and then to expel her from it. In the process the institution is weighed against a human relationship which has all of its attributes but none of its sanctions. Indifferent to his daughter's feelings though presumably acting in her social interest, Will Varner pays Flem to marry his pregnant daughter and to give her illegitimate child a name, thereby making a mockery out of the marriage ritual and incidentally showing him how easy it is to contrive the appearance of respectability. Flem himself compounds the mockery by agreeing to a marriage which he cannot consummate. In contrast, Eula and De Spain establish what is a marriage in all but name since it is marked by more than a decade of constancy, fidelity, and devotion. But while Jefferson is perfectly prepared to applaud the cuckolding of Flem and to sympathize with the lovers in secret, publicly it must rise to the defence of its institutions. For De Spain has done more than violate Flem's wife; "he had not only flouted the morality of marriage which decreed that a man and a woman cant sleep together without a certificate from the police, he had outraged the economy of marriage which is the production of children, by making public display of the fact that you can be barren by choice with impunity." (338) Thus Eula is the scapegoat which must be sacrificed in order to ensure society's own life and purity.

It is by removing Eula from the context of society and by reversing the moral judgment of her that the poetic view finds scope for creating its own legend. Actually there are two legends, one topical and comic, the other universal and tragic. The former focusses on the destruction of social order which Eula's mere presence engenders and the absurdities to which Eula's suitors are reduced in their rivalry. In a series of highly comic scenes, Jefferson watches spellbound as Gavin and De Spain, the county attorney and the mayor, play sophomoric tricks on each other. The rivalry culminates in a public brawl which makes chaos out of the formality of the Cotillion Club as Gavin protects Eula's honor against his more successful rival while Flem, "the husband, the squire, the protector in the formal ritual," (75) characteristically effaces himself. What gives these incidents the quality of legend or folklore is that they are recurrent. De Spain's use of a cutout on his car to annoy Gavin recalls McCarron's splendid horse and buggy and anticipates Matt Levitt's use of his gaudy racing car to express his displeasure with Linda. Gavin is but the polished version of Labove, the football playing teacher in *The Hamlet* who dreamed of becoming a lawyer. Like Labove, he finds that his education and his sense of decorum and propriety vanish as he is drawn into the vortex of Eula's attraction. But unlike Labove, Gavin has the added bitterness of being forced to witness the success of his rival. Ratliff underscores the basic similarity when he states that Gavin is "faced with a simple natural force repeating itself under the name of De Spain or McCarron or whatever into ever gap or vacancy in her breathing as long as she breathed; and that wouldn't never none of them be him." (101)

Yet when Eula, De Spain, and Gavin are viewed in an essentially romantic and tragic light, they enter the timeless world of pure legend as attested by the frequency of allusions to classical and medieval literature. The two lovers re-enact what is almost a modern version of courtly love, setting up "a kind of outrageous morality of adultery, a kind of flaunted uxoriousness in *paramours* based on an unimpugnable fidelity." (270) Each, according to Charles, has found in the other his single ordained fate, and that fate is inevitably associated with doom since death is at the very heart of the romantic passion. Even Gavin finds a place in the archetypal pattern: "Because there was more folks among the Helens and Juliets and Isoldes and Guineveres than jest the Launcelots and Tristrams and Romeos and Parises. . . . Not ever body had Helen, but then not ever body lost her neither." (101) It is thus in and through poetry that Eula escapes the narrow strictures of social and moral judgment to become synonymous with that submerged world of passion " 'which down all the long record of man the weak and impotent and terrified and sleepless that the rest of the human race calls its poets, have dreamed and anguished and exulted and amazed over.' " (226)

The voice of the past reminds man of his true nature and society of what it has lost or is in danger of losing by too great a preoccupation with its own forms. For though respectability is central to any culture, its strength and its life depend, as Gavin

Stevens points out, on its production of " 'an incorrigible unre-constructible with the temerity to assail and affront and deny it.' " (182) And in Eula there is found one who stands up to society's internal enemy—the person who, like Flem, callously and hypocritically invokes its norms only that he may contravene their moral intent for his own ends. She resists society's projec-tion of Flem's sham not only in her own person but also by her capacity to incite others to dream and so to temper that reality which they have long identified with those impossibly ideal mores espoused, though not practised, by their community. It is out of this tension that there emerges a fresh perspective on the interrelation of society and the individual, Flem and Eula, and all the antecedent perspectives from which they have been viewed in the novel. The necessity is not of choosing between persons, attitudes, or causes but of understanding the balance life achieves between them. For though Flem's rise entails Eula's fall, nevertheless, she leaves to the town as her social and moral legacy not only the memory of her person but the legend of her actions—courage, love, pride, and honor.

*

The Mansion continues to explore the themes of sex and eco-nomics though on a different level. In *The Hamlet,* for example, each of these themes is examined as if it were relatively inde-pendent of the other. Each reveals its own problems, generates its own kind of violence, and finds its own resolution. Their jux-taposition serves mainly to illuminate through contrast. Sex is identified in *The Town* with the natural world of impulse and the potency of the individual, whereas economics is related to the social world of conformity and power. Because they are repre-sented as antithetical, warring elements, the victory of one de-pends on the destruction of the other. Significantly, Faulkner does not abandon these concepts in *The Mansion,* but he does mute their importance. Sheer, undeviating drive for money is re-stricted to minor characters like Jason Compson even as sexual obsessions are confined to the indefatigable Virgil Snopes. The rise to power through conformity is burlesqued in that great American joiner, Senator Clarence Snopes. And romantic passion is the province of Charles Mallison, a narrator rather than an actor.

As these familiar concepts recede into the background, Faulkner provides his final definition of their evolving interrelationship. Though the economic drive is clearly restricted to the social world, nevertheless it is given a different weight and emphasis in each of the novels. *The Hamlet* presents this motif under the emblem of the acquisitive drive for money; *The Town* concentrates on the related drive for power. In *The Mansion*, however, as befits the final stage of the saga, the focus is on the drive for preservation of those achieved goals that were sought in the earlier parts of the trilogy. The sexual pattern, on the other hand, reveals less a capacity for variation than for metamorphosis. It moves from sex to passion to that charitic emotion shared by Linda and Gavin Stevens, from the need to enslave to the desire to liberate.

In so doing it suggests that the potency of the individual is not derived solely from the world of nature. For though Mink may have been motivated originally by a primitive urge to get even and Linda by a determination to avenge her mother's suicide, these do not emerge as either the sole or the primary explanation. Instead, as the narrators' speculations make amply clear, man sees his personal motives in a context larger than himself, which may be animate, as with Mink's "Old Moster," or inanimate, as in Linda's notion of Marxian social justice. In essence, this context is the moral world of a transcendent humanity. In it, man acts in terms of what is fitting for himself as a human being in the given situation. Over and beyond the natural and the social dimensions of man, there is, as Faulkner reiterates, a transcendent humanity in which each individual shares and with reference to which he may act. Only through this dimension do we grasp the wholeness of man and the totality of his experience.

Since this concept of a transcendent world is not immediately dramatic, readers of *The Mansion* have been quick to point out its relative loss of power and slow to recognize that such criticism would restrict Faulkner's treatment of the trilogy to simple continuation of plot and character. But with the completion of the Snopes saga it is clear that in addition to the expected linear development, there is also Faulkner's characteristic circling over material already presented. Explored from different points of view in different moments of time, such material is appreciably enriched. But that the line and the circle delineate one of the main themes and dominate the structure of each successive book as well as of the trilogy as a whole will bear close examination as a measure of Faulkner's achievement.

Most simply: the line and the circle provide a metaphor of the juxtaposition of discrete action against continuing plot and of archetype against history. With respect to the latter, the trilogy conveys as vivid an impression of cumulative change and the inexorable movement of time as the prose sections of *Requiem for a Nun.* From Flem's first appearance in *The Hamlet* to his death in *The Mansion,* Faulkner's canvas, paralleling the growth of America itself, gets larger and more crowded. Certain characters die, move away, or simply disappear from the scene; but others, at times only tenuously connected to the plot, emerge to take their place. As the horse and buggy yields to De Spain's horseless carriage and finally Linda's Jaguar, Colonel Sartoris is succeeded by Manfred de Spain and Flem Snopes as president of the bank. Concurrently, the center of political power shifts from the county to the city to the state; and the agrarian economy of Frenchman's Bend merges into the urban economy of Jefferson until both are absorbed by the impersonal and unlocalized big business, U.S.A. From Varner's store to Wallstreet's chain of wholesale and retail outlets, from personal loans of two dollars to G.I. insurance, from isolated shacks to the shoddy, jerry-built development of Eula Acres—a pattern is formed involving three distinct stages: the community of *The Hamlet,* the complex but homogeneous society of *The Town,* and finally the amorphous Americanism of *The Mansion.*

Passing through these stages, Yoknapatawpha County loses its insularity if not its identity. For Frenchman's Bend, Memphis had represented the outer edges of the world, and Ratliff, making his round of four counties, had been its most seasoned traveller. In *The Town,* Jefferson had constituted its own world, complacently tolerating the eccentricity that had led some of its members to Harvard, Heidelberg, and Europe. But the Jefferson of *The Mansion* can no longer preserve its isolation or guard itself from the insidious infiltration of the alphabet: the F.B.I., the N.R.A., the I.W.W., the C.I.O. absorb the local in national concerns. Furthermore, as part of America, it is also part of the international scene. The sense of uniqueness cherished in and through memories of the Civil War collapses under the onslaught of Franco, Hitler, Mussolini, and Stalin: fascism, socialism, and communism. In fact, Jefferson itself assumes a small scale internationalism by virtue of the presence of two Finns, a Chinaman, and the widow of a New York Jew.

Yet, paradoxically, Jefferson remains unchanged while in the very process of changing simply because it is, as it has always been, impervious to new ideas. For to recognize any real change is to accept the breaking up of the world as one has always known it and the destruction of all that gave it an identity. Thus Mr. Nightingale, the unreconstructed Rebel, can and does repudiate his son for joining the Yankee army during the First World War. And Tug Nightingale, the son, who manages not only to join the army but to fight in France, yet shows his father's stubbornness when he refuses to acknowledge that the world is indeed round. In view of this humorous though still characteristic resistance to history, the two Communist Finns pose no threat. Their lunacy couched in a foreign language and divorced from action has no relevance to the "native-born Jefferson right to buy or raise or dig or find anything as cheaply as cajolery or trickery or force could do it, and then sell it as dear as the necessity or ignorance or timidity of the buyer would stand." (214) Linda's communism implemented as a humanitarian effort to help the Negroes improve their education would constitute a more serious threat were it not that the Negroes themselves preserve the status quo. In short, while Jefferson has been transformed externally, its ideological identity seems untouched by the rapidly accelerating changes of the twentieth century.

Adding a new dimension to this theme of permanence in the midst of change, various patterns of circularity, repetition, and recurrence dominate the trilogy. For example, what at first appears to be a simple linear presentation of Flem's career is actually circular and self-repetitive. Each successive book thus contributes to the comic view of Flem by using the same pattern of external symbols. As he rises from a tenant farmer to a bank president, he progresses from overalls to a white shirt and a black bow tie and from cap to a suit and "a black felt hat that somebody told him was the kind of hat bankers wore." (65) Concurrently, his rented room, lunch pail, and horse are ultimately replaced by the mansion, the dining room, and the Cadillac. But the emphasis on the externality of these changes serves to point out the absence of any real progress or achievement. Since Flem uses only the back room of the mansion and rarely rides in his Cadillac, he is at the end of his career what he was at the beginning. The comic repetition thus leads to a caustic irony evident in the smallest details: "When he had nothing, he could afford to chew tobacco; when he had a little, he could afford to chew gum; when he found out he could be rich . . . , he couldn't afford to chew anything." (66) As he sits, feet propped on the ledge built to protect his expensive mantelpiece, he evokes Will Varner sitting on his flour barrel throne wondering what fool had wanted or needed the baronial splendor of the old Frenchman Place just to eat and sleep in. While apparently moving not only through space and time but through the economic and social structure of Jefferson, Flem has begun and ended with nothing.

The circular pattern is even more striking in the case of Mink. The first chapter of *The Mansion* once more concerns itself with the events leading up to Houston's murder as related in the two earlier books. But since the retelling is from Mink's point of view, discrepancies become immediately apparent. Certain distortions and simplifications of the kind inevitably present in any public version of truth are reexamined and corrected or clarified. There are also, however, some flat contradictions that cannot be explained away by invoking a shift in point of view, narrator, or time. Thus Mink draws our attention to what should have been obvious all along—that Houston's wild grief for Lucy does not keep him from buying another stallion as untamed and dangerous as the one that killed her. On the other hand, Houston's retreat into a completely masculine and Spartan world as described in *The Hamlet* is contradicted in *The Mansion* insofar as he has both a Negro helper and a housekeeper in his home. More important, the pound fee, originally the sole motive for murder, is now seen in the context of thirty-seven and one-half days of furious labor with which Mink had paid Houston for the cow at its appraised value. For it is not the work but Houston's arrogance in demanding the extra dollar that makes Mink spring to an embittered defense of his manhood. Clearly, then, the very presence of such contradictions indicates that *The Mansion's* recounting of the murder serves a purpose other than reminding new or forgetful readers of past events. In essence, it reinforces the thematic continuity of the trilogy by establishing a parallel between the passionate arrogance of Houston and the cold ruthlessness of Flem Snopes. Both deny to Mink even a minimal recognition of his humanity and thereby diminish their own.

Accordingly, both evoke not only the same response from Mink but the same complex of events, though there is a recognizable shift from the grotesque to the moral. The parallels between *The Hamlet* and *The Mansion* are further extended insofar as the pattern of action recalled in "Mink" is imposed on the "Flem" section of *The Mansion*. In both cases Mink fulfills certain legal requirements without complaint or self-pity. He digs post holes for a specific number of days and hours as determined by Varner, and he serves a specific number of years and days first for murder and then for attempted escape. After he has decided on revenge, nothing can make him lose the edge of his determination or his belief that he will be given his chance. The first time he is forced to make a long and exhausting trip to buy bullets, the second time to get bullets as well as a gun. And both times the money, pathetically small though accumulated over a long period, is stolen from him. In both cases he spends the night in a depot watching the trains enter and leave the station. After incredible physical exertion, denying his need for food or rest, he reaches his goal, undergoes the same agonizing experience of having his first shot fail, and on the second attempt gets his revenge.

These similarities have a macabre interest of their own; they also reveal the compulsiveness of Mink's actions. But beyond this they establish both murders as being in some sense ritualistic. After forty years of prison, Mink does not kill Flem in the heat of anger. Indeed he kills with regret and almost with pity for himself and his victim: "What a shame we cant both of us jest come out two old men setting peaceful in the sun or the shade, waiting to die together, not even thinking no more of hurt or harm or getting even, not even remembering no more about hurt or harm or anguish or revenge. . . . *But I reckon not* he thought. *Cant neither of us help nothing now. Cant neither one of us take nothing back*." (94) The pattern of retribution established in *The Hamlet* demands its reenactment in *The Mansion* up to the culminating moment of Flem's death. And as part of the ritual, Flem, too, transcends his own nature, for as he waits for Mink to pull the trigger for the second time, his characteristic impassivity is not without courage and dignity as well.

There are, of course, countless other parallels within the trilogy as a whole and in each of its individual books. Ratliff, for example, frequently comments that various characters are to be identified by virtue of the role they play. Thus there are certain basic similarities between Hoake McCarron, Manfred de Spain, and Barton Kohl and a certain family resemblance between Labove, Gavin Stevens, and later Charles Mallison as each in his turn suffers the anguish of his obsession and his failure. Furthermore, both groups are continually related to Helen of Troy, to those who have won her under whatever name or form she has assumed and to those who continue to love without hope of recompense. In terms of episodes, there is no question of the resemblances between the various scenes of rivalry over Eula and Linda, whether involving buggies or cars with cutouts. But in addition, Ratliff's maneuvering Flem into buying unsalable goats antici- pates Gavin's ingenious scheme for saddling Flem with a new but rapidly depreciating Cadillac which he cannot sell. Mrs. Hait's feud with I. O. involving a trespassing cow resembles that of Meadowfall and Orestes Snopes over a trespassing pig. Lump Snopes's snickering exhibition of his cousin's "stock-diddling" finds its counterpart in Senator Clarence Snopes's profitable ex- ploitation of Virgil Snopes's sexual prowess.

These repetitions, whether of character, action, or episode, dramatically juxtapose the permanence of myth against the fluid- ity of history. And out of this juxtaposition come the striking tonal differences of the three books, moving from pastoral to tragedy to elegy. The world of *The Hamlet,* as its very name sug- gests, is pastoral. Frenchman's Bend is a community that has not yet lost its contact with nature. Ike, for example, moves through an idyllic setting of pleasant pastures opulent in their fertility and beauty. The sale of the spotted horses is conducted within hearing of a mockingbird in a blossoming pear tree, and the horses are pursued through a magically beautiful moonlit night throb- bing with the renewed life of spring. The moon itself is invoked as part of a fertility ritual whether for the single meeting of Eula and McCarron, for Houston and Lucy, or for Will Varner and his wife. Even the imagery, especially as it focuses on Eula, re- inforces the pastoral through references to the rich, fecund land and the fertility of nature.

In this pastoral world of Frenchman's Bend the peasants lead a simple life ordered by the patriarchal Will Varner. The store ledger, forever postponing final payment, lessens their responsi- bility. The emphasis is thus placed not on their work but on their play. Hence the dominant tone is one of youthfulness, of vitality and exuberance that are exploited for their full comic potential both in scenes of love and of barter. Though some of their con- sequences may be pathetic if not tragic, the various trades con- tinue to have some of the quality of a game. Flem's exploitation of "the peasants" is all but submerged in the general feeling of exhilaration as Mrs. Littlejohn breaks her washboard over the head of the same horse that impels half-dressed Ratliff to leap out a window, as Tull's wagonfull of women folk is upended, and as almost every man in the hamlet joins in the all night mass pursuit of the spotted horses.

As for sex—a second dominant element in the pastoral—Frenchman's Bend is full of successful and unsuccessful lovers. Eula is for the time being restricted to her role of a fertility goddess, a Venus or Persephone. Through her presence, whether in the classroom or the church, nature asserts its power and disrupts those rules, conventions, and moral codes with which society seeks to tame it. Will Varner, as yet only in his forties, serves as Eula's male counterpart, a satyr as active in his pursuit of women as the most avid neophyte. But it is Ike who provides the pastoral with its ultimate definition by literally effecting a union of the natural, the human, and the divine.

Flem, then, who is without youth and who displays a total indifference to sex and to nature, has no place in this world. He can only pervert, destroy, or exploit it. But in so doing he also exposes the reality beneath the literary conventions of the pastoral. The idyll crumbles in the face of injustice, folly, and crime as barter ceases to be a game and the Armstids emerge into horrifying prominence. The joyful celebration of sex yields to the barren mockery of Eula's marriage to Flem. The pastoral, seen in its purest form in the episode of Ike and the cow, becomes itself the object of satire as his love is reduced to a mere perversion. Thus, Ike's pasture is replaced by Mink's dark and terrifying forest and by the barren land despoiled by an insane Armstid. As the comedy grows darker, the idyllic is overshadowed by the grotesque, the macabre, and the demonic, producing the complex tonal quality of *The Hamlet*.

In contrast to Frenchman's Bend, the society of *The Town* is more complicated and further removed from its sources in nature. The characters are more mature and the dominant tone is not the exuberant laughter of youth nor even the flashing wit of satire but rather a deep, pervasive, and sombre irony. Comic scenes are, of course, still present, but they tend to be isolated episodes. There is, for example, Tom Tom's pursuit of his wife's lover, Mrs. Hait's feud with I. O., or Gavin's rivalry with Manfred de Spain and Matt Levitt. But in all of these, as Gavin points out in connection with his own romantic extravagances, there is an element of childishness and irresponsibility. Significantly, even Ratliff becomes less inventively witty and more reflective as he explores the moral and social implications of Snopesism.

The shift from the pastoral simplicity of Frenchman's Bend to the social complexity of Jefferson and from laughter to irony is evident in the very first episode of *The Town*: Flem's theft of the power-plant brass. His ingenious use of Tom Tom and Tomey's Turl to do his stealing for him is pure Frenchman's Bend strategy predictably rich in comedy. The irony lies in the fact that Judge Stevens, Gavin Stevens, and Manfred de Spain, the foremost representatives of Jefferson and protectors of its civic virtue, confederate in order not to prosecute him. From this experience Flem learns that if he can become Jefferson's defender and champion, it will of necessity become his. This unholy alliance is the source of Gavin's mounting frustration and the center of that most agonizing of ironic visions which fails to match clarity of perception with opportunity for action.

If Flem's confederation with society is treated with bitter irony, Eula's alienation from it is tragic. For she is the isolated individual writ larger than life who is at odds with her time and her place by virtue of her nature rather than her choice. Swiftly she had passed from the pre-social stage of her identification with natural fertility and sex to a brief acknowledgment of the communal power to regulate sexual matters to a transcendence of the social structure and its morality for the sake of a purely personal, human commitment. In full maturity she reveals an infinite capacity for love, devotion, fidelity, and self-sacrifice. But those qualities cannot circumscribe or define that power in her that stirs men's desire and awakens their capacity for dreaming. Like Helen, what she represents is meant to be felt intuitively as beauty, as freedom, and above all as the inexhaustible possibilities of life. Her strength, however, also makes her vulnerable since transcendence is also defiance. Her doom is inevitable because as Gavin states in *The Town*, no one can "stand against the cold inflexible abstraction of a long suffering community's moral point of view." (312) Time and again he weeps over the tragic waste of her death, tragic because society has failed to match the dream she embodied and tragic because it is markedly diminished by her death. Yet hers is also a victory since she could not be defeated, only destroyed.

With *The Mansion* Faulkner establishes his final tonal variation by stressing the elegiac. Comic scenes are relatively few and, in a sense, anachronistic. Actually, of course, the comedy both here and in *The Town* has been transposed to a minor key from the major one it occupied in *The Hamlet*. Thus, to look for the

same measure of humorous intensity in the later books is to mis-
conceive the complexity of the trilogy's genre and the subtleties
of Faulkner's exploration of mutiple perspectives. In *The Mansion* references to earlier episodes, no matter how humorous, tend
to be imbued with the nostalgia of reminiscence. The feud of
Orestes Snopes and old Meadowfill belongs by virtue of the characters as well as their concern with pigs and pound fees to the
world of Frenchman's Bend. Similarly, Ratliff's elimination of
Clarence Snopes from the senatorial race displays the childlike
ingenuity and delight in a prank of a younger, less sophisticated
age.

In general, then, the tone is one of diffused melancholy, weari-
ness, and sense of loss that permeates both the human and the
natural worlds. The triumphant celebration of youth, nature, and
sex in *The Hamlet* and the intense passions of *The Town* are only
memories shared by childless people. The Linda who left Jefferson to find her future returns having met her doom: "To love
once quick and lose him quick and for the rest of her life to be
faithful and to grieve." (158) And in urging Gavin into an
autumnal marriage, she sums up his life: "You haven't had very
much, have you? No, that's wrong. You haven't had anything.
You have had nothing." (424) Ratliff's brief meeting with Alla-
nova comes too late and leaves nothing but a memento: a red tie
with yellow sunflowers under a glass case. So pervasive is the
melancholy that it touches and softens Mink, an old, tired man
moved by past compulsions and even Flem Snopes, who had
never asked for pity and perhaps had never recognized that his
was the most wasted life of all. The private losses swell to a single
note of mourning for a vanished past, for the golden time of Eula.

Nature itself, particularly in the first and last sections of *The
Mansion*, contributes to the same sense of loss. In an alien world
of neon lights, asphalt roads, and strange words like "Krauts,"
"Japs" and "P.O.W.'s," Mink remembers the landscape of his
childhood, all "gold and crimson with hickory and gum and oak
and maple, and the old fields warm with sage and splattered with
scarlet sumac." (104) But what he passes through is the flat
Delta country, just cotton stalks and cypress needles. It is, however, in the very last scene that the elegiac mood fuses the human
and the natural most movingly. Mink is found in what Gavin
agrees could at one time have been a house. Nearby is one worn,
gnarled cedar and what had once been a fence fiercely choked
with roses long since gone wild again. Around him is "the night,

the moonless dark, the worn-out eroded fields supine beneath the first faint breath of fall, waiting for winter." (433) The very cosmos is involved as "beyond cold Orion and the Sisters the fallen and homeless angels choired, lamenting." (433) And, after the departure of Gavin and Ratliff, Mink accepts his own mortality, sinking to rest on the earth which will make him finally "equal to any, good as any, brave as any, being inextricable from, anonymous with all of them: the beautiful, the splendid, the proud and the brave, right on up to the very top itself among the shining phantoms and dreams which are the milestones of the long human recording—Helen and the bishops, the kings and the unhomed angels, the scornful and graceless seraphim." (435–6)

In *The Mansion,* then, the elegiac mood is projected against an enlarged social background and increasingly complex historical changes. Indeed, it is the participants' very awareness of this tension between background and foreground that makes them inherently elegiac. Their regret for the simplicity and humor they believe redolent of the past intensifies the melancholy inspired by the complexity they feel is inevitable in the present. Appropriately, the narrators and secondary characters are caught up in time and their environment, though to differing degrees. Charles, for example, has his war, his first love, and his first grief. And Clarence succeeds by joining each new organization and by being mindlessly attuned to shifts in public opinion. On the other hand, the major characters—Flem, Mink, and Linda—are almost completely isolated from society. For them time has in effect stopped; they are anachronisms whose motives, responses, and actions derive from a vanished past. Mink's imprisonment keeps him unaware of the changing world and free of its influences: "It didn't change what he brought with him. It just made remembering easier because Parchman taught him how to wait." (92) Hence his actions are the result of drives and emotions arising out of Frenchman's Bend forty years earlier. Similarly Linda's involvement in history and her development as an individual seem to have been terminated in Spain when she was wounded. Like Mink, she acts out of old commitments, compulsions, and regrets because "she had the silence: that thunderclap instant to fix her forever inviolate and private in solitude." (211) Even Flem, though he may still engage in an occasional skirmish with Jason Compson, is a man whose achievements are part of the history of Jefferson rather than of its present. It is only fitting that these three characters representing the three continuing themes of the saga—money and power, violence and death, sex and love—should bring their conflict to a resolution that is almost entirely personal. And through such resolutions an added elegiac quality is glimpsed—that provided by the perspective of the author as distinct from that provided by the characters themselves. Here the dominant tone of the work as a whole registers Faulkner's regret that even the shrewdest, most dedicated, and most compassionate of his characters should fail to mesh their fundamental convictions with the reality of man's total experience. Each retires into a settled conviction whose certitude betrays even in the most sympathetic of ideals the stultifying effect of dogma that has been anathema to Faulkner throughout his career. To recognize, then, that the author's elegy is essentially for the humanness of man's nature is to avoid identifying him with his characters' regret for the pastness of the past.

Nowhere is his detachment more clearly seen than in his final handling of Flem Snopes. As an index of his growing isolation, Flem recedes not only from the foreground of action but even of attention. The primary reason is that unqualified success has eliminated conflict, passion, drive and left only a reflexive habit. He has gained *"the only prize he knew since it was the only one he could understand since the world itself as he understood it assured him that was what he wanted because that was the only thing worth having."* (240) He has dispossessed Jody, disarmed Will Varner, and displaced De Spain. Thus there is no one for him to challenge and, equally important, no one to seriously challenge him. Economic rivals have been eliminated or subdued, and moral antagonists such at Ratliff and Gavin Stevens have been forced to recognize the status quo.

Accordingly, though his omnivorous greed is in no way diminished, yet it is rendered in some sense trivial because it is deprived of further goals. Position, status, power, and all the external trappings that accompany them are already in his possession. High finance can provide ample scope and incentive for its adventurers, of course, but it is not fitted to Flem's country-nurtured talents. He has outlived the time in which success depended upon outmatching and outwitting individual competitors or victims. Thus his shrewdness, his ability to bluff, anticipate, and outmaneuver, is only fitfully and somewhat listlessly employed against an occasional challenger like Jason Compson. In short, Flem has destroyed his purpose in life by achieving it.

Inevitably, then, he must fall back on the urge to keep, to protect and conserve. Such conservation depends on not spending, not using, and not risking. Aside from his two extravagances necessary to consolidate his position in Jefferson—Eula's tombstone and De Spain's mansion—Flem apparently lives on less than he did as a clerk at Varner's store. Furthermore, his house is unlived in, his car rarely driven, his tobacco unchewed. His very hat is unsweated though, according to Montgomery Ward, he has worn it night and day for three years. Finally, the bank's money offers considerable protection to his own. The only departure from the pattern of conservation is in his deal with Jason Compson, and that is a Frenchman's Bend anachronism. Flem recovers his early self as Jason assumes the role of Jody Varner outsmarting himself and thus providing Flem with his opportunity.

Though there is no real threat to his economic power, Flem's façade of respectability leaves him vulnerable. It is satisfyingly ironical that Flem too can be caught in a trap of his own making. Respectability is finally turned against him. For, having forced Eula into that suicide which reasserted in the eyes of society that Linda was his daughter, he has made it necessary to continue the charade unless and until Linda herself chooses to terminate it. Thus once every week he is faced with "the dilemma of whether to let every prospective mortgagee in Yoknapatawpha County hear how he would sit there in the car and let his only female child walk into a notorious river-bottom joint to buy whiskey, or go in himself and with his own Baptist deacon's hand pay out sixteen dollars' worth of his own life's blood." (221) And almost as frequently he must witness her using his house for entertaining her Communist friends or otherwise behaving in a way most unbecoming to the daughter of one of the leading citizens of Jefferson. But in contrast to his role in *The Town,* his strategy, though highly ingenious, is defensive. By stealing Linda's Communist party card, he hopes to gain some measure of control over her. More important, according to Gavin, it is he who scrawls on his own sidewalks the words "Nigger Lover" and "Jew Communist Kohl" in order *"to bank a reserve of Jefferson sympathy against the day when he would be compelled to commit his only child to the insane asylum."* (240) Clearly Flem can still call upon his native shrewdness and his familiar techniques when his position is threatened.

There is only one thing other than his money and his respectability that Flem feels called upon to defend, and that is his own life. He does so with characteristic economy and precision. By maneuvering Montgomery Ward into Parchman Prison, he buys "twenty more years of life with that five gallons of planted evidence." (368) In addition he offers the smallest possible bribe: one hundred dollars and a one-way ticket out of Mississippi, judiciously reinforced by a little blackmail. The cost of Mink's continued imprisonment is thus considerably lower than the five-thousand-dollar price for his death, apparently the standard fee set by the Chicago Syndicate.

Yet eighteen years later, knowing Mink has been released, Flem makes no effort to preserve his life. It is Gavin Stevens who tries frantically to have Mink found and murder averted. It is Luther Biglin, in lively expectation of Flem's gratitude, who spends his nights guarding the mansion. Flem himself asks for no protection and refuses either to leave Jefferson or to take any precautions. Indeed, confronted by Mink in his own room, he sits impassively even when the gun misses fire. That he does so is not caused by any recognition of guilt or acceptance of moral retribution. He has simply lost his reason for living. He has surpassed his models and achieved his goals; life can offer him no hope, no challenge except the perfunctory one of preserving the status quo. His death, of course, leaves no one bereaved, for he has simply vacated a place and a position. Yet his funeral is marked by an elegiac note, a bizarre recognition of mortality, a parody of mourning for the loss of great men. Gavin sees the spectators as "*wolves come to look at the trap where another bigger wolf, the boss wolf, the head wolf, what Ratliff would call the bull wolf, died; if maybe there was not a shred or scrap of hide still snared in it.*" (421)

Viewed against the expanded account of Houston's murder in the first section of *The Mansion*, Mink Snopes becomes the only possible nemesis for Flem. For what is needed to destroy him are certain characteristics which he himself possesses. Ratliff and Gavin Stevens are too conscious of limitations and possibilities, too concerned with balance and proportion; their own reasonableness diminishes their ability to cope with Flem. Mink, however, has that singleness of purpose which enables him to devote his life to waiting for one moment of revenge. Like Flem he can ignore all those factors which might interfere. The claims of his wife and children cease to matter. Living itself is reduced to waiting because "nobody, no man, no nothing could wait longer than he could wait when nothing else but waiting would do." (22)

In short, Mink and Flem both reveal the same implacable self-sufficiency and the same ruthless determination.

On the other hand, Mink, in his own fashion, replaces Eula as an antithesis to all that Flem stands for. If Linda perpetuates her mother's capacity for love, Mink represents that potency of the individual, though at its irreducible minimum, that she had embodied in all its opulence. Like Eula, he finds his values in himself and not in his society. He has rejected the church and its God on the basis of his own experience: "He had seen too much in his time that, if any old Moster existed, with eyes as sharp and power as strong as was claimed He had, He would have done something about." (5) And he has refused to be circumscribed by the law though he acknowledges its punitive power. Above all, he has repudiated the social and economic definitions of man.

Accordingly, Mink's pride, the sense of his own integrity, depends on his willingness to engage in "the constant and unflagging necessity of defending his own simple rights." (7) These rights consist of being accepted and treated as a man by other men. By his arrogance Houston denies that the dealings between them must be based on mutual respect. And by his continued absence, Flem denies "the ancient immutable laws of simple blood kinship." (5) In both cases Mink is asking for recognition, and when it is withheld, he resorts to the ultimate violence of murder. His response is, of course, demonic, yet it is nevertheless firmly grounded in his recognition of the value of the individual man. Accordingly, he can wait for almost forty years, confident that he will be given his chance, since there must be "a simple fundamental justice and equity in human affairs, or else a man might just as well quit." (6) By accomplishing his vengeance Mink affirms the significance of his life though, ironically, at the cost of losing twenty years of it.

Though Mink is prepared to act any time, it is Linda who enables him not only to do so but also to escape and thus to regain that feeling of communion with the earth and all mankind that precedes his death. As Ratliff notes, "She could a waited two more years and God His-self couldn't a kept Mink in Parchman without He killed him, and saved herself not just the bother and worry but the moral responsibility." (431) But she accepts that responsibility not for the sake of revenge but to affirm those values embodied by Eula and herself.

It is clear that Linda is, in some sense, a repetition somewhat muted of Eula. However, while continuing the theme of love, she also extends its definition. Certainly in her adolescence, despite all Gavin's efforts to improve her mind, she exists in and through her sex as Eula did. Gavin finds himself going through the now familiar ritual of rivalry involving, inevitably, a car with a cutout and a fist fight in which he is defeated. Later, her affair with and subsequent marriage to Kohl, a relationship that fuses sex, passion, and fidelity, recreates the love of Eula and De Spain.

Linda can and does, however, go beyond her mother in the scope of her love. After the death of Kohl she too can offer herself to Gavin, but when that offer is characteristically refused, she can find a new basis for their relationship. Since it does not involve sexual desire or possessiveness, it obviously differs from the familiar concept of love. Indeed, Charles and Ratliff attempt to treat it as the latter by assuming that Gavin and Linda are having an affair or that they will eventually marry. But what Linda does is to free love from its ritual enactment. Released from the traditional role of either husband or lover, Gavin is able to be wholly himself with regard to her. And Linda can urge him to marry not only for the sake of his happiness but to preserve their own love: "I want you to marry. I want you to have that too. Because then it will be all right. We can always be together no matter how far apart either one of us happens to be or has to be." (252) With this plea Linda effectively distinguishes the emotion they share not only from sex but from that type of Platonic love which by denying the physical also denies life itself.

The final form of love worked out, in and through Linda, may, for lack of a better word, be called humanistic. In any event it fuses the moral and emotional, the imaginative and the real, the contemplative and the active into a single response. Its inception lies in her meetings with Gavin which, according to *The Town*, inserted "into her mind and her imagination not just the impractical and dreamy folly in poetry books but the fatal poison of dissatisfaction's hopes and dreams." (285) With Kohl she had attempted to enact that "folly," committing herself to causes and attempting to change the Snopes-dominated world. Whether it involves the Loyalists in Spain, the Communists in Russia, or the Negro in Jefferson, she is not simply a misguided political radical. What moves her is the eternal "hope, millenium, dream: of the emancipation of man from his tragedy, the liberation at last and forever from pain and hunger and injustice, of the human condition." (222) This vision is preserved despite the clamor of a world that has made her ideals obsolete and has left "nothing for her to tilt against anywhere now." (351)

Gradually she ceases to act, withdrawing into her silence and solitude, though at no time does she deny her own involvement. Thus, just as she had urged Gavin to find fulfillment in marriage so she is responsible for Mink's achieving the consummation of his life in the moment of revenge. In killing Flem, Mink avenges a personal slight. In facilitating that killing, Linda is contributing to the destruction not of a specific Snopes but of Snopesism itself —the destroyer of life, love, human values, and human dreams.

In other words, Linda's act transcends the purely personal. For like Eula, she too is imbued with mythic proportions and attributes. But hers are the qualities not of Venus but of Diana. From the beginning she has been "the virgin bitch" immune in her virginity. And that quality of chastity persists despite her marriage and her love of Gavin. Furthermore, her status as Jefferson's first female wounded veteran, her work in the shipyard, her preference for trousers, all serve to separate her from the conventional woman, to minimize sex without destroying the power to attract. Charles sees in her the warrior-maid, the knight marked by "a collapsed plume lying flat athwart her skull instead of cresting upward first then back and over." (350)

Accordingly, it is appropriate that Linda should be the patroness of marriage. The marriage of Gavin and Melissandre makes her "happy, satisfied, like when you have accomplished something, produced, created, made something." (357) And it is also appropriate that she should be the agent of Mink's release from Parchman and of his escape from the mansion after the murder. For she is the protector of small, wild animals with whom Mink is consistently identified. But above all, she is the dispenser of a justice which seems capricious if not incomprehensible by ordinary human standards insofar as she not only uses Mink but makes Gavin her agent and her accomplice. With a final kiss for Gavin, at once chaste and passionate, she withdraws from the human world, away from "the ceaseless gabble with which [man] has surrounded himself, enclosed himself, insulated himself from the penalties of his own follies." (236)

That Linda as well as Eula can assume mythic proportions is due in part at least to Faulkner's handling of the narrators. For the main characters are magnified by virtue of the fact that the narrators act within the recognizable limits of the moral and social norm. Though Ratliff, Gavin, and Charles are capable of individual aberrations, together they represent social man at his best. Their responses are grounded in knowledge of human nature both in themselves and others and in an acceptance of the logic of social convention. Thus, they are able, for the most part, to balance the claims of the individual and of society, to temper reason with emotion, impulse with precept. Accordingly, they can accept moral responsibility: "So what you need is to learn how to trust in God without depending on Him. In fact, we need to fix things so He can depend on us for a while. Then He wont need to waste Himself being everywhere at once." (321) These victories may seem slight since "even when you get rid of one Snopes, there's already another one behind you even before you can turn around," (349) but Ratliff does eliminate one Snopes from politics and Gavin does save Linda from another. In brief, they may err, falter, suffer defeat, and even lose hope, yet their efforts constitute a promise that each new Snopes will be confronted with a Roland. Thus, in a significant fashion, they qualify the elegiac sense of the other characters by refusing to accept human affairs as irredeemable. They do so, however, by intuitively recognizing the limited, piecemeal character of change for the better. That is, they see and demonstrate that it is a matter of specific concrete actions in individual moments.

Against the limitations of their humanity imposed on the narrators, the main characters stand out in vivid relief. They are fixed, isolated in their deviation from the norm. Flem, Mink, Eula, Linda—for good or for evil, these are the giants who, while still living, become part of the folklore of Yoknapatawpha County. With the death of Mink and Flem and the departure of Linda, the elegiac note reaches its diapason. There is a melancholy sense not simply of personal loss but of the passing of time and the ending of an era.

12 : CULMINATION AND CRISIS

A Fable

In A Fable Faulkner transcends his role as chief chronicler of Yoknapatawpha County and demonstrates conclusively that his subject is not merely the South and its history but man and his problems. In the interest of universality, he restates abstractly most of the ideas developed in dramatic fashion in his preceding novels. Similarly, he subdues the particular and therefore unique aspects of his situation and characters and eliminates that profusion of detail which creates the illusion of reality for Jefferson and its inhabitants. Furthermore, he makes no effort to employ language as a stylistic equivalent to the characters. The speeches whether of the Marshal or the peasant girl Marthe tend to be generalized in content and similar in tone. The same suppression of individuality is evident in the fact that few of the characters are named and that though dates are occasionally mentioned the emphasis is on the days of the week rather than a specific year. Nor is any effort made to suggest the uniqueness of World War I or to document its events. What is important is not what took place at Verdun or Valaumont but the fact of war. This blurring of the historical outline by fusing the realistic present with the mythic past points up the essential unity of human experience. The characters therefore belong simultaneously to the historical world of the drama and the timeless world of the fable. As part of the former, they work out their individual destinies in a particular place and time; as part of the latter, they re-enact a pattern which is not and cannot be exhausted by any one of its temporal manifestations. Stated in its simplest terms, that pattern consists of the conflict between authority and individual freedom. The quest for freedom is presented on three different levels. The first and archetypal quest is Christ's, which is primarily religious and divine. For the Christ whose life is paralleled in the Corporal's is essentially the rebel, pitting his own personal faith in God and man against the authority of the church and its traditions. The Corporal's quest, on the other hand, despite the suggestions of the supernatural, is purely human and moral. Hence his disobedience is directed at paternal authority, military discipline, and civil law. Finally, the groom and his two Negro companions engage in a quest for physical freedom on the natural level through their frantic efforts to keep the magnificent lame horse out of the hands of its owner. Totally different, taking place at different times in different countries, Christ's conflict with the established church, the Corporal's defiance of the army, and the groom's evasion of the law, all reveal "truth, love, sacrifice, and something else even more important than they; some bond between or from man to his brother man stronger than even the golden shackles which coopered precariously his ramshackle earth." (165)

In its implications the story of the horse and the English groom constitutes a profane version of Faulkner's sacred fable. The connection between the two is made by the Runner, himself a fugitive from army rank and authority, who embarks on a "pilgrimage back to when and where the lost free spirit of man once existed." (148) But the story he hears from the Reverend Sutterfield reveals the same worship of the word "freedom" and the same willing submission to control in America that had made him despair of man in the old world. From it he learns that freedom is never to be found in a pure state, that in fact, it is always being threatened with suppression or extinction. Appropriately, the horse, which is a symbol of natural freedom, is maimed and its liberty is contingent upon the evasion of various groups of men dedicated to its capture. Helping its owner assert his legal title are five separately organized but grimly unified groups: the Federal government, the successive state police forces, and the three sets of detectives employed by the railway, the insurance company, and the owner himself. Though all these groups are concerned with restoring a valuable piece of property to its owner, they also have a more personal stake. To preserve their own function, they must see to it that no single law is broken and no one lawbreaker left uncaught and unpunished lest the whole vast system of laws and law enforcement be placed in jeopardy.

Because the abduction of the horse is an act of love and self-sacrifice, the flight from law becomes no mean search for safety but a triumphant procession drawing new converts into its wake. The Reverend Sutterfield, though dedicated to opposing all forms of sin, nevertheless abets theft and gambling for the sake of the horse in the belief that God understands and approves his reasons. The Federal Deputy resigns his post and though he is not able to join the fleeing group, does his best to protect them from the legal consequences of their actions. The Masons work effectively to impede pursuit and later to spirit the Groom and the two Negroes out of jail. And at the very moment that the prosecutor exults in his control of the mob, the people ignore him and due process of law as well and free the Reverend Sutterfield in the very courtroom they themselves have erected as a symbol of legal justice.

Yet despite all such help, the horse itself is destroyed and with it the Groom's capacity for love and trust. It thus becomes the self-appointed duty of the Reverend Sutterfield and later the Runner, to recall him to a spirit of resistance, a love of freedom, and a willingness to sacrifice himself and to transfer these qualities from the natural to the human world. They, however, can but prepare the way with argument and persuasion. It is the Corporal's mutiny, offering a living proof of faith in man, which rouses him from his moral apathy to risk his life in a gesture of affirmation in spite of his own conviction that any such gesture is doomed.

In contrast to the Groom's quest for physical freedom, which is presented as a simple flight from the law, the Corporal's quest is rendered extremely complex by virtue of his relationship with the Marshal. As the latter suggests, they are " 'two articulations, self-elected possibly, anyway elected, anyway postulated, not so much to defend as to test two inimical conditions which, through no fault of ours but through the simple paucity and restrictions of the arena where they meet, must contend and—one of them—perish.' " (347–48) This opposition is worked out in various contexts, but in all of them the Marshal represents the voice of authority and power, the Corporal that of individual freedom and love. In terms of their personal relationship, the Marshal is the father, traditionally a symbol of authority, the arbiter of his family's conduct, and the defender of the *status quo.* In effect, he stands for both the order which supports civilization and the tyranny which oppresses it. An attempt to perpetuate the order which he himself has inherited and preserved is implicit in the Marshal's offer to make the Corporal heir to his wealth and position. The son must, however, challenge the father and renounce his inheritance if he is to find his own identity even though, ironically enough, he himself replaces the father and assumes his power and authority. The spiritual quest for freedom of the individual is forever being transformed into collective dogma and order into regimentation. Regarded in this light, the Marshal and the Corporal are both archetypal figures, exemplifying a pattern that is eternally present—an irresoluble tension that is the essence of man's history and a condition of his future.

Within the religious context, the Marshal and the Corporal are both related to Christ though in quite different ways since a distinction must be made between the religious impulse which Christ awakened in man and the church founded in his name, between Christ as rebel and as lawgiver. Obedient only to God, Christ found himself pitting his instinct, his mind, and his heart against the entrenched authority of the church. In defiance of it, he transformed the Old Testament God of wrath into a God of love and forgiveness and made ethics a matter of conscience rather than law. But most important he sought to effect the fulfillment of God's promise which would dispense with the church as an intermediary between God and man: "I will put my law in their inward parts, and in their hearts will I write it; and I will be their God, and they shall be my people" (Jer. xxxi. 33). But the faith he awakened was not permitted to remain " '*snared* in that frail web of hopes and fears and aspirations which man calls his heart.' " (364) Once more it was translated into dogma, once more channelled into a church which assumed direction and control over the faith and conscience of mankind. Obviously it is to the living Christ that the Corporal is related, a fact borne out by the repetition in his own life of the events of the Passion Week and by the nature of his mission. The Marshal, on the other hand, is the defender of the church and its dogmas if only because it is part of the established order. In his concern to defend and preserve the institutions of religion, he becomes a mock savior, deified and venerated by his people.

The distinction between a religion of authority demanding personal obedience to law and a religion based on personal responsibility and conscience is worked out in yet another Biblical context. The Marshal and the Corporal are related respectively to the Old and the New Testaments and to the prophecies of the savior as a Warrior King and as the Prince of Peace. In the Old Testament the emphasis is almost wholly on God's omnipotence of which the most characteristic expression is military might. Complete submission of His chosen people to His laws brings rewards of military conquests and spoils; lack of obedience results in His wrath and the swift triumph of their enemies. The leaders of the people are divinely chosen heroes, combining power and wisdom as befits His representatives. The resemblance of the Marshal to these hero-saviors is clear as is the correspondence of modern nationalism to the concept of a people proving themselves divinely chosen not only by their religious fervor but by their military prowess. From this point of view, it is not strange that the Marshal is able to gain the love of the Quartermaster General and the worship of the people.

It is also quite evident that the Corporal is in the tradition of another prophecy, that of Jeremiah's vision of the prince of peace. Like Christ, the Corporal is not concerned with the salvation of a single country or the glorification of a chosen people. And like him, he comes not in the guise of a warrior-hero but as the meek son of man. It is simply as a man that the Corporal succeeds in reminding some few others of their humanity, leading them to recognize their moral nature and to accept the responsibility for ethical decisions. In the process codes and traditions lose their sacrosanct quality. The filial obligation to conform and preserve is countered with the individual's duty to judge and, where necessary, to alter. The implications of this are enormous: if the power to effect changes is man's, then the future is no longer predetermined by the past. Love rather than force, peace rather than war becomes possible though not necessarily inevitable. The Corporal's successful though brief rebellion offers the hope that man will once more take his destiny into his own hands and shape it to his own needs. For the moral responsibility of the individual encompasses not simply his own self but his society, the past, and the future.

There is little difficulty in choosing between the Old Testament heroes and Christ since the differences are readily apparent. It is difficult in the extreme, however, to choose between two men who profess the same sentiments and claim the same faith and ideals. It is in the guise of a false savior that the Marshal appears in *A Fable*. This explains why it is he rather than the Corporal who re-enacts such events connected with the life of Christ as the renunciation of the world, the trial in the desert, the ascent of the mountain, and the *noli me tangere* incident. Since all the features for the Messianic mission appear to be present, it is little wonder that the Marshal arouses both faith and hope in the Quartermaster General: " 'I believed from that first moment when I saw you in that gate that day forty-seven years ago that you had been destined to save us. . . . that you in your strength would even absolve us of our failure due to our weakness and fears.' " (328) Yet the Marshal mocks even as he fulfills this prophecy. Like the warrior kings of the Old Testament, he saves his nation, giving it victory over its enemies; and like them, his military leadership is endowed with religious significance. Standing with the other two Allied generals, he is one of "a triumvirate consecrated and anointed, a constellation remote as planets in their immutability, powerful as archbishops in their trinity, splendid as cardinals in their retinues and myriad as Brahmins in their blind followers." (239)

But when he saves France, not man, he reveals himself as a mock savior whose initiation is into the mysteries of power rather than of love. It is in this light that his apparently Christlike actions must be seen. His being chosen is qualified by the fact that evil also " 'chooses the men and women by test and trial, proves and tests them and then accepts them forever.' " (286) Only the hedonism of Paris, unworthy of a hero, is renounced; its matchless and immutable power is held in reserve for later use. Nor are the temptations in the desert rejected, for by exercising the authority vested in his rank, he denies simultaneously the brotherhood of men and the sovereignty of God. In arranging with the enemy to send them a scapegoat, he presumes to judge the value of the men under his command and to dispose of them accordingly. This act, for which the Marshal is decorated despite vigorous signs of divine disapproval, constitutes his assumption of God's power. In so doing, he becomes the antithesis of Christ who had " 'absolved poor mortal man forever of the fear of the oppression, and the anguish of the responsibility, which suzerainty over human fate and destiny would have entailed on him and cursed him with.' " (363) The betrayal of trust is followed by the betrayal of love as he seduces and abandons the woman who is to bear the son whom he will send to his death some thirty years later.

Each of these betrayals of the individual and personal relationships appears, however, in the guise of contributing to a greater good. The death of the man at the desert outpost preserves the security of that outpost and, symbolically, of France itself. The abandonment of the woman is merely an extreme instance of that breaking of ties with home and family which is expected of any soldier called by his country. The execution of the Corporal does, as Gragnon points out, ensure the future safety of men in front lines by enforcing discipline and a disciplined army ensures in its turn the victory of France over her enemies. In each case the interests of the individual are subordinated to the interests of the group and the nation which is its ultimate expression. Each would seem to be, accordingly, an example of altruism and self-sacrifice. What prevents its being so is that no choice is involved; and to be a moral act, sacrifice must be willingly rendered, not exacted.

When people are denied choice and make no protest, the result is a closed society in which ethics are replaced by a code backed by both authority and tradition. As defender and savior of this society, the Marshal has almost unlimited power which is again challenged by the Corporal in his role as soldier. The quest for freedom is thus shown to possess more than a religious dimension; it involves a conflict between the individual and society and between personal values and the greater or social good which is presented in military terms. For the army with its rigid hierarchy, its countless rules and regulations, and its disregard for the individual as such is the very nadir of the type of society which Faulkner has explored in the plantation system of the ante-bellum South. Like the Old South, the army separates man from man by imposing its own categories on humanity. Indeed, its very identity is dependent upon maintaining the distinction between itself and the civilians. And since it is a hierarchy founded on authority, its preservation is contingent on maintaining a similar distinction between officers and men. The military categories of officers, men, and civilians constitute an equivalent to the South's classification based on an economy of plantation owners, slaves, and poor whites. In both cases, men find themselves in mutually exclusive groups, each with a particular code binding on its members and determining their behavior both within the group and with respect to other groups.

The creation of a military aristocracy, looking "at the anonymous denizens of the civilian world . . . with a sort of contempt as alien intruders, rightless, on simple sufferance," (10) is achieved by fostering that sense of alienation felt by the Runner, who finds that his rank bars him from all that confederation of fellowship which enables man to support the weight of war. Significantly, the Marshal, the Quartermaster General, Bidet, Lallemont, and Gragnon, all begin their army career by serving in the desert whose effect is to isolate them from mankind and to transform them into members of that " 'repudiated and homeless species about the earth who not only no longer belong to man, but even to earth itself.' " (327) This isolation is not only affirmed but established as a principle of conduct. Thus Gragnon claims that in order to lead them, a commander must be hated or at least feared by his troops. His assertion is but a step to Lallemont's enunciation of the doctrine of the superman. The latter's contemptuous view of the civilian and the common soldier as unreliable but necessary adjuncts to the hero is matched by Bidet's view of them as functioning machines to be kept in good working order and by the Marshal's conviction that they can always be controlled by their triumphant and ineradicable folly, their deathless passion for being led, mystified, and deceived.

In return for raising them above the base anonymity of mankind and giving them a more heroic world to live in, the army demands complete loyalty from its members. For this reason, the soldier ideally is an orphan, an individual like Gragnon, who has no record whatever of his parentage. Absence of family ties or even friends leaves him free to dedicate himself to the army with no conflicting loyalties of the kind that plague the young Airman who is forced to postpone his search for glory in order to placate an obstinate and tearful mother. For these orphans, the army recreates the rituals of family life. The army group becomes a fraternal organization, a brotherhood of heroes suffering the same experiences, moved by the same ideals, offering and receiving the same aid and encouragement. At their head is the Marshal, the surrogate father, source of power and authority, agent of reward and punishment, and defender of the motherland. Quite appropriately, the Marshal addresses each of his subordinates as "my child," irrespective of their age or their acquaintance with him. With these concepts the army can and does engage the unquestioning allegiance of its soldier-sons. Thus, the

German general can claim proudly that he is a soldier first, then a German, and that the uniform he wears is more important than any German or even any victory.

The pattern of exclusion and division evident in the army is repeated on a larger scale in the world of nations, each jealously guarding its identity and maintaining its exclusiveness. By its very essence, the state can exist only by contrast with other states, a contrast which finds its ultimate expression in conflict over those geographical boundaries which serve both to create and to preserve national identity and unity. Paradoxically, then, war which appears to be an instrument of destruction is in reality an instrument for preserving the *status quo*. This, in effect, is the lesson Lallemont teaches the naively nationalistic Gragnon: " 'The boche doesn't want to destroy us, any more than we would want, could afford, to destroy him. Cant you understand: either of us, without the other, couldn't exist?' " (28) If one nation were to destroy the national identity of another, it would, of necessity, lose its own. Wars, then, must result only in a rearrangment of elements which leaves the pattern itself unchanged.

Under these conditions war inevitably becomes a formal engagement or a national ritual. The formalism is stressed in the comparison of war to "an unfinished cricket or rugger match which started according to a set of mutually accepted rules formally and peaceably agreed on, and must finish by them." (79) There are rules, for starting, for conducting, and for terminating wars, rules which even specify which weapons may or may not be used. And because war is a national ritual, the soldier is transformed into a hero, killing into a sacred duty, and death into a glorious sacrifice. To this ritual young men are dedicated from the moment of birth and even "transported free of charge and even with pay, to die violently in places that even the map-makers and -dividers never saw." (80) Insisting on the physical aspects of war, the torn flesh and the agony of dying, rather than on its ritual significance is to be guilty of a lack of decorum so monstrous that it constitutes betrayal.

Since ritual demands the scrupulous observance of its forms, it precludes choice. When it is operative, there is a discipline enforced by authority and tradition. The young Airman is thus informed, somewhat testily, that his squadron is run by people especially appointed and even qualified for that task and that they together with the King's Regulations make it unnecessary for him to do any thinking. But even blind obedience is not enough since it must be linked with proper respect for procedure. The lieutenant who bypasses his immediate superior to inform Army Headquarters of the threatening mutiny is described ironically by the Marshal as " 'a blatant and unregenerate eccentric whose career very probably ended there also since he held the sanctity of his native soil above that of his divisional channels.' " (331) Obviously, procedure ceases to be a means of securing order and efficiency and becomes an end in itself.

Certainly Gragnon makes obedience and procedure into positive values in the observance of which he finds his integrity as a soldier, if not as a man. To begin with, he carries out, or at least attempts to carry out, an order that his experience tells him is not only doomed but intended to be a failure. Even that failure must be achieved by observing the rules and since his regiment breaks the rules while providing the failure, it must suffer the specified consequences. Stubbornly, he refuses all compromise, demanding the execution of every one of his men from each of his superiors and even more stubbornly insisting that his own record receive justice if not by court-martial then at least by the manner of his death. He refuses to let himself be glorified by the fraud of a bullet in the chest as a hero killed by the enemy while gallantly and recklessly leading his men into battle. By a last desperate wrench of his body, he succeeds in affirming his record and preserving his integrity which, strangely enough, is threatened not by the men who mutinied but by his superiors or rather by the very principles of obedience and procedure which he had venerated. For intent on fulfilling orders to the letter, his executioners plug the bullet hole in his back with wax and place another in the position specified by authority.

Even a soldier perfect in obedience as Gragnon is, might yet prove an inadequate warrior unless he is moved to a passionate acceptance of the ritual in which he is engaged. That can be achieved by offering glory as an incentive and the nation's need as a reason. Levine longs to go off to the wars in search of glory because there is no way in which it can be earned so splendidly. It is a heroic adventure, a chivalric tourney with all Europe for a field and an audience. And death is not destruction but merely a passport to immortality in "Valhalla's un-national halls" inhabited by "the un-national shades, Frenchman and German and Briton, conqueror and conquered." (89) There are no ene-mies intent on killing, only opponents, each providing the other with an occasion for displaying valor and attaining glory.

If Levine's romantic vision of a glorious war can be discounted as the product of youth and naïveté, his idealism manifested in his willingness to sacrifice himself for his country cannot be, for it is equally shared by all the citizens of any country. But such self-sacrifice is not a matter of choice; quite the contrary, it is expected and demanded by the nation. Altruism whose object is the abstraction, the nation or state, is the gesture of the citizen bound by his code, not of man freely expressing his moral nature. And when the nation or the state converts man into a citizen, it also succeeds in destroying or at least atrophying his moral sense. First of all, it is obvious that whatever authority the state as-sumes must be at the expense of the individual's freedom. War simply intensifies this situation, increasing the authority of the government and drastically decreasing the area in which the in-dividual is still permitted to exercise moral choice. The phrase "Render unto Chaulnesmont" recurs with manifold irony throughout A *Fable*. Secondly, the state not only appropriates certain of man's moral sentiments but alters them completely by enlisting them in the service of the nation. Love of land is trans-formed into patriotism, the feeling of kinship with neighbors into nationalism, and pride in local traditions and achievements into chauvinism. In other words, all these perfectly natural hu-man emotions are drawn to a central core, the nation, and formulated into a dogma of exclusion.

Implicit in the citizen's surrender of moral choice and re-sponsibility is the surrender of the right to moral judgment as well. It is the state which acts as the repository of truth and justice and as the final judge of right and wrong. Taking human life, forbidden by both religious and civil law, becomes a duty to the state which cannot be evaded without incurring legal and social punishment. Ironically, the refusal to kill during war re-sults in a procedure as formal and ritualistic as the act of murder in peace. There are specialists trained "to preside with all the impunity and authority of civilised usage over the formal orderly shooting of one set of men by another wearing the same uni-form, lest there be flaw or violation in the right." (136) This inversion of values is sanctioned by the danger to the state which is made to appear a danger also to the people. Such iden-tification of state and people is not, however, justified. Man and the motherland, the place of his birth and the soil which gives him sustenance, endure through all political changes. It is the state or the "Fatherland" which must preserve its identity and protect its authority by war. Significantly, "Fatherland" is used to refer to both France and England as well as Germany, despite the customary feminine gender of *la France, la patrie*, and Britannia. Bidet, as spokesman for authority, is thus quite right in saying, " 'It's no abrogation of a rule that will destroy us. It's less. The simple effacement from man's memory of a single word will be enough.' " (54) The word, of course, is "Fatherland."

Such destruction is far from likely. The whole complex of ideas and emotions which constitute a nation has been so long unquestioned that it has assumed a sacred quality, engaging the emotional allegiance of the people, channeling their thoughts and directing their actions, establishing its own rituals and glorying in its own traditions. It is little wonder, then, that the French regard the Corporal as a traitor to his country: in effect, he is precisely that since he places the value of man above that of the nation. In contrast, they understand and condone Gragnon's behavior even though they are its victims. His actions and their reactions are both predetermined, for they are all part of a single entity, the nation. Acquiescing to their own bereavement, they willingly submit to authority and surrender the regiment to its laws for the sake of those clichés which " 'carry the torch of man into that twilight where he shall be no more; these are his epitaphs: They shall not pass. My country right or wrong. Here is a spot which is forever England—' " (436)

That the power of the state remains unchallenged is accounted for by the firm belief that it corresponds to the needs and limitations of human nature. The Quartermaster General, for example, claims that the state is simply a collective expression of man's rapacity. Lallemont exults in the fact that some few men are born to lead and that others are forever doomed to be part of the inchoate mass that is shaped into a body of followers. War, according to Bidet, is an expression of man's inherent greed or, according to the Marshal, " 'a vice so long ingrained in man as to have become an honorable tenet of his behavior and the national altar for his love of bloodshed and glorious sacrifice.' " (344) Even the people are committed to this view, accepting war as "a fact or condition of nature, of physical laws." (125) Rapacity, inequality, and war are thus assumed to be natural conditions of existence and the state is regarded as the best possible means of establishing order and keeping some check over these destructive aspects of man's life.

By regaining for himself his free will and its attendant responsibility, the Corporal posits a threat to all mass control of human values and conduct and without denying man's capacity for greed, violence, and injustice, demonstrates his equal capacity for pity, compassion, and self-sacrifice. At first glance, the threat seems to be successfully countered: the Corporal is executed, the mutiny is quelled, and the *status quo* is re-established. But certain reverberations of the Corporal's action cannot be confined or suppressed. The mutiny compels the Marshal to take emergency measures which reveal the true nature of authority and of that complex structure of institutions and ideas which it supports. The meeting of the Allied generals with the German commander provides that moment of shock, found in almost all of Faulkner's novels, which drives various characters to re-examine themselves and their shibboleths. The Marshal himself, Bidet, and Lallemont feel no need for such a re-examination precisely because the meeting is no shock to them. There can be no disillusionment where there has been no illusion. Accordingly, all three take a kind of pride in facing facts and in dispensing with those beliefs by means of which the people are both deceived and controlled.

The case is obviously different with respect to men who suddenly discover the hollowness of values which they have accepted sincerely and in good faith. Gragnon, slowly and stubbornly, examines the course of events leading to his disgrace, testing each step of the way by army protocol and by the comments of Lallemont and Bidet. Having no frame of moral reference other than the army, he is finally compelled to reaffirm its values by insisting that his disgrace and failure be made evident in the manner of his death. Vulnerable by reason of his youth and his passionate commitment to the nation, Levine suffers the most complete form of disillusionment. At one stroke he is deprived of his ideals and, more important, of faith itself. Suicide is his despairing attempt to escape from a world in which everything seems false. The Quartermaster General cannot escape as Levine does, but neither can he follow Gragnon in affirming values which have been proven manifestly unworthy. His is the difficult task of continuing to live with his disillusionment and his sense of personal guilt. In varying degrees, Gragnon, Levine, and the Quartermaster General each make some effort at critical evaluation and moral judgment of their society; they are, however, still trapped within it, unable to make the bridge from knowledge to action and from criticism to re-creation.

It is the Corporal who, like Christ, reveals through his own life the way and the truth. In contrast to the Marshal, the temporal hero-savior, he is associated not with the city and the desert but with the fruitful land. And the land, as Faulkner's earlier novels insist, is the constant underlying the dissolving patterns, the arrangements and rearrangements of political structures, just as man is the constant underlying the changes of political history. With this background, the Corporal comes to France, willing and even eager to believe in and to serve her. He becomes a French citizen and, to repay that honor, a French soldier since "all France asked of him in return for that dignity and right and that security and independence was his willingness to defend it." (299) That he succeeds in becoming a loyal Frenchman and a courageous soldier is indicated by the medal he receives from his grateful adopted country. It is evident, then, that the Corporal does not come in the spirit of destruction, nor does he deny the value of the community and the responsibility of the individual to it. But he does insist that the responsibility must be for as well as to society, and that this involves the right to alter as well as the duty to preserve, the right to criticize as well as defend. History is not preordained, traditions are not sacred, systems and codes are not immutable. Whatever is made by man can also be altered by man; his moral responsibility consists in deciding what he is prepared to tolerate and what he is determined to alter. So long as individuals are moved by a desire for perfection, society serves as an accurate mirror of their growth and development and so long as they accept moral responsibility for it, it reflects their essential and unchanging character as men. When they cease to do so, they themselves become static reflections of a fixed social system within which they find their identity as citizens and as members of different groups and classes.

The Corporal refuses, however, to be an uncritical reflector of his society, its norms, and its values. Accordingly, his gesture of rebellion is at once a criticism of the existing society and an affirmation of man. Because that society is composed of interlocked and interdependent elements, disobedience on any level or at any point poses a threat to the whole complicated structure. The Corporal's refusal to attack thus initiates a most impressive series of reactions. Simply as disobedience, leaving aside for the moment the question of war and peace, it constitutes a challenge to authority and asserts the right of the individual to make his own decisions. Even though he has no voice in what he is to do, he can still assert his right to consent or disobey. This does not mean, of course, that disobedience is to be undertaken lightly and with impunity; the Corporal does in effect "Render unto Chaulnesmont" insofar as he makes no attempt to evade the disapproval and punishment which his action incurs. Any such evasion would separate decision from responsibility and hence would perpetuate the need for external controls, law, and discipline. The challenge to authority is also a challenge to the hierarchy. If each man asserts his moral right to choose, then the division of men into those who command and those who obey is rendered impossible. The Runner need no longer despair because his rank gives him " 'not only the power, with a whole militarised government to back [him] up, to tell vast herds of man what to do, but the impunitive right to shoot him with [his] own hand when he doesn't do it.' " (61–62) In recognizing their own moral nature, men also recognize their equality as moral beings.

In addition to defying authority and repudiating the hierarchical organization of men, the Corporal challenges the codes binding upon the citizen and the soldier. Refusal to kill other men even though they are Germans and designated enemies signals his declaration of the right to heed his own conscience and to make his own moral judgments. The national directive enjoining killing is weighed against God's commandment and found wanting. War is not a glorious ritual in which man finds glory but a horrifying physical reality of which he is the victim. The survival of the nation does not justify the destruction of its people. For man's meaning is not exhausted by his place in an organized society. As an individual he transcends all categories, as a man he transcends all societies. By his example, the Corporal conveys the fact that heroism need not consist of shouldering a gun and marching off to battle, that there is a moral as well as a physical courage, and that loyalty and self-sacrifice need not be linked with the nation and its ideologies. In the wake of his action, categories are nullified as Frenchmen and Germans leave their trenches to discover that " 'all we ever needed to do was just to say, Enough of this—us, not even the sergeants and corporals, but just us, all of us, Germans and Colonials and French-

men and all the other foreigners in the mud here, saying together: Enough.'" (68) Acting together out of faith in man,
men can change the world because it is their world to change.

In the temptation scenes of *A Fable* the opposition between
the Marshal and the Corporal assumes its final and perhaps most
compelling form. No longer father and son or commander and
soldier, they face each other as two individuals with totally different views of man. The Marshal articulates the nature of this
contrast: "'I champion of this mundane earth which, whether
I like it or not, is, and to which I did not ask to come . . . you
champion of an esoteric realm of man's baseless hopes and his
infinite capacity—no: passion—for unfact.'" (348) First of all,
the Marshal insists on his own knowledge of men, claiming
repeatedly, "'I dont fear man's capacities, I merely respect
them.'" (329) His own position proves both the extent of his
knowledge and his ability to use it for practical purposes. The
nature of his respect for man is suddenly clarified by his description of Polchek, the traitor, as a creature capable of speech,
movement, and above all, self-interest. Obviously it is man's
capacity for evil which he has probed. He points out to the Corporal that he has been betrayed by one of his men, deserted by
another, and repudiated by the people who clamor for his execution. These acts of betrayal, he suggests, have been, are, and
will be the essence of man's history. On this assumption he sets
up a false antithesis. By implying that his own view of man is
realistic, he suggests that the Corporal's must be a delusory and
naïve belief in the goodness of man which excludes recognition
of the reality of evil.

But the Corporal is far from naïve; from the beginning he had
foreseen the curses of the crowd and his own betrayal by his men.
His answer to the Marshal is to point to the other reality: the
ten men who have kept faith. In other words, he shares the
Reverend Sutterfield's conviction that "'evil is a part of man,
evil and sin and cowardice, the same as repentance and being
brave. You got to believe in all of them, or believe in none of
them. Believe that man is capable of all of them, or he aint capable of none.'" (203) Isolating either of these two aspects of
human nature leads inevitably to distortion. To see only the
good is to render oneself incapable of coping with the world of
men. But to see only evil is to perpetuate that evil by excluding
all possibility of change.

Swiftly the Marshal shifts ground from a false antithesis to an equally false identification of interests. He too professes faith in man and his ability to survive. If a man is destined to endure, then, of course, he has no need of being saved, no need of the sacrificial death which the Corporal is prepared to offer. The Marshal elaborates on the nature of that endurance in a passage that closely resembles part of Faulkner's Nobel Prize speech. Man " 'will survive . . . because he has that in him which will endure even beyond the ultimate worthless tideless rock freezing slowly in the last red and heatless sunset, because already the next star in the blue immensity of space will be already clamorous with the uproar of his debarkation, his puny and inexhaustible voice still talking, still planning.' " (354) The Corporal does not explain why he rejects this vision of man, but Faulkner himself does in the Nobel Prize speech: "I refuse to accept this. I believe that man will not merely endure: he will prevail. He is immortal, not because he alone among creatures has an inexhaustible voice but because he has a soul, a spirit capable of compassion and sacrifice and endurance." The Corporal is more interested in the nature of man's endurance and the form of his prevailing than in the fact of survival itself.

While the Marshal is concerned largely with expounding a view of man, the Priest explores, for the Corporal's benefit, the relationship between the individual and his society. According to his argument, the individual is ephemeral, inconstant, and unreliable; in contrast, the various institutions of an organized society are permanent, stable, and secure. It is therefore the task of the latter to provide a stable pattern, to provide " 'a morality of behavior inside which man could exercise his right and duty for free will and decision.' " (364) It is the church which saved Christ's oral teachings from being lost precisely by its transformation of a faith into a dogma. Similarly, it is the state which transforms man's moral instincts into a law which transcends the individual and which by limiting freedom saves it.

By accepting this "morality of behavior" with its limited form of free will, the individual eludes the terrible burden of responsibility. As the Priest points out, the Corporal's defiance of law involves others. This, in effect, constitutes the Priest's strongest argument: " 'Save that other life. Grant that the right of free will is in your own death. But your duty to choose is not yours. It's his. It's General Gragnon's death.' " (366) But the fear of implicating others by one's own actions and decisions leads ultimately to isolation and a negative goodness, a condition rightly rejected by the Corporal. At the same time his response to all the Priest's best points, " 'Tell him [the Marshal] that,' " suggests the flaw in this argument. Like the Marshal's view of man, it is incomplete rather than false. The relationship between the individual and his society must be reciprocal, each having equal right to judge the other.

In short, no matter what the level, personal, religious, or social, the relationship between the Marshal and the Corporal indicates the continuing necessity of protest. And this is always the task of the individual since the majority of men, concerned with safety and security, actively fear and distrust personal liberty. But there are the ten who accompany the Corporal into prison and who serve as witnesses to as well as symbols of faith and hope. To these ten might be added the old Quartermaster General, shaken by his loss of faith in the Marshal and appalled by his own guilt, weeping over the battered body of the Runner whose laughter is a triumphant affirmation of the spirit of resistance. Representing various nations and ranks, these men offer a composite picture of man becoming aware of his servitude, proclaiming his freedom and his humanity.

Paradoxically, protest is an affirmation rather than a negation of the social order. For protest is a moral act, and if each man realizes his moral nature and accepts his responsibility, or even if enough men do, the community as a whole discovers, of necessity, its essential character as a moral rather than an authoritarian organization. Only then does the relationship of father and son become one of love rather than force, fulfilling Marthe's vision of the Marshal and the Corporal: " 'You and he together to be one in the saving of France, he in his humble place and you in your high and matchless one and victory itself would be that day when at last you would see one another face to face.' " (299) This, however, is an ideal—nothing less than the establishment of the kingdom of heaven on earth—and as an ideal, it is always out of reach. In the meantime the conflict between society and the individual, authority and freedom, dogma and faith, is both inevitable and necessary, for it is by virtue of that conflict that the moral nature of both man and society is recognized. Hence, the resolution of the struggle between the Marshal and the Corporal on the personal level merely effects its continuance on the general level. The Marshal's victory is in reality a defeat, for the death of the Corporal is a triumphant affirmation of that principle which the Marshal had sought to destroy by tempting the Corporal to save his life.

At the conclusion of A *Fable* the two opposing forces of authority and freedom, explored through the complex relationship between the Corporal and the Marshal, appear once more, thus suggesting the continuance of the struggle despite the death of any of its protagonists. The Marshal's funeral conducted with full military, civilian, and religious honors seems to indicate the unqualified triumph of his ideas. But suddenly disturbing the universal sorrow of the mourners comes the indomitable voice of protest heard in the terrible laughter of the Runner who accuses the savior of France of having helped to " 'carry the torch of man into that twilight where he shall be no more.' " (436) And beneath the Arch of Triumph, "vast and serene and triumphal and enduring," (434) is the small flame burning above the grave of the unknown soldier. If the Corporal is indeed that soldier, then the flame becomes a symbol of the individual's love, faith, and freedom preserving itself in the very heart of that shrine dedicated to the army, the nation, and its heroes.

13: THE REALITY OF ROMANCE

The Reivers

In *The Reivers* Faulkner has created his enchanted land; it is Prospero's island compounded of the innocence of youth and the wisdom of old age, of dream, imagination, and fantasy, which are, nevertheless, firmly anchored in the reality of Jefferson and Yoknapatawpha County. It encompasses elemental good and elemental evil, but above all it is a world of infinite freedom and therefore of infinite possibility.

The enchantment is woven by Lucius Priest, an aging man who, like Prospero, regards the adventures of youth with amused detachment as well as compassionate understanding. For what he recollects is his own youthful self responding to the "brave new world" of Parsham, Tennessee, and passionately embarking on a venture that is at once painfully real and absurdly unreal. Thus the boy's innocence and the old man's wisdom serve to balance the wonder of discovery against the deeper note of mature reflection and comprehension. This complexity of tone is also related to the pattern of chivalric romance which shapes Lucius Priest's reminiscences—the departure, the perilous journey complete with fabulous adventures, and the triumphant return. As in *Don Quixote*, the journey is conducted in a naturalistically real world, and the result is rich and often very broad comedy; yet the parody of the chivalric romance is not permitted to destroy the shining thread of idealism which is its very essence. And it is this idealism that moves both the reader and the narrator as he evokes a vanished world preserved through memory, transformed by imagination, and contemplated with the serene judgment of old age.

Jefferson offers an appropriate point of departure for Lucius, Boon, and Ned, the three adventurers, since it represents a fixed social order, defined and buttressed by conventions, traditions, and habits. Each individual has and knows his place and each recognizes that authority which sets limits to his freedom. Thus Jefferson can yield comedy but not romance, eccentricity but not self-expression, tolerance but not freedom. The comedy arises out of a sudden disordering of familiar patterns, the validity of which is not itself challenged. Boss Priest's acquisition of a car initiates a series of comic surprises until the new rituals designed to cope with it become habitual themselves. For example, Miss Alison's ingenious contrivance for protecting backseat passengers from the Boss's chewing tobacco is accepted as a normal accessory of driving. Much more significant, however, is Ludus' "borrowing" of a team and wagon since it anticipates Boon and Lucius "borrowing" the automobile. In both cases the consequences verge on the improbable. But Ludus' adventure is confined to the social world, and the laughter it provokes lacks the dimension of wonder and discovery that accompanies it in the world of romance.

The absence of Boss Priest and Mr. Maury from Jefferson occasions the emergence of as strange a trio of knights-errant as has been witnessed since Don Quixote and Sancho Panza—an eleven-year-old boy, a simple-minded giant, and a shrewd Negro servant. There is, of course, no question of their desire to take advantage of this unexpected opportunity for adventuring; for those "dedicated to Virtue, offer in reward only cold and odorless and tasteless virtue: as compared not only to the bright rewards of sin and pleasure but to the ever watchful unflagging omniprescient skill —that incredible matchless capacity for invention and imagination—with which even the tottering footsteps of infancy are steadily and firmly guided into the primrose path." (52–53) Non-virtue offers freedom, unlimited possibilities of action and experience, and, above all, life grasped in its immediacy rather than through those rules and codes designed to encompass and control it.

But first Lucius, Boon, and Ned must prove their fitness for their venture into the fabulous world of non-virtue by undergoing the trials attendant upon separation from the ordinary life of Jefferson. For Ned this consists mainly of guessing at the intentions of the other two and suffering the discomfort of hiding under a tarpaulin for the first part of the trip. Boon is required to persuade Lucius and to control his own impatience which courts disaster since it leads him to a "clean shirt and collar and necktie and the shave in the middle of the day and all the rest of the give-away aura of travel, departure, separation, severance." (59) The trial is, however, most difficult for Lucius, who must overcome the handicaps of both his youth and his training. He must resist his desire to "return, relinquish, be secure"; (66) he must ignore his own ingrained rules of conduct by defying Aunt Callie and by lying to Uncle Ike and Uncle Zack; and finally he must risk all the consequences of helping Boon "borrow" the car.

Even with Jefferson behind them, the period of testing is not complete. The passage into the world of romance is marked by three preliminary adventures, each offering an obstacle to further advances and hence, implicitly, a temptation to relinquish the quest. The first, the mudhole of Hurricane Creek, offers a simple, physical challenge to which Boon is more than equal. With one Herculean effort, he lifts the automobile bodily and shoots it forward onto dry ground by main strength. The second, the Iron Bridge, seems much more promising as adventure since it is associated with "an ancestryless giant calling himself Ballenbaugh" (73) who sweeps into his lair not only horses and cattle but stray federal revenue agents. But the giant has been replaced by a more subtle temptress, his daughter Miss Ballenbaugh. For the sake of her cooking, hunters and fishermen have given up their manly pursuits, and Lucius is tempted to do the same. Since Boon, however, is intent on satisfying a different kind of appetite when he arrives in Memphis, the three knights resume their journey.

It is, then, the third adventure at Hell Creek bottom that provides the greatest test of their strength, will, and determination. For here the natural and the supernatural seem to combine to frustrate them. The mudhole assumes all the mysterious terror and implacability of Scylla and Charybdis, especially since there is no way of avoiding it: "Go one way and you'd wind up in Alabama; go the other way and you'll fall off in the Mississippi River." (80) Boon can exert the effort of a demon, a titan, without making headway. It is only when the exacted tribute of six dollars is paid that they are permitted to pass the final obstacle to their quest: "Because the die was indeed cast now; we looked not back to remorse or regret or might-have-been; if we crossed Rubicon when we crossed the Iron Bridge into another county,

when we conquered Hell Creek we locked the portcullis and set
the bridge on fire." (93) At the same time, this experience reveals the pervasive comic note of the novel, for here the archetypal trial involves only money, not human life.

Behind that locked portcullis is the real world defined as the
familiar and the predictable; before them is a world in which the
laws of nature are intermittently suspended to accommodate the
fabulous and the magical. For example, Miss Reba, a perfectly
respectable madam, is confronted with one child who has a pen-
chant for drinking beer and stealing gold teeth and another who
drives her girls "into poverty and respectability." (209) Even
stranger, "a whore, a pullman conductor and a Mississippi swamp
rat the size of a water tank leading a race horse through Memphis at midnight Sunday night" (136) reach the station and load
the horse into a boxcar without being stopped. And if all this is
accepted or at least entertained, there is clearly no reason to balk
at a sardine-loving race horse who prefers companionship to competition or at Ned's ingenious scheme "to use the horse to win
the automobile back from the man that has already give [him]
the horse for it." (119) By some sleight of hand worthy of Ned
himself, reason is disarmed and the incredible becomes plausible.

This thin edge of plausibility is maintained by permitting the
real and the unreal to merge. It constitutes a way of defining the
function of illusion, one of whose forms is the tendency to that
idealization which permeates the story. Thus the apparently
magical is given some simple explanation. Certainly there is no
mystery, only mechanical ingenuity, in starting the car without
an ignition key and removing it from Miss Reba's house. The
whip that spurs Lightning into the boxcar is after all only a boy's
vocal trick. And Ned's "preliminary incantation or ritual of rub-
bing Lightning's muzzle" (296) is reduced to a tin of sardines.
Conversely, however, the real frequently becomes the magical.
Lucius wears a right-footed sock on his hand both to protect his
cut and to ensure luck since, according to Ned, a left-footed sock
(however one goes about identifying it) is bad luck if worn
alone. Minnie, an attractive woman to begin with, becomes irresistible by virtue of her gold tooth. And Butch's badge is, of
course, his talisman, the source of his strength and his power.

What is true of the plot is also true of the characters. Their
basic reality is altered by their assuming one of the three roles
typical of romance. The result is predictably hilarious because of
the disparity between their social definition or nature and the

roles they embrace. Thus Everbe and Minnie are both maidens in distress no matter how bizarre the cause of their distress may be. The three adventurers do indeed undertake to protect the virtue of a prostitute and to recover the gold tooth of a Negro maid. Bobo, another orphan like Everbe, is also trapped, about to see "the end of everything—job, liberty, all" (290) and unable to extricate himself without their help so providentially offered by Ned. Extending the element of romance, their persecutors, Otis, Butch, and Bobo's anonymous creditor, are all referred to as demons. Finally, when they are rescued from these demons, the spell of evil is broken. Minnie recovers her beauty, Everbe her virtue, and Bobo his dependability as a servant.

However much the villains differ, they are alike in being tyrants and bullies. As in *The Tempest*, the antagonists are those who would seize power to exercise it brutally and selfishly. They are oppressors not specifically of the virtuous but certainly of the weak. Moreover, by virtue of their role, they can neither be placated nor reformed. Bobo, for example, finds that the fifteen-dollar tribute he pays to his "demon" merely increases the demands. Indifferent to her kindness and generosity, Otis exacts from Everbe five cents a day, soon to be raised to ten, for keeping silent about her name. Butch, of course, is not only implacable but successful in his designs on Everbe. Significantly, the only real punishment meted out to these ogres is that of being humiliated and deprived of their prize.

The role of the remaining characters is to assist the heroes and ensure their triumph. As Lucius points out: "Who serves Virtue works alone, unaided, in a chilly vacuum of reserved judgment; where, pledge yourself to Non-virtue and the whole countryside boils with volunteers to help you." (143) Miss Reba offers entertainment at her palace of pleasure to the road-weary travellers as well as opportunity for further adventure. For suddenly Lucius finds himself fighting Otis and defending Everbe from Boon's advances. But most important, she finances the trip to Parsham, making the final adventure possible. In short, the dominant mode of contributing to the heroes' triumph is through a bizarre series of metamorphic acts of transformation which intensify the growing recognition that reality is both dubious and fluid.

But Miss Reba's money would be to no avail without other help. It is Everbe who knows Sam, once described as an "errant pullman conductor," (252) though he is only a simple flagman

with an uncle who is division superintendent. It is Sam who performs the magical act of spiriting a horse from Memphis to Parsham, of commandeering box cars, and of stopping trains at
unscheduled places. And it is Uncle Parsham who provides a
basis of operation for Ned as well as princely hospitality, since it
includes not only food and rest but the services of his son, Lycurgus, as squire. Finally, Mr. Poleymus, the constable, who interrupted the race to put everyone but Lucius into whatever make-
shift dungeons he could contrive, turns into their friend and
protector. He frees Ned, rips the badge off Butch, offers a job to
Everbe, and places a two-dollar bet on Lightning.

As Lucius, Boon, and Ned assume their role as knights, the
customary social definition of their relationship is soon forgotten.
As knights they are peers, and indeed all three of them can claim
to be of noble birth. Lucius himself belongs to the royal family
of McCaslin-Edmonds-Priest and his status is never questioned.
But Ned can claim a more direct descent, never letting the Priests
forget that he "was an actual grandson to the old time-honored
Lancaster where we moiling Edmondses and Priests . . . were
mere diminishing connections and hangers-on." (31) Similarly,
Boon, "depending on the depth of his cups, . . . would declare
himself to be at least ninety-nine one-hundredths Chickasaw and
in fact a lineal royal descendant of old Issetibbeha himself." (19)
And on those occasions when he denies having any Indian blood,
it is still possible to fall back on the mystery involving his birth
and lineage, which in itself is sufficient to link him to the hero of
romance.

It is, then, partly on the basis of their character and ability that
a new relationship is formed. Boon is conceded any task which
requires strength and courage, leaving all intellectual exercise to
Ned and all moral assessment to Lucius. Thus the distinguishing
characteristics of each determine the level of his quest: romantic
and physical in Boon Hogganbeck who becomes the knight as
warrior; inventive and intellectual in Ned McCaslin who is the
knight as leader; and moral and spiritual in Lucius Priest who is
the knight as exemplar. At the same time, this new relationship is
also partly a result of the narrator's perspective. In recounting a
tale of his earlier life, the narrator dramatizes for us the way in
which past events, when recalled, tend to group themselves into
literary patterns. The choice of which pattern (in this case, romance) should be employed is determined by the narrator's pre-

cise relationship to his own present and to his community. It is something of this order that Faulkner conveys through subtitling the novel "A Reminiscence."

The fact that the hero is threefold suggests that each is a knight *manqué*, at least in relation to the original medieval pattern of romance. Yet it is the distinctive kind of lack inherent in each of the trio that determines the novel's comic form and the nature of the ideal in the modern world. Thus, though Boon does possess certain knightly qualities, the fact that he lacks a chivalric code is both painfully and humorously apparent. Lucius describes him as "tough, faithful, brave and completely unreliable; he was six feet four inches tall and weighed two hundred and forty pounds and had the mentality of a child." (19) It is therefore not surprising that his concept of adventure is totally unimaginative. He is willing to risk Mr. Maury's anger, steal or at least borrow the Boss's automobile, and involve an eleven-year-old boy in his scheme apparently for the excitement of driving from Jefferson to Memphis. To achieve this goal, he performs marvellous feats of strength. Once in Memphis, his goal is equally simple and direct—Miss Reba's house and one of her girls, preferably Miss Corrie with whom he has already conducted business if not shared adventures.

But in the world of romance, the knight must win his lady not by offering money but by overcoming all obstacles and defeating all challengers. In effect, he must prove his own worthiness. Initially, Boon is convinced that Miss Corrie regards him with favor and that the only obstacles are the practical details of disposing of Otis and getting Lucius settled for the night. With all that attended to, however, he is still repulsed, for Miss Corrie has suddenly stopped being "in the paid business of belonging to [him] exclusive the minute she sets her foot where [he's] at." (197) The evil of the past has been dispelled by the magic of a young boy's faith and his beautiful but absurd code which makes him treat a whore like a lady and defend her honor with his own blood. Miss Corrie, the prostitute, is transformed into the chaste and even virginal Everbe Corinthia.

Boon's consequent frustration is not only intense but varied. He cannot buy her because she has "reformed from the temptation business." (280) He cannot seduce her because she is protected by Lucius and the promise she made. Furthermore, he cannot even fight it out with his rivals, for, humorously, he is thwarted equally by the goodness of one and the evil of the other.

Sam is not only necessary to their joint venture, but his behavior is irreproachable. Preoccupied with the adventure of the horse race, he is simply too busy to make those advances which would justify Boon's suspicions and jealousy. Thus the latter finds himself engaged in rivalry without a rival. In contrast, Butch Lovemaiden glories in his role of competitor or indeed victor. Convinced in advance of his own success, he refuses to recognize Boon as a rival. For the sake of the group, Boon must endure Butch's malicious taunts and witness his lustful stalking of the helpless Everbe Corinthia.

Yet frustration is a necessary prelude to Boon's growth since it forces him into "restraining himself who never before had restrained himself from anything." (176) At the same time, Butch's predatory lust offers Boon a mirror image of his own, providing he recognizes it. He does so when Everbe sacrifices her new-found virtue for her three knights, effecting the release of Ned and the return of Lightning. Paradoxically, Butch's success terminates the rivalry for physical possession of Everbe and frees Boon to perceive the true nature of his feelings. He can blacken Everbe's eye for her lapse from purity, but he also repeats Lucius' quixotic gesture by fighting Butch. In doing so, he demonstrates that he has finally learned his own meaning of "chivalry: to shield a woman, even a whore, from one of the predators who debase police badges by using them as immunity to prey on her helpless kind." (176) He has proved himself the equal of Lucius in chivalry if not elegance of speech: "God damn it . . . if you can go bare-handed against a knife defending her, why the hell cant I marry her? Aint I as good as you are, even if I aint eleven years old?" (299)

Through love, one of the eternal verities common to both the real and the fairy worlds, Boon is changed from an unrestrained, lustful male to a knight in shining armor. He claims Everbe Corinthia not because of his conquest of others but because he has conquered himself. He is willing to devote whatever he is or has become to her love and service. In so doing he gains certain magical powers; for if Lucius could make Everbe a virtuous woman, Boon can transform her into a wife, and that transformation which signals the conventional happy ending is accepted not only by the "reivers" but by Jefferson as well.

While Boon is discovering the proper object of his quest, Ned McCaslin finds an adventure of his own. What drives him, however, is not love but a burning desire to spread the glory of his

name and deeds. His weapons are simply his own native shrewdness, his willingness to take risks, and his incredible perseverance.
It is almost as if he welcomes each new obstacle for the sheer
pleasure of overcoming it and to give further magnitude to his
triumph.

Dedicated to his pursuit of fame, Ned treats other adventures
as distractions or problems to be coped with. Thus he is a squire
of ladies or, as Minnie defines it, "nature-minded." (134) He is
unfailingly gallant whether at Miss Ballenbaugh's or in the
kitchen of the Parsham hotel. But not even Minnie, "a high
priestess worth dying for," (117) can engross his full attention.
Sexual conquest is simply a pleasant diversion which cannot be
permitted to interfere with his quest for glory.

Indeed, Ned subordinates everything and everyone to the one
end. When Otis reveals his cowardice, Lucius is pressed into
service as a jockey despite his cut hand and his growing fatigue.
Boon's jealousy is ignored because Sam's help is needed. Everbe's
sacrifice is accepted because, as Ned sees it, it was the only thing
she could do. It is important to notice that all of this activity
and all of the sacrifices are made primarily for the sake of running
the race and only secondarily for rescuing a victim. Clearly Bobo
could have been saved in a less spectacular fashion. Moreover,
Ned's own retrospective comment is instructive: if he had lost
the race, "That would a been Bobo's lookout. . . . It wasn't me
advised him to give up Mississippi cotton farming and take Memphis frolicking and gambling for a living in place of it." (293)

If the true knight is simply a man of tender sentiments, a protector of the weak, a defender of virtue, then Ned must give up
his claims to such a title. Certainly he is not blind to moral or
spiritual values, but he does subordinate them to the single objective of winning the race. For that alone will vindicate his
actions and justify the demands he has made of others. It will
give meaning to the time during which he "had carried the load
alone, held back the flood, shored up the crumbling with whatever tools he could reach . . . until they broke in his hand."
(304) Yet this very emphasis on the race defines Ned's role as a
knight. He is the doer of glorious deeds, achieving what is essentially a personal triumph. He is the knight-as-leader who subordinates all to the single-minded realization of one overriding purpose.

It is a triumph that will transform Ned's life in Jefferson; by
making him the main figure in a legend it demonstrates far be-

yond reasonable doubt his own superiority. Amusingly and yet in keeping with a sense of his role as leader, he lets the lesser folk do the work. For example, even Everbe and Lucius help to move the ramp into place while Ned deliberately waits to perform the magic ritual that will make Lightning leap into the car. Indeed he has a small army of helpers busily engaged in various minor tasks while he plans the strategy that will culminate in his own brief but dramatic appearance behind the finishing line at the race track.

It is, however, in his handling of individuals that Ned proves himself to be without peer. Through his ironic responses he makes Butch Lovemaiden seem not only stupid but foolish. With one quiet, dignified remark—"There's somewhere the Law stops and just people starts" (243)—he makes Mr. Poleymus concede that personal relationships take precedence over social or racial ones. But his headiest triumph comes in dealing with the gentlemen—Mr. Van Tosch and Mr. Maury Priest. For it is Ned who makes the decision relieving Mr. Maury of Lightning, "Because what in the world would we do with him [the horse], supposing they was to quit making them stinking little fishes?" (298) He can even afford to disguise his superiority by refusing to repay Mr. Maury since such repayment would prove that the latter did not have sense enough to bet on the right horse. Thus, despite his cumulative betting, he is quite truthful when he tells Ned that "we never done it for money." (282) What is important is the victory won on the very verge of defeat and the creation of a legend preserving his name and his fabulous deeds throughout time.

Unlike Ned the leader and Boon the warrior, Lucius Priest is the knight as moral exemplar, the individual who is pure of heart, noble in thought, courageous in deed. High principles are part of his tradition, part of "that inviolable and inescapable rectitude concomitant with the name [he] bore, patterned on the knightly shapes of my male ancestors as bequeathed—nay, compelled—to [him] by [his] father's word-of-mouth, further bolstered and made vulnerable to shame by [his] mother's doting conviction." (50-51) Accordingly, in him the code of ethics and the code of manners are one and the same. Not stealing, not referring to people by their race or religion, not breaking promises is as much a matter of inner compulsion as outward conformity. Hence the pathetic absurdity of Everbe's hope that Otis can become like Lucius simply by observing and imitating his manners, including the courtly gesture that Ned describes as to "drug his foot." (100)

Yet because he is only eleven years old, Lucius' adventure is almost purely educative. He returns with no rescued maidens to his credit. But in a very real sense, without him neither Everbe nor Bobo would have been saved. Everbe informs him: "I've had people—drunks—fighting over me, but you're the first one ever fought for me." (159) By fighting for her, Lucius makes her worth fighting for; by defending her honor, he makes it a reality. He does so by committing her to an ideal of herself through seeing it objectified in his behavior. The possibility inherent in fantasy and idealization is replaced by the actuality of observation. It is, then, her responsibility to make sure that his action becomes more than a quixotic gesture, that her conduct be such as to vindicate his faith. Similarly, Ned's scheme to rescue Bobo can only be realized through Lucius. He is called upon for courage, endurance, skill, but above all belief, since "if the successful outcome of the race this afternoon wasn't really the pivot; if Lightning and I were not the last desperate barrier between Boon and Ned and Grandfather's anger, even if not his police, . . . then all of us were engaged in a make-believe not too different from a boys' game of cops and robbers." (229–230)

Without Lucius, the Memphis-Parsham journey could not rise above the trivial and absurd. For Lucius is the true Don Quixote figure spurred by his idealism to recreate the world nearer to the heart's desire. Because of him we are forced to match experience against preconception, the essential against the incremental, the indestructible golden age of innocence against the recalcitrance and skepticism of the iron age. In the very impracticality of his childish code—defending prostitutes and racing stolen horses—one discovers its ultimate value and reality.

Accordingly, Lucius makes us realize that there is no neat dividing line between the ideal and the real or the desirable and the practical. Everbe is both a prostitute and a virgin, Boon a lustful lover and a tender husband, Ned a Negro servant and a leader of men. People are not only what they have been but what they are capable of becoming. And the agent that transforms them or, perhaps more accurately, recovers their essence is faith. In a sense, the world becomes what the individual has either believed or wished it to be, providing he has the courage to act out of his convictions.

The fact that Lucius has managed to influence or change the world he found means that he has outgrown his eleven years.

A difference must have been made: "if all that had changed nothing, was the same as if it had never been—nothing smaller or larger or older or wiser or more pitying—then something had been wasted, thrown away, spent for nothing." (300) What would have been wasted is an individual's dreams, his capacity to aspire, to be a little better than even he expects or hopes. Mr. Maury attempts to judge his son's actions conventionally and finds himself checkmated; as Lucius recognizes, "if after all the lying and deceiving and disobeying and conniving I had done, all he could do about it was to whip me, then Father was not good enough for me. And if all that I had done was balanced by no more than that shaving strop, then both of us were debased." (301) It is Boss Priest who, with the wisdom of old age, breaks the impasse by realizing that Lucius' childish prank demonstrates not only disobedience and irresponsibility but courage, fidelity, and responsibility. Thus Lucius too has undergone a transformation during his adventure as he passes from conventional virtue to non-virtue to the ideal virtue grounded in the self.

With the qualities of their adventures in mind, it is possible to comment on the reentry of the three heroes into the normal, non-heroic world of Jefferson. Boon brings with him a concrete prize: Everbe Corinthia is the reward for his courage and strength and love. Ned has the satisfaction of knowing that he has established a legend; using whatever tools were at his disposal, meeting every obstacle, and countering every opponent, he has proven himself the leader. Lucius wins applause for his victory, but more important, he receives from Boss Priest the accolade of responsibility for his own moral nature.

This triumphant reentry into an established society serves to unite the world of romance and reality. And in his reminiscences, the aging Lucius seems fully aware of the fusion. Thereby he establishes the dominant tone of *The Reivers*. It is a blending of innocence and experience and of acceptance and wonder. But above all, it offers a heightened, poetic awareness of the beauty of normal humanity, simultaneously splendid and absurd but always worthy of man's faith. It is a tribute to Faulkner as well as *The Reivers* that in this, his last book, he should have created his "brave new world" by describing man not tragically, satirically, or comically but simply lovingly.

PART TWO

THE GRAND PATTERN

14: TRUTH, LEGEND, AND FACT

In addition to his specifically Southern themes, Faulkner has explored in detail the instinctual, emotional, and mental behavior of man. Throughout his novels he reveals an urgent preoccupation—shared by many of his characters—with the problems of perception, language, and time, all of which constitute modes of apprehending and ordering experience. It is precisely this preoccupation which makes Faulkner more than a regional novelist meticulously delineating the topography and recounting the history of one segment of America. For even as he brilliantly renders the particulars of place and time, he manifests his interest in the permanent and unchanging aspects of human nature. As early as *Mosquitoes* one of his characters establishes that principle which is central to all Faulkner's subsequent novels: " 'Life everywhere is the same, you know. Manners of living it may be different . . . but man's old compulsions, duty and inclination: the axis and the circumference of his squirrel cage, they do not change. Details don't matter, details only entertain us.' " (243)

This vision of man as related to both the particular and the universal, to time and eternity, underlies Faulkner's examination of perception, truth, and reality. Every man is fixed at birth by the specific co-ordinates of time and space, through which he comes to share in the history of his people and the geography of his land. History itself is a record of events and changes in the life of the individual, of society, and of the very land as the wilderness slowly retreats, as cotton and tobacco replace corn, as the scars of the Civil War are annealed. But beneath such surface changes the land nevertheless preserves its own identity, maintaining its own rhythms through the seasonal cycle of life and death, growth and decay. Similarly, human nature provides the unchanging constant in the evolution and dissolution of social and economic forms. In one sense, then, time and place merely provide the setting for the drama of mankind; but at the same time, those individuals who contribute profoundly to the panorama of history find their hearts—the permanent and unchanging aspect of human nature—continually revivified by the primordial land with which they are intimately related as a result of deep and abiding connections with a specific place.

Obviously neither the particular nor the universal can be slighted without a consequent dislocation of moral vision. While the mind concerns itself with the various possible arrangements of purely temporal phenomena, the heart must grasp the permanence and the reality behind them. For the province of the mind is knowledge, while that of the heart, as so many of Faulkner's characters reiterate, is a truth which transcends even as it is manifested in the particular. Such truth is simple and universal, and it carries its own immediate conviction, bypassing reason, logic, or verification. Moreover, it is the source of all truly humane and ethical conduct, based on an intuitive understanding of the harmony between the human and the natural, the temporal and the timeless. Though only a few, like Dilsey, Isaac McCaslin, or the French Corporal, both recognize and attempt to live by this truth, yet it does provide the touchstone against which are tested all the partial truths with which men delude themselves.

These partial truths are relative to the mind of the observer who simultaneously observes, remembers, interprets, and modifies the object of his awareness. His interpretation is in turn shaped by his personality, his past experiences, and the patterns of thought unconsciously absorbed from the various groups of which he is a part. The result is a multiplication of partial truths —personal, social, institutional, historical—ranging all the way from private conviction to public dogma. Their truncated nature is indicated by their tendency to substitute rigidity and opposition to change for universality, logical coherence for organic unity, and either intellectual conviction or authority for immediate recognition of truth. Inevitably man is trapped in a world created by his own mind, alienated from nature and the land, and unable to readjust himself and his thinking to reality.

Clearly the greatest barrier to his recognition of truth as experiential rather than metaphysical is his own passion for categorical solutions which seem to offer an end to the perplexities imposed by the problematic character of existence. Longing both to know and to be free of the burden of learning, he frequently resorts to short cuts to the truth. Facts are appealed to as undeniable, while their limitations as media for conveying truth are ignored. History becomes the same touchstone projected into the past so that knowledge may be extended and a greater authority invoked. And when facts and history lack the material for ineluctability, legend is sought as a means of completing the search for truth. Where these valid approaches to the truth of man fail is in the user's oversimplification and confusion of their modal values. Fact, history, and legend are regarded as synonymous with the universal truth prized by Faulkner, whereas in reality they are but limited modes of commenting on it, modes which when employed as self-sufficient and mutually exclusive lead to human disaster by encouraging distorted and insensitive attitudes.

From the moment of his birth, man is confused in his search for truth by his reliance on his senses and his reason, both of which tend to deal with the more purely temporal manifestations of the world. As part of the natural world of occurrence, events present him with a barrage of sensations and impressions. Caught up in a welter of physical and mental stimuli, he finds himself in the position of Mrs. Hines in *Light in August*, bewildered by her experience and unable to make sense of it: " 'It was all coming down on her too fast. There was too much reality that her hands and eyes could not deny, and too much that must be taken for granted that her hands and eyes could not prove; too much of the inexplicable that hands and eyes were asked too suddenly to accept and believe without proof.' " (390–91) Too much is happening for any clear-cut, much less neatly articulated, impression or reaction to be possible. Hence Faulkner's emphasis on those frozen moments of "horror," "outrage," or "amazement" with which his characters greet a new experience.

It is man who imposes an order on sense data and shapes the chaotic world into an intelligible form. Exercising his reason, he assimilates events by translating them into facts, massive, solid, and immutable, impervious to time because they have been lifted out of time. But he can do this only after the event has receded into the past, for the passage of time alone provides him with the necessary mental distance. The value of such facts is entirely pragmatic. They have to be "usable" as part of a total pattern if they are to be accepted as facts, and invariably there are degrees of usability. Some facts are automatically accepted by all people, some are entirely unacceptable, but the majority are accepted by at least some individuals. In the first case, we have public facts, in the last, private conviction. Clearly, then, facts do not exist; they are created by the reasoning mind which interprets what it sees and hears, and on this basis deduces other facts, the accuracy of which frequently cannot be tested. In other words, events are a part of immediate experience while facts are related to the world of thought or language. Since immediate verification is impossible, for all practical purposes facts are determined by their ability to compel belief and initiate action. No one questions, for example, that a man named Thomas Sutpen rode into Jefferson one day, that he created an estate out of the wilderness and married a woman named Ellen Coldfield who bore him two children. From this point, the three narrators of *Absalom, Absalom!* go on to select or, if need be, invent those facts which fit their preconceptions. Obviously both the selection and the arrangements of facts depend to a large extent on the personality of the narrator as influenced by his age, his experience, and his society. Conversely, in *Pylon* the Reporter presents a number of conflicting facts about the pilots in the hope that if they cancel out or at least modify each other, something of the real truth might emerge.

It is not only in reconstructing a story of the past that this process of subjective interpretation is evident. Each new event can only be ordered and made comprehensible in terms of the individual's present beliefs and past experience. Certainly the varying attitudes to Donald Mahon's scar in *Soldiers' Pay* depend on whether or not the characters have themselves been subjected to the violence of war. Nor is Joe Christmas able to comprehend what he is seeing for the first time at the restaurant: " 'I know that there is something about it beside food, eating. But I dont know what. And I never will know.' " (153) Perhaps even more striking is the young Thomas Sutpen trying to translate his rebuff at the manor house into something he can comprehend, " 'seeking among what little he had to call experience for something to measure it by.' " (233) He does manage to fit this new fact into his thinking, but only by making certain basic and far-reaching changes in his habits of reacting to and assessing events.

And having done so, he finds that this new fact provides a vantage point for the re-evaluation of his whole past, as if he were "rushing back through those two years and seeing a dozen things that had happened and he hadn't even seen them before." (230) The relation between memory and perception is clearly indicated. As the individual is changed by his experience, his interpretation of remembered events or facts also changes, and this in turn modifies his view of the present.

When there is substantial agreement about a number of related facts, the result is a pattern of response and thought which encompasses and transcends the individual. Such patterns, having all the authority of dogma and all the prestige of tradition, possess a disastrous tendency to absolve men of the responsibility for grappling with and assimilating experience. Logic, ethics, economics, theology—all are systems by means of which society and the individual order and interpret their experience. They are, of course, necessary if society is to have continuity and if the past is to survive into the present, but they must continually be re-examined so that they do not destroy the life they are meant to order. For if the individual and the society of which he is a part forget the intellectual and moral limitations of the conscious mind, they risk confusing reality with an intellectual pattern and truth with dogma.

The collective mind of the community tends to cling to the old, familiar patterns of thought and action and to resist innovation or change. As in the case of the individual, there is no comprehension of or reaction to an event until it has been translated into a fact which can be measured against past experience or fitted into some habitual system of interpretation. Indeed, it is a complex of such systems (Calvinism, racial purity and white superiority, Southern provincialism and insularity, Civil War chauvinism) and their interrelations which in effect constitutes the communal mind and thought of the South. As *Light in August* makes clear, society lives and thinks in terms of an amalgam of dogmas because varying levels and groups in the community embrace various aspects of various systems and with various degrees of intensity. Unable to understand or deal with Gail Hightower, the people of Jefferson first speculate and then assert that he is an "unnatural" husband. The moment this is assessed as fact the Ku Klux Klan and Jefferson are able to take appropriate actions. Again, the crowd watching Miss Burden's burning house has its bewilderment and uneasiness transformed into familiar action by Brown who points out all the elements of the Negro-sex-crime pattern. Such subtle communal pressures are forever forcing individuals to assume social masks which depersonalize both their natures and their words. Their language takes on the vocabulary, tone, and even rhythm of a catechism, a catechism of society. Against a background of conflicting emotions, they rehearse a litany founded on fear, insecurity, and hate; ordered by oversimplification; and invoked by mass hysteria.

Whenever a habitual interpretation of and response to events assumes control, a quality of play-acting makes its appearance, indicating an absence of concern with either truth or reality. The lynching of Joe Christmas is simply one more rehearsal of a drama in which the action and the dialogue are invested with the prestige of a long tradition. The formal pattern of this drama has its own coherence and carries its own style of conviction. Thus the innocence of Lucas Beauchamp in *Intruder in the Dust* or the guilt of Joe Christmas in *Light in August* are equally irrelevant to the society seeking to judge them. Hence the peculiar helplessness and foreknowledge of such characters as Joe Christmas and Lee Goodwin of *Sanctuary*, both branded as murderers. One is guilty and the other innocent, but once they have been cast in the role of guilt, they cannot step out of that character; society, which is the audience as well as a participant in the drama, will not permit it. It is only rarely that a Byron Bunch or a Horace Benbow recognizes that there is an individual human being behind the actor's mask and that such type-casting perverts truth, justice, and humanity. Even more rare is the occasion when the play is interrupted midway because a stubborn Chick Mallison listens to truth instead of logic. Usually the formal pattern is too strong to be so disrupted, even by reason.

It is the aggregate of these formalized patterns of response that gives the communal mind its social continuity through history and its perspective on experience. Unfortunately, however, it preserves both the good and the bad, the meaningful and the destructive rituals of the past. This whole burden of fossilized traditions and rigid formulae descends on the individual, smothering any spontaneous response to experience. Religious instinct is forced into the Calvinistic credo in the name of which Ruby Lamar's child is threatened with damnation, Joe Christmas is persecuted by McEachern and Hines, and the Negro is condemned to eternal servitude by such men as Wash Jones and Joanna Burden's father. Similarly, ethical conduct becomes a matter of unswerving adherence to certain forms of behavior. Jackson, described in *The Sound and the Fury*, for example, asserts not the reality of his wife's honor or chastity "but the principle that honor must be defended whether it was or not because defended it was whether or not." (4) A concern with propriety thus replaces any genuine concern with decisively ethical actions. Narcissa Sartoris and the ladies of Jefferson who drive Ruby out of the hotel are simply acting in conformity with their moral and social code which blinds them to the true ethical significance of their action. Others, like the fanatics, Rosa Coldfield, McEachern, and Doc Hines, are moral cripples who have confused a system of belief with experiential reality. In each of these cases, the individual takes his own habit of thought for granted and identifies his own particular bias with truth. Nor is this identification ever challenged since no experience is permitted to make its own distinctive impression. Instead its unique character is obscured by its being automatically assimilated to and subsumed under some general concept or category.

Similarly, when an individual translates a personal ideal into a formula or a pattern of behavior, he falsifies experience and substitutes private conviction for truth. In effect, he ceases to cope with experience and the crude data of existence. He confronts instead the illusions of consciousness which, whether they appear in the guise of dreams, reiterated legends, or rational convictions, steadily entice him further and further into a house of mirrors. Hightower, Quentin Compson, and young Bayard Sartoris, all identify eternal human values with a specific period of history and thereby replace reality with outmoded gestures. All three regard their fictions and their designs as a kind of revealed truth which abrogates the necessity of continual self-criticism, re-evaluation, and education. Each finds in his ideal world a superior reality insofar as it resolves the conflict and uncertainty which is an essential part of experience. In it truth, beauty, and goodness can be separated from their opposites and endowed with the same tangible solidity as objects of sense perception. Reality, however, cannot be formalized into a system nor truth translated into a dogma, for they are a condition of existence and not of thought. Significantly, all three characters are incapable of feeling love or affection or of meeting the demands of the external world. There is a hardness and rigidity in them that is recognized most clearly by the women—Narcissa, Caddy, Mrs. Hightower—who have a right to their love.

The extent to which these and related characters such as Horace Benbow or the Reporter have denied their involvement with circumstance and isolated themselves in a private and incommunicable world is charted by certain recurrent images embedded in the narrative texture. The feeling of restrictive confinement is rendered through images of a circle, a gray corridor, or isolated rooms. This sense of being trapped is reinforced by a phrase that seems to recur in almost every Faulkner novel—"tomorrow and tomorrow and tomorrow"—which carries in context the suggestion of time circling back on itself. From within their cramped, solitary worlds these characters see the rest of the world and frequently themselves as shadows or as actors in a play. This is true even of such minor characters as Ellen Sutpen making a lawn charade out of her position as the lady of the manor or Belle Mitchell in *Sartoris* creating a world of sentimental tragedy for herself. Charles Bon exists as the joint creation of the Sutpens, "a myth, a phantom . . . as though as a man he did not exist at all." (104) And Miss Rosa Coldfield, a shadow among shadows, creeps into a deserted room to look at Bon's portrait *"not to dream, since [she] dwelt in the dream, but to renew, rehearse, the part as the faulty though eager amateur might steal wingward in some interim of the visible scene to hear the prompter's momentary voice."* (147)

The most effective element, however, the richest in nuance and implication, of this cluster of images is that of the mirror which is used most effectively in *Sanctuary, The Sound and the Fury, Absalom, Absalom!* and *Light in August*. It acts at once as a reflection and a distortion of reality by presenting a shape, a formal arrangement of color and line, devoid of substance. Moreover, it reflects not only the scene but the observer himself. Thus, the degree of distortion that emerges provides an insight into the particular world of the observer as well as of what he observes. No matter how faithfully the mirror reflects appearances it is still relative to the particular angle of vision of the observer.

These shadow worlds which exist in defiance of reality are, nevertheless, at the same time vulnerable to reality. Time is constantly weaving a pattern of events and presenting situations which threaten to destroy the individual's "design" because they cannot be fitted into that design. Change is a necessary concomitant of time and experience: consequently, no order imposed on experience is immune to change. It is, therefore, of the utmost importance that the individual orientate himself and his perception to reality. If he sees his world only as a stream of unpredictable and continually changing events, he will not be able to deal effectively with his experience. Instead he finds himself in the position of the tall convict in *The Wild Palms*, reacting instinctively to each new stimulus and devoting all his energies to simple physical survival. As a means of circumventing uncertainty, each of the three Compson brothers emphasizes his own stability. Each equates truth and reality with his own habits of perception and belief, thereby achieving a kind of permanence though only at the expense of his humanity. But as Faulkner suggests, if man is to know truth and not simply facts, he must recognize and yield himself and his world to change, as Dilsey does, while still holding firm to their continuity.

On occasion some event or complex of events shocks the individual out of his self-imposed rigidity and forces him out of his isolation. Lena Grove's needs, for example, make Byron Bunch ignore the routine of his life; they transform him into an eager though somewhat awkward man of action. Her pregnancy brings an unwilling Hightower to her assistance and prepares the way for his genuine, though unsuccessful, attempt to save Joe Christmas from the lynch mob. Again, in *Sanctuary* a woman involves Horace Benbow in a series of events that compels him to re-examine his dream-like ideals just as Hightower is forced to re-examine his vision of the charging cavalry. Though both men once more retreat from the living world, it is not before they have gained a bitter kind of knowledge concerning themselves and their worlds. No dream or ideal, no matter how enthralling, can be substituted for reality and for action; and since their ideals had been cherished at the expense of life, it is a kind of poetic justice that they should also be destroyed the moment they are put to the test of experience.

The relationship between the individual, his society, and the natural world of events, both of which implement his vision, can best be illustrated through a comparison of Isaac McCaslin in *Go Down, Moses* and Chick Mallison in *Intruder in the Dust*. In them we have a paradigm of the problems by which Faulkner conceives the culture hero to be confronted. As white Southerners of the same social class, both of them have been molded by the same historical and geographical influences. Presumably, both begin by accepting the patterns of thought and behavior they have inherited. A single event, however, jolts each of them out of his complacence and innocence. In Isaac's case the dramatic immediacy with which he envisages this incident permanently dislocates his cultural vision. By an act of the historical imagination he is induced to deny history, time, and change. The explicit gesture which embodies this denial is Isaac's repudiation of the social order. For him this is inherently and essentially the same society as that which countenanced old Carothers McCaslin's right to call his Negro daughter to his bed simply because she was his possession. His self-imposed cultural deracination is accompanied by a geographical retreat into the wilderness. Here his life is devoted not to the complexity of experience but to the preservation of a ritual which quickly reveals limitations of a serious kind once it is disengaged from its symbolic function.

In essence Chick Mallison's problem is to avoid the *cul de sac* into which McCaslin permitted himself to be drawn. The culture hero must maintain his imaginative flexibility at all costs if he is to realize his cultural vision not only in the world of myth but also in the context of history. Chick's first rage and indignation at finding that his people are less than perfect threaten to catapult him, like Isaac McCaslin, into self-willed isolation. His spiritual and cultural return to society occurs at the precise moment he realizes that each individual is responsible for all men's thoughts and actions. He accepts the specific conditions of the place and time into which he is born as the framework within which he must maintain his humanity.

With Chick's decision Faulkner affirms the basic interdependence of the individual and society, of personal ethics and public morality, of the natural world of time and the social world of history. If perception is a matter of habit and pattern which intervene between the observer and the observed, then obviously each element of these paired opposites modifies the pattern of the other. Ideally, there should be a balance between them, but that balance has been destroyed by a number of factors. Hence Faulkner's reiterated plea to man to recover his dignity, his integrity, and his humanity. Man cannot, of course, control events or regulate time, but he can shape his historical destiny insofar as he can control his thinking. It takes one man to set in motion the pattern which culminates with the lynching of Joe Christmas, but it also takes only one boy to prevent that pattern from recurring in the case of Lucas Beauchamp. Significantly, Chick's acceptance of responsibility prompts a change of attitude in the older and rather complacent Gavin Stevens. In contrast, Isaac's repudiation of society merely confirms Edmonds in his defense of it. It is the individual who must remake the world nearer to the heart's desire because, as Faulkner declared in his Nobel Prize speech, he believes "not only in the right of man to be free of injustice and rapacity and deception, but the duty and responsibility of man to see that justice and truth and pity and compassion are done."

The relation of the individual to his present experience is, as has been suggested, crucial in the implementation of this process, but no less crucial is the relation of the individual to the past experience of others. Immediate experience and facts contribute to the realization of truth but so do history and legend. History, at least in the textbook sense, is relentlessly factual. Indeed, there is a sense in which history is merely the temporal continuum in which facts exist. Regardless of how distant or how recent, such history cannot be the entire truth. The historian deliberately removes the human aspect from history; his collection of data is intellectually ordered in terms of laws which are as general and abstract as possible. The result is, of course, intellectually convincing, but such a pattern cannot command emotional allegiance since it misses the core of truth and reality. When the Civil War is reduced to names of battles, military strategy, and lists of casualties, it loses all its stirring, evocative power and becomes simply information fixed in dead words.

In submitting to the tyranny of the factual the historian reveals his human fallibility: he accepts a part for the whole and thereby, of necessity, embraces an illusion as the ultimate reality. His positive contribution to the realization of truth is simply the essential raw material which he presents as fully as possible to the imagination of humanity. It is only when this material is enshrined in legend, which alone is capable of growth, that the very names of battles and casualties attain a reality which is immediately convincing. Even though the legend is still fixed by words, these words are evocative rather than definitive. Accordingly, they are susceptible to new interpretations from generation to generation. The events of the past, as *Intruder in the Dust* suggests, are woven into an explanation "not in facts but long since beyond dry statistics into something far more moving because it was truth: which moved the heart and had nothing whatever to do with what mere provable information said." (50)

In origin legends are attempts to clear up the confusion of and to impose a form on past events. But since the legend is a product of a number of narrators, each with his own preconceptions, the result, at least temporarily, is factual confusion and a multiplication of alternatives. Ultimately, however, the human impulse for pattern and order asserts itself through a quasi-communal effort on the part of the story-tellers to make the legend of the past a coherent and convincing whole. In effect, aesthetic unity imperceptibly assumes an existence independent of any single narrator and becomes part of the communal memory and tradition. Quentin Compson finds that he has absorbed the legends of his people without any effort or volition on his part. Similarly, Chick Mallison in *Knight's Gambit* relives the Civil War and makes certain legends his own "by means of childhood's simple inevitable listening." (143)

Whatever ethical or religious overtones the legend may display, its form is necessarily dramatic and, providing enough time has elapsed, heroic. Colonel John Sartoris, Carothers McCaslin, Jason Lycurgus Compson, Thomas Sutpen, all these men have been lifted out of history into legend where they stand, in the words of *Absalom, Absalom!*, "possessing now heroic proportions, performing their acts of simple passion and simple violence, impervious to time and inexplicable." (101) All the confusion, hesitation, and vacillation of the living man vanish and what is left is the demi-god and hero, carving an empire out of the wilderness and establishing his dynasty within it.

Since the legend of Colonel John Sartoris is seen both from different points in time and from different perspectives, it illustrates most exhaustively the gradual transformation of history into legend and of the individual into the hero. In *The Unvanquished* the Colonel already possesses for Bayard Sartoris the glamor of the strange and unfamiliar. He is the warrior hero returning from mysterious and intriguing adventures with "that odor in his clothes and beard and flesh too which I believed was the smell of powder and glory, the elected victorious." (11) But the warrior returns, grows older, more familiar and more approachable, for even he is not immune to gray hair and a paunch. Finally, however, death removes him from time and its plethora of accidental, concrete details. So that in *Sartoris* there are now no stubborn facts, no "clumsy cluttering of bones and breath" (23) to impede the imaginative definition of Sartoris. Only the name and a series of remembered actions remain—his flight from the Yankees, his killing of the two carpetbaggers, his death at the hands of Redmond.

Each of these actions provides a focus for the elaboration of a story or legend. As Bayard recounts the story of the Colonel's flight from the Yankees, it has already been pared down to its bare essentials since a number of years intervene between the experience and the memory of it. The Colonel displays shrewdness and courage in outwitting the Yankees, but he is also fully aware of the danger to himself and the family he is forced to abandon. In *Sartoris* many of the same details are used by Will Falls, but the whole point of the later account is not the danger which the Colonel must evade but rather the dramatic moment in which he faces his pursuers and outwits them. In this version the Colonel's parting words become less truthful in the factual sense but more dramatic: *The Unvanquished's* " 'Take care of Miss Rosa and the chillen' " (84) is replaced by *Sartoris's* " 'And then he tole you to tell yo' aunt he wouldn't be home fer supper.' " (22) With this the historical context becomes largely irrelevant; the Colonel's adventure has become a part of folk literature.

In *Light in August* the legend of Colonel John Sartoris is suddenly presented from a completely different and somewhat disillusioning perspective. Will Falls had seen the shooting of the two "carpetbaggers" as an act of personal courage and heroism. But when Joanna Burden gives the two victims an identity, the heroics are deflated. The contest between the Colonel and the "carpetbaggers" is too unequal despite their pistols on the table: " 'So I suppose that Colonel Sartoris was a town hero because he killed with two shots from the same pistol an old onearmed man and a boy who had never even cast his first vote.' " (218) In these words of Joanna's there is the seed of a counter-legend. With a measure of Rosa Coldfield's gift for "demonizing," narrators could easily transform Colonel Sartoris into another "demon-ogre."

As symbols of the human capacity for love, honor, pride, and courage these legends are a fundamental and important aspect of man's heritage and experience. Yet there is always the danger that the individual may reverse the process by which history is transformed into legend and find himself mistaking the legend for history, the symbolic truth which commands belief with the experiential fact which commands action. As an extreme instance, Hightower isolates himself from the living world because he has found in the legend of his grandfather, shot with a fowling piece in a henhouse—an incident that may be tawdry or comic but certainly not heroic—the epitome of youthful daring and bravery. The facts of the past can be selected and events and characters arranged to make a satisfying and enthralling aesthetic pattern, whereas the present overwhelms us with a barrage of events all of which clamor for recognition. Hightower's dead grandfather can carry any symbolic and emotional weight with which the young boy's imagination endows him. His father, on the other hand, continually interferes with the symbol and the unconscious process of myth-making by his very physical presence.

Clearly the danger of confusing legend and history increases in direct ratio to the degree of importance which the individual attaches to the legend. This confusion of modes can be seen operating on the comic level in the sporadic searches for the gold reputedly buried on the old Frenchman place during the Civil War. Since there is nothing to prove or disprove the legend, it persists as possible fact, one of the many embedded in the numerous Civil War tales. A single coincidence is sufficient, however, to prove not of course that the story is true but that the individual can be moved to a literal acceptance in spite of himself. Finding one coin, Lucas Beauchamp in Go Down, Moses spends subsequent nights digging furiously and employing with ceremonial solemnity his newly acquired divining machine. His actions lend new credibility to the story; observers are quick to assume that no man would be fool enough to spend his nights digging unless there was something to be found. Later in the history of the legend it is the shrewd Ratliff who in The Hamlet reasons himself into believing in the existence of the gold. His belief in turn convinces two others so thoroughly that they ignore the evidence against it which they hold in their very hands.

The consequences of the confusion of legend and reality are far more serious for such characters as Bayard Sartoris, Quentin Compson, and Gail Hightower. The legend must serve as a symbol of humanity and not as a criterion of conduct or an absolute blueprint for behavior. Otherwise it becomes a barrier between the individual and his experience and so subverts its own purpose. Legends exist as the result of humanity's efforts to order and channel its imaginative energy into the primary and formidable task of heroically liberating itself from its own shortcomings. If the individual recognizes and accepts his humanity, he must be prepared to build his dream out of the intractable materials provided by his own historical place and time. But if he mistakes the dream for reality, if he tries to impose an ideal pattern on experience, it is at the expense of humanity, his own and that of others. Only by meeting life with a total human response, not an attitude, can man aspire to the vision of an open society, which is the only truly human society.

Central to such a response is the perception of truth which for Faulkner is ultimately experiential rather than metaphysical or linguistic. Chick Mallison implicitly realizes this when he insists in *Intruder in the Dust* that truth is simple "and so there was not needed a great deal of diversification and originality to express it because truth was universal, it had to be universal to be truth and so there didn't need to be a great deal of it just to keep running something no bigger than one earth and so anybody could know truth; all they had to do was just to pause, just to stop, just to wait." (89) Women, Negroes, and children recognize this truth instinctively because they are prone to react wholeheartedly to their experience. At the same time they are indifferent to all attempts to state definitively what truth must inevitably be. Instead they make their recognition depend on the specific situation in which they find themselves. In order to avoid a complete falsification of reality and a distortion of truth, the individual must continually readjust his thinking in the light of his everincreasing and everchanging experience. Faulkner's doomed characters are those who lack the necessary flexibility and resilience to admit and mend their errors in perception. Those who survive and triumph are the ones who, unfettered by facts and uncommitted to legends, respond to the truth which is within them.

15 : THE CONTOURS OF TIME

Faulkner's concept of time determines, in part at least, the structure of his novels even as it constitutes another facet of his concern with the truth of man. The former has been discussed in the analyses of individual novels. With respect to the latter, time, as Faulkner sees it, is a necessary condition of existence in that it provides a medium for as well as the essence of man's experience. Like events, it has both an objective and a subjective aspect. Objectively, time exists and continues weaving its patterns regardless of the presence or absence of any one person; subjectively, it is dependent for its very existence on the individual's awareness of it. Since time manifests itself through events and change, it is identical with man's experience; but insofar as man can examine that experience, at least in retrospect, all time is contained in his own consciousness. Yet as with thought and action, words and deeds, consciousness of time and time itself must be meshed if the individual is to enjoy a harmonious and fruitful relation with his world and his experience.

Although Faulkner's interest in time is psychological rather than metaphysical, he does insist on the existence of a time which is independent of any observer. This kind of time can be grasped intuitively as that vital impulse behind all things, manifesting itself in change yet not to be identified with change. Because it is independent of man, Faulkner uses it to provide a focus for a range of possible human reactions and attitudes as well as a basis for judging them. Since it is related to the land and actualized in the steady progression of the seasons, it may be called natural time. Endlessly, it moves through the recurrent cycles of creation and destruction, each of which is implied in the other, so that although there is continual change and destruction of particular objects and individuals, there is no end to the process itself. In addition, natural time is characterized by its immediacy. Because its movement is cyclical and because it appears as a continuous process, all time exists in any one moment of it. Past and future possess an independent identity only in the world of logic; actually, they are both contained in and their contours subtly altered by an eternal growing present.

In the Faulknerian world, it is through logic applied introspectively that man arrives at his concept of linear time, for with respect to his own fixed position as spectator, events seem to recede in a regular temporal sequence. The whole apparatus invented for telling time, the clocks and the calendars, enables him to determine the precise point currently reached by linear time. Clocks are perhaps the central symbol, especially prominent in *The Sound and the Fury* and *Pylon*, of mechanical linear time because of their duplicity in concealing their true nature. The clock face disguises its linear quality by assuming the spatial figure of a circle; by analogy it hopes to suggest the cyclic form of natural time. It is, however, an incomplete symbol, for its hands in themselves are merely reflexive, indicating nothing beyond the repetition of a particular angle obtaining between two straight lines. Like the calendar and all the other instruments of linear time, it lacks a recurrent polarity, a systole and diastole, such as the seasons and natural time possess. This attempt to assimilate natural time to an alien form not only obscures but falsifies it, if only because events are thereby regarded as isolated and discontinuous. As Mr. Compson points out in *The Sound and the Fury*, "time is dead as long as it is being clicked off by little wheels; only when the clock stops does time come to life." (104)

All that such mechanical devices for measuring duration can do is to record history which consists of events in time, not time itself. If man confuses the two, the inventions meant to order his relation to time completely destroy it. For Faulkner, the essence of time, as of truth, lies in people's actions and behavior. It is simply the medium in which an individual has the opportunity of living in accord with his humanity, an opportunity taken advantage of by all too few. Thus if he relies exclusively on the clock, he becomes, in the extreme case, a mechanical man, like

Mr. Hooper of *Mosquitoes,* murmuring, " 'Well, well. I must run along. I run my day to schedule.' " (37) Or else he becomes a Quentin Compson who, even on the threshold of death, attempts to construe his experience of natural time in terms of his obsession with mechanical time. The folly of such attitudes is realized by the Reporter in *Pylon* who despairs over the succession of days and lives rigidly controlled by the hands of a clock.

Though man's measurement of time is logical, his comprehension of it depends not only on reason but on memory and hope. The former defines his past, while the latter anticipates his future. The future is, however, necessarily uncertain; hope, therefore, is inextricably fused with fear lest some unexpected stroke of fate or circumstance destroy that familiar order to which man clings precariously but persistently. In contrast to this uncertain and incalculable future, the past seems infinitely reassuring in its completeness. Forgetting that each moment of the present places the past in a new perspective, man believes that whatever he holds in his memory is finished and unchangeable and that it can be invoked and re-examined at different points in time without suffering any alteration. This, unfortunately, is possible only if the individual himself remains static, a condition which he cannot achieve without isolating himself from the world of natural time. Those who make the act of remembering a consecration or a sacred duty gladly accept this isolation for the sake of gaining immunity from time and change for some cherished event or person. Thus, young Bayard Sartoris, Harry Wilbourne, Gail Hightower, and Rosa Coldfield, each in his own way lives in and through his memories. The latter two are, in addition, extreme representatives of a society which, as *Requiem for a Nun* observes, has turned its face "irreconcilably backward toward the old lost battles, the old aborted cause, the old four ruined years whose very physical scars ten and twenty and twenty-five changes of season had annealed back into the earth." (239) Clearly, an excessive concern with the past can destroy the continuity of time and paralyze the capacity for action not only in the individual but in society as a whole.

Whereas memory confines the individual to the past, imagination can free him or, conversely, confirm his bondage. It alone can recreate the events of the past and transform them into reality. As *Requiem for a Nun* points out, "so limitless in capacity is man's imagination to disperse and burn away the rubble-dross of fact and probability, leaving only truth and dream." (261)

Lifted out of the context of accidental detail, truth and dream are recognized as eternally present and eternally compelling. Since imagination alone is free of time, it can transcend and abrogate all categories of time and space and thereby rescue man not from time but from his temporal delusions. If, on the other hand, it is not permitted to function in perfect freedom, it merely intensifies those delusions. Such is the case with Hightower and Quentin Compson, for example, who place imagination and all the truth and beauty with which it endows experience in the service of the past. In *Go Down, Moses* a similar delusion, though directed to the future rather than the past, leaves Fonsiba's husband completely, almost wilfully, blind to immediate needs. Instead of bending every effort to making his ideal of a new Canaan a reality, he immerses himself in the dream, scarcely seeing and totally indifferent to "the empty fields without plow or seed to work them, fenceless against the stock which did not exist within or without the walled stable which likewise was not there." (279)

Each individual is confronted with the problem of somehow adjusting memory and imagination and of reconciling the natural and mechanical, the cyclical and the linear modes of time. But since there are degrees of awareness, there are also degrees of concern on the part of the individual. A Jim Bond or an Ike Snopes, reduced simply to a physical existence by idiocy, lives in time without being conscious of it. Others, particularly women of limited intellectual capacities such as Jenny in *Mosquitoes*, Lena Grove, and Eula Varner of *The Hamlet* can be completely absorbed into the rhythms of natural time. This quasi-vegetative existence constitutes a pre-conscious state which must necessarily be transcended; even Benjy Compson is aware of change and loss, though unable to develop any concept of time or to understand that he also is changing. The ultimate relationship between man and time is one that will admit man's involvement in time while leaving scope for distinctively human dreams and aspirations. Deliberate reduction to the purely physical, vegetative life is stultifying, for it is out of conflict and struggle that understanding of himself grows.

Man's dignity consists of submitting to time and change while preserving his identity and his sense of continuity. Once this subtle balance is destroyed, only the land can restore it. By forcing man to respond to the changes of season, the cyclic rhythm is re-established in the human body and psyche. In *Sartoris* even young Bayard with all his eagerness for mechanical speed finds that for a brief interlude planting and tending crops leaves him "with the sober rhythms of the earth in his body." (203) At the same time mere proximity to the earth is not in itself sufficient to restore the harmony of man and nature. Putting forth no effort of his own, Harry Wilbourne in *The Wild Palms* finds himself vitiated, not strengthened, by his contact with nature. Gradually he sinks into lethargy, "a drowsy and foetuslike state, passive and almost unsentient in the womb of solitude and peace." (110) In contrast, Armstid of *The Hamlet* becomes overactive, violating the land and destroying its rhythms as he extends his digging for the buried gold "into the waxing twilight with the regularity of a mechanical toy." (419) Clearly, man's own attitude toward nature plays an important part in determining what he derives from it.

It is in the interaction of natural and human time that Faulkner's concept of "doom" finds its source and its meaning. At its simplest it is synonymous with death, and as such it is shared by all creatures. Thus in *Sartoris* not only the characters but even the fowls appear to have "a foreknowledge of frustration and of doom." (107) Yet doom is not merely an awareness that the inevitable goal of life is death. It is also time seen as the medium which not only leads to but also determines the mode and manner of the conclusion of life. It is the realization of this that is back of the conviction of such characters as Charlotte Rittenmeyer and Laverne Shumann that as much living as possible should be compressed into each day. They share Gavin Stevens' conviction, expressed in *Intruder in the Dust*, that "all man had was time, all that stood between him and the death he feared and abhorred was time." (30) Doom, however, exists throughout all time, not solely at the extreme end of a rapidly diminishing future. As Gavin suggests in *Requiem for a Nun*, it also is identified with the past. This is seen most dramatically in the case of Joe Christmas whose death is the inevitable but not preordained result of his past. Here doom as action or event is fused with doom as time or process.

Rather than face the annihilation of their individuality implicit in the concept of doom, some of Faulkner's characters evolve various strategies of evasion. All of these are based on the paradox, enunciated by Harry Wilbourne, Quentin Compson, and Darl Bundren, that though man is in time, he yet contains time within himself. So long as he exists, he preserves the past through memory; with his death the past is either obliterated or altered. Ironically enough, then, such strategies can have but a limited success. Such characters as Labove in *The Hamlet* and Quentin Compson can evade doom as time only by seeking it as death. The same is true of Gowan Stevens in *Requiem for a Nun* who, like Quentin, envisages drowning as the means by which he can "stop having to remember, stop having to be forever unable to forget." (74) Harry Wilbourne, on the other hand, chooses doom as time in order to avoid the obliteration of love and his memory of Charlotte which would follow were he to accept death.

A quite different strategy is employed by Faulkner's patriarchs, the hero-founders of dynasties, such as Thomas Sutpen, Colonel John Sartoris, and Carothers McCaslin. They attempt to evade doom as time by exerting control over the future rather than the past. Although they cannot escape their own involvement in time nor the doom which must ultimately overtake them, they can and do seek to impose their "designs" on the future by means of their descendants. Sutpen builds his plantation and establishes his dynasty to outlast time. Similarly, Sartoris bequeaths his name and his dream through his son Bayard to all succeeding generations. Both men's actions constitute a defiance of time's destructiveness through an attempt to match man's achievements against time. Though they cannot wrest a personal immortality from time, they can, they think, perpetuate themselves through their descendants. John Sartoris still continues to "stiffen and shape that which sprang from him into the fatal semblance of his dream." (23) Time has changed both the appearance of the land and the customs of its people, but still the Sartorises, inevitably named after the first John and Bayard, continue to play the game of Sartoris, "a game outmoded and played with pawns shaped too late and to an old dead pattern." And Sutpen's descendants, whatever their personal feeling about him, affirm his design through their own actions even at the cost of their happiness and very lives.

But each dynasty carries the seeds of its own destruction; not only individuals but also the Sartorises, Compsons, and Sutpens are doomed. Their disintegration is reflected in the fate of their splendid estates. Ironically, the Old Compson place retains its name even after the old square mile has been transformed into a housing development. And finally even the name disappears. The same is true of other families. Thus the owner of Frenchman's Bend is forgotten by all in *The Hamlet*, "his pride but a legend about the land he had wrested from the jungle and tamed as a monument to that appellation which those who came after him in battered wagons . . . could not even read." (4) All that remains of the Grenier family in *Knight's Gambit* is a man who "could not even spell the Lonnie Grinnup he called himself." (66) And the last of the Maingaults appears in *Requiem for a Nun* as Nancy Mannigoe, a drunkard and casual prostitute.

The stages of the dynasty as it passes from creation to destruction reflect those ascribed to the individual by Fairchild in *Mosquitoes*. Elemental being is succeeded by stages of doing, thinking, and finally remembering. The first stage, that of simple existence, preceded the building of the plantations. It was the period of the frontiersmen. As these men and the wilderness which sustained them vanish, the men of action, the Sartorises and Compsons and Sutpens, take their place. They devote themselves to building a world in accord with their "design" and to actively assuring its perpetuation. To this end virtually all their deeds, which comprise the bulk of their lives, reveal what *The Unvanquished* calls a "violent and ruthless dictatorialness and will to dominate." (258)

In the third stage, usually represented by lawyers, there is a considerable diminution of the capacity to act and a substantial increase in ratiocination. These lawyers are the theorists of the clan and the strategists of kinship. Their dominant concern is to abstract and therefore to universalize the tradition they have inherited. Caught up in their own rationality, however, such men as Horace Benbow, Jason Compson III, and, to some extent, Gavin Stevens find it difficult to act simply, directly, and immediately. They show evidence of that paralysis which sets in when a man sees so many sides of a question and so many possible alternative actions that he is unable to come to any decision. Accordingly, like Mr. Compson, they retreat from the world of events into a world of books, philosophical generalizations, and rational speculations. Or else, if they do attempt to establish contact with events, as Horace Benbow does, they find their rational world with its concepts, hypotheses, and ideals utterly devastated and shattered. They know what is right

and just in theory, but they falter badly when it comes to applying their theories to concrete and usually urgent situations.

The final phase is that of characters like Quentin Compson,
Bayard Sartoris, and young Gail Hightower for whom time is
remembering. Despite their own youth, they represent the old
age of their respective families and in this lies their tragedy.
Instead of days filled with new experiences arousing new reactions, they relive the lives of their ancestors; instead of
gathering memories for their own old age, they devote themselves to remembering and so preserving legends of a past they
have never seen. The disparity between their actual youth with
its anticipation of the future and their psychological and
genealogical old age with its memories results in either the
frustration of Quentin, the indifference of Hightower, or the
despairing recklessness of Bayard. With the death of each, his
family tradition dissolves to all intents and purposes.

From this it is obvious that no more than the individual
can the dynasty evade time without having to accept death.
And yet man is not consigned to ultimate extinction. Instead
his only immortality is seen to lie in the continuity of the
species through which each man is linked to all past and future
time. Faulkner's novels have consistently and insistently dramatized the fact that immortality is, in the broadest sense,
human. Neither the individual, the family, the society, nor even
the race can hope to overcome time. Humanity, on the other
hand, is above and beyond genera and in this inclusiveness
(temporal as well as spatial) it finds its supreme test and
triumph. For recognition of the nature of man's immortality
and of his relation to time constitutes the fundamental basis
for ethical conduct upon which both the individual and society
must depend for survival. Thus conscience, as *Intruder in the
Dust* indicates, is seen to be " 'that belief in more than the
divinity of individual man . . . in the divinity of his continuity as Man.' " (202)

Time manifests itself to man not only as change and destruction but also as event. Chronologically arranged, these
events constitute the history of the individual and his race.
Such an arrangement, however, further contributes to the delusion that time is linear. Yet actually past and future are both
implicit in the present; therefore the event, the cause, and the
effect exist simultaneously. Consciousness that both cause and

event derive from a past that is always present explains why certain of Faulkner's characters appear to be reliving something which has already happened or to be watching from a distance the rehearsal of a play whose ending they already know. Joe Christmas, for instance, accepts as accomplished the murder which he has not yet committed or even consciously planned. Even before he enters the house, he finds himself saying, "*I had to do it* already in the past tense; *I had to do it*." (245) Nevertheless, in this seeming determinism the individual is not relieved of responsibility. With respect to each of his actions, man has free moral choice; but once committed, that act becomes the nucleus of an increasingly complex chain of events, the reverberations of which cannot be confined to a single individual. Representative of this pattern is Narcissa Benbow's retention of Snopes's letters, Temple Drake's decision to break the college rules, and Rosa Millard's first acquisition of the Union mules.

It would seem, then, that the characters in Faulkner's novels are not nearly so helpless nor so victimized by supra-human forces as the numerous references to doom, fatality, and the Player would indicate. Man bears his destiny in his own character and his motives shape the contours of his life except, of course, for the sudden, unexpected eruption of the irrational both in himself and nature. His talk of determinism is, therefore, but one more stratagem of evasion whereby he hopes to shift responsibility from his shoulders to that of some supernatural power. In *Light in August* Brown's frustration expresses itself in his outrage at an "Opponent who could read his moves before he made them and who created spontaneous rules which he and not the Opponent, must follow." (383) On the other hand, the exposure of this stratagem is seen in Bayard Sartoris and Temple Drake Stevens, both of whom are finally forced to admit their own responsibility, if only for a fleeting moment.

The complex of such single acts in turn constitutes the pattern of history into which the individual is born. The sins of the fathers are expiated by their children throughout all time, for the history of a people is, properly speaking, not a matter of abstract laws of economics, politics, or social science. It is rather the feelings, motives, characters, and actions of individuals and their cultures that shape the course of human history. Accordingly, the pattern of history is neither inexorably deterministic nor immutable. Though the guilt is passed on from generation to generation, each individual is free either to prolong or to expiate it. Each present action reshapes or confirms the design of the past. It is this that Gavin Stevens suggests in *Intruder in the Dust* when he remarks that " 'It's all *now* you see. Yesterday wont be over until tomorrow and tomorrow began ten thousand years ago.' " (194) What is inherited from the past must be assimilated if it is to be possessed. The Civil War may become for one person a blaze of glory and for another an agony of shame. On a more personal level, Henry and Judith Sutpen are caught in the wake of their father's rejection of his first wife. In this act of his they find their own test and make their judgment and decision; and like their father, they perpetuate the guilt by committing fresh crimes against their humanity by initiating new moral outrages. Conversely, Bayard Sartoris of *The Unvanquished* refuses to continue the pattern of violence and death promulgated by his father. He goes through the vendetta motions expected by Jefferson, but in a decisive and considered gesture he refrains from drawing fresh blood.

This pattern of expiation, however, is seen most clearly in the McCaslin saga of *Go Down, Moses*. Old Carothers McCaslin initiates his particular familial guilt, Uncle Buck and Uncle Buddy then begin the process of expiation, and Isaac carries it a step further though he does not complete it. Since it is a part of time, the guilt can, in fact, never be completely erased. Accordingly, the decision to expiate must inevitably be a recurrent one. This decision, however, is complicated by the strong pressures to conformity exercised by the society into which the individual is born. Yet that the effort can be made is revealed by the actions of such disparate characters as Chick Mallison and Nancy Mannigoe. The former flouts every rule, every convention of Jefferson, and risks the combined wrath of the Gowries and Beat Four; yet he manages to make the saving of Lucas Beauchamp a part of the history of the South. And for the sake of a child not her own, not even of her own race, Nancy Mannigoe, "the nigger, the dopefiend whore, didn't hesitate to cast the last gambit . . . she knew and had: her own debased and worthless life." (208) It is thus that the expiation can be written into man's history and therefore into time.

When man realizes that *the* past and *the* future alike are unattainable fictions, he is disenchanted of his mania for linear time. Left with only individual past experiences to recall and specific future happenings to anticipate, man finds the continuity of time once more established in all its primacy. The communal and anonymous brotherhood of man can be reestablished if each man individually cherishes not his social but his human identity and accepts responsibility for all time as well as for the particular time into which he is born. Bayard Sartoris' rejection of his familial pattern of violence, Isaac McCaslin's repudiation of his heritage of guilt, Chick Mallison's efforts to save Lucas Beauchamp, Nancy's self-sacrifice, and even Gail Hightower's futile attempt to save Joe Christmas, all provide conclusive and irrefutable evidence of man's capacity for assuming responsibility for all events, all people, and all time. He possesses this capacity because he holds the secret of time in his hands, and he exercises this capacity because he understands the nature of that secret.

16: LANGUAGE AS THEME AND TECHNIQUE

As part of his attempt to render the truth of man, Faulkner has assiduously explored the problem of language, both from the point of view of technique and as an index to human behavior. The latter involves the examination of the verbal patterns that dominate the South and subtly mold the individual, his society, and his tradition. Since language is at once the foundation and the product of social intercourse, it cannot be separated from the matrix of personal and communal experience. Without such experience, physical, mental, and emotional, to give them content, words are simply empty sounds. The veterans of *Soldiers' Pay*, for example, find that they can talk only with one another; communication has completely broken down between them and the civilians who have not been touched by the actual fighting. The "public" character of language has been destroyed by the war which has provided the one group with an inescapable pattern of experience and the other group with but a verbal pattern. Age itself also causes a shift in perspective and therefore in definition. Thus Chick Mallison in *Knight's Gambit* with unshaken conviction rejects his uncle's description of the brutality of war. Obviously words derive their meaning both from the object or event to which they refer and from the subjective reaction of the speaker or listener to that object or event. A single word conveys different things to different people as it reflects not reality but their own particular angle of vision.

Over and over again Faulkner returns with a kind of brooding fascination and amazement to the experiential foundation of language. He probes and traces its various forms in an effort to reveal why and how such a foundation is necessary in order for communication through language to be effected. Quentin Compson, for example, repeatedly asks in *The Sound and the Fury*, "Did you ever have a sister," as if that were the prerequisite for understanding his mental and emotional agony. Joe Christmas recognizes the words used by Bobbie's friends, but they convey no meaning to him. There is as yet nothing in his own experience in terms of which he can understand and respond to the verbal counters they employ, just as there is nothing which could have prepared him for the old Negro's resentment when he asks, " 'How come you are a nigger?' " (336) To break out of her silence and isolation Temple Drake hires Nancy Mannigoe "for the reason that an ex-dopefiend nigger whore was the only animal in Jefferson that spoke Temple Drake's language." (158) In all these cases some community of experience seems to be the prerequisite for communication. And this, as Chick Mallison suggests in *Intruder in the Dust*, holds true not only for individuals but in the national and international contexts as well. A dramatic version of that North-South immersion in linguistic solipsism which Chick merely contemplates appears in *Absalom, Absalom!* where Quentin attempts to convey to Shreve the particularly Southern qualities of his experience and language.

The existence of such a problem indicates decisively that there is no direct relationship between the word and its referent. The object is itself involved in the process of change and the word is continually acquiring additional connotations, personal, social, and historical, in order to make it conform to the speaker's view of that object. Even proper nouns are not free of these clusters of secondary meanings and associations. Thus the final, the ultimate meaning of the word "Caddy" in *The Sound and the Fury* involves the whole complex of private associations belonging to Benjy, Quentin, Jason, Dilsey, the librarian, and, in fact, the whole town of Jefferson. Yet neither singly nor in combination can words capture the elusive reality of the person who is Caddy. The concrete vocabulary of Benjy, the convolutions of Quentin, and the logical precision of Jason provide an index to their own character rather than a reflection of their sister. Moreover, their feelings and emotions are attached not to the real Caddy but to their self-created image of her. At this point communication breaks down for language has become a matter of personal symbols, unrelated to objective reality. In the same way the accretion of meanings attached to a proper name can be traced in the case of Thomas Sutpen or Colonel John Sartoris.

Since the proper noun has a concrete and specific referent, it does possess a certain ineluctable relation to reality. But when a more abstract level of language is employed, when words representing categories and concepts are brought into play, man, according to Faulkner, finds himself wholly in a verbal and logical universe. Because there are no objects corresponding identically to the concept but only representative instances which approximate it, the number of associations the concept can carry is incalculable. Once these secondary meanings are accepted publicly as part of its meaning, the concept ceases to function as an abstraction; it takes on the substance and authority of experiential truth and reality. If the concept is then permitted to provide the incentive and generate the motive for individual actions, a vicious circle is completed. Language which should be used to order man's experience now controls it, and in the process, as Julius points out in *Mosquitoes,* men are reduced to " 'that species all of whose actions are controlled by words.' " (130)

The relationship of the concept to reality is readily demonstrated by the attitudes of various characters to virginity. Only Mr. Compson recognizes that virginity is both a symbol and a physical condition and that each is subject to quite different laws. The former is eternal and immutable, the latter necessarily yields to time and change. Will Varner in *The Hamlet,* on the other hand, adopts a thoroughly realistic attitude about his daughter's virginity since he "cheerfully and robustly and undeviatingly declined to accept any such theory as female chastity other than as a myth to hoodwink young husbands with." (160) In contrast, Quentin Compson and Jody Varner are concerned solely with the symbolic value of virginity. But such symbols are continually threatened by the very objects with which they are identified. Not only Quentin but Jody Varner and Byron Bunch are forced to admit that Caddy, Eula, and Lena have qualities and drives of their own. The arbitrary identification of the symbol with a specific person is destroyed. As reality asserts itself, the spell is broken, causing the brooding despair of Quentin, the comic outrage of Jody, and the humble acquiescence of Byron.

The danger of confusing the generalized term with the proper noun or the concept with the object is, however, most frequently illustrated in Faulkner's novels in connection with the word "Negro." Thus at one stroke Faulkner both documents the process outlined above and dramatically recapitulates the quiddity of his Southern inheritance. A major part of *Light in August*, in fact, is devoted to Joe Christmas' painful exploration of the various implications and ramifications of that single word. During the period of childhood, as Faulkner repeatedly points out, the word "Negro" carries no connotation except possibly that of strangeness or physical difference stemming from the observation of people with dark skins. This accidental characteristic arouses curiosity but neither approbation nor disapproval while the emphasis is placed entirely on the individual and proper names. Since it takes some time to learn words and even more time to grasp their total meaning, for a little while at least, the white child and the black react to and judge each other strictly on their individual merits. Bayard Sartoris and Ringo, Roth Edmonds and Henry, Chick Mallison and Aleck Sander—all these share a close personal friendship before yielding to a mutual recognition of color and status.

But even among children language is capable of reflecting basic attitudes and elemental feelings. Hence the term "nigger" implies opprobrium as the cruel game of calling Joe Christmas a "nigger" or Miss Burden "nigger-lover" suggests, but it is opprobrium through mimicry. Only later do the children learn what they implicitly and unconsciously meant by the epithets. By that time it is too late to retract even if they wished to, for habit has rendered language almost invulnerable by establishing it as an autonomous authority in private and personal as well as social experience. Paradoxically, this subtle and unconscious exaltation of language has the effect of diminishing the individual's awareness of and sensitivity to words, their meanings, and uses. This is exemplified by the dietitian in *Light in August* who initially uses "nigger" as no more than an expletive hurled at the child Joe Christmas to relieve her own emotions. As is apparent from this case, words thus become arbitrary and undifferentiated counters to be used carelessly and therefore dangerously.

Ringo, Henry, and Lucas Beauchamp can maintain their individuality and personal identity only in the experiential world. Logic and reason place them in a category, that of "Negro," which is, in origin at least, a scientific effort at descriptive definition. As long as it is remembered that "Negro" and other similar terms merely specify a particular logical, verbal class, the word cannot possibly provoke any emotional response or elicit any action. If, however, they are regarded as exhaustive accounts of the individual's nature, they become an instrument of division, destroying that communal anonymous brotherhood in which alone man can express his true nature. Confusion of a verbal category with experiential reality leads Roth Edmonds, like his father before him, to reject and in turn be rejected by his Negro foster-brother, causes Thomas Sutpen to deny his wife and child, and impels Carothers Mc-Caslin to call his own daughter to his bed. Even the intelligent Gavin Stevens ignores the character of Lucas Beauchamp and sees in his story to Chick the cliché explanation of "any other Negro murderer." (79) No matter how sensitive a man may be to the injustices perpetrated in the name of these categories, he yet tends to accept and perpetuate them in his own thinking. Isaac McCaslin, for example, renounces his patrimony in protest against slavery, but he still sees the relationship of Roth Edmonds and his Negro mistress as controlled by the traditional pattern of black and white. Clearly the most insidious feature of linguistic categories is their initiating of a large scale policy of exclusion.

That this formal category of Negro has other dangers in its application is suggested by the fact that there is some doubt as to whether Velery Bon and Christmas are actually Negroes. Velery's mother is believed to be an octoroon by the various narrators of *Absalom, Absalom!* Sharing this belief, Judith Sutpen sends the pale, delicate youth into an inferno of conflict with both black and white worlds. But even after he commits himself to the black world through marriage, the uncertainty continues and even his wife is not really sure that he is not a white man. Similarly, Joe Christmas goes through a violent period of alternately affirming and denying his black blood, though in answer to Miss Burden's questions he is forced to admit that he may not be a Negro. In both cases the category of Negro is impressed on their consciousness by the convictions or actions of others. Judith and Clytie, faithful to their tradition, do so in all sincerity; the dietitian and Doc Hines, however, force Joe into an ethnic and social category as a means of justifying their own actions.

When secondary meanings begin to attach themselves to the category, it develops into a concept. "Negro" ceases to be a logical term and becomes a cultural idea encompassing a number of accidental, associative implications that have little to do with the original descriptive definition. This change is indicated by the transformation of the word itself: "Negro" becomes "nigger." In the latter form, the word has acquired and continues to acquire historical, political, religious, and ethical ramifications. In short, "nigger" is no longer a descriptive or generic term but a compressed myth to which the plantation system, the Civil War, and the Reconstruction have all contributed shades of meaning. Concomitantly, from being a description of a certain color, blackness becomes first a symbol and then an actual and incontrovertible sign of slavery, the mark of Cain and evil. For Hines, Joe Christmas is the "devil's spawn" because he thinks him the son of a Negro. Both Wash Jones and Calvin Burden, the one a Southerner, the other a Yankee, use the Bible as authority and precedent for their attitude to "niggers." With this addition of religious as well as racial fanaticism, the word "nigger" is charged not only with an immense number of associated ideas but also with powerful emotions which periodically erupt into violence.

The final transformation of the word is from concept to precept. At this stage language ceases to be descriptive or logical and becomes rhetorical, persuading or compelling people into certain specific modes of feeling, thought, and action. "Negro" begins to imply a pattern of behavior as well as a complex of ideas. Different though interrelated patterns for the two races extend even to such minutiae as personal cleanliness. Eventually these patterns acquire an ethical significance. The "good" Negroes are the ones who scrupulously modulate their behavior to the conventional pattern until it becomes a series of habitual responses. They accept the role of faithful family retainers whose affection for the white master compensates for the expected and therefore inevitable laziness and petty dishonesty. Dilsey in *The Sound and the Fury* and Simon Strother in *Sartoris* provide the serious and the comic, the dignified and the ludicrous embodiments of this type.

Conversely, the "bad" Negro, the "nocount nigger," is not necessarily the one who has committed a crime; he is simply the individual who does not accept the role of the Negro as the South construes it. In a sense, Caspey of *Sartoris* and Loosh of *The Unvanquished* display too much individuality to be regarded favorably by the whites or even by the other Negroes. More important, however, they take Negro freedom and equality a little too literally. Loosh welcomes the Yankee liberators of the Negro and Caspey returns from Europe with some highly radical ideas which would be dangerous if they were not essentially comic in their exaggeration. Significantly, both whites and Negroes unite in deflating Caspey's delusions of grandeur just as they unite in grim disapproval of Loosh and later, in *Intruder in the Dust*, of Lucas Beauchamp. Lucas, however, maintains his personal integrity by conforming to the pattern of Negro behavior only when it is convenient for him to do so. Implicit in his observance of Southern precepts and shibboleths concerning Negro conduct is a sardonic amusement and contempt for the white man whose preconceptions of Negro behavior must not be challenged lest it endanger his cherished belief in white supremacy.

The usual reaction to these compressed myths, of which "Negro" is but one example, is the cliché response which might in its turn be called a compressed ritual. Chick Mallison notices that the same verbal formula is used over and over again with regard to the stiff-necked "nigger" who finally shot a white man in the back, a form of violence which is particularly associated with and accepted as part of "Negro." Certain actions become as standardized as the words which form their verbal equivalent. Accordingly, the violence that flares up between Negroes and whites is always formalized and wholly impersonal. When Joe Christmas or Velery Bon provoke white men by asserting their own Negro blood, the ensuing fight is not between two individuals but between the antithetical concepts of black and white. When Christmas is finally lynched or Lucas Beauchamp threatened, it is as an effigy of the Negro which submerges the individual identity of the victim and his executioners alike. In such situations language is no longer a means of communication. Instead it serves as a way of circumventing the recalcitrance of experience by fixing a code or formula which clearly, definitively, and finally orders that experience and hence all reactions to it. The result is a kind of linguistic determinism inflicted on himself by man because of his desire for order.

The shift in language from the concrete and descriptive to the abstract and logical is accompanied by a corresponding shift in man's attitude to experience. As long as the individual restricts himself to the level of immediate action and intuitive knowledge, language can present no very pressing problems. It is reason or the conscious mind that attempts to articulate and so order its own reactions to experience. Those persons who most nearly approximate the pre-conscious and therefore pre-verbal state of "just being" are women, children, and Negroes, as well as those individuals possessing simple or even limited minds. In this somewhat incongruous collection, the common factor is a concern, almost a passion, for the concrete, though, of course, for very different reasons. Benjy Compson, Ike Snopes, and Jim Bond, for example, are incapable of passing from the concrete objects which they handle to generalizations, and consequently, they are wholly bounded by the physical world in which they live. A similar sense of limitation is present also, though to a lesser degree, in Cash Bundren and the tall convict of *The Wild Palms*. Both are capable of working and of tremendous physical effort and both have difficulty in finding words with which to express themselves. It is as though their physical capacities and skills leave no room for the cultivation of their linguistic potentialities. Byron Bunch is another whose mental activities are of a pre-conscious nature. He, however, represents the furthest possible development of that habit of mind which appears in its most limited form in Benjy Compson; beyond Byron lies the conscious, rational mentality. In him we see intuitive perception on the verge of articulation.

Women, children, and Negroes are not necessarily more limited in mental capacity than other people, but they are more interested, according to Faulkner, in practical affairs and in the non-verbal world of experience. In contrast to the intellectual sophistication and verbal sophistry of the man, they possess an intuitive knowledge of truth as it is manifested in the act. Thus Bayard Sartoris does not need to inform Drusilla or Miss Jenny of his plans because, as *The Unvanquished* remarks, "they are wise, women are—a touch, lips or fingers, and the knowledge, even clairvoyance, goes straight to the heart without bothering the laggard brain at all." (274) In the same way Miss Habersham instinctively understands what Chick fails to communicate to his uncle. Because they are not encumbered by an awareness of logical possibilities, women and children are able to act quickly and decisively. While Gavin Stevens hesitates in *Intruder in the Dust*, Chick Mallison proves the soundness of old Ephraim's advice: " 'If you ever needs to get anything done outside the common run, dont waste yo time on the menfolks; get the womens and children to working at it.' " (71–72)

There are, naturally, exceptions, but these represent deviations from the essential nature of the class as a whole. Thus Rosa Coldfield was never really a child, and Jason Compson seemed to have been born a miniature version of the rational man. Similarly, Joanna Burden is the product of "man-training" and "man-thinking" and in the process the woman has been submerged. Perhaps the most ludicrous exception is Sophonsiba's husband, a Yankee "nigger," whom Isaac McCaslin discovers reading a book through lensless spectacles while his farm is reduced to a muddy waste. Nevertheless, Faulkner does choose a single representative from each of these groups not only to believe but to save Lucas Beauchamp despite all logic and evidence. As Gavin Stevens remarks, " 'It took an old woman and two children for that, to believe truth for no other reason than that it was truth.' " (126) And it is Nancy Mannigoe who makes the final distinction between rational and intuitive knowledge: "Jesus is a man too. He's got to be. Menfolks listens to somebody because of what he says. Women dont. They dont care what he said. They listens because of what he is." (274)

A parallel distinction is drawn by Isaac McCaslin who in *Go Down, Moses* juxtaposes the experience of truth, immediate and intuitive, against its articulation, logical but mediate and indirect since it is at a remove from the experience itself. In so doing, he suggests the necessity of realizing that words and language constitute a particular kind of experience, namely, a linguistic experience. As such, it has its own truth which consists primarily in a sense of awareness and comprehensiveness embodied in a verbal medium. Linguistic truth operates most unrestrictedly in the realm of literature where the texture of possibilities inherent in human experience is most fully elaborated. Isaac McCaslin's recapitulation of history, Gavin Stevens' analysis of the position of the Negro in the South, the narrative passages in *Requiem for a Nun,* all provide instances of this particular kind of truth.

Clearly, then, despite his awareness of the perils and deceits inherent in language, Faulkner does not suggest that truth cannot exist in a verbal formulation. He does insist, however, that it should not be taken as the only or the whole truth since, as Addie Bundren observes in *As I Lay Dying,* "the high dead words in time . . . lose even the significance of their dead sound." (467) Non-verbal experience must always provide the ground or basis for truth, for in the last analysis truth for Faulkner is the inseparability of the word and the act. The word by itself issues in the mind's running amok and indulging in the logic spinning and verbal acrobatics of a Jason Compson or in the empty rhetoric of the Reverend Whitfield. An excessive preoccupation with language tends to vitiate the capacity for action until, in Addie's words, "the two lines are too far apart for the same person to straddle from one to the other." (465) Januarius Jones, Talliaferro, Anse Bundren, and the Reporter, for example, are so dominated by words that they are almost totally incapable of carrying through any vital action. On the other hand, the act by itself degenerates into random and haphazard psychological responses to one's external and internal environment. Thus, though the nature of their activity varies considerably, such men as the tall convict in *The Wild Palms* or Jewel Bundren in *As I Lay Dying* dispense with words for the sake of action.

A few of Faulkner's characters, most notably Horace Benbow, Gavin Stevens, and C. V. Ratliff, make an effort, with varying degrees of success, to fuse the two modes in their own lives. This is complicated by the difficulty in recognizing and clinging to truth which cannot be fixed permanently nor stated finally despite the fact that it is universal and eternally accessible. In one's actual physical experience truth can be known but not communicated, though it can be shared. In linguistic experience it can in addition be shown or presented in such a way as to produce an immediate, intuitive conviction. These two ways of arriving at the truth are dramatically rendered in *Requiem for a Nun.* Saying simply "Believe," Nancy Mannigoe offers to share, though she cannot convey, the truth which she herself has painfully grasped. It is Gavin Stevens who articulates and interprets the significance of Nancy's gesture, thus leading

Temple to the point where she herself can comprehend and accept that truth.

Since this intuitive but comprehensive knowledge of truth dispenses with logic and words, it posits a difficult problem in technique for the artist. Whatever a character is conscious of, he can express for himself in his own idiom, though in a number of instances this involves a groping for words, a struggle to fuse the word with the feeling and the act. It is in broken phrases that Lena Grove tries to tell Hightower why she is worried by Mrs. Hines's confusion of her child with Joe Christmas. Rosa Coldfield uses a voluble speech in her repetitive verbal circling around certain key points in her narrative. In each case, however, this search for the word is rendered in both dramatic and stylistic terms. Yet there is always a residue of experience and personal feeling which resists formulation if only because of the nature of language. Addie Bundren, for example, finds that words obscure or even falsify the quality of experience. Similarly, the Reporter in *Pylon*, despite an extensive vocabulary, is unable to convey to the editor the intense drama of the airport. This problem of communication or self-expression is intensified where there is an actual lack of vocabulary. Yet the inability to articulate does not argue a limited experience or a shallowness of feeling. That Ike Snopes cannot give expression to his love and longing for the cow does not mean that the feeling itself has no reality. Similarly, Benjy Compson's wail is "nothing. Just sound," (303) but at the same time it is "all time and injustice and sorrow become vocal for an instant by a conjunction of planets." (303–304)

Whenever the character is unaware of the problem of articulation or whenever, for one reason or another, he is incapable of expressing himself, the author's voice assumes control. At times, as in *The Wild Palms*, Faulkner clearly indicates what he is doing. Repeatedly he comments, usually in parentheses, that this is what the convict would have said "if he had been able to phrase it, think it instead of merely knowing it." (266) Thus, what the convict remembers having done or thought is continually enriched by Faulkner's revelation of what he knew and felt. The simple, colloquial language of the one fuses with the imaginative lyricism of the other to produce that style which is so distinctively Faulkner's. This same technique is handled somewhat less successfully in "The Long Summer" section of *The Hamlet*, for here the weight of Faulkner's rhetoric is not balanced by colloquial realism. All Ike Snopes contributes is "the one sound which he knew, or at least was ever known to make, and that infallibly when anyone spoke to him." (204) On the other hand, Faulkner's most striking use of this technique is in *As I Lay Dying* where he gives a formal lyrical representation of the unconscious minds and subliminal selves of the inarticulate Bundrens without destroying the sense of their physical reality.

It is also the author's voice that speaks when the communal consciousness or memory is to be articulated. The individual necessarily contributes to and shares in the mass consciousness, but the moment he begins to talk, it is his private world which he is formulating verbally. Accordingly, it is impossible to present the mass mind dramatically. Chick Mallison may describe the mob as it affects him, Gavin may explain its rationale, but it is Faulkner who conveys its essence through the play of rhetoric. Similarly, it is Faulkner's voice which expresses the thought, feeling, and impulses of Jefferson throughout *Light in August*. Since he alone is not restricted by the dramatic context or confined to a single mode of expression, he is able to see and present lyrically the whole complex of relationships which obtain at any given moment. In other words, Faulkner's voice is the only one in the novels which is not bound by a limited perspective. In the same fashion and for the same reasons, Faulkner articulates the communal memory at length in *Requiem for a Nun* and more briefly in such novels as *Absalom, Absalom!* where he relates what Jefferson learned and remembered about Sutpen. Isaac McCaslin inherited his memories even "as Noah's grandchildren had inherited the Flood although they had not been there to see the deluge." (289) His account of history, however, is necessarily private, for he can only discuss it as it has affected him. Using the same material and occasionally even the same phrases, the author's voice in *Requiem for a Nun* recounts that history as it has affected all mankind.

Obviously such a technique demands an almost incredible range of style and vocabulary if the modulation from factual description to lyric revelation is to be effected. It is essential that the writer have complete control over dialect and the nuances of common speech, and Faulkner's skill in this field is undisputed. Even in the elaborately overwritten *Soldiers' Pay* the conversation between Joe Gilligan and young Robert Saunders about Donald's scar shows promise of his gift for dialogue, vivid and sharply individualized. The necessarily limited and repetitive vocabulary of such people as the Bundrens or the farmers clustered around Varner's store is enlivened by its absolute concreteness and by the humorous turn of phrase. In *As I Lay Dying* the idiomatic language of the characters serves to relieve the genuine horror of the funeral journey, while in *The Hamlet* the mock-tragedy of Eula Varner's loss of chastity is heightened by her father's pithy comments.

The style Faulkner uses to render the abstract thought of his characters is somewhat more formal; its vocabulary is less concrete and individualized. There is both gain and loss involved in this shift from the realistic and colloquial to the formal level of language. The range of vocabulary is extended, thereby increasing the flexibility of language as an instrument of communication. On the other hand, all the vividness and immediacy of dialect with its heavy reliance on concrete nouns is lost. Furthermore, language no longer expresses the individual personality but rather thought in general. As a result, it loses much of its ability to provide a stylistic equivalent to individual characters. Hence, in *Intruder in the Dust* it is almost impossible to tell when Gavin Stevens' analysis of the South stops and Chick's begins. Similarly, one can only with difficulty distinguish between Isaac McCaslin's statements and Cass Edmonds' comments in "The Bear." Stevens, McCaslin, Edmonds, Mr. Compson, all speak the common, accepted language of educated men in which the rules of grammar, syntax, and logic are assiduously, almost monotonously, followed. Of these, Stevens alone has the ability to move from the logical and the abstract to the simple and concrete, as suggested in *Knight's Gambit*, "so that all the people in our country—the Negroes, the hill people, the rich flatland plantation owners—understood what he said." (87)

In formal language used to express abstract thought, the individual and the concrete are secondary. These, however, are once more restored in the language of symbols which makes its appeal not to reason but to emotion and imagination. Symbols are created out of and operate through images which possess that concreteness in the verbal universe that objects and events have in the non-verbal. At the same time, they are suggestive rather than definitive. Accordingly, the symbol provides an immediate and incommunicable verbal and aesthetic experience in the same way that the object or event provides an equally incommunicable non-verbal experience. Because the symbol cannot be confined within any single system or formula, it serves to free man's imagination and because it is evocative rather than definitive, it provides a verbal stimulus to that totality of human response which reason and logic destroy. Its tremendous power to move is illustrated by Hightower's reaction to Cynthie's story of the Civil War or by *Requiem for a Nun*'s description of the haunting effect produced by a girl's name scratched on a pane of glass. In effect, the symbol provides the antidote as well as the antithesis to the cliché response and formula. And since it does not depend on logic but on intuitive comprehension, the language of symbols is the only one common to all men, to the lawyers and plantation owners as well as to those whom Isaac McCaslin calls " 'the doomed and lowly of the earth who have nothing else to read with but the heart.' " (260)

The language of reason with its attempt to fix and define reality is limited to science and related fields. Symbolic language which does not seek to translate reality but to create a reality of its own is primarily the language of literature and art, both on the formal and informal levels. Faulkner's novels are filled with characters who are themselves unconscious creators of folk literature. The source of folk literature is man's capacity to use words imaginatively without conscious effort or deliberate technique. In the very process of using words, there is an element of unconscious fiction, if only because language is itself metaphoric. In addition the play of fancy and imagination and the desire for some recognizable pattern ensure an almost imperceptible shift from fact to fiction. The tall story with its frank attempt to render the fabulous credible, the anecdote with its humorous understatement, and the tales of heroes and wars provide the forms so long familiar to generations of story-tellers, lounging on the courthouse steps, that using them is almost second nature. Gavin Stevens, for instance, finds no difficulty in continually passing from the rational to the imaginative, from logical to aesthetic order. Fairchild telling his story of alligator-men, Will Falls and his legends of Sartoris, Cynthie and her stirring account of the Civil War,

Ratliff with his casual anecdotes, all contribute to the growing body of folk-tales.

It is in literature whether created by peasants and old men or by professional writers that the racial memory is preserved. The act or event becomes permanent in language, for, in a sense, the word *is* the act existing in a verbal universe. The physical deed and its repercussions gradually subside and become part of the lost past in accordance with the laws of change and succession which operate in the world of space and time. Yet the reverberations of the act continue and become a part of the human consciousness; thus, the act itself persists in the mental world whose co-ordinates are memory and imagination. Language, when used creatively, is a pictorial representation of the mental world just as graphs and diagrams are of the physical world. Thus, the three sections of *The Sound and the Fury* picture Caddy Compson's reactions only as they exist in the memory, the mental world of her three brothers. Quentin and Shreve give verbal and aesthetic form not to the actual story of Henry Sutpen and Charles Bon but to the impact that the story has on them. Through language they are externalizing their own emotions and aspirations, identifying themselves with the shapes they have created so that "there was now not two of them but four, the two who breathed not individuals now yet something both more and less than twins, the heart and blood of youth." (294)

Since the deed persists only in memory, language constitutes the sole possible communal memory insofar as it denies the notions of uniqueness and privacy affirmed by the individual memory. For this reason, Judith Sutpen gives Bon's letter to Mrs. Compson in the hope that "at least it would be something just because it would have happened, be remembered even if only from passing from one hand to another, one mind to another, and it would be at least a scratch, something, something that might make a mark." (127) Similarly, emotion and thought acquire objective reality only after they have been stated. Jefferson forgives Mrs. Hightower because "no crime or transgression had been actually named." (56–57) Conversely, Dewey Dell Bundren refuses to say that she is pregnant because, as Darl suggests, " 'when you say it, even to yourself, you will know it is true.' " (365) Mrs. Hines does not really know her past until she relates its story to Hightower, thereby simultaneously externalizing it and making it a part of the communal memory rather than of her own recollections. Language has made her memories public and therefore objectively real.

The only way in which language can be private is through style which alone can render the individuality of the writer. In a sense, the author borrows his words from the communal language and makes them his own through style. This, however, does not deprive them of the weight of communal memory and emotional associations that attach themselves to each word. The personal and the communal are thus fused into one aesthetic whole. The result is that literature and literature alone presents the reader with a language of memory and hence with the means of reading his own past and so of understanding his own actions. By the very nature of language the writer cannot invent but only invoke that which is already present in the memory of all men. He aims at becoming an instrument of evocation for his readers. In Faulkner's own novels, the paradigmatic image of this is to be found in the Negro preacher of *The Sound and the Fury* who conjures up before his congregation a vision of the Passion of Christ "until he was nothing and they were nothing and there was not even a voice but instead their hearts were speaking to one another in chanting measures beyond the need for words." (310) The task of the man dedicated to language is to reveal to man his endless potentialities and to make him more cognizant of the quality of his experience. Ultimately, it is through the word that man becomes aware of his knowledge, for in language he projects his wisdom beyond his own mind. And it is precisely this task that Faulkner has been fulfilling consciously and deliberately in all his novels.

17 : THE DEFINITION OF MAN

Out of Faulkner's sharply realized portraits of individual men and women, there gradually emerges a view of man which involves making a crucial distinction between the social and moral definitions of his nature. The former simply places the individual in certain exclusive categories, the latter restores to him his identity with all humanity. The one provides a formula for morality and enforces it with law, the other leaves moral action undefined and therefore unfettered. In short, the social definition of man predetermines the individual's response to experience by creating an expectation of conformity to certain codes which govern the behavior of each social unit. The moral definition forces man to assume responsibility for recognizing and enacting his own moral nature. At the very heart of the Yoknapatawpha novels and *A Fable* is the problem created by the conflict between the inflexible morality of society and the ethics of the individual based on experience, grounded in specific situations, and usually incapable of formulation beyond the simplest of maxims and platitudes. Isaac McCaslin and Chick Mallison, each acting according to his conscience and risking the certain disapproval of society, anticipate the Corporal in his role of rebel.

Since any social system or moral code tends to replace internal morality with external controls, the only healthy relationship between men and their society is one of mutual suspicion and unrelaxed vigilance. Only such an attitude can ensure the continued existence of a critical revaluation of the former's behavior and the latter's conventions. If this balance is destroyed, the result is either anarchy or social and governmental dictatorship. Because it completely obliterates freedom, because it reduces the individual to an unquestioning automaton, the second is more dangerous. Faulkner levels some of his bitterest and most forthright criticism at this accelerating process of regimentation which he describes in almost all of his novels, though it becomes increasingly prominent in the later works, beginning with *Go Down, Moses*.

Far from idealizing the Old South, Faulkner sees in it, as in the army, an instance of the paralyzing influence that a rigid caste system and a closed society can exert on the individual. Born into such a society, men are automatically labelled and cross-filed in terms of color, class, clan, and possibly religious and political affiliations. Each of these categories defines a separate world and a distinct code of behavior; all of them together constitute the Southern way of life. In fact, the most general and inclusive of these categories is the South itself with its attendant myth of uniqueness. It is, of course, a truism to say that the South is not simply a geographical locale but that it has a certain identity quite independent of its position on the map. Yet this truism is itself a disguised myth of unusual power because accepted by North and South alike. Acceptance of this myth represents the initial and basic step towards a comprehensive pattern of social compulsion which influences the individual through a definition of his status.

Gavin Stevens makes a convincing argument in *Intruder in the Dust* for the necessity of maintaining such national or regional myths since " 'only from homogeneity comes anything of a people or for a people of durable and lasting value.' " (154) A common language and customs establish unity within the group, while common memories of the past, whether of triumph or defeat, glory or shame, intensify the feeling of kinship. It is the memory of guilt, of slavery and injustice, and the present need of expiating it that gives the people of the South their communal character which at times almost obliterates their individual identity. Under these conditions the group has a continuity and flexibility that permits change without subsequent loss of identity. And each of its members, like Chick Mallison in *Intruder in the Dust*, reveals not "just a man's passions and aspirations and beliefs but the specific passions and hopes and convictions and ways of thinking and acting of a specific kind and even race." (151)

In actuality, however, the South does not achieve this ideal since it seeks to preserve its identity not through the homogeneity of its people but through the perpetuation of its structure—the mathematically precise organization of human beings with a place for each and each in his place. Descending from the mountains where " 'the land belonged to anybody and everybody,' " Sutpen is amazed to find himself in a country whose people are rigidly stratified by property and race. Whether or not the institution of slavery exists, classification by color can continue and can be used to determine social, economic, and even moral status. The absolute exclusiveness of the two groups thus formed is, of course, tellingly documented through Joe Christmas and Velery Bon. With the exception of a few Negroes, such as Lucas Beauchamp and Sam Fathers, and a few white men, such as Isaac McCaslin and Chick Mallison, no one questions or challenges such classification despite the pattern of alienation which it instigates.

Further stratification is apparent within the white world itself. The plantation owners, the independent farm holders, and the tenant farmers form three distinct social classes determined in this case not by color but by wealth. And as the prose sections of *Requiem for a Nun* make clear, these divisions remain constant despite changes in the source of wealth or its distribution. The infrequent occasions on which an individual moves from one class to another has no effect on the economic structure itself. Since there is no difference in color or race to act as a convenient explanation for the economic ordering of society, the possibility of tension, resentment, and violence is increased. Ab Snopes spends his life in a state of constant irritation and resentment which has its roots not only in his own past but in the history of the South. Gentlemen, as Gavin Stevens learns in *Knight's Gambit*, no longer have their horses shot from under them " 'from behind a fence—for a principle,' " (54) but the memory and the tradition of hatred still exist. Certainly there is a principle, no matter how distorted, involved in the barn burning of Ab, the murder committed by Mink, and the sudden explosive and fatal violence of Wash Jones.

If we can accept the premise that Will Varner in *The Hamlet* is a symbol of the continuing brigandage of the past, then the significance of the Snopeses as of the Sutpens in Yoknapatawpha County becomes clearer. They are at once the product and the doom of the Old South. The only way they can break out of their class is by applying themselves with a frightening single-ness of purpose to an intensified economic exploitation of the land or of its people. Success, significantly enough, transforms them in their turn into defenders of the *status quo*. To preserve his newly acquired status, Sutpen repudiates his oldest son, while Flem, with his usual thoroughness, not only repudiates but makes victims of all his kin.

The Snopeses would thus appear to be in direct line of descent from the Sartorises though working in a different context inso-far as exploitation of the land and the Negro has given way to the cannibalistic preying on one's own kind. Yet the emotional re-sponse these two families engender forms a sharp contrast which cannot be explained solely in terms of moral judgment. Flem's willingness to victimize his relatives is more than matched by Carothers McCaslin's cavalier treatment of his daughter. We applaud the robber barons of the past, in part at least, because of their daring, their splendor, and their manifest success. We admire the honor, justice, and dignity displayed in their world and forget what Isaac McCaslin points out in *Go Down, Moses*, that it was "founded upon injustice and erected by ruthless rapacity and carried on even yet with at times downright savag-ery." (298) On the other hand, we deplore the solitary sneak thief dressed in a soiled white shirt instead of scarlet and lace, robbing for pennies instead of empires. In comparison with old Carothers' autocratic rule over his slaves, the power Flem Snopes wields, though no less real, seems petty and ignoble. It is the difference between the conqueror who makes a whole country his booty and the camp follower who patiently picks over the leavings. Both may be equally reprehensible, but the former captures the imagination while the latter prompts only revul-sion.

Whereas movement is still possible within the social structure of the South, the clan completely restricts the activity of the individual. At the same time, since its membership is deter-mined by birth, it is as rigidly exclusive as definition by color. Sutpen, for example, cannot force entry into a clan, though he can through sheer ruthlessness and determination establish one which will bear his name and tradition. The influence of the clan is exercised not only through established patterns of social conduct but through concepts of language. The name itself compels its bearer to act in accordance with the tradition. As young Loosh Peabody ironically comments in *Sartoris*, each new Sartoris means " 'another one to grow up and keep his folks in a stew until he finally succeeds in doing what they all expect him to do.' " Eventually the family tradition, the old masculine hierarchy, becomes stronger than any of the individuals in it, until it is scarcely worthwhile distinguishing them by specific names. Just as MacCallum has stamped each of his six sons with his physical likeness, so the other patriarchs—Sartoris, Compson, Sutpen, McCaslin, and most recently Snopes—have handed down gestures, attitudes, and concepts along with their blood and name.

In ordinary circumstances, the precepts which belong to the community as a whole are not nearly so strong as those which belong to one's own class and family and which are sustained not only by words but by example. The aristocratic class, in particular, stresses conformity in its members, for only by so doing can it maintain and perpetuate its distinctive position. But the pattern of behavior which this class advocates involves the more sensitive of its members in a conflict which is almost irresolvable. The primary flaw in the Old South was not slavery but a false concept of class with its resultant double standard of ethics. Within the limits of the class, a gentleman's code was established which not only permitted but demanded honor and justice and dignity in its adherents. The restrictive nature of the code helps explain why the Sartorises and the Sutpens are said to have "false" pride, why their honor so often appears to be "formal," and their courage recklessness. For the Southern code permitted the existence of slavery at the same time as it demanded freedom for its own members. This paradox is most fully explored through the attitudes of the successive McCaslins and Edmondses in *Go Down, Moses*.

The conflict between the code and the individual who suddenly questions its validity is perhaps best revealed in the final scene of *The Unvanquished*. To meet the expectations of George Wyatt and the other men of Jefferson and to vindicate his "honor," Bayard must kill Redmond. The code demands a death for a death in the case of a Sartoris as well as a Gowrie. Yet Bayard feels that there is another precept which transcends the code, that "if there was anything at all in the Book, anything of hope and peace for His blind and bewildered spawn which He had chosen above all others to offer immortality, *Thou shalt not kill* must be it." (249) In a sense, Bayard avoids choosing by effecting a compromise. He confronts Redmond, but to adhere to his own convictions, he does so unarmed. Simultaneously he preserves Sartoris honor and his own integrity. The further extension of Bayard's action is found in "The Bear," in which Isaac McCaslin scorns the gesture of conformity and makes a clear-cut choice between honor and integrity.

This obligation to live up to and in terms of a family tradition can prove isolative and stultifying. Young Bayard, for instance, is cut off from responding to experience naturally and consequently from any constructive activity by his compulsion to define his identity not in terms of humanity but of "Sartoris." A particularly clear instance of the clan's pressure is found in Sartoris Snopes, whose very name suggests his particular problem. His nature and instincts draw him to an admiration of a world other than his own, but Ab, his father, allows no deviation from the Snopes norm in his family. From these and other examples, it is clear that Faulkner makes approval of the family or clan contingent on its acknowledging the freedom and individuality of its members. For him, its gravest shortcoming is the rigid and compulsive patterns which it tends to engender and perpetuate.

Since the clans are based on a male hierarchy, women naturally play a secondary role. It is, however, a clearly defined role which is integrated into the whole complex structure of the South. In one sense, women are merely transferrable property passing from clan to clan. Through marriage, they lose the name of their father's clan and become simply the instrument for the perpetuation of their husband's line and name. In a characteristic, forthright comment, Sutpen reveals the position of the woman in the design: " 'To accomplish it I should require money, a house, a plantation, slaves, a family—incidentally of course, a wife.' " (263) His crude proposition to Rosa and his use of Milly Jones, whom he compares to a brood mare, present the position of the women of the clan. To fulfill her position, the woman must possess two qualities—purity of blood and chastity —since both of these are necessary to ensure the uncontaminated continuance of the male hierarchy. Clearly, when stripped of all social niceties and bereft of the ritual and rhetoric of courtship, the lot of the woman appears menial and shabby.

It is not surprising, then, that the wives in Faulkner's novels are shadowy, unreal figures. Usually they die young in child-birth, like Mrs. Zack Edmonds, or waste away, like Gail High-tower's mother. Colonel Sartoris, Major de Spain, and General Compson are vividly and vibrantly alive even in memory; their wives, on the other hand, are scarcely mentioned before they sink into the anonymity of the past. The fate of the woman is to be a pale reflection of her husband. Thus, Ellen Coldfield loses all individuality when she assumes her role of wife to Sutpen, living "from attitude to attitude against her background of chatelaine to the largest, wife to the wealthiest, mother of the most fortunate." (69) It is only during the absence of the father and the husband that the woman exercises her latent and re-pressed strength and asserts her own identity. The Civil War brought to the fore a number of indomitable women capable of guarding and preserving the achievements of their men. Dru-silla Hawk in *The Unvanquished* is the extreme example of the "emancipated" woman emerging from the shadowy background of sheltered femininity. Usually, however, it is only the older women who show this strength and determination. Miss Jenny Sartoris, Miss Rosa Millard, and Miss Habersham come readily to mind as instances. It is as if the woman's individuality can only be expressed after the termination of her function as a childbearer. Only then can she rise, as *Absalom, Absalom!* notes, "to actual stardom in the role of the matriarch, arbitrating from the fireside corner of a crone the pride and destiny of her family." (69)

In contrast to these matriarchs who win for themselves a unique position in the masculine hierarchy of the South are those women who, consciously or not, threaten its very existence. Because they are associated with sex, unrestrained by social con-ventions, they are the object of mixed fear and fascination on the part of the men. Their concern with feelings and emotions and their reliance on the immediate intuitive response to experi-ence has no place in a rationally ordered society based on power and authority. Significantly, all these women have lost their virginity and with it their usefulness to the hierarchy. The preg-nant woman in *The Wild Palms*, Lena Grove, and Eula Varner exist as embodiments of nature. They are wholly creative beings absorbed in the immemorial ritual of sex and reproduction. It is this quality in them that arouses the distrust of the tall con-vict, of Hightower, and of Jody Varner. As *The Hamlet* makes clear, their whole way of life is threatened by the female, "serene and intact and apparently even oblivious, tranquilly abrogating the whole long sum of human thinking and suffering which is called knowledge, education, wisdom, at once supremely unchaste and inviolable: the queen, the matrix." (131)

Ruby Lamar, Laverne Shumann, and Charlotte Rittenmeyer are related to this group even as they constitute a departure from it. Though they are deeply involved in the sexual and emotional aspects of life, they are more sharply individualized. And though all three have children, they bear no resemblance to that great earth-mother, Eula Varner. Charlotte, in particular, attempts to terminate her bondage to nature and childbearing. Each of these women is attempting in her own way to develop her own individual and human potentialities. In this, they are anticipated by Margaret Powers of *Soldiers' Pay*, who recognizes that she has upset men's fixed ideas about women and their capabilities. With Charlotte of *The Wild Palms*, these women have discovered " 'that love and suffering are the same thing and that the value of love is the sum of what you have to pay for it.' " (48) Out of this knowledge comes a certain kind of integrity and a certain firmness of purpose that elevates them above the society which rejects them.

In one sense, the Negroes bear the same relation to the plantation system as the women do to the clan. They are at the very basis of its structure, and, like the women, they have no individual identity. They are simply indistinguishable faces which can be bartered or sold at the white man's will. Though they may share the blood and even the name of Sartoris or Compson or McCaslin, a position in the hierarchy is denied them because of their color. Like the woman, however, the Negro acquires social position and status in his own world from the white man with whom he is associated. Much of the comedy of Negro behavior in Faulkner's novels thus arises out of their literal translation of white modes of behavior into the black world and out of their self-identification with their masters. The parody of the white man's ways is sketched in broad clear strokes in *Sartoris* where Simon Strother feels it his duty as a Sartoris Negro to "sot de quality" (114) for the Negro world. During her stately progress to church, Dilsey, acting as representative of the Compsons, reveals her consciousness of caste and the social rituals of condescension and exclusion. Finally, Lucas Beauchamp has the distinction of being not only a McCaslin Negro but a McCaslin by blood. The gold toothpick, the worn handmade beaver hat, the high bridged nose, all contribute to his role as a Negro Carothers McCaslin.

As the behavior of both women and Negroes suggests, the social hierarchy cannot easily be maintained without active protection. One method of protection already noticed is that of familial pressure on individual members. Two other means are the church and law, and these receive the same sort of detailed analysis in *Requiem for a Nun* and *A Fable* as the familial did in *Sartoris* and *Go Down, Moses*. The church and law, however, are not identified with the religious and moral impulse of mankind. The latter exists as part of man's immediate experience; the former are social institutions, enshrining a complex of rituals intended to order experience. The one belongs to the realm of being, the others to the realm of thinking. The religious consciousness is associated with the moral definition of man and an awareness of the human condition. As a moral being, man is capable of all good and therefore all evil. The Reverend Sutterfield in *A Fable* merely states explicitly what Isaac McCaslin, Gavin Stevens, and Nancy Mannigoe also suggested. The price of man's capacity for bravery and repentance is his ability to sin and to be a coward. As Addie Bundren and Nancy Mannigoe demonstrate, to see one's own nature and therefore one's own deficiencies clearly is the first step in feeling humility before God and compassion among men. In short, one form of the religious impulse is ethical behavior.

Rather than giving free expression to this religious impulse, the church stifles or distorts it by subjecting it to a process of abstraction and formalization. For the moment faith is externalized, it begins to lose its spiritual powers and to assume temporal ones. Belief is now imposed from without and enforced by the authority of the church. In this sense, Hightower is quite right in suggesting that "that which is destroying the Church is not the outward groping of those within it nor the inward groping of those without, but the professionals who control it." (426) At this point, the church becomes an end in itself and hence a barrier between man and God. Worship and faith are placed in the service of the church, its dogmas and its rituals, until man "seems to see the churches of the world like a rampart, like one of those barricades of the middleages planted with dead and sharpened stakes, against truth and against that peace in which to sin and be forgiven which is the life of man." (426–27) What Hightower gradually discovers about faith and the church is also presented in the argument between the Corporal and the Priest in *A Fable*, culminating in the Priest's repudiation of his office and his suicide.

As faith is translated into dogma and as the church replaces God, good and evil are isolated and localized. Satan becomes not the creature but the powerful opponent of God, while their epic conflict is reproduced in detail on earth. Those within the church gather themselves into the ranks of the righteous whose duty it is to vanquish sin both in themselves and others. There is nothing personal or vindictive in McEachern's treatment of Joe Christmas. In its most extreme form, however, this righteousness looks for its complement and antithesis in the scapegoat. By piling all sin on the scapegoat, the righteous free themselves of all blame and at the same time become liable to pride, intolerance, cruelty, and hatred. Old Hines believes himself to be God's instrument in removing all "pollution and abomination" from the earth, and this conviction blinds him to the brutality of his actions. The whole town of Jefferson finds its scapegoat in Joe Christmas and its purification in his death. This same attitude, though less fanatical, is present whenever cruelty is performed in the name of virtue. The cold disapproval of Lena and the more active persecution of Ruby Lamar indicate the extent to which the ethics of righteousness can delude itself.

Just as the church and its dogmas gradually replace God and the religious consciousness, so justice and the moral law give way to legal authority. The distinction between the two is perhaps best illustrated by two references to the commandment "Thou shalt not kill." For Bayard Sartoris in *The Unvanquished* this injunction is part of his very being "since it went further than just having been learned." (249) Thus, the moral impulse and the religious behest coincide and issue in his refusal to kill Redmond. On a larger scale, the same decision is reached by the Corporal and his regiment. But in their society the commandment, separated from its religious and moral source, is simply a verbal precept. As such, it is enforced by the external authority of the law and can, as the need arises, be temporarily abrogated by the supreme authority of the state. Its original significance can be restored only through the faith and actions of each new generation and each individual in it.

The increasing externalization of the moral law is exhaustively documented in the prose sections of *Requiem for a Nun*. Slowly man relinquishes his responsibility for seeing that justice is done to the courthouse and the state capitol, relieving himself of the necessity for making any further effort to realize his dream of justice. Simultaneously he denies his own nature and relinquishes his freedom by accepting the theory, expressed in *Go Down, Moses*, that moral behavior is the result of the fear of detection and punishment. Eventually a complex system of laws and precedents provides a detailed blueprint for conduct. The King's Regulations, described in *A Fable* as having "winnowed and tested and proved every conceivable khaki or blue activity and posture and intention, with a rule provided for it and a penalty provided for the rule," (58–59) merely offers a paradigm for the legalistic aspect of society.

The result is a static morality in which the moral is identified with the lawful. Because he pays scrupulous attention to the legal aspects of his actions, Jason Compson considers himself not only legally blameless but morally right. The same attitude is revealed in *Sanctuary* and *Requiem for a Nun* by Temple Drake's inability to see the moral significance of her actions. This diminution of the moral involves also a shrivelling of the concept of sin to a mere violation of a formal law for which an exact and often arbitrary punishment is meted out. It is Nancy Mannigoe's trial that most dramatically juxtaposes the moral and legal aspects of sin. Her concern is with God and her own soul not with the judges, lawyers, bailiffs, and jury. With her quiet words, "Guilty, Lord," she acknowledges her sin as distinct from her legal culpability. Through her action, responsibility and dignity are once more restored to man.

The church and the courthouse are merely two instances of the way in which a symbol is replaced by collective dogma and traditional forms. The individual is thus born into an imposing system of myths and rituals, all of which exert their coercive pressures on him. They inevitably become barriers between man and truth since they force him to react to his experience in terms of cliché responses. Thus, Roth Edmonds' instinctive affection for Henry and Mollie Beauchamp is replaced by the traditional code which governs the relations between Negro and white, master and servant. The child, relying on his instincts, possesses integrity and a sure sense of right and truth which the adult must labor to regain. Perhaps the most striking instance of the child's betrayal by the man is found in Sutpen who accepts so completely the concepts of a class and a tradition not even his own that in one brief moment the child who was turned away from the plantation house door ceases to exist.

The pressure of society compelling the individual to submit to its categories and rituals would be too overpowering a burden if the land itself did not teach him virtue and lend him strength. What it teaches is a sense of perspective and hence of values. In the land's persistence throughout all change, man sees that those values which are most truly his are themselves eternal and capable of being enacted by anyone in any situation. They are made to live and flourish by the individual's practicing them without regard for the prevailing climate of public opinion. And if there are enough such individuals, then the group or society also is capable of moral commitments and a responsible existence. Thus, though it is a mob that lynches Joe Christmas in *Light in August*, it is also a mob that frees the Reverend Sutterfield in *A Fable*. From *Soldiers' Pay*, his very first novel, to the present, Faulkner has continually emphasized that violence and destruction and even death become fully significant only when set over against the larger rhythms of birth and renewal that order the natural world. The land, however, is not a mystical panacea for the ills of man, nor is it a never ending picnic. What it does provide is an image of faith which dramatizes the conviction that man is capable of replacing the concepts of an artificial social structure with the values of humanity which create "the communal anonymity of brotherhood."

18 : THE FIGURE IN THE CARPET

With *The Reivers* Yoknapatawpha County, consisting of some 2400 square miles and inhabited, according to William Faulkner's private census, by a population of 15,611 has received its last topographical, historical, and legendary delineation. Accordingly, Faulkner's works, so often placed in the tradition of the fictional saga, can now be set over against and distinguished from the achievements of Balzac, Zola, and Galsworthy as well as of his own contemporaries such as C. P. Snow or Anthony Powell.

The chief interest in linking him to this tradition is not to see what he has assimilated or copied but what he has achieved that is uniquely his own. And this involves identifying what Henry James called "The Figure in the Carpet," "the thing that most makes [the writer] apply himself, the thing without the effort to achieve which he wouldn't write at all, the very passion of his passion, the part of the business in which, for him, the flame of art burns most intensely." Certainly Faulkner's uniqueness is not to be found in a chronological rendering of events and characters such as Malcolm Cowley suggests in his introduction to *The Portable Faulkner*. Nor is it revealed in the essentially topographical arrangement of material in the *Collected Stories of William Faulkner*. Such patterns, whatever their intrinsic value, fail to penetrate to the heart of his work if only because they ignore the formal strategies invoked by Faulkner. Similarly, the attempts, beginning with George Marion O'Donnell, to focus on Faulkner's morality, social criticism, or philosophy fall short of the mark. There is, of course, no doubt that ideas, moral judgment, and social criticism do exist or can be derived from his work. Yet they too are part of the texture of the carpet as Faulkner himself implies when he states quite categorically that the character is more important than the idea and that "the writer is not really interested in bettering man's condition. . . . He's interested in all man's behavior with no judgment whatever." (267)† In other words, moral and social dimensions emanate from the character and not vice versa.

Even the most casual of glances shows us that Faulkner's ability to "create flesh-and-blood people that will stand up and cast a shadow" (47) is a prominent part of the figure in the carpet. The sense of the density and complexity of life, the tremendous range and variety of character in his works has not been equalled in American literature. The Sartorises, the Snopeses, the Compsons, and the McCaslins; young Temple Drake sowing her wild oats (if such a metaphor can be disengaged from the male sex) in a house of prostitution; Lena Grove serenely licking sardine oil from her fingers; Ike Snopes ambling after his beloved cow through the long, golden afternoon; Dilsey, Nancy Mannigoe, Ringo, T. P.—the list seems endless at least partly because even minor characters, merely rounding out a scene or two, clamor for the reader's attention and understanding.

That they do so is a result of Faulkner's concern with the possibilities—including self-contradiction—inherent in character. As he has stated: "Those characters to me are quite real and quite constant. They are in my mind all the time. I don't have any trouble at all going back to pick up one. I forget what they did, but the character I don't forget, and when the book is finished, that character is not done, he still is going on at some new devilment that sooner or later I will find out about and write about." (78) In adition to this independence and ingenuity, these characters also have the delightful ability to create their own milieu by dragging in a number of people whom Faulkner claims he had never anticipated, never seen nor heard before. For example, Byron Snopes in *Sartoris*, writing lewd letters to Narcissa Benbow and absconding with the bank's cash, has called forth a whole swarm of Snopeses, including a senator, a murderer, and an idiot, as well as his own spawn—a foursome precociously ingenious in their viciousness, eating pedigreed dogs and busily attempting to burn one of their kinsmen at the stake.

† All quotations of Faulkner's personal opinions are from F. L. Gwynn and J. L. Blotner (eds.), *Faulkner in the University* (Charlottesville, Va., 1959).

Clearly, then, Faulkner's major concern is not with manipulating his characters nor with documenting the stages in their development. Instead, having granted them their autonomy and having assumed that all men are capable of all things, he has concentrated on exploring and revealing their complexity. For instance, one thinks of Boon Hogganbeck first as the camp buffoon, the hunter incapable of hitting a barn door at twenty paces or the petulant child intent on protecting his tree full of squirrels from other hunters. Yet he is also the man who has enough courage and patience to tame Lion and enough love to avenge his injuries by killing Old Ben with only his knife for a weapon. Demanding a rarer courage as well as compassion and understanding is his willingness to help Sam Fathers fulfill his wish not to outlive Lion and Old Ben—a willingness that Shakespeare's Antony could not command in his faithful servant, Eros. In *The Reivers* Boon's marksmanship is once more presented in highly comic terms, but beyond that he achieves his final definition, surprisingly enough, as Yoknapatawpha's Don Quixote finding his Dulcinea in Everbe Corinthia, one of Miss Reba's girls, but without the good knight's subsequent disenchantment. For in the world of *The Reivers*, the real and the ideal can be reconciled and so lead to the fairy-tale conclusion—the marriage of Boon and Everbe.

Boon is, of course, representative of many of Faulkner's characters who disconcert critics looking for consistency and the logic of cause and effect. But Faulkner's indifference to such formal patterns of history frees him to recognize an integral, experiential unity which can encompass both change and apparent contradiction: "To me they are people, and they have grown older as I have grown older, and probably they have changed a little—my concept of them has changed a little, as they themselves have changed and I changed. That they have grown. I know more about people than I knew when I first thought of them, and they have become more definite to me as people." (108) Accordingly, he as well as the reader may discover a latent characteristic that manifests itself only under the pressure of some new stimulus or situation. For example, there is development but no inconsistency in Gavin Stevens from *Light in August* to *Requiem for a Nun*. But in *The Town* under the impact of Eula, herself transformed by virtue of her devotion to her child and De Spain, he discovers a hitherto unsuspected capacity for dreaming and for suffering the agony of frustration and failure.

Perhaps a more characteristic way of exploring the latent possibilities of character is Faulkner's repeated use of juxtaposed scenes involving either a lapse of time or a change of place, leading the reader to recognize both simultaneity and progression. Caddy, the child, getting her panties dirty or observing Nancy Mannigoe's mounting panic and despair in "That Evening Sun" coexists with "the ageless and beautiful, cold serene and damned mistress of a German staff general" described in the appendix to the Modern Library edition of *The Sound and the Fury*. (12) And Nancy herself is at once the fearful wife whose infidelities have been discovered, the raucous voice that refuses to be stilled as it demands payment for services rendered to the Baptist deacon, the murderer of Temple Drake's child, and the embodiment of faith asking Temple only to "Believe."

Equally effective is Faulkner's technique of a fallible narrator or point-of-view figure who recognizes and attempts to correct his own mistakes in perception or his own limitations of understanding as the narrator does in "Hair," or the use of multiple narrators who contradict, correct, supplement, and even invent as they do in the Snopes trilogy. And finally, rhetoric itself can serve to modulate or transform the reader's view of a character. In "The Long Summer" the animal-like viciousness of Mink Snopes (suggested by his very name) is lined to his obsessive determination to revenge himself first on Houston and then on Flem. In *The Mansion* the comic horror of these scenes modulates into the vision, still comic but replacing horror with pathos, of his abortive escape from Parchman prison, wearing a woman's dress and bonnet, to the unmodified pathos of his release. The smallness of his figure and his almost total ignorance of the world into which he has finally been released introduce a child-like quality into his composite portrait, a child who must perform the act he has set himself though he has long ago forgotten his own reasons for so doing.

Yet if the limitless possibility of character is a striking and significant part of the Faulknerian carpet, an equally important aspect is Faulkner's concern with the personal identity and common humanity of his characters. The fascination exerted by the problem of identity is nowhere more graphically rendered than in those conscious, deliberate exercises in self-definition embarked upon by so many of Faulkner's characters. Here we see another facet of the author's concern with human possibilities, for not only does he probe for the uniqueness, the quiddity of individuals, but he also charts the variety of ways in which the knowledge of identity both is and is not acquired. Chick Mallison, Isaac McCaslin, Lucas Beauchamp, Joe Christmas, and Charles Etienne Bon, each in his own way exhibits the successes, the hazards, and the failures involved in human identity. But in each case identity is contingent upon a precise relationship to the common humanity of mankind. For Faulkner, common humanity seems to resolve itself into the capacity to aspire and so to choose acceptance, rejection, or evasion of the eternal verities—courage, honor, pride, compassion, pity. Because of his freedom to choose and because his identity is the sum of his choices, the individual character is both intricately woven into the warp and woof of Faulkner's carpet and rendered in a variety of poses and actions that reflect their author's quizzical delight and curiosity at the products of their freedom: "the writer is learning all the time he writes and he learns from his own people, once he has conceived them truthfully and has stuck to the verities of human conduct, human behavior, human aspiration, then he learns—yes, they teach him, they surprise him, they teach him things that he didn't know. . . ." (96)

If Faulkner is indeed concerned not only to explore the range of possibility in character but to probe for its essential humanity, no matter how shrivelled, he must have complete freedom to proceed in any order, in any temporal or spatial direction, and to recall and reexamine any action, situation, or character from a new perspective. Consequently, he experiments endlessly not because, like Henry James, he is interested in form and technique as values in themselves but because no single method can accomplish his purpose of rendering the unique figure of his carpet. The difference between the two is clear. James is the most conscious and consummately skillful craftsman America has ever produced; Faulkner is the most dedicated student of human nature, driven by the demon of compassionate curiosity to literary experimentation.

It follows, then, that Faulkner's interest in form and technique cannot be divorced from his interest in character, his determination, as in *Absalom, Absalom!* or *Light in August*, to make the reader aware simultaneously of consistency and contradiction, immersion in and transcendence of time, simplicity as well as complexity, depth as well as scope. To do this he resists any temptation to circumscribe, define, or interpret his characters from a position of authority since that would immediately destroy their autonomy. Thus, he goes a step beyond the Joycean artist who refines himself out of existence. In Faulkner, authorial exclusion is replaced by authorial transcendence. The anonymous Voice so often detected in his fiction is the author seeing himself distanced as one more perspective on the scene, one more legitimate but not conclusive point of view. It is also his mature version of the omniscient narrator founded upon the conviction that freedom for the self is freedom from the self. Throughout, his aim is to avoid limiting the freedom of character, reader, or author.

An apparent contradiction, often pointed out by critics, actually serves to reinforce these statements. Popeye, the cardboard figure, the two-dimensional character, the mechanical man, seems completely circumscribed, an impression that is supported by the awkwardly introduced "case history" summarizing his heredity and environment. But this Zolaesque tendency to "explain" is held in check by Faulkner's own and apparently instinctive desire to provoke simple curiosity. The sociological-psychological mold is broken as Popeye passively accepts death for a crime he can prove he has not committed and by his final words to his executioner "Fix my hair, Jack." The inhuman monster conditioned to callousness shows a fleeting trace of wry irony if not humor as he repudiates that minimal life so precariously and persistently maintained at the expense of living.

Faulkner's proper concern, then, is to preserve the heart of the mystery by ordering his material to provide a maximum of concentration, illumination, and implication. In other words, Faulkner, the self-styled "failed poet," (22) makes prose fiction approximate poetry which he equates with the lyric and defines as "some moving, passionate moment of the human condition distilled to its absolute essence." (202) Such an attempt does not simply demand absolute exactitude; it also encourages the soaring design of rhetoric, the evocative condensation of imagery and symbolism, and the variety of textural richness as well as dramatic immediacy, all characteristic of Faulkner's style at its best.

In viewing the carpet one therefore moves inevitably from an awareness of vibrantly living characters to the perception of an intricately related series of lyrical stases. Individually these recall Keats's Grecian Urn capturing the essence of the moment, while collectively they constitute a modern prose equivalent to the Renaissance lyric cycle such as the *Amoretti*. It is with this that the place and significance of Faulkner's short stories in his total canon begin to emerge. In terms of content, we distinguish between stories, like "Turnabout," that are completely outside the

Yoknapatawpha saga and those that contribute to it. The former serve as a variegated peripheral frieze that frames the panorama of the central saga. At the same time, the thematic and narrative similarities between a story like "Honor" and a novel like *Pylon*, both concerned with a bizarre solution to a sexual triangle, suggest the possibility of alternative or additional sagas that were never developed.

It is, however, the Yoknapatawpha stories that show the three-fold function of the short story in Faulkner: as a narrative unit in its own right, as an element of structure, and as a method of thematic and character exploration. These stories may be classified roughly as adjunctive, projective, and parodic. The first, the adjunctive, are stories that simply add more information about certain characters, situations, or the history of Yoknapatawpha County: for example, the MacCallums in "The Tall Men," the Griers in "Two Soldiers" and "Shall Not Perish," or Miss Emily in "A Rose for Emily" and Miss Minnie Cooper in "Dry September." Others, such as "There Was a Queen" or "All the Dead Pilots," examine a new aspect of characters already established and so project new demands of action on the characters and new demands of understanding on the readers. Thus, the laughing face of Johnny Sartoris is replaced by an inarticulate, humorless man incapable of seeing the comic aspects of his rivalry with a superior officer for the favors of a girl so eager to accommodate all men that she is nicknamed "Kitchener." The final group, consisting mainly of the Indian stories, parody the white man's follies and ways so as to counterpoint the design of the primary saga itself. A pair of useless red shoes serves as a symbol of status and authority, the wilderness and the vanished past form a subject of nostalgic reminiscence; while the "Negro question," that is, the question of his position in the Indian economy, is the subject of a hilarious debate about whether cannibalism offers a sensible solution to Negro fecundity. But most impressive as illumination through parody is the ritual pursuit of a Negro slave in "Red Leaves." The desperate terror, the agony, the pain of his gangrenous arm leap out of the scene with a dramatic immediacy that both points up and is underscored by the essentially comic view of his pursuers moving in their decorous, stately, untroubled course.

In addition to the pattern of content there is a pattern of form and structure. Its first aspect consists of a group of conventional stories depending on plot complication and action leading to some sort of resolution, as in "Dr. Martino," "The Brooch," or "Artist at Home." Since most of these stories are unrelated to the Yok-napatawpha saga and its techniques of presentation, they can fairly be viewed as providing a bold relief background for the scenes, actions, and characters that dominate the center of the carpet. A second group approximates the lyric insofar as it tends to focus on a single effect and a single impression. The emphasis is on situations rather than plot and on revelation rather than definition of character. Typical of these are "A Rose for Emily" and "That Evening Sun," surely two of Faulkner's finest stories. In the latter the situation is so vividly rendered and Nancy's fears so powerfully communicated that her death has, at times, been taken for granted and her corpse identified with the bones picked clean by buzzards in *The Sound and the Fury*. But in view of her disconcerting resurrection in *Requiem for a Nun*, a careful re-reading discovers how much emphasis is placed upon the foolishness of her fears. As in "That Evening Sun" so in "Dry September" or "Wash," Faulkner's refusal to dramatize the conclusive action serves both to intensify the dominant emotion and to project it beyond the story itself. By this last Faulkner makes the reader implicitly accept the possibility of future continuation of the narrative and recognize that his characters' lives extend beyond the formal confines of individual works. Questions remain unanswered as to the fate of young Sartoris Snopes fleeing from his barn-burning father, Dewey Dell still carrying her child as the Bundren family begins its homeward journey, or Byron Bunch whose inept but earnest advances are firmly repelled by Lena Grove.

With the third type of story, a new element in the design of Faulkner's carpet can now be detected. In addition to living characters and frozen moments of concentrated emotion, the carpet also contains a series of recurring designs. For, surprisingly enough in view of his concern with freedom, the third kind of story is formulaic. Faulkner describes its genesis and function to a University of Virginia student: "There are so few plots and what you read—the plot has not changed too much, only the people involved in it have changed, and to see the same plot repeated time after time with different people motivated by it or trying to cope with it, you can learn about people that way, to match your own experience with living people." (117) What would seem to reveal a paucity of imagination becomes in his hands a highly sophisticated technique, a most subtle method of exploring character and delineating its uniqueness. The formula, which Faulkner calls "the dead skeleton," is born of curiosity meeting the challenge to human freedom and imaginatively evoking characters whose vibrancy animates and fleshes out the dead skeleton resident in the human situation.

The skeleton or formula consists of two main patterns or types, each of which possesses three sub-types or variants. And since each is capable of interrelation, there are at least nine possible formulaic modes. The first main pattern is that of the contest, whether involving cards, horses, or women. If emphasis is placed on the formal aspect of the contest—the complicated moves and countermoves of a card game, the intricate maneuvers of bargaining, the wild ingenuity of sexual rivals—and if the opponents are evenly matched, the result is likely to be comic. *The Reivers* offers the purest form of comedy, for in the inherently absurd process of exchanging a car for a horse in order to regain the car, nobody wins and nobody loses. Similarly, Ab Snopes, before he becomes soured, and Pat Stamper are, in the story "Flem," so evenly matched in ingenuity and so obviously enjoying their contest that the elaborate swapping of horses and mules and even milk separators is hilariously funny.

In contrast, Miss Rosa's ability in "Raid" to dupe the Yankees into providing her with a steady stream of mules fuses the comic with the heroic. The increasing stakes in "Was" ultimately involving the fate of a confirmed bachelor, a frustrated spinster, and two Negro slaves introduce an element of irony. Of greater mordancy is the game of checkers in "The Long Summer" between Mink and Lump Snopes, played in an atmosphere of macabre humor and nightmare pressure. It is, however, "Spotted Horses," the most famous of Faulkner's horse-trade stories, pitting amateurs against professionals and introducing the themes of greed and exploitation, that offers the widest range of tones. The absurdity of the situation, the irrational behavior of the participants, and the exaggerated humor of incident is qualified by the pathetic suffering of Mrs. Armstid, the horrifying transformation of her husband, and the accidental involvement of Tull and his family. Thus, the simple formula is made to yield a complex insight into human behavior, morality, responsibility, and justice.

The final version of the contest formula involves some form of sexual rivalry. The Queen Bee—the irresistible, elusive She—as exemplified by Mink Snopes's wife making a private harem out of her father's lumber camp is broadly comic. As Eula Varner unleashes a frenzy of desire and frustration in the young men of Frenchman's Bend, comedy is fused with myth and symbol, but as Temple Drake alternates between provocation and retreat, the dominant tone is horror. The classic triangle, like the mass pursuit, appears in many guises. In "A Courtship" Herman Basket's sister marries her uncompetitive suitor while the other two are busily engaged in eating and racing contests. When the triangle involves adultery, the range of response becomes more complex. In "Centaur in Brass" Tom Tom farcically chases Turl, his wife's lover, until both fall breathlessly into a ditch and reestablish their friendship and male solidarity. In "Wild Palms," however, the attempt of Charlotte's husband to help the man who has not only run away with but also inadvertently killed his wife is developed not as knock-about comedy but as shrill, highly-colored melodrama. And beyond it the basic triangle reappears in *Pylon* as the continuing *ménage a trois* in which not even Laverne knows who has fathered her child. Here melodramatic situation is used to develop with the artless simplicity of a morality play the theme of paternity as an emotional and moral rather than legal commitment. When adultery is set in a racial context, the formula develops added ramifications including those of ambiguity and uncertainty. Thus Lucas Beauchamp regains his wife from Zack Carothers in "The Fire and the Hearth" and simultaneously recognizes that his victory may be transitory; indeed, his very suspicion may be groundless. And at the furthest extreme from the comic there is the unrelieved horror of incest compounded by miscegenation in "The Bear" as Ike relives the scene of old Carothers McCaslin calling his Negro daughter to his bed.

The other main pattern used by Faulkner is the hunt in which the prime objects are buried treasure, wild game, or human beings. Thus, as engaged in by Lucas Beauchamp, the search for buried treasure provides a wide spectrum of humor. But a similar hunt contrived by Flem Snopes results in a shattering experience for the Armstid family and a chastening one for Ratliff. Accordingly, both the victim and the victimizer evoke a horror which replaces the original comic response.

In contrast the ritual pursuit of game is almost always treated seriously, though the mode may vary from heroic to elegiac to low mimetic. The heroic culminates in the poetic rhetoric of "The Bear" where through Sam Fathers, Isaac McCaslin, Old Ben and Lion, the story acquires a symbolic universality, testing not only courage but humility and integrity. In an elegiac mood, the aged Isaac in "Delta Autumn" watches the wilderness receding, the hunters refusing to discriminate between worthy game and does and fawns. On the periphery are such stories as "A Bear Hunt" that degenerates into a private joke or "A Fox Hunt" in which a cuckolded husband relieves his jealousy and mounting frustration by chasing a fox and finally killing it in a particularly brutal fashion.

The final object of the chase, that of another human being, may be pursued with two different aims. The hunt can either issue in death, as with lynching or scapegoat tales, or in life, as with the Reluctant Lover stories. And in either case they too range from comedy to tragedy. The vigorous chase of Tomey's Turl by Uncle Buck and Uncle Buddy, parodying the lynch tale, is comic because there is no possibility of violence or death. Comedy through parody is also used in "Red Leaves." Unhurried, patient, and meticulous about the rules to be followed, the Negro's Indian pursuers prefer to wait for their quarry to surrender rather than to track him down. But in "Dry September" and "Pantaloon in Black" as well as in *Light in August* and *Intruder in the Dust*, humor is either entirely absent or reduced to a caustic irony, for here there is no parody, only naked inhumanity to man.

When the human being is pursued as a sexual object, the stories offer brilliant variations on the theme of the Obsessed and the Reluctant Lover. The former, as in "Eula," frequently plays a complimentary role to the Queen Bee. But he is also seen in Philip St. Just Backhouse ("My Grandmother Millard") overcoming Melisandre's modesty, Hawkshaw ("Hair") patiently waiting for his Susan Reed to grow up, or Ike ("The Long Summer") happily following his beloved cow. When the Obsessed Lover is a woman, humor is replaced by an intensity bordering on hysteria whether it involves Miss Emily's ("A Rose for Emily") bizarre manner of claiming Homer Baron for her own, Miss Elly's determination ("Miss Elly") to kill herself and the recalcitrant Paul Montigny, or Joanna Burden pursuing Joe Christmas through her garden. The Obsessed Lover may also find that his obsession does not prevent him from feeling reluctant to satisfy it because of fear of involvement, difficulty of removing ingrained conviction, or loss of dignity, detachment, and simple male freedom. The strategies of evasion may encompass Houston's departure from Jefferson, Labove's attempted rape which will permit him to be forceful instead of humbly tentative, or the Reporter's conviction that he can become part of Laverne's world without sexual involvement. Depending on his character, then, we may feel a greater or lesser degree of sympathy for the

lover, but we are rarely, if ever, free of a sense of the absurdity
with which his obsession and his evasions surround him.

Broadly speaking, these formula stories, whether separate units
or episodes within novels, contribute three major qualities: revelation of character, as in "Dry September," "Death Drag," or
"The Bear"; recurrence of patterns, as in "Centaur in Brass," "A
Courtship," and "Artist at Home," each of which issues in a
reconciliation of husband and lover; and diversity of tones as
exhibited in "Was," "Pantaloon in Black," "Dry September" or
in the love stories beginning with the romantic comedy of Melisandre and Lieutenant Philip St. Just Backhouse in "My Grandmother Millard" and its parody in the homosexual relationship
of "A Divorce in Naples" and in Ike's attachment to the cow.
The first of these qualities reiterates in a graphic, sketch-like
fashion the centrality of character and personal identity. The
second, the perception of the recurrence of a relatively limited
number of patterns of human action, introduces into the Faulknerian design the perdurable limiting conditions of human existence. We become aware of our common humanity through
perceiving the anatomical similarities of skeletons. Or, to put it
otherwise, because in one sense there are so few courses of human
action and they are pursued so repetitively, we see both the limitations of life and its ritualistic significance as the embodier of
the eternal verities. If this awareness of recurring patterns suggests a straitening of human freedom and variety in the Faulknerian design, it is more than offset by the third quality, that of
the brilliant diversity of tones exhibited in and through the formulas. By varying his tone and attitude from comedy through
irony, heroism, pathos, and elegy to tragedy, Faulkner reveals
in a deeper light the true nature of human freedom. It consists
not so much in limitless opportunities for all conceivable actions
as in an infinite variety of responses to those actions which man
either can or must perform. In short, the diversity of tones constitutes that virtually unparalleled range of shading and color which
amazes and delights every viewer of Faulkner's carpet.

This somewhat lengthy discussion of the types of short story
simplifies our consideration of the novels since the short story for
Faulkner is not only a genre but an element of structure. For
Faulkner would accept Poe's statement that "unless a book follows a simple direct line such as a story of adventure, it becomes
a series of pieces." The author's function, then, is to exercise
"his judgment and taste to arrange the different pieces in the

most effective place in juxtaposition to one another." (45) It is therefore possible to argue, as Malcolm Cowley does, that all of Faulkner's novels reveal some structural weakness, some absence of unity, and that he has no talent for sustained narrative and hence his reputation will eventually rest on his superbly structured short stories.

But it is also possible to assert that such criticism is irrelevant in that it uses the criteria of the well-made novel in discussing a form which deliberately rejects that particular tradition. In other words, Faulkner was creating a new form which would suit his own purpose: "You write a story to tell about people, man in his constant struggle with his own heart, with the hearts of others, or with his environment. It's man in the ageless, eternal struggle which we inherit and we go through as though they'd never happened before, shown for a moment in a dramatic instant of the furious motion of being alive, that's all any story is. You catch this fluidity which is human life and you focus a light on it and you stop it long enough for people to be able to see it." (239)

Clearly the light focussed and held is one of the structural principles underlying the form Faulkner evolved. In virtually all his works there are scenes which dramatically render a character's individuality so powerfully and unforgettably that they are climactic moments regardless of where they occur in the narrative. It is this principle which Faulkner developed out of the short story with its emphasis on the single incident and the character scrupulously revealed in a specific but universal moment of history. At the same time, he recognized that fiction could not truly exist as merely dramatic scenes involving individual human beings: "I mean that love and money and death are the skeletons on which the story is laid. They have nothing to do with the aspirations and conflicts of the human hearts involved. But the story has got to have some skeleton, and the skeletons are love or money or death." (198) The skeleton, then, is Faulkner's other structural principle, the one which provides the varieties of narrative development out of which emerge the recurrent themes and the characters' link with "man in the ageless, eternal struggles." When the two principles are mastered, Faulkner begins to bring his new form to fruition. Their presence and the result appear most obviously in his story-novels: *The Unvanquished, The Hamlet, Go Down, Moses,* and *Knight's Gambit.* To see them as ordered by the concepts of universal pattern and unique character is to grasp the true relationship of their parts and to avoid seeing nothing but what Cowley has called "a series of beads on a string."

Closely related to the story-novel is the novel of formal juxtaposition as seen in *The Sound and the Fury* and *As I Lay Dying*. But instead of focussing on a significant action, the emphasis is on a single, fixed attitude or state of mind, revealing itself through interior monologues as it responds to certain focal experiences in the past as well as to the demanding present. Each member of the Bundren family, for example, reacts in his own individual manner to Addie's death and to the crises of the funeral journey, just as each of the Compson brothers copes with the present while he reveals himself as in some sense molded by his past response to Caddy and her loss of virginity. The brilliant juxtaposition of psychological perspectives enables Faulkner to introduce and reinforce certain obvious comparisons and contrasts, to provide an infinite number of variations, and to achieve an incredible richness of texture and shading. To use but one example, Jason Compson's compulsive greed for money is juxtaposed against Quentin's guilt about the financial sacrifice involved in his attending Harvard, Benjy's loss of the pasture—one of the three things he loved—Dilsey's indifference about whether or not Jason pays her, and Luster's anxious search for the lost quarter which will enable him to attend a travelling show.

When we turn to the counterpoint novels such as *The Wild Palms*, *Requiem for a Nun*, and *Light in August* (which, however, bears certain resemblances to the next type), the separateness of the stories is deliberately stressed. The very absence of narrative bridges creates that sustained comparison and contrast which leads to recognition of the uniqueness of character. It also bears in upon us in tentative, hypothetical fashion the possible metaphysical significance of the pattern in the carpet through recurring but sudden glimpses of the relation of identity and diversity, of the particular and the universal. Whether we call it point and counterpoint or theme and variation, the balancing of disparate stories is necessary in order to prevent a definitive, completed statement of theme or a single, sustained tone, which, in effect, would limit or predetermine the reader's response.

Thus, in *The Wild Palms* the romantic love of Henry and Charlotte results in a mismanaged abortion, her death, and his imprisonment. The emotional impact of their love is balanced by the Tall Convict, the ultimate version of the Reluctant Lover, forced into responsibility for a pregnant woman whom he neither knows, loves, nor desires. Tragedy and comedy; abortion and death as well as birth and life; prison as punishment and prison as reward: the evocative parallels can, of course, be multiplied. And yet they are without point unless the material's diversity is also fully recognized. Alternation between opposing character attitudes (as in *The Wild Palms*), differing authorial points of view (as in *Requiem for a Nun*), or disparate concepts (as in *Light in August*), all point up striking variations in surface configurations and disparate, multi-levelled clashing planes much after the manner of a Cézanne or cubist painting. The aim is simultaneously a perception of hitherto unnoticed similarities and a renewed awareness of the incontrovertible differences that exist both in the physical and in the more broadly human worlds.

Unlike the other counterpoint novels, *Light in August* does connect its three stories through plot, though only tangentially. But the real richness and coherence in this novel is due to the recurrence of the scapegoat pattern with its evocation of mythology and religion as it is enacted by Gail Hightower, Joanna Burden, and Joe Christmas. In the same way, the angular contrasts of diversity, providing a wide spectrum between the poles of life and death, are seen in the varied sexual relationships as well as in their conceptual clash with the religious modes of the novel.

The final distinguishable form, one that is among Faulkner's most original and certainly most misunderstood is what (for lack of a better word) I have called the "fused novel" which combines the virtues of the short story possessing its own "unity and coherence, the proper emphasis and integration which a long chronicle doesn't have" (108) with the illusion of density and complexity of life typical of the novel proper. This form may attempt to incorporate already existent stories or to make the illumination but embryonic or potential story an integral part of the novel. As a separate story, for example, "Barn Burning" emphasizes the vengefulness of Ab Snopes and the agony of the child, Sartoris Snopes, who can neither approve of nor betray his father. When it recurs in *The Hamlet*, it is narrated by Ratliff with his usual sardonic humor. The boy is not mentioned and the viciousness of Ab is transferred to Mink. What remains is a comic story which stresses the mounting frustration of De Spain, the imperturbability of Ab, and an indirect warning to Will Varner, his son Jody, and Frenchman's Bend. In addition, it is precisely because Jody hears this story that he begins that process of placating Flem that leads to his own dispossession. The integration of the story into a large unit is thus completed.

The use of the embryonic or potential short story is most clearly seen in *Absalom, Absalom!* Quentin and Shreve provide the novel's formal unity by virtue of their concern to explore the past as seen in the history of the Sutpen family. But there are at least three different accounts of Sutpen which could stand independently. In addition, because Quentin and Shreve are attempting an aesthetic reconstruction, they tend to think in terms of scenes and episodes: Miss Rosa's reaction to Sutpen's brutal proposal, Charles Etienne's tragic inability to define himself racially, Wash Jones and his daughter Milly, Sutpen's adventures in Haiti, Charles Bon's doomed relationship with his mistress. Yet one is not conscious of the separateness of these stories because they are caught up in the fluidity of time and because they are an integral part of the total pattern of the book.

These unremitting efforts at formal experimentation testify to Faulkner's passionate effort to enshrine in his carpet the full quiddity of the living character, the lyrical exaltation of the moment that epitomizes, the sobering (even when most humorous) recognition of the unsought recurrence of human actions, and the emancipatory release afforded by the diversity of tones. Perhaps most important of all, in their integrating the dramatic immediacy and concentration of the short story with the sweep of sustained narrative, they reveal the carpet as containing the reconciliation of what George Steiner in *Tolstoy or Dostoyevsky* has described as antithetical if not mutually exclusive traditions of fiction. To summarize from Steiner's long list of contrarities: Faulkner, like Dostoyevsky, distrusts reason and loves paradox, distrusts total understanding and seeks to preserve some element of mystery, plunges into the labyrinth of the unnatural and the morass of the soul, and hovers on the edge of the hallucinatory, of the spectral, always vulnerable to demonic intrusions into what might prove, in the end, to have been merely a tissue of dreams. On the other hand, like Tolstoy, he is the poet of the land and of the rural setting, the man thirsting for the truth and engaging in excessive pursuit of it, the writer evoking the realness, the tangibility, the sensible entirety of concrete experience. Admittedly, to assert he is both a Tolstoy and a Dostoyevsky is a large claim but so is Faulkner's achievement.

That he was able to risk and still to achieve so much brings us full circle to the figure in the carpet, to "the very passion of his passion" that is the unifying principle for all his works. The one indispensable element that seems best to explain the characteristics identified in the preceding pages is, put most simply, the inquiring mind, that quizzical, reflective prober of persons, places, and things who simultaneously ventures into the unknown and interrogates the known. To use his own words once more: "The most important thing is insight, that is, to be—curiosity— to wonder, to mull, and to muse why it is that man does what he does." (191) It is at this point that author, character, and reader meet and see their own images reflected each in the other and in the carpet. In this we can see perhaps why the Yoknapatawpha saga remains incomplete necessarily and not simply because of Faulkner's death. For each new reader, each new critic who takes up Faulkner's task of wondering, musing, and mulling, and each new interpretation that proves less than definitive is in some sense a contribution to the saga as well as a tribute to its founder.

INDEX